Reflections on Kurt Gödel

Reflections on Kurt Gödel

Hao Wang

A Bradford Book
The MIT Press
Cambridge, Massachusetts
London, England

This book was set in Palatino by Asco Trade Typesetting Ltd., Hong Kong, and printed and bound by Halliday Lithograph in the United States of America.

Library of Congress Cataloging-in-Publication Data

Wang, Hao, 1921–
  Reflections on Kurt Gödel.

"A Bradford book."
Includes index.
  1. Gödel, Kurt. 2. Logicians—United States—Biography. 3. Logicians—
Austria—Biography. I. Title.
QA29.G58W36   1987   511.3'092'4 [B]   86-21095
ISBN 0-262-23127-1

Contents

Preface

In a century and more Kurt Gödel has been unique in combining truly fundamental contributions to science with exceptionally profound and precise philosophical work. Very much a private person, his remarkable results have been receiving increasingly broader attention since his death in 1978. But comparatively little of his life is generally known, and his bold speculations on several perennial issues of universal concern remain buried in unpublished material, except for a few scattered brief statements inserted in rather specialized contexts. My reflections are meant to be a first attempt to consider his life and work as a whole within an inclusive context that is accessible to most thoughtful people. Gödel exemplifies, I think, a way of life and work that inspires a greater faith in reason, questions the 'prejudices of the time,' and stirs our imagination to strive for more autonomy by examining our largely derivative sense of what is important in life.

I am fortunate to have had close contact with Gödel in his last years. Through this contact I have acquired some familiarity with him as a person as well as with that part of his thoughts that goes beyond the universally admired mathematical results. The task of thinking extensively about an object of admiration is gratifying. But the incentive to write on Gödel has come more from a belief that reflections on him would also be an effective means of clarifying my own philosophical thoughts, by sorting out where and why I agree or disagree with him. Once, however, the decision to do so was made, there has been a natural tendency to wish to learn more about him and to consider other aspects of him. For this purpose, I have consulted several informed individuals, read written material (published and unpublished) about Gödel, taken some quick looks at his Nachlass (literary estate), and reconstructed my conversations with him.

A version of the projected book was completed in February 1986, but the parts having to do with Gödel's unpublished thoughts were not satisfactory. Chiefly I was not happy with the organization of the reconstructed conversations and especially my failure to obtain and present a coherent understanding of the various facets of what Gödel told me. After a period of frustrated efforts to mend this defect, I finally decided to remove the chapters having to do with the details of Gödel's private sayings (oral or

written) and use them as the basis for a separate book, to be entitled
Conversations with Kurt Gödel. The present book is a somewhat revised
version of the chapters that are less dependent on unpublished material. By
leaving the other parts for a separate book, I shall be able not only to
improve the organization of both books but also to continue my attempt
both to reflect on Gödel's outlook and to formulate an alternative one of
my own.

Both books aim to render Gödel accessible to those who are not specialists in logic or philosophy, without refraining from considerations of new
ideas on a level that is challenging to the experts. In the present book
the material that is primarily of interest only to professional logicians and
philosophers is largely relegated to the detailed parts in the two chapters of
the supplement (chapters 10 and 11), in which the text of five of Gödel's
famous papers is examined with a view to improving the appreciation of
them. Of the nine chapters making up the body of the book, only chapter 6
concentrates directly on the meaning and implications of Gödel's major
mathematical results. The other eight chapters fall, I believe, mostly within
the realm of things that are fully and equally accessible, without the need of
mediation, to every thoughtful person.

A project to publish Gödel's *Collected Works* (briefly, *CW*) was started
in 1982, of which the first volume appeared in early 1986. More volumes
are forthcoming. A film and a volume on Gödel's life and work are being
prepared in Vienna. The film is under the guidance of Peter Weibel and
Werner Schimanovich; the volume is also edited by them, together with
Eckehart Köhler. All these works are in many respects complementary to
my books. I am grateful to the editors and directors for sharing some of
their information with me.

For permission to use quotations and photographs from the Gödel
Nachlass, I am grateful to the Institute for Advanced Study, its director
Harry Woolf, and its committee responsible for these papers: Enrico Bom-
bieri, Armand Borel, and John Milnor. The Nachlass, which had been, after
Gödel's death in 1978, donated by his widow Adele to the institute, was
catalogued during 1982–1984 by John Dawson, who issued also an inven-
tory (in typescript) in July 1984. Both he and Cheryl Dawson have given
me generous and indispensable help not only in connection with using
the Nachlass but also in sharing with me some of their factual knowledge
and in other ways. The Nachlass was placed on indefinite loan to the
Manuscripts Division of the Firestone Library at Princeton University
early in 1985 and became available to scholars on 1 April, with the Institute
retaining all rights for its use. Jean Preston, the curator of manuscripts at
Firestone Library, is in charge of the Nachlass, and I have found her and
her colleagues most courteous and helpful.

In response to my inquiry, Rudolf Gödel has sent me an elegant letter on his brother. Köhler and Schimanovich have helped my efforts to familiarize myself with facts related to Gödel in various ways. In particular, they have made available to me Gödel's letters to his mother (and brother), the script for the Gödel film, and Karl Menger's memoir, as well as some photographs. I am very grateful indeed to all three of them. The letters are kept at the Wiener Stadt- und Landesbibliothek, and Dr. Franz Patzer has kindly granted me permission to quote.

The quotations from the Carnap papers (see section 2.2) are from the Rudolf Carnap Collection in the Special Collections Department of the University of Pittsburgh Libraries. For the privilege of using the material I am grateful to the university and to Richard Nollan, who has arranged to have the permission granted to me. In addition, I wish to thank Stephen Kleene and Olga Taussky-Todd for allowing me to make use of typescripts of their lectures at a Salzburg symposium of July 1983.

Marie Grossi has made my share easy throughout the whole process of turning handwritten pages into the printed text. Indeed, of my various writings so far, this book is her favorite. She and Antai Ko have also improved the presentation.

Abbreviations and references

A. *Abbreviations*
Except for a few obvious ones, the following are the main items.

BA	Wang 1985
BP	Benacerraf and Putnam (BP2 for the revised second edition)
CG	*Conversations with Kurt Gödel* (under preparation)
CP	Carnap
CW(I)	Gödel 1986
FG	J. v. Heijenoort
GQ	Gödel 1975
HA	Hilbert and Ackermann
HB	Hilbert and Bernays
I.A.S. (or the Institute)	The Institute for Advanced Study, Princeton, NJ
JSL	*The Journal of Symbolic Logic*
LM	Gödel 1945–1966
MP	Wang 1974
PM	Whitehead and Russell
PNAS	*Proceedings of the National Academy of Sciences of the U.S.A.*
RG	Dr. Rudolf Gödel's letter to me, quoted in section 1.1
WS	Weibel and Schimanovich

B. *Writings of Gödel*
Only the main items considered in this book are included.

1929	The doctoral dissertation (for more details, see section 10.1). Reprinted in *CW*.

1930(1929)	The completeness paper, completed in 1929 and published in 1930 (see section 10.1). Reprinted in *FG* and *CW*.
1931(1930)	The incompletability paper. Also referred to as the famous paper, the celebrated paper, the 1931 paper, etc. (see section 10.2). Reprinted in Davis, *FG*, and *CW*.
1939	Consistency proof of the generalized continuum hypothesis, *PNAS*, vol. 25, pp. 220–224. Reprinted in *CW*.
1944	The Russell paper (see section 11.3), Reprinted in BP.
1945–1966	*LM*. Letters to his mother (and brother).
1947 and 1964	The Cantor paper (see section 11.2). Reprinted in BP.
1949	The Einstein paper. A remark about the relation between relativity theory and idealistic philosophy, Schilpp 1949, pp. 447–450. For related papers, see section 6.5.
1958 and 1969	The Bernays paper (see section 11.1).
1970	'My notes 1940–70,' quoted in the introductory pages of part I, courtesy of the I.A.S.
1974	Contributions to *MP* (as specified in its preface).
1975	*GQ*. The Grandjean questionnaire. The completed form and related material are quoted in section 2.2, courtesy of the I.A.S.
1986	*CW. Collected Works*, vol. I (publications 1929–1936), edited by Solomon Feferman, John W. Dawson, Jr., Stephen Kleene, Gregory H. Moore, Robert M. Solovay, and Jean van Heijenoort. Additional volumes are forthcoming.

C.   Writings by Others

References that occur in isolated contexts are mostly given only in the body of the book.

Paul Benacerraf and Hilary Putnam, editors
> 1964. BP. *Philosophy of Mathematics: Selected Readings* (BP2, second edition, 1983).

Georg Cantor
> *Works. Gesammelte Abhandlungen*, 1932.

Rudolf Carnap
CP. The Carnap papers (the pages related to Gödel), quoted in section 2.2, chapter 4 (under *1929*), and section 6.2, courtesy of the University of Pittsburgh.

Ronald W. Clark
1971. *Einstein: The Life and Times*, Avon Books edition, 1972.

Paul J. Cohen
1966. *Set Theory and the Continuum Hypothesis.*

Martin Davis, editor
1965. *The Undecidable.*

John W. Dawson, Jr.
1983. The published work of Kurt Gödel, *Notre Dame Journal of Formal Logic*, vol. 24, pp. 255–284 (addenda and corrigenda, vol. 25, pp. 283–287).
1984. Kurt Gödel in sharper focus, *The Mathematical Intelligencer*, vol. 6, no. 4, pp. 9–17.
1986. A Gödel chronology, *CW*, pp. 37–43.

Richard Dedekind
1888. *Was Sind und Was Sollen die Zahlen?*

Solomon Feferman
1986. Gödel's life and work, *CW*, pp. 1–36.

Gottlob Frege
1879. *Begriffsschrift*, reprinted (in English translation) in *FG*.

Jean v. Heijenoort, editor
1967. *FG. From Frege to Gödel: A Source Book in Mathematical Logic.*

David Hilbert and Wilhelm Ackermann
1928. *HA. Grundzüge der theoretische Logik*, first edition.

David Hilbert and Paul Bernays
HB. *Grundlagen der Mathematik*, vol. 1, 1934 and 1968; vol. 2, 1939 and 1970.

Douglas R. Hofstadter
1979. *Gödel, Escher, Bach.*

Gerald Holton and Yehuda Elkana, editors
1982. *Albert Einstein: Historical and Cultural Aspects.*

Stephen Kleene
Gödel's impression on students in the 1930s, *Gödels Wissenschaftliches*

Weltbild, proceedings of a Salzburg symposium held July 1983, to appear.

Eckehart Köhler
Gödel und der Wiener Kreis, to appear.

Georg Kreisel
1980. Kurt Gödel, 28 April 1906 to 14 January 1978, *Biographical Memoirs of Fellows of the Royal Society*, vol. 26, pp. 148–224 (corrections, vol. 27, p. 697, and vol. 28, p. 718).

Karl Menger
(1981). Recollections of Kurt Gödel (English translation by Eckehart Köhler, 1982), to appear.

Abraham Pais
1982. *'Subtle Is the Lord . . . ,' the Science and Life of Albert Einstein.*

Frank P. Ramsey
1931. *The Foundations of Mathematics.*

Constance Reid
1970. *Hilbert.*

Bertrand Russell
1903. *Principles of Mathematics* (second edition 1937, with new introduction).

Paul A. Schilpp, editor
1949. *Albert Einstein, Philosopher-Scientist.*

Carl Seelig
1960. *Albert Einstein.*

Thoralf Skolem
1970. *Selected Works in Logic*, edited by Jens E. Fenstad, several relevant papers reprinted in *FG*.

Olga Taussky-Todd
Remembrances of Kurt Gödel, to appear in the proceedings mentioned above under Kleene.

Alan M. Turing
1936. On computable numbers, *Proceedings of the London Math. Soc.*, vol. 42, pp. 230–265 (corrections in vol. 43, pp. 544–546), reprinted in Davis.

Hao Wang
1962. *Survey. A Survey of Mathematical Logic* (reprinted in 1970 as *Logic, Computers, and Sets*).

1974. *MP. From Mathematics to Philosophy.*

1981. *Popular Lectures on Mathematical Logic.*

1985. *BA. Beyond Analytic Philosophy.*

Peter Weibel and Werner Schimanovich
 WS. Drehbuch für den Film 'Kurt Gödel: Ein Mathematischer Mythos,'
 1986 manuscript.

Alfred North Whitehead and Bertrand Russell
 PM. Principia Mathematica, 3 vols., 1910–1913 (second edition of
 volume 1, 1925, with additions by Russell).

Ludwig Wittgenstein
 1922. *Tractatus Logico-Philosophicus.*

Harry Woolf, editor
 1980. *Some Strangeness of Proportion.*

Chronology

The chronological account of Gödel (in chapters 3 and 4) has grown so much that a summary is needed to see things in one glance, which was one of the original purposes of the account.

1906.   Born on 28 April at Brünn in Moravia.

c. 1911.   Had 'at about the age of five a light anxiety neurosis.'

1912.   On 16 September, enrollment in Evangelische Privat-Volks- und Burgerschule, Brünn. A very inquisitive child, the family called him 'Mr. Why,' der Herr Warum.

c. 1914.   At about the age of eight, a severe joint-rheumatism with high fever.

1916.   On 5 July, graduation from the Evangelischeschule. In the autumn, entrance to Staats-Realgymnasium mit deutscher Unterrichtsprache, Brünn.

1919.   1919–21, formal study of Gabelsberger shorthand. While in school, a romantic interest in a family friend ten years older (year and duration indefinite).

c. 1920.   Began interest in mathematics (at 14). His brother Rudolf went to the University of Vienna to study medicine.

c. 1921.   Interest in mathematics and philosophy started (about 15). Read Goethe's theory of colors and his criticisms of Newton, which, according to G, indirectly influenced his choice of vocation (see chapter 3, under 1921).

c. 1922.   First study of Kant's work.

c. 1923.   At 16–17, had already mastered university material in mathematics. In school, at first an outstanding pupil in the languages, later in history, and later again in mathematics.

1924.   On 19 June, graduation from Realgymnasium. His powers of concentrated work and sustained interest were already evident at school.

Autumn, entrance to University of Vienna, intending to specialize in theoretical physics.

1925.   Attendance of 1925/26 course in history of philosophy by H. Gomperz and adoption of the philosophical position of 'mathematical realism.' Also attended M. Schlick's course or seminar on the philosophy of mathematics. Probably also began courses in number theory by P. Furtwängler; possibly course in relativity theory by Hans Thirring around this time. Beginning of close association with H. Feigl and M. Natkin, two older students in philosophy. Requested from the library Kant's *Metaphysische Anfangsgründe der Naturwissenschaft* (1785).

1926.   Shift of primary interest from theoretical physics to mathematics. Beginning of participation in some activities of the Moritz Schlick Circle (later known widely as the Vienna Circle). Association with a younger girl with intellectual aspirations probably around this time. Local reputation of brilliance; ready to help fellow students.

c. 1927.   First acquaintance with Adele, his future wife. First reading of the *Tractatus* (never thoroughly). Library request slips indicate his interest in number theory.

1928.   Attended one or both of Brouwer's lectures on 10 and 14 March. Shift of interest to mathematical logic. Attendance of Carnap's course on 'the philosophical foundations of arithmetic' in the winter semester of 1928/29. Publication of HA in which the completeness and decision problem of elementary logic are formulated as open problems. Hilbert's Bologna lecture (September), in which questions of completeness and consistency of mathematical systems are explicitly posed. Library request slips for reading in logic, including books by E. Schröder and Frege (both in October).

1929.   Unexpected death of his father on 23 February (born on 28 February 1874). Release from Czech citizenship on 26 February and acquisition of Austrian citizenship on 6 June. Dissertation (proving the completeness of elementary logic) approved on 6 July by Hahn and Furtwängler. Revised dissertation received for publication on 22 October. Attended the first regular meeting of Menger's colloquium on 24 October.

1930.   Degree of Dr. Phil. granted on 6 February. A combinatorial version of the first completeness result was obtained in the summer. It was announced in public on 7 September at Königsberg. Afterward the first theorem was made into the familiar form and the second theorem was discovered. An abstract was communicated to the Vienna Academy of Sciences on 23 October and the full famous paper was received for publication on 17 November. The I.A.S. was formally established in late autumn but actual operation was only to begin on 2 October 1933.

1931.   Correspondence with Herbrand and Zermelo. Probably tried to write the second part of his famous paper, as well as began work on the continuum hypothesis and on intuitionism. According to his brother, he had a serious nervous depression around the end of the year. Prepared notes for Hahn's logic seminar of 1931/32.

1932.   The famous paper was submitted on 25 June as his Habilitationsschrift to the University of Vienna, and Habilitation was granted on 1 December. Obtained and presented three interesting results on the formal systems of intuitionistic logic and arithmetic (see the notes listed as 1932, 1933e, and 1933f on p. 421 of *CW*).

1933.   Became Dozent on 11 March and gave his first course ('The foundations of arithmetic') shortly afterward. A full-length paper (on the Entscheidungsproblem), the first since the 1931 paper, was submitted (22 June) and published (the paper listed on p. 422 of *CW* as 1933i). Sea voyage to America 30 September to 6 October. Met Einstein for the first time in autumn. Address at the annual meeting of the Am. Math. Soc. ('The present situation in the foundations of mathematics', 30 December).

1934.   Lectured at the I.A.S. from February to May; general recursive functions were introduced and his 1930 idea on the concept of truth was presented. Lectured to the NY Philosophical Soc. (18 April) and the Washington (DC) Acad. of Sci. (20 April) on his incompleteness theorems. Sea voyage back to Europe from 26 May to 3 June. Hahn died on 24 July. Admitted in autumn to sanatorium (Purkersdorf) for treatment of depression. Apparently there were also problems with his teeth.

1935.   Discovered the constructible sets and their property of being a model of the usual axioms of set theory (including the axiom of choice); told these ideas to v. Neumann in autumn. Lecture course ('Selected topics in math. logic') in Vienna (started 4 May). Presented paper on the length of proofs (19 June). Sea voyage to America from 20 to 28 September, with Bernays on the same ship. Sudden resignation (17 November) from the I.A.S. on account of a severe depression. Voyage to Le Havre from 30 November to 7 December, followed by rest and recuperation back in Vienna.

1936.   More time in sanatoria. This was a year when his health was exceptionally poor. Schlick was assassinated on 22 June.

1937.   Third and last lecture course ('Axiomatik der Mengenlehre') in Vienna (May and June). Crucial step in verifying the (generalized) continuum hypothesis (CH) was, according to the first volume of the Arbeitshefte in the Nachlass, discovered on the night of 14–15 June; told

v. Neumann the (outline of) proof in July. Worked to bring the proof into a satisfactory form and began to tackle the independence of CH.

1938.   Austria annexed to Germany on 13 March. Married Adele on 20 September. Sea voyage to America from 6 to 15 October, leaving Adele in Vienna. Lectured at the I.A.S. on the relative consistency of GCH from October to December; revised notes of these lectures were published 1940 as a monograph, his only publication in book form. Announcement of results on constructible sets (communicated 9 November) in *PNAS*, vol. 24, pp. 556–557. Lecture at the annual meeting of the Am. Math. Soc. (28 December) on the consistency of GCH.

1939.   Taught at Notre Dame from January or February to May. First publication of his consistency proof of GCH (communicated 14 February) in *PNAS*, vol. 25, pp. 220–224. The title of Privatdozent was abolished probably in March and Gödel was upset over the violation of his rights. Return sea voyage from 14 to 20 June. World War II began on 1 September, and Gödel was found 'fit for garrison duty.' Applied for Dozent neuer Ordnung on 25 September (not granted until 28 June 1940). Lectured at Göttingen on 15 December. Received German exit permits (together with Adele) on 19 December.

1940.   Non-quota US immigration visas were issued to Gödel and Adele on 8 January. They left Vienna on 18 January and arrived at San Francisco on 4 March (by way of Russia and Japan). They arrived at Princeton (probably toward the end of March) to begin a continuous residence for the next four decades or so. Lectured at Brown University on 15 November. Probably also gave a series of lectures in set theory at the I.A.S.

1941.   Discovered the main idea of his interpretation of arithmetic (first published in the Bernays paper) apparently on 1 January. Lectured on this interpretation at Yale University on 15 April. A course of lectures on this subject was given at the I.A.S. in the spring.

1942.   Began frequent contacts with Einstein (continued till Einstein's death in 1955). According to Arbeitsheft 15, discovered his idea of proving the independence of the axiom of choice in the summer (at Blue Hill House, Hancock County, Maine). Tried to extend the proof to the CH without success. Was invited (18 November) to write a paper on 'Russell's mathematical logic,' and accepted the invitation soon after.

1943.   Studied Leibniz from 1943 to 1946. Sent in the manuscript of his Russell paper on 17 May; the revised version was ready on 28 September.

1944.   The series of notebooks marked 'Max' is taken to be the philosophical notebooks. As far as I know, these have not yet been deciphered.

Over two hundred pages were written this year, including Max 11 (28 January to 14 November, 153 pages) as well as parts of Max 10 (12 March 1943 to 27 January 1944, 93 pages) and Max 12 (15 November 1944 to 5 June 1945, 119 pages).

1945.   It is conjectured that it was during this year that Gödel delayed proper treatment of a bleeding duodenal ulcer until blood transfusions had to be administered. Invited on 30 November to write what later became the Cantor paper.

1946.   Became a permanent member of the I.A.S. on 1 July. A typed draft of the Cantor paper had been completed by 31 August, which undoubtedly was revised again over many months. Invited by Schilpp (10 July or perhaps orally in May) to write a paper to honor Einstein. Lecture at the Princeton University bicentennial conference on problems of mathematics (17 December, text published in Davis).

1947.   Worked on general relativity and Kant's philosophy. Publication of the Cantor paper in December. Adele was away in Europe for about seven months (May through November).

1948.   Granted US citizenship on 2 April (together with Adele). Continued to work on the mathematical and philosophical aspects of general relativity, obtaining new solutions to Einstein's field equations.

1949.   Publication of a mathematical paper (July) and a philosophical one (December) on general relativity (and the concept of time). Lecture at the I.A.S. (in May) on his new solutions of the field equations. Einstein was hospitalized around the beginning of the year. Purchased house at 129 (later changed to 145) Linden Lane on 3 August.

1950.   Continued work on cosmology and the concept of time (till the beginning of 1951). Addressed the International Congress of Mathematicians on 31 August at Cambridge, Massachusetts, on 'Rotating universes in general relativity theory.'

1951.   Was sick and hospitalized between January and March. Received the First Einstein Award on 14 March (together with Julian Schwinger). Honorary D. Litt., Yale University (in June). Planned to visit his mother in autumn but changed his mind, saying that he had to spend more time on his Gibbs Lecture (given 26 December at Brown University, on 'Some basic theorems on the foundations of mathematics and their philosophical implications').

1952.   Honorary Sc.D., Harvard University (19 June). Liked the citation calling him 'the discoverer of the most significant mathematical truth of the century.' Summer vacation at Asbury Park, NJ. Reported on 31 October, 'My acquaintances tell me, I had for a long time already not looked so well [as now].' Einstein was ill for a couple of weeks.

1953.   Became professor at the I.A.S. on 1 July. Adele went to Europe in March for an extended visit. Accepted (2 July) Schilpp's invitation (15 May) to write a paper on Carnap's philosophy, on which Gödel was to work for several years. Carnap was at the I.A.S. from 1952 to 1954. Brouwer visited the I.A.S. in autumn.

1954.   Worked a good deal on the Carnap paper, which, by the way, remains unpublished to this day. Summer vacation at Asbury Park. Poor health in autumn.

1955.   Elected to the National Academy of Sciences (of the US). Einstein died on 18 April, a great personal loss to Gödel, who was quite disturbed for the next two months or so. Responded in autumn to Carl Seelig's request with two letters about Einstein. Adele went to Vienna in February and brought her mother back with her in March.

1956.   Accepted an invitation to write a paper for a Bernays Festschrift (on his 70th birthday in 1958), resulting later in the Bernays paper. Received a long congratulation on his 50th birthday from the board for culture and education of the city of Vienna. Again planned (only) to visit his mother in Europe.

1957.   Elected to the American Academy of Arts and Sciences. Death of v. Neumann (8 February, at age 53). Invited his mother to visit him (in letter of 11 November).

1958.   Visit by his mother and brother in May. Publication of the Bernays paper (submitted around 10 July).

1959.   Began to study Husserl's work. Adele's mother, who had been living with them for several years, died in Princeton around 13 March. Adele went for a summer vacation in the White Mountains and visited Europe again in autumn. Bernays and Kurt Schütte visited the I.A.S. during 1959/60.

1960.   Probably continued with his study of Husserl's work. Adele took a trip to Europe in autumn.

1961.   Elected to the American Philosophical Society. Apparently had trouble with his stomach early this year. Spoke of liking better his new schedule of sleeping and rising early. Wrote four 'theological' letters to his mother (compare section 8.1). Adele visited Italy and Spain from July to September. Clifford Spector, who discussed logic with Gödel during 1960/61, died at the I.A.S. (29 July, at a young age).

1962.   Spoke of having been immersed in a philosophical book that specially interested him (in his letter of 4 July), but did not name the book. Visit by his mother and brother in autumn.

1963.   In April Paul J. Cohen circulated a preliminary version of his independence proofs in set theory. Gödel studied the work and communicated a revised version of the paper (in two parts, 30 September and 27 November) to the *PNAS*. An expansion of Gödel's Cantor paper had been completed before April and a postscript was added later with a reference to Cohen's result.

1964.   Publication of the expanded Cantor paper. Added a postscript (dated 3 June) to his 1934 lectures for their publication in Davis (1965). Visit by his mother and brother in May. Adele took a summer vacation at the seaside.

1965.   Pleased with the new library of the I.A.S. and his new office attached to it. Adele was away (in Europe) July and August.

1966.   Symposium organized by the Ohio Academy of Sciences to celebrate Gödel's 60th birthday took place at Ohio State University (21–23 April). Declined honorary professorship of the University of Vienna and honorary membership in the Austrian Academy of Sciences. His mother, Marianne (Handschuh), who had wanted very much to be in Princeton on Gödel's 60th birthday, died in Vienna on 23 July (born 31 August 1879). Carl Kaysen became the (new) director of the I.A.S. on 1 July. Adele was in Europe in July.

1967.   Elected honorary member of the London Math. Soc. Honorary Sc.D., Amherst College (in June). Wrote me a letter (dated 7 December, commenting on material sent by me on 27 July and 14 September) to explain the important role of his philosophical position in his mathematical work. A supplementary second letter was sent to me on 7 March 1968.

1968.   Elected foreign member of the Royal Society (of London). Worked on an expanded English version of his Bernays paper.

1969.   According to Oskar Morgenstern, Gödel confessed that, after the late 1960s, he could no longer understand the work of younger logicians.

1970.   Health was exceptionally poor this year, especially during the early months.

1971.   Began regular discussion sessions with me in October, which continued till the end of 1972. Some of the discussions from the initial months resulted in Gödel's contributions to *MP* (as specified in its preface).

1972.   Elected corresponding fellow of the British Academy and corresponding member of the Institut de France. Honorary Sc.D., The Rockefeller University (1 June).

1975.   Awarded National Medal of Science by President Ford (18 September). Arranged to have me visit the I.A.S. for 1975/76, and we had extended discussions during this period, mostly by telephone.

1976.   Became professor emeritus on 1 July. Was hospitalized around the end of March. There were proposals to treat his health problems at the University of Pennsylvania Hospital, but he did not consent.

1977.   Adele had surgery in July and stayed away from home till 18 or 19 December. She then persuaded Gödel to enter the Princeton Hospital (29 December). O. Morgenstern, a close friend, died in Princeton on 26 July (born 1902). Bernays died in Zurich on 18 September (born 1888).

1978.   Died in the hospital on Saturday, 14 January, at one in the afternoon, of 'malnutrition and inanition.' A small private funeral was held a few days later. The I.A.S. organized a memorial meeting on 3 March.

1979.   A meeting of the Association for Symbolic Logic was devoted to Gödel's work (24 March). Publication of D. R. Hofstadter's *Gödel, Escher, Bach*.

1981.   Adele died on 4 February (born 4 November 1899) and bequeathed Gödel's Nachlass to the I.A.S.

1983.   Two sessions at an international congress dealt with Gödel (July, Salzburg).

1984.   Cataloguing of Gödel's papers was completed in July.

1985.   On 1 April, the Gödel papers became available to scholars at the Firestone Library of Princeton University.

1986.   Publication of the first volume of Gödel's *Collected Works*. Conferences devoted to Gödel at Vienna (April), Kirchberg (Austria, August), and Bucharest (October).

PART I

Facts

The facts of Gödel's life and work suggest considerations that are of interest beyond the academic world and, indeed, call for a historical perspective in terms of centuries.

Everyone eats, sleeps, needs a shelter, is healthy or not, has a family and other contacts with people, works or earns a living in one way or another, confronts the question of money, relaxes, makes decisions, judges, errs, conjectures, suffers, experiences joy, grows, ages, dies, etc. This shared humanity provides a channel of communication with every person, relating him to how anybody, G in this case, with his particularity of being a recluse and a profound thinker, copes with the universal components of human needs and wishes. The restrictedness of the range of people who are interested in a life (in particular, G's) is determined by its specificity, which at the same time increases the intensity of appeal to those who fall within the range. What distinguishes G from most people are the several meaningful ways in which he transcends his own century: in terms of his thoughts, concerns, life-style, and the spiritual company he keeps in his mind.

It is common to think of G as a mathematician, and as such, he has been compared with Archimedes and Gauss. For example, Professor E. Hlawka, of the University of Vienna, observes that G shares with Gauss the habit of procrastinating over the preparations for publication but that G's judicious attitude toward the discovery of the independence of the continuum hypothesis may be said to differ from Gauss's reaction toward the discovery of non-Euclidean geometry. It is, however, more appropriate to view G as a 'philosopher-scientist.' To find work of comparable caliber in both science and philosophy, one has to go back to Descartes (31 March 1596 to 11 February 1650) and Leibniz (3 July 1646 to 14 November 1716). Indeed, it appears that G identifies himself with Leibniz more than with anybody else.

The impact of G's scientific ideas and philosophical speculations has been increasing, and the value of their potential implications may continue to increase. It may take hundreds of years for the appearance of more definite confirmations or refutations of some of his large conjectures. For example, he speaks of the need of a physical organ to handle abstract impressions and suggests the possibility of philosophy as an exact theory emerging 'within the next hundred years or even sooner' (*MP*, p. 85). There will be, he believes, scientific disproofs of what he calls 'mechanism in biology' and of the proposition that 'there is no mind separate from matter'; moreover, he thinks it practically certain that 'the physical laws, in their observable consequences, have a finite limit of precision' (*MP*, p. 326). In his conversations he recommends the important project of finding what might be called a 'rational religion.'

(A question raised by G on a public occasion in 1972, which I had also asked myself before, is the feasibility of a computer 'knowing' its own program. One difficulty is to give the idea a less elusive meaning, perhaps by relating it to ideas that lack its seeming simplicity. Recently it occurred to me that one could conceivably approach the problem by attempting to find an analogue of the hidden 'rational core' in Hegel's *Phenomenology of the Spirit*, namely, in terms of a journey toward self-knowledge within a world consisting of computers. Such a project ought to do something to reconcile the antagonism between the humanists and the technologists.)

The fundamental character of G's work, fortified by his beautiful friendship with Einstein, makes it harder to resist the inclination to pair him with Einstein and create a two-membered 'natural kind' consisting of the leading 'natural philosophers' of the century. One indulgence leads to another. Given the familiar association of Einstein with Newton, why not extend the pair by analogy? The riddle is then to look for an x such that Einstein is to G as Newton is to x. The obvious candidates are Descartes and Leibniz. G's own hero is Leibniz and both of them are great logicians. Moreover, G considers Leibniz's monadology close to his own philosophy. At the same time, the clean and conclusive character of his mathematical innovations may be said to be more similar to Descartes's invention of analytic geometry, and his sympathy with Husserl appears to be closer to Descartes's predominant concern with the methods of a new way of thinking and the beginning of a new type of philosophy.

In a letter to his mother (dated 9 December 1953, in *LM*), undoubtedly in response to a question from her, G comments on the burden of fame:

> Meinen "Ruhm" hab ich bisher in keiner Weise unangenehm empfunden. Das fängt erst dann an, wenn man einmal so berühmt, ist dass einen jedes Kind auf der Strasse kennt, wie das bei Einstein der Fall ist. Dann kommen ab u. zu Irrsinnige, die ihre Wahnvorstellungen erklärt haben wollen, oder sich über die Zustände in dieser Welt beschweren. Aber wie Du siehst, ist auch das nicht gefährlich, da ja Einstein bereits das Alter von 74 Jahren erreicht hat. [In rough translation: I have so far not found my 'fame' burdensome in any way. That begins only when one becomes so famous that one is known to every child in the street, as is the case with Einstein. Insane ideas then set in, having

to explain away one's mistakes or weighing onself down by the plights of the world. But as you see, the danger is also not so great; after all, Einstein has already managed to reach the venerable age of 74 years.]

G's fame has spread more widely since his death in 1978. By coincidence the surprisingly popular book *Gödel, Escher, Bach* was published in 1979. A number of conferences have been or will be devoted to his life and work. The first volume of his collected works has appeared, and additional volumes are expected. Undoubtedly the growing attention to him and his work is related to the increasingly widespread applications of computers. For instance, one symposium to honor him advertises itself by offering the topic 'Digital Intelligence: From Philosophy to Technology' as its theme.

It is possible that the connection between G's work and computers is closer than that between Einstein's work and the atom bomb, about which G says (in his letter of 11 May 1950 to his mother), 'That just Einstein's discoveries in the first place made the atom bomb possible, is an erroneous comprehension. Of course he also indirectly contributed to it, but the essence of his work lies in an entirely other direction.' I believe G would say the same thing about the connection between his own work and computers.

The 'entirely other direction' is fundamental theory (in 'natural philosophy'), which constitutes the (central) purposes of life for both G and Einstein. This common dedication, their great success with it (in distinct but mutually appreciated ways), and their drive to penetrate deeper into the secrets of nature: the combination of these factors undoubtedly provides the solid foundation of their friendship and their frequent interactions. Each of them finds in the other his intellectual equal, who, moreover, shares the same cultural tradition. By happy coincidence, they happened to have been, since about 1933, thrown into the same 'club' (namely, the Princeton Institute for Advanced Study).

It is hard to find in history comparable examples of intimacy between such outstanding philosopher-scientists. The friendly relations of Newton with Locke and Leibniz with Huygens were not nearly so close. Faraday and Maxwell admired and complemented each other, but they had little personal contact. Among intellectuals of other types we do find a few famous instances: Goethe and Schiller, Hegel and Hölderlin, Marx and Engels.

How does the dedication to fundamental theoretical work condition one's life? In G's case the concentration on theory implies a decisive distancing from affairs of the world, thereby excluding nearly all participation in practical activities beyond the universal range of what is needed for everyone's daily life. The focus on the fundamental means a selection and a restriction of the objectives and commitments, in order that each path may receive correspondingly a larger portion of one's attention. The guiding principle is to undertake fewer types of activity, which are in some sense of higher quality. Unlike Einstein, G extends this restriction to all aspects of his outside life and work: to have contacts only with a few persons, to publish little and concisely, to give few lectures, to accept few invitations, to travel little, to write fewer but better (and even longer) letters (e.g., than his mother in their correspondence), etc. When he does make a commitment (to others), he is conscientious about fulfilling it to perfection, so that he generally keeps his promise even though he is usually late in completing what is required. A notable exception was the paper to honor Carnap ('Is mathematics syntax of language?'), which he had spent years writing but finally decided to withhold. In 1951 G more or less promised to visit his mother but failed to do so (then or later).

As one would expect, G (also) did not complete all the major projects he had set for himself (or, in other words, fulfill all the major commitments to himself). A famous example is his unfinished work toward proving the independence of the continuum hypothesis. In philosophy he said that he had never arrived at what he looked for. G's Nachlass contains several unfinished manuscripts and massive private notes, which reveal the wide range of his reading and research. This material and his conversations all point to a willingness to pursue and experiment with a wealth of alternative goals (or at least subgoals) and pathways.

G's exceptional talent of knowing what to disregard (in the quest for fundamental theory) appears to be combined with the thoroughness of his preparations, which include an extensive collection and examination of what he considers relevant in the literature. His advice against 'collecting data' (in doing philosophy) is apparently not meant to exclude reading or scanning a broad range of material and an imaginative use (as a comparison) of selected previous attempts at 'knowing oneself.'

G's dedication to theory and his faith in reason appear to be exceptionally all-inclusive and confident (and independent). By this I mean a readiness to think through all aspects of life and knowledge, to arrive at reasoned conclusions that often go against the current, to follow up even the remote logical consequences, and to adhere staunchly to what he takes to be consistency and especially truth. Since we are all so ignorant about many fundamental and crucial questions, on which our wishes and emotions inevitably play a part in determining our belief and attitude, it is perhaps to be expected that the all-pervading exercise of G's powerfully logical mind would lead to tentative and probable (for him) conclusions that are seen by most people to be implausible, irrelevant, contrary to common sense (or the acknowledged authorities), or even 'crazy.'

On broad theoretical issues I have just mentioned some of G's conjectures (on a separate mind, on 'mechanism in biology,' etc.). I shall later in this book consider also his attention to the hypothesis that there is a next life; he has also (I do not know how seriously) spoken of rocks having experience and the spirits hiding out today. (He is right to the extent that these three examples have not been demonstrated to be 'logically' impossible. But most of us do not pay much attention to what is merely 'logically' possible. In the case of the rocks, one may construe the suggestion as a proposal to extend the use of the word 'experience' for the purpose of a unified philosophy, as is done by Leibniz in his monadology.) There is a story that G tried to explain at his citizenship examination how the American Constitution permits actions that could lead to fascism (see chapter 4, under *1948*). Admittedly that was not quite the occasion to give such an explanation, which, however, could very well be a significant contribution (of possible practical relevance) to political theory.

Most of us tend to take over commonly accepted associations or links of one belief or attitude with another. When we have chosen the one, we generally adopt the other without further reflection. This is more frequently not the case with G. While not questioning the broad validity of current science in its more familiar aspects, he distrusts some of the fundamental assertions and attributes them to the 'prejudices of the time' (as can be seen from some of his conjectures mentioned a while back). In this regard his attitude resembles Einstein's unpopular skepticism toward the definitive character of quantum theory. In politics his admiration of Roosevelt was shared by the majority of his colleagues, but he favored Eisenhower in opposition to most of them (including Einstein). Like Einstein, G's outlook was cosmopolitan and he was very much peace loving.

The correspondence with his mother contains also G's observations on his own experience in the realms of film, art, and literature (mostly biographies). These undoubtedly present an aspect of G as a person but are probably of little intrinsic interest. According to WS, G was interested in surrealist and abstract art (often visiting the Museum of Modern Art in New York), and his favorite authors include Goethe, Kafka, Gottfried Kästner, Stefan Zweig, Arthur Schnitzler, Franz Werfel, and Heimito von Doderer. His preference for 'light' music (Richard and Johann Strauss, Franz Lehar, Spanish dance music, 'pop' music, Carmen, etc.) and his enthusiasm for Disney films (especially *Snow White*) are commonly thought to be surprising and in poor taste (or perhaps 'retarded'), since most of his colleagues are likely to cultivate and acquire more 'sophisticated' enjoyments under the influence of the tradition of highbrow culture. Yet G's independence in this regard may also be seen to be a greater readiness to acknowledge what one actually likes and in part a result of his more intensive concentration on other matters.

G's wife Adele had little formal education or intellectual pretension.

Their close association and then marriage were apparently not favored by G's parents and his brother. (For more details, see chapter 3 under *1938*). In a letter to his mother (14 April 1953) G says, 'Adele is by nature certainly thoroughly harmless and good-hearted, but evidently has a nervous streak that was greatly aggravated by her experiences (especially the excessively strict upbringing at home and her first marriage).' G certainly trusted Adele fully, and Adele attended to G's everyday needs satisfactorily and devotedly. The marriage probably conformed to G's wish to concentrate on theoretical work and to separate it as much as possible from other aspects of his life.

A rational consequence of the choice to dedicate oneself to fundamental theoretical work is to reduce, as much as possible, involvements with other activities and to eliminate, with regard to the necessities of everyday life, all avoidable complexities. Being thoroughly rational along this line, as G undoubtedly attempts to be, contains the potential danger of a conflict with the holistic criterion of rationality in terms of a balanced life that eschews all forms of fanaticism. Indeed, this potential conflict seems to point to an intrinsic ambiguity in the concept of rationality.

To compensate for the excessive energy devoted to theoretical innovations, the simplest and least demanding way to handle one's daily affairs appears to be cultivating and following a routine according to a familiar and accustomed pattern. On the whole G's home life has all the appearance of a bourgeois family, typically concerned with house and garden, food and digestion, household helpers, weekly accounts, summer vacations, (G's and Adele's) families and relatives, birthdays and anniversaries, cinema, radio and then television, rests on Sunday, etc.

Somewhat exceptional are their limited social contacts, the absence of children, the great attention to G's health, not driving a car, and G's modesty toward his official titles and compensations. Indeed, G's attitude toward money, spending, and material possessions is hardly typical, and agrees well with his own priorities. He conforms to his own assertion that money is not the only problem and 'also never the most important' (letter of 25 March 1953). He spends little on himself not because he limited himself to the bare necessities but because, for instance, he had 'no need to travel' and for him 'buying books would have little sense when I get all those of interest to me more easily and quickly from the libraries' (letter of 14 April 1953). Moreover, his choice to leave, along with his other belongings, also his papers to Adele (who knew little about such things) would seem to suggest that he was not even particularly concerned with the proper handling of his unpublished work.

There is of course nothing unusual for an originator of novel theoretical ideas to be at the same time ordinary and old-fashioned in everyday activities. A more striking juxtaposition of the new with the old is G's preference and talent to obtain original ideas to illuminate perennial issues and approaches by penetrating more deeply into traditional concepts and concerns, which are often considered out of date on the basis of less careful responses to past exaggerations. Examples include the significance of metaphysics, the appeal to intuition, the concept of mathematical (in particular arithmetic) truth, the concept of time, the nature of logic and the concept of concept, etc. The emphasis on precision does not for him exclude what is intuitive and rich in content.

G's originality and ability to be precise are accompanied by an inclination to caution and privacy, both of which may be seen as ways to shun complexities in human relations (in particular, controversies). He is known to have permitted himself exceptions in cases of major misconceptions, either to criticize by conspicuous omissions or even to defend his own work in public when he found that his important published ideas had been unintentionally misrepresented and that the errors could be corrected in a pretty definite and convincing manner. As is well known, he often did not publish his views that are controversial or hard to communicate fully. This probably has something to do with his estimate that criticisms of his views are likely to be conducted on a level and in a vocabulary not congenial to him, particularly since what he calls the 'prejudices of the time' would make it hard to understand some of his views. Moreover, he appears to be exceptionally sensitive to criticism, a tendency undoubtedly connected with his being a 'private person.' (For instance, E. Köhler talked with Adele after G's death and reports that G had on his death bed urged Adele to shun journalists and biographers.)

The concept of consistency has a precise meaning when applied to formal systems. With respect to the beliefs, actions, words, and attitudes of a person, the corresponding concept is much more complex. There are stronger and weaker beliefs, self-awareness of inconsistencies varies widely with situations and individuals, etc. In most cases G is aware of more logical connections than most people, and he is more consistently rational in the special sense of being more concerned with finding reasons everywhere. In philosophy he distinguishes consistency from truth and criticizes Kant's work on the ground that it is consistent but pays insufficient attention to truth. In saying this G may have in mind his dissatisfaction with Kant's ambiguous position on religion, his detachment of phenomenal objectivity from the transcendent Ding-an-sich, and his inadequate philosophy of arithmetic, which is based on an unduly restricted notion of intuition.

There are four chapters in this first part of the book, which considers some of the facts about G. It begins with a discussion of G's life from the perspective of his dedication to fundamental theoretical work. In order to obtain a more concrete focus, I quote and discuss three documents relevant to his life and work. Also included is a section that makes a preliminary attempt to compare G with Einstein and to report on some aspects of their relation to each other. The next chapter reproduces a brief account of G's life and work as he told it to me in 1976, which is accompanied by a consideration of his relation to the Vienna Circle (using some records kept by Carnap), a review of Hilbert's program leading to G's response, and some comparisons of G with Wittgenstein. The remaining two chapters offer a more detailed chronological account, with 1940 as a dividing line between life in Central Europe and the Princeton years.

Apart from brief visits (notably five months or so in 1939 to Notre Dame and summer vacations in the 1940s and 1950s), G spent his life in Brünn (1906–1924 plus vacations in 1924–1929), Vienna (autumn 1924 to January 1940, with three visits to Princeton and periods in sanatoria), and Princeton (1940–1978, almost 38 years). G became an Austrian citizen in 1929 (on 6 July) and a US citizen in 1948 (on 2 April, together with Adele). Roughly speaking, he completed his education in spring 1929, did mathematical logic from summer 1929 to perhaps the end of 1942, and occupied himself largely with philosophy (including his work on relativity theory, probably from 1946 to the beginning of 1951) over the remaining thirty-five years.

Once I looked up a few biographical dictionaries and found some information of interest that was, I conjecture, derived from completed forms prepared by G himself before 1970. One interesting aspect is not so much the content as G's selection and formulation of the material. For instance, in all three entries I consulted, he dated his membership at the I.A.S. as 1933, 1935, 1938–1953 (and professor, 1953–   ). A particularly interesting piece of information is the item on his leisure interest, under which is listed ancient history. I have a vague recollection that he told me of this interest once or twice. Of his professional employment, the only item other than his association with the I.A.S. is Dozent, University of Vienna 1933–1938.

What is of more contentual significance is how G chose to list his work prior to 1970. In *International Who's Who 1971–72*, he listed under publications only three items: Über formal unentscheidbare Sätze 31, the consistency of the continuum hypothesis 40, rotating universes in general relativity theory 50. In *Who's Who 1970–71*, he listed *Dialectica* (re the Bernays paper) among the few journals to which he contributed.

In *World's Who's Who in Science*, he described his principal work as follows:

> Gave proof of completeness of predicate logic; method of finding, for any given formalized axiom system of math, a question of Diophantine analysis undecidable in that system; proof that consistency of system cannot be proved in the same system; proof of consistency

of axiom of choice and of Cantor's continuum hypothesis with currently assumed axioms of set theory; constrn. of rotating universes on basis of Einstein's theory of gravitation.

To obtain a more complete picture of G's work one has to supplement the above description by adding his philosophical publications and especially his unpublished work. G chose to list only those aspects of his work that had been definitely completed and generally accepted. This does not mean, I think, that, in his own mind, he did not consider his philosophical work important. Of his philosophical views, he had an occasion (around 1975) to answer a query (see GQ) on where to find published accounts of them. In reply, he listed his contribution to my MP (1974, pp. 8–12, 84–86, 186, 189–190, and 324–326, totaling about 10 pages), and about 6 pages in his Cantor paper (1947 and 1963, BP, pp. 262–265, 270–272). I have read these 16 pages many times, and am convinced that these terse statements are extraordinarily rich in content and yet at the same time precise in the sense of delineating accurately some basic aspects of the world as he sees them.

But what is likely to be of greater importance in philosophy is his unpublished work. My reconstruction of the conversations with him (to be included in CG) is meant to be a small step toward making his unpublished views more broadly accessible. The major task of selective publication from his vast Nachlass will undoubtedly be arduous and valuable.

Of special interest is an undated sheet on which G summarized his unpublished work from 1940 on. It appears probable that the list was made around 1970. Hence, it is likely that a major portion of G's unpublished work is included. Roughly in G's own words, the list can be given as follows:

1. About one thousand 6 × 8 inch stenographic pages of clearly written philosophical notes (= philosophical assertions).
2. Two philosophical papers almost ready for print. [His paper on relativity and Kant's philosophy and his paper on syntax and mathematics.]
3. Several thousand pages of philosophical excerpts and [notes on the] literature.
4. The clearly written *proofs of* my [his] cosmological results.
5. About six hundred clearly written pages of set theoretical and logical results, questions, and conjectures (to some extent *outstripped* by recent developments).
6. Many notes on intuitionism and other foundational questions.

[The first item is probably the most important for philosophy. Mentioned on the sheet are also his ontological proof, five minor mathematical works, his general consistency proof of the axiom of choice, and his rewritten 1958 paper with three appended notes. A more detailed account of this sheet is given in *CG*.]

It is clear from G's handling of his results and manuscripts that he was exceptionally exacting in the publication of his work (especially after 1950). He also declined several invitations to consider publication of his collected papers, on the ground that the important ones were all easily available. But this, I believe, does not mean that he thought all of his unpublished work unimportant, but rather that he considered most of it not finished enough for publication.

At some stage (probably in 1970) G spoke to Dana Scott of his desire to have certain papers published posthumously and even asked Scott to prepare typescripts of some of them. Also he told me in 1976 that my notes 'Some facts about Kurt Gödel' could be published after his death. Hence, it appears that he preferred the posthumous publication of a wider range of his sayings than during his lifetime. I am sure this is because he did not wish to be bothered by criticism and controversy.

Chapter 1
A life of fundamental theoretical work

Gödel's was a life (1906–1978) devoted, as much as is humanly possible, and with success, to the doing of fundamental theoretical work. Compared with others who have done fundamental theoretical work that is known to be of interest to him, G's life may be said to be even more exclusively centered on this one type of work. He was more consistently after the important, and he published relatively little. He engaged himself in very few other activities, whereas, for example, Plato was active in politics, Newton served as master of the mint, Leibniz was, among many things, also diplomat and historian, Kant served as librarian and rector, and Russell and Einstein were active in various directions. Unlike Kant or Husserl, G did not do much teaching or lecturing.

In doing important things, talents, choices, and circumstances all play their parts. Of those who do fundamental theoretical work, some show exceptional abilities in a more definite direction when young, while others appear to have abilities in several directions. G appears to belong to the second category: when he was in college, it was clear to people who knew him that he had mastered a wide range of subjects and that he was going to do important work in one field or another. Indeed, it seems that he wanted to make fundamental conceptual advances that are at the same time conclusive and noncontroversial. Such advances are of course rare. Up to 1939, he was fortunate enough to get results that meet both requirements, even to his own satisfaction. From 1940 on there appears to have been a constant struggle between these two requirements in the line of his work. He discontinued very promising work in logic in 1943 and then spent much energy in doing philosophy (in the familiar sense), but little was completed (according to his own ideal) and even less was published.

Speaking mechanically and misleadingly, one may delineate a few different stages in G's life of intellectual work. The first 23 years (1906–1929) were devoted to learning and preparation. This was followed by 14 years (1929–1943) of intensive and most productive research in mathematical logic. The next few years witnessed his deep-rooted interest in philosophy coming to dominate his intellectual activities. He was not only interested in the philosophy of mathematics but took it as central to philosophy. His papers on Russell (1944) and Cantor (1947) are in this area, and he spoke of his work on relativity theory (and also its relation to Kant's philosophy), probably from late 1946 to the beginning of 1951, as a 'digression.' For the next eight years the philosophy of mathematics occupied a conspicuous place: the Gibbs Lecture, the Carnap paper, and the constructivity paper. In 1959 he began to study Husserl, probably to look for a deeper foundation of human knowledge in everyday life. It was presumably at this time when he 'realized that philosophy calls for a different method from science.' Overlooking fine points, one might distinguish a period of science-centered philosophy (1943–1958) and one of more autonomous philosophy (1959–1978). It is clear, however, that many of his views had remained the same not only since 1943 but even since 1925, according to his own account and other records.

To get a closer look at G's life, I would like to consider three documents: a letter from his brother Rudolf on G's youth (29 April 1985), G's unsent responses to a questionnaire (1975), and an evaluation by me (1972).

1.1 Letter from Dr. Rudolf Gödel (RG)

This is a response to my inquiry. An English translation of the letter is broken up and its pieces are distributed under the years 1911, '14, '16, '20, '24, and '45, in the chronological account below.

Wir (mein Bruder und ich) lebten mit unseren Eltern in Brünn in einer Villa mit schönem Garten.

Es war ein harmonisches Familien-Leben, ich verstand mich mit meinem Bruder sehr gut und ebenso wir beide mit unseren Eltern.

Wir spielten meist miteinander und hatten wenige Freunde, ruhige Spiele—Baukasten, Eisenbahn, im 1. Weltkrieg natürlich auch mit Zinnsoldaten.

Mein Bruder war ein fröhliches Kind, hatte allerdings mit etwa 5 Jahren eine leichte Angst Neurose, die später vollkommen zurück ging. Er war ein ausgezeichneter Schüler der anfangs an Sprachen, später an Geschichte und noch später an Mathematik interessiert war. Auf lateinischen Schularbeiten hatte er *immer* die beste Note. In Mathematik war er mit 16–17 Jahren seinen Kollegen weit voraus und beherrschte schon den Stoff der Universität.

Mit seiner Mutter hat er sich bes. gut verstanden, sie spielte ihm oft am Klavier seine lieberlings Melodien vor (leichte Musik). Wenn ich mit meinen Eltern spazieren ging blieb er oft lieber mit einem Buch zuhause.

Im Alter von etwa 8 Jahren hatte mein Bruder einen schweren Gelenk-Rheumatismus mit hohem Fieber und seither war er etwas hypochondrisch und bildete sich ein einen Herzfehler zu haben, was aber medizinisch nie nachgewiesen wurde.

Später, in Princeton, hatte er ein Ulcus duodeni mit einer schweren Blutung. Seither lebte er *so streng* Diät, dass er dauernd an Gewicht verlor und unter-ernährt war.

Im Alter von etwa 10 Jahren spielte er gerne Schach und war im Spiel sehr ergeizig und sehr traurig oder ärgerlich wenn er verloren hat, was nicht oft der Fall war.

An unserem schönen Garten hatte er nicht viel Interesse, während ich dort gerne arbeitete.

Im Alter von 18 Jahren ging er zum Studium an die Univ. Wien wo ich schon seit 4 Jahren Medizin studierte, wir wohnten als Stundenten beisammen jeder in seinem Zimmer, waren aber nicht viel beisammen da er an die Univ. und ich ans Krankenhaus ging, er sprach mit mir nur selten über seinen Beruf. Ich erfuhr spät, als er schon in Princeton war, durch Bekannte(!) dass er in seimem Fach ein bedeutender Mann war.

Unsere Eltern kamen uns in Wien oft besuchen und wir gingen dann oft ins Theater wofür mein Bruder grosses Interesse hatte.

Warum mein Bruder nach dem 2. Weltkrieg nie mehr nach Wien zu Besuch gekommen ist, habe ich nicht verstanden. Er gab als Ursache an dass er in Wien vielleicht nicht die entsprechende Diät einhalten könnte(?).

Er hat aber seine Mutter und mich mehrmals nach Princeton eingeladen und wir haben mit ihm und seiner Frau viele glückliche Stunden verbracht.

From this letter it is clear that G grew up in a happy and quite wealthy family. His intimacy with his mother continued over the years till her death in 1966. In later years he developed close relations with some of his seniors, particularly Hahn (died 1934), Schlick (died 1936), Einstein (died 1955), and Bernays (died 1977). Of his contemporaries (all somewhat older than he), he is known to have been familiar with M. Natkin, H. Feigl, K. Menger, J. v. Neumann, and O. Morgenstern. Over the last 25 years of his life, he was quite comfortable with about half a dozen logicians who were about 15–20 years younger than he. All these known personal contacts have a base in shared intellectual interests. Judging from the little I know, his marriage was on the whole a happy one. His wife was not an intellectual but apparently helped him greatly also in his work by making it possible for him to concentrate on it; a greater help, I believe, than one partner commonly gets from the other in a marriage. The marriage appears to resemble more Einstein's second one (rather than his first). [Einstein also came from a harmonious and loving family (Pais, p. 36).]

The happy and wealthy family undoubtedly helped to strengthen G's self-confidence and give him a stronger sense of security. There was less of the distraction of having to make a living at an early stage in his career, which is often accompanied by the need to produce results and advertise oneself. For example, Einstein had to economize in college and to manage to make a living immediately afterward. The other side of the coin was the danger of being spoilt, yielding a tendency to expect things to be taken care of by others and to limit personal contacts to those of a quality comparable to what he had been accustomed in the happy family.

G's school career shows the normal responses of an extraordinarily talented and methodical child. His shift of interest from the languages to history and then to mathematics seems natural for one who had all-around intellectual abilities. The attraction of a school subject is determined by the combination of its intrinsic appeal (in its full richness) and what can be taught and pretty thoroughly grasped at the school stage. Since G was able to absorb all that was taught and more, the succession of the subjects that interested him appears to fall under a pattern more or less to be expected. For example, science or theology can rarely be taught in schools in such a way as to produce in the mind of a brilliant pupil a sense of really understanding the subject.

Another point is obvious: G's ability was far above the maximum demand in the schools. This is clear from the additional amount of mathematics he learned by himself. This great surplus over what is required seems to be an experience shared by all who go on to do important theoretical work later in life. People differ in how they use this surplus. Einstein certainly had such a surplus, but his choice to use it in studying physics and mathematics was more exceptional than G's choice. Apart from the famous enchantment with a pocket compass at 4 or 5, (his paternal) Uncle Jacob posed mathematical problems after Einstein was 9; at the age of from 10 to 14 Max Talmud introduced him to some good reading material on physics and spent hours every week discussing science and philosophy with him (Pais, pp. 37–38). As far as I know, G did not have comparable extracurricular encounters.

It is amusing that G's brother had to learn about G's important place so indirectly. I was once told that G's wife considered G's brother more of a success than G. Clearly G rarely spoke with his family about his work or his profession. More generally, G was willing to answer questions (and answer them well), but tended to limit his replies to what he considered directly relevant. Unlike most people, he seldom brought in related material, which it would be reasonable to expect to be also of interest to the questioner. One reason for this reluctance to broaden the topic may be the fact that he knew so much and had so many ideas, and that he did not want to say things that did not interest the person. According to my limited experience, he volunteered information only in exceptional cases, such as on his state of health, when he felt misrepresented, or, less frequently, when he took an interest in educating somebody.

An important factor in G's life and work was his frail physique and his relatively poor health. Both he and Kant were frail and somewhat hypochondriacal. Both of them paid a good deal of attention to their health, but apparently Kant was more successful, probably because he was more 'rational.' G's brother remarked on the excessively stringent diet and its bad effects. It is generally known that G did not obey the doctors' orders even in situations where most people would. Sometimes G himself admitted that he was a difficult patient. In his daily life, especially in the matter of food, he depended, at least in his later years, very heavily on his wife. On one occasion when his wife was away he told me that he cooked once every few days. During the last half-year of his life, his wife was, because of her health, away from home most of the time. This was very hard on him, and when friends had arranged for nurses to come to help him, he did not open the door to them. It is widely believed that he was paranoid and had a constant suspicion of food poisoning. His wife returned home before Christmas 1977 and persuaded G to enter a hospital, where he died on 14 January 1978. He died of 'malnutrition and inanition' caused by 'personality disturbance,' according to the death certificate (on file in the Mercer County courthouse, Trenton).

Like Kant, G did not travel very much. Indeed, he only traveled when he had to, and traveling, especially away from home, seems to have been hard on his nerves, as can be seen from the fact that both in 1934 and in 1935, he fell sick upon returning to Vienna from Princeton. After his arrival in Princeton in March 1940, he never left Princeton, except for short brief trips and summer vacations (once or twice in Maine but mostly in New Jersey). His brother wonders why G never visited Vienna again. G's reluctance to travel appears to have been the decisive reason. (He declined an honorary degree from Cambridge University for this reason.)

G's relation to Vienna and the university there is complex. In 1939 he was, to his surprise, found to be fit for military service and he applied for but did not obtain (until much later) the changed position of Dozent. But apparently he bought (or leased) an apartment in Vienna and had work done to it as late as November 1939. It seems that up to even that time he still intended to stay in Vienna. Later in his life he declined honors from Vienna on more than one occasion.

Evidently G was satisfied with living in Princeton and in America. But he is much better known for his work done in Vienna than what he did in Princeton. If circumstances had permitted, he would undoubtedly have preferred to live and do his life's work, like Kant, all at one place or at least within one more or less homogeneous cultural region. His philosophical views would probably have found more sympathy and encouragement on the European continent and, as a result, he might have been induced to publish more of them. Along a different direction, if he had held only a position with teaching duties, especially one in philosophy, his philosophical views would probably have been more widely known through his students.

1.2 The Grandjean questionnaire (GQ)

Burke D. Grandjean designed a special questionnaire for G in 1974. He wrote to G on 16 July and 19 September of 1974, as well as on 12 February, 2 May, 15 September, and 2 December of 1975. He also telephoned G on 24 February 1975. There is a letter addressed to Grandjean dated 19 August 1975 in G's papers, answering only a few questions. But the reply was not sent. There are also two variants of a moderately complete set of answers drafted in pencil (not entirely legible) to the questions. I shall try to reproduce here all three documents (all contained in folder 01/55 of the Nachlass). Presumably these replies were written in 1975.

1.2.1 The form with answers

Intellectual and Biographical Information: Kurt Gödel.
  1.   Please sketch for me your educational background. My research indicates that your primary school was at Brünn (now Brno, Czechoslovakia), that you took a degree in engineering at a Brünn technical college, and that in 1924 you began your studies in mathematics at the University of Vienna, where you received the Ph.D. degree in 1930. How complete and accurate is this account?
    G crossed out the clause 'that you … technical college,' wrote 'wrong' on the margin, and drew a line from between 'studies' and 'in mathematics,' connecting it to 'first in physics 1 to 2 years.'
  2.   (a)   As well as you can recall, when did your interest in mathematics begin?
      '14 years of age.'
    (b)   Are there any influences you would single out as especially important in the development of your interests?
      'Introduction to calculus included in [the] "Görschen" collection.'
  3.   When did you first study Principia Mathematica?
      '1929.'

4.   (a)   As well as you can recall, when did you become interested in the problem, central to your 1930 and 1931 papers, of the completeness of logic and mathematics?

'1928.'

(b)   Are there any influences you would single out as especially important in this regard?

'Hilbert-Ackermann's Introduction to mathematical logic, Carnap's lectures of metalogic.'

5.   When, if at all, did you first study any of the works of the following:

(a)   Ludwig Boltzmann. 'phil[osophical] papers 1960.'
(b)   Jan Brouwer. '1940.'
(c)   Paul Finsler. '1932' [followed by some indistinct words, probably to indicate that the work is of no value to him.]
(d)   Immanuel Kant. '1922.'
(e)   Karl Kraus. '1960.'
(f)   Fritz Mauthner. 'Never.'
(g)   Jules Richard. 'Never.'
(h)   Ludwig Wittgenstein. '1927 (never thoroughly).'

6.   How much importance, if any, do you attribute to each of the scholars in the above list, in the development of your interests?

'Only Kant was imp[ortant].'

7.   Your name is frequently mentioned in connection with the 'Vienna Circle,' which began to meet in 1924 and included Rudolf Carnap, Hans Hahn, Otto Neurath, Moritz Schlick, and others.

(a)   When did your association with this group begin?

'1926.'

(b)   How close was this association?

'1926–28 frequ[ent] disc[ussions] with some younger members but mostly (very often) I took a non-pos[itivistic] pos[ition] & attendance of seminars.'

(c)   Do you regard this group or some of its members as influential in the development of your intellectual interests?

'Yes, this group aroused my interest in the foundations but my views about them differ fund[amentally] (subst[antively]) from theirs.'

8.   Your philosophical leanings have been described by some as 'mathematical realism,' whereby mathematical sets and theorems are regarded as describing objects of some kind.

(a)   How accurate is this characterization?

'Correct.'

(b)   In particular, how well does it describe your point of view in the 1920's and early 1930's, as compared with your later position?

'Was [has been] my position since 1925 before [followed by two words, presumably to indicate "joining the Circle"].'

(c)   Are there any influences to which you attribute special significance in the development of your philosophy?

'By phil[osophical] lectures (introduct[ory]) of Gomp[erz] and math[ematical lectures] by Phil. Furtwängler.'

9.   Is there a published source, either written by yourself or by another author, which you regard as a particularly apt statement of your philosophical point of view?

'Book by Wang, paper on cont[inuum] probl[em], on Russell.'

10.   (a)   When and where were your parents born?
[left blank]

(b)   What was their native language?
'German.'

11.   (a)   What was your father's occupation during your child-hood?

'Manager of cloth factory.'

(b)   What was your mother's occupation (if employed)?
'Not employed.'

12.   What was the highest level of education attained by each parent?

$\left\{\begin{array}{l}\text{'Father technical school} \\ \text{Some educ[ation] equi[valent] with coll[ege] courses.'}\end{array}\right.$

13.   (a)   What was your parents' religion?
'Father Old Cath[olic], mother Luther[an].'

(b)   What is your religion?
'Baptist Lutheran (but not member of any rel. cong.). My belief is *theistic*, not pantheistic, following Leibniz rather than Spinoza.'

14.   (a)   How many other children did your parents have?
'1.'

(b)   In what year was each born?
'1902.'

(c)   What is the highest level of education attained?
'Doctor of Medicine (x-ray spec.).'

15.   (a)   How would you characterize your family's financial situation during your childhood: quite poor, poor, average, above average, wealthy?
'Close to wealthy.'

(b)   To what extent was your family affected by World War I and the post-war inflation?
'Not much affected.'

16.   (a)   To what extent were you and your family affected by the Czech nationalist movement for independence from the Austro-Hungarian Empire?

'Emigrated to Austria 1929 (after my father's death).'

(b)   To what extent were you and your family aware of or affected by the anti-Semitism in the period from 1910 to 1935?

'Not affected.'

17.   Before you enrolled at the University of Vienna, how much contact did you and your family have with the cultural and intellectual life in Vienna?

'Little contact except through the newspaper *Neue freie Presse*.'

Your time and attention to these questions are much appreciated, Professor Gödel. Thank you very much.

Sincerely,

(signed)

Burke D. Grandjean

1.2.2   *An alternative and supplementary reply*

Dear Sir,

I am sorry I have no time for an interview. Moreover I have not been so well recently.

Here are some answers to your questions (excluding those that are too personal or too complicated to answer). In part they are given on the form you sent me.

2a.   14 years of age.

2b.   Current textbooks in calculus.

3.   1929.

4a.   1928.

4b.   Hilbert-Ackermann Introduction.

Lectures by R. Carnap.

5.   (a)   ca. 1960 (phil writings)   (b)   1940

(c)   only 2 papers, 1932 and later.

(d)   1922   (e)   ca. 1960   (f) (g)   not at all

(h)   ca. 1927 only very superficially.

As to 6 I would like to say that only Kant had some infl. on my phil thinking in gen & that I got acq. with him about 1922, that I know Wittg only very superficially, & that I read only two papers by Finsler (in or after 32); finally that the greatest phil. infl. on me came from Leibniz which I studied about 1943–46.

7.   (a)   1926.

(b)   1926–28 reg. att. of meetings & frequent disc. with some of the younger members. After 1930 the assoc became more & more loose. Generally speaking I only agreed with some of their tenets. E.g. I never believed that math is syntax of lang. In the course of time I moved further & further away from their views.

(c) Yes, they aroused my interest in the found of math.

8. (a) accurate.

(b) held such view since 1925

(c) Heinrich Gomp. Prof of Ph of Vienna

Wittg's views on the phil of math had no inf on my work nor did the interest of the Vienna Circle in that subj. start with Wittgenst [but rather went back to Prof. Hans Hahn.]

1.2.3 The letter

Finally G's typed but unsigned and unsent letter of August 1975 follows.

August 19, 1975

Mr. Burke D. Grandjean
Department of Sociology
University of Texas
Austin, TX 78712

Dear Mr. Grandjean:

Replying to your inquiries I would like to say first that I *don't* consider my work a "facet of the intellectual atmosphere of the early 20th century," but rather the opposite. It is true that my interest in the foundations of mathematics was aroused by the "Vienna Circle," but the philosophical consequences of my results, as well as the heuristic principles leading to them, are anything but positivistic or empiricistic. See what I say in Hao Wang's recent book "From Mathematics to Philosophy" in the passages cited in the Preface. See also my paper "What is Cantor's Continuum Problem?" in "Philosophy of Mathematics" edited by Benacerraf and Putnam in 1964; in particular, pp. 262–265 and pp. 270–272.

I was a conceptual and mathematical realist since about 1925. I never held the view that mathematics is syntax of language. Rather this view, understood in any reasonable sense, can be *disproved* by my results.

I am enclosing a brief biographical sketch. I never studied in Brünn [This refers to the crossed-out part in Grandjean's question 1 but does not mean to deny that he attended primary and secondary schools in Brünn.] My interest in mathematics and philosophy started in high school at the age of about 15. None of the scholars mentioned under 5 in your questionnaire, except perhaps Kant, had any direct influence on the development of my interests.

I am of German-Austrian descent, but my family and I were always friendly disposed toward the Jews. My family was upper middle class. My father was engaged in the manufacturing industry.
Sincerely yours,
Kurt Gödel

KGcdu
Enclosure

There are a few variations in these documents. For example, to question 2a about the beginning of his interest in mathematics, the answer was 14, but in the letter the age was 15 for mathematics *and philosophy*. To question 8c about influences on the development of philosophy, the answer includes the professor of number theory in the first version but lists only the philosophy professor in the second version. The inclusion in the first case is, I believe, related to G's belief that number theory offers the strongest evidence for his mathematical objectivism.

Of particular interest are the references to Leibniz and Wittgenstein volunteered in the second document. Even though it is well known that he studied the works of Leibniz carefully, the date of 'about 1943–46' is helpful. The observation about Wittgenstein's work gives an explicit answer to a question often asked.

Let me try to make a picture of G's intellectual development. He became interested in mathematics at about 14 and to this was added philosophy at about 15. He read Kant at about 16. By the time he entered university at 18, he had acquired a good command of several languages, a familiarity with history, a good deal of advanced mathematics, and, presumably, an understanding of science well above the norm at that stage of education. It is perhaps not surprising that he planned to study theoretical physics in the university. This could be a way to combine his interest in mathematics and philosophy. The concern with giving an account of the mysterious success of physics is certainly central to Kant's philosophy. In terms of the fundamental conceptual issues, physics appears to complement and even contain mathematics.

Judging from the library slips, G requested primarily books on theoretical physics during his first two or three years in Vienna. There was an unmistakable inclination toward what might be called the philosophical foundations of physics. For example, he asked for Kant's *Metaphysical Foundations of Natural Science* on 26 January 1925. Given G's preoccupation with thoroughness, however, there is a certain lack of neatness in physics that calls for a breaking up of the conceptual issues involved, and mathematics seems a natural choice, at least for a prior concentration, as a way of dividing up the difficulty. This I take to be what G means in saying that his interest in *precision* led him from theoretical physics to mathematics.

There are other reasons. He attended the lectures by Gomperz on the history of European philosophy (at least) during 1925/26. At about this time, he became a 'conceptual realist,' presumably under the influence of Plato. From such a viewpoint, it would appear that, by reflecting on mathematics, we get to the heart of fundamental conceptual analysis, which was, for G, at the center of philosophy. He also enjoyed Furtwängler's lectures on number theory, which offers the strongest evidence for and the clearest application of conceptual realism. Indeed, in 1927 he requested largely books on number theory. The pursuit of number theory as a specialist is, however, quite remote from the study of philosophy using its concepts as an important ingredient.

At this stage what might be regarded as more of a historical accident came to play an important part. It so happened that at this time some of the leaders of what was later known as the Vienna Circle of logical positivists were actively developing their novel and influential views, precisely within the community to which G belonged. Given G's interest in philosophy, he attended Schlick's lectures on the philosophy of mathematics and became friendly with the advanced philosophy students Natkin and Feigl, all in 1925. He also became friendly with his mathematics teacher Hahn and began to attend the meetings of the Schlick Circle in 1926. Carnap also came to Vienna in 1926 and there were detailed discussions of Wittgenstein's *Tractatus* in the meetings of 1926/27.

G was apparently not sympathetic with the empiricist orientation, nor impressed by the *Tractatus* and the philosophical work actually done by members of the Circle. But undoubtedly he was sufficiently influenced to sense that logic might be important for philosophy and to see gradually that logic promised to deal with the fundamental concepts of mathematics in a concentrated manner. But it was only in 1928 that he became intensely interested in logic. I believe the reason to be G's concern with looking for points at which definite advances could be made. It was probably in 1928 that he acquired some idea of the Hilbert program as well as the work of Frege and Russell, and saw that logic could be *precise* yet at the same time quite comprehensive. It was then natural for him to explore logic seriously. This is apparently the sense in which G's interest in precision led him from mathematics to logic.

Carnap offered a course, 'The philosophical foundations of arithmetic,' in the winter semester of 1928/29 (listed in the catalogue of the University of Vienna, two hours weekly), which was undoubtedly the one on 'metalogic' attended by G. It was probably only at the beginning of 1929 that the first edition of Hilbert-Ackermann (published in 1928) became available to G and Carnap. Both the course and the book included questions of a mathematical character that bear directly on basic logical concepts. It was probably also in 1929, when G became acquainted with Hilbert's Bologna lecture (of September 1928) in which four central problems of proof theory were explicitly formulated. The dramatic story of how G settled all four problems in less than two years (1929 to 1930) is familiar. I shall give a more detailed account of this below (in section 2.3).

In Vienna, apart from the valuable intellectual stimulus of the Schlick Circle, there were other factors that were good for G's work. He was liked and admired by many of his teachers and fellow students (and, in particular, by the members of the Schlick Circle). His work was quickly appreciated and recognized. His discoveries were rapidly announced and published through the Vienna Academy, the *Monatsheft*, and Menger's colloquium. (Under less favorable circumstances, the effort needed to get things published would have greatly frustrated him, and he would probably have published much less during his Vienna period.) He was very fond of Hahn and Schlick and certainly a few other colleagues as well. His brother was there and his mother lived in Vienna from autumn 1929 to autumn 1937. Before autumn 1929 he often went back to Brünn for vacations. He had known his wife for over ten years before they were married in 1938. Probably he was close with her also for most of that period.

The philosophical aspect of G's completeness and incompleteness results can best be understood in the contexts of Hilbert's formalism and of logical positivism. If it had turned out that mathematical formal systems were complete and decidable and their consistency were provable by finitist means, one would have made an astonishing advance, conclusive in our understanding of mathematics and tremendous in our understanding of human knowledge. Hence, given the prominent position of Hilbert and the enthusiasm of Hahn and Schlick, it is philosophically important to settle the matter if possible, and the fact that the issue was brought into a mathematically approachable form added greatly to its attraction for G.

G's negative solutions of the problems show that we cannot have such exhaustive clean answers to these fundamental questions about the nature of mathematical knowledge. He demonstrated only that mathematics *is not* 'syntax,' but we are still a long way from a fairly clear picture of what mathematics *is*. In this connection, it is of interest to reflect on G's statement that 'the philosophical consequences of my results, as well as the heuristic principles leading to them, are anything but positivistic or empiricistic.' The heuristic principles are explained in his two letters to me (*MP*, pp. 8–11). The philosophical consequences are mentioned in scattered remarks (*MP*, p. 324, here and there in his conversations, to be reported in *CG*; compare also *BA*, p. 15). Apparently his two unpublished papers written in the 1950s (the Gibbs Lecture and the Carnap paper) consider these consequences more extensively.

By 1931, there were, as far as I can see, several factors that were beginning to exert their influence in determining G's course of further work. He was more deeply into logic. The spectacular early and quick success of his work from 1929 to 1930 undoubtedly created an inclination to look for conceptual problems that can be elucidated by mathematical considerations. In this regard a natural choice is the foundations of mathematics on account both of his expertise in logic and of the central place of mathematics in his philosophy. There was, for instance, the problem of evidence and, in particular, its relation to intuitionism.

A more attractive direction was set theory. With regard to number theory he felt that he had settled the mathematical issues of the major conceptual problems (except for the one of seeing clearly the concept of computability). Set theory presents new problems and opens up a vast new vista. Moreover, the continuum problem is definite, challenging, and conceptually so pregnant that any decisive clarification of it cannot but enrich our understanding of the concept of set. He first heard of Hilbert's proposed solution of the problem most likely in summer 1930. And the problem occupied him, off and on, for the rest of his life. He probably thought much about the problem between 1931 and 1943. In the late 1960s he returned to this problem, thinking about it sporadically, probably from 1969 to 1975.

In 1938 G proved the consistency of the continuum hypothesis (and its generalized form) and in 1942 he obtained a sort of method that appeared promising for proving the independence of the hypothesis. He could not see how to clinch a proof and developed a distaste for it. By that time, his continuing attention to his strong interest in philosophy had generated enough momentum, by combining force with the impasse, to turn his attention away from research in logic.

On intuitionism and the problem of evidence, he obtained in 1932 three easy (for him) but illuminating results on the formal system of intuitionistic logic (and number theory). He began to make a close study of Brouwer's work in 1940, which, by the way, apparently suggested to him his idea of proving independence in set theory. In 1941 he obtained a more substantive result that gives an informative interpretation of formal intuitionist number theory. He added philosophical considerations on the problem of evidence and published the result in 1958. In the late 1960s he spent much time in further improving the philosophical part to strengthen the reasoning for his conclusion that the interpretation does make the proofs of (intuitionist, and therewith classical, by one of his 1932 results) number theory more evident (for more on this, see section 11.1).

To return to the 1930s. During this period, he also continued his study of pure mathematics, theoretical physics, and philosophy. While the main thrust of his work appears to be largely autonomous (apart from the great influence, mentioned above, of his contact with the Schlick Circle), his publications, apart from a few, were largely conditioned by external circumstances. Most of his shorter publications from 1931 to 1936 were reports of his presentations to Menger's colloquium. (He also spent the first five months of 1939 at Notre Dame at the invitation of Menger.) After 1940, nearly all his publications were responses to invitations.

Along a different direction, the impact of the 'Princeton connection' on G's work is hard to evaluate. Certainly the visits of 1933/34, 1935, and 1938 helped to spread the influence of G's work more widely and more effectively, as well as to pave the way to his settling down in Princeton from early 1940 on. But the visits apparently put a good deal of strain on G, who fell ill in 1934 and again from 1935 to 1936. It is not easy to estimate how much damage to G's health and disruption to G's work these extended trips away from home created. It appears that in the 1930s no new discoveries were made while he was away from Vienna.

The uncertainties during the second half of 1939 forced G to do several things that were exceptionally hard on him: applying for the changed position of Dozent, contemplating the prospect of a position in industry, drafting a letter (to Veblen) to appeal for help, traveling to Berlin for visas, and, at the beginning of 1940, undertaking the long journey (via Siberia) from Vienna to Princeton. Fortunately, he was accompanied by his wife on the long journey. The difficulties of that period must have much enhanced the relief and satisfaction experienced at the end of the journey, when he and his wife could look forward to a settled and secure life for years to come.

Indeed, the notebooks in G's papers seem to show that in 1940 G began intensive work both in logic and in philosophy, with a major part of the notebooks all filled during the next few years. As I mentioned a moment ago, G became tired of his efforts to prove the independence of the continuum hypothesis, probably around the end of 1942. From 1943 on, G essentially stopped doing research in logic and nearly all his work afterward may be said to be more philosophical than mathematical.

This seems to be a good place to introduce an evaluation of G's work, which was made by me and approved by G himself (contrary to regulations), for the occasion on 1 June 1972 at which he received an honorary degree from The Rockefeller University. This citation gives a listing of G's major contributions in logic that may serve as a summary of his work before 1943. It also mentions in general terms his work in physics (with a philosophical orientation) and in fundamental philosophy, which largely originated since 1943. Hence, it appears appropriate to insert this document and then resume my story of G's lifework.

1.3 My 1972 evaluation

A theoretical man with intellectual talents of the highest order, Professor Gödel is concerned with nothing less than what is fundamental. He succeeds in attaining a level of accomplishment supreme in science, profound in philosophy, and noble in human relations. In the foundations of mathematics, his work gave rise directly or indirectly to most of the major developments during the past few decades. And his interest in foundational questions is by no means confined to mathematics. For example, he has done significant work in physics, namely the construction of rotating universes on the basis of Einstein's theory of gravitation. Yet probably more of his energy has been devoted to fundamental philosophy than to science. Applications of his philosophy in conversations and in his published papers give evidence of a truly comprehensive and forceful grand structure, which has points of contact with the philosophies of Plato, Leibniz, and Husserl. In the human sphere, he is as meticulous in his dealings with people as in theoretical matters, and notably generous to his friends both of his time and of his knowledge. Those who are fortunate enough to come into personal contact with him are struck by his warmth, charm, and wit. The deep respect he enjoys among diverse groups is of a kind rare in the modern world. In a world of people very much competing with one another, he is above competition.

Professor Gödel's work has revolutionized modern logic, greatly raising its level of significance both mathematically and philosophically. And mathematics and philosophy as done by him are exceptionally meaningful, beautiful, and free from rancour. In all current branches of logic, his work is a foundation and a life force. An incomplete list of his contributions to logic must include (1) his proof of the completeness of predicate logic (1930), (2) his method of constructing, for any formalized axiom system of mathematics, a question of number theory undecidable in the system (1931), (3) his proof that the consistency of any of the systems of classical mathematics cannot be proved in the same system (1931), (4) his proof of the consistency of the axiom of choice and of Cantor's continuum hypothesis with the currently assumed axioms of set theory (1938), and (5) his constructive interpretation of classical number theory (1958). On broader issues, his celebrated paper of 1931 on undecidable problems dealt a fatal blow to Hilbert's formalist approach to the foundations of mathematics. Moreover, this paper, supplemented by Turing's definition of computing machines, led to the surprising consequence that even in such restricted fields as the theory of Diophantine equations, no machine can decide all propositions. It is indeed a privilege and an honour to present Professor Gödel for his honorary degree from The Rockefeller University.

While I was preparing the above presentation, G asked to read its various drafts and volunteered comments. In particular, I recall his objecting to a previous formulation to the effect that his work 'dominated' mathematical logic. Also he smilingly expressed skepticism over the phrase 'above competition' but permitted me to retain it. Bradford Dunham and Stanley Tennenbaum both helped me in finding the appropriate language on several points.

According to G's conception of philosophy, all his more important work is closely related to philosophy: in philosophy or philosophically motivated or having philosophical consequences or using philosophy as heuristic principles. It may even be supposed that, for him, all fundamental theoretical work is related to philosophy in one or more of the four nonexclusive alternative ways. It is noteworthy that in G's work there is a strange and exceptional mixture of the new and the old. While his scientific results are novel and surprising, they bear on familiar traditional concepts such as proof, truth, formal (systems), set, time, and intuitive evidence; moreover, in philosophy he is said to be 'old-fashioned.' Of course, to be able to say radically new things about familiar old concepts and questions is specially attractive and indeed a sufficient condition for fundamental theoretical work.

As quoted above, G studied Leibniz around 1943–1946. In 1944 he published his first philosophical paper, using the occasion of an invitation to consider Russell's work in logic to collect and set down many of his own thoughts on logic, its history, and philosophical issues suggested by or relevant to logic. This was followed by a lecture at Princeton University on the concepts of absolute definability and provability (1946) and a paper (1947) on the continuum problem in which the iterative concept of set is formulated (BP, pp. 262–265). In 1963, G further expanded the last paper to give his 'mathematical realism' a fuller exposition (BP, pp. 270–272). From late 1946 to 1950, G considered the relation of relativity theory to the views of Kant and 'the modern idealists,' who 'deny the objectivity of change' and that of time and space. This 'digression' in G's work included new solutions of the field equations, which may be seen, according to him, to support such a philosophical view. It is likely that G's interest in this matter was also related to his study of Leibniz, who was undoubtedly one of the modern idealists he had in mind. However, the distinct features of the views of Leibniz (contrasted with those of the physicists, from Newton to Einstein) seem to go beyond the idea of space and time being subjective (shared by Leibniz and Kant) to require a more comprehensive concept of force. Conjecturally, G was dividing up the difficulty of moving from the physicists' concepts to the Leibnizian, using Kant's view as a point in between.

Apparently G worked on his Gibbs Lecture in 1951, followed by extensive work, probably from 1953 to 1956, on a paper criticizing the syntactic view of mathematics, shared by G's teachers Hahn, Schlick, and Carnap. Then he worked on the problem of evidence, publishing the fruits in his paper of 1958 to honor Bernays. These three papers all center on the philosophy of mathematics. G discussed with me some of the ideas in his Gibbs Lecture (*MP*, p. 324). But the bulk of the lecture and the Carnap paper appears to be devoted to a settling of accounts with the Schlick Circle, by offering arguments that prove conclusively that mathematics cannot be just the syntax of language. They also point, less conclusively, to his own objectivism or mathematical (or conceptual) realism, with its somewhat indeterminate range of applicability, supported by different degrees of evidence. The 1958 paper may be viewed as a positive argument to show that we at least have strong evidence for realism in the domain of natural numbers (by way of the intuitionist number theory).

It is clear that G did other things from 1951 to 1958 besides working on the three papers. He said that his work was divided into three parts: philosophy, mathematics, and affairs having to do with the Institute for Advanced Study (where he became a professor in 1953). Apparently he was not doing much mathematical research during this period, though he kept up with what was going on in logic. On the whole, I do not have a good picture of G's working habits or of the various directions of his studies (particularly since 1951). A careful examination of his Nachlass may give us a better idea of the reading material and his reflections on it at different stages of his life. I believe that on the whole G organized his life (in particular, from 1951 to 1958) around fundamental theoretical work and was most of the time capable of an exceptional methodical concentration (except when eclipsed by his concern with his health). For example, in 1978 his wife told me that they used separate bedrooms because G got up (to work) in the night. This is undoubtedly an indication of G's continuous preoccupation with his work.

According to G, he began to study Husserl in 1959. There are in the Nachlass extensive study notes on the work of Husserl and others. What is commonly known about G's work since 1959 is quite fragmentary and can only add up to a fraction of what he did. Presumably he studied Husserl intensively during 1959 and 1960. He said that his health was exceptionally poor in 1961. He wrote additions and notes on the occasion of the republication of a number of his early papers throughout the 1960s (including additions to his 1958 paper in the latter part of the decade). In 1963 his interest in the continuum hypothesis was revived by Paul J. Cohen's work and (from 1969 to 1975) he returned to this now and then. From late 1967 to early 1968, he spent some effort in composing his two letters to me (*MP*, pp. 8–11). During the academic year 1971/72 he decided to use the occasion of discussing the manuscript of my *MP* to collect his thoughts and formulate some of his more definite philosophical views, as well as to have the formulations published in the book. His extensive conversations with me during 1975/76 may also have been motivated in part by the idea of having me write up some of them in a form suitable for publication.

1.4 Aspects of the life work

The combination of science and philosophy, the reluctance to publish, and the wide range of unfinished projects: all these are striking features of G's life work. In addition, the way he dealt with his health problems and his sensitivity to external circumstances are also rather exceptional.

G's early success set a standard of work that is hard to attain: fundamental and definite results of great conceptual significance (scientifically and philosophically) that were presented in a form acceptable (with different meanings) to conflicting perspectives. But G appears to have sometimes aimed at an even higher level of achievement: doing for metaphysics what Newton did for physics (*MP*, p. 85) or finding a 'scientific foundation' of science or an analysis of fundamental concepts that not only captures the 'axioms' but also yields methods of derivation from them (in some of his conversations). I am not able to determine how far G progressed toward such ambitious goals or what evidence he had for believing them attainable. Once or twice he said that had he started to pursue such goals at the beginning of his career, he might have had a better chance of success. In practice, G must have used, most of the time, more moderate guiding principles in selecting the topics of his research. He seems to have looked for suggestions in the work of Leibniz and Husserl.

G would probably have published more in philosophy if he had found himself living in a more sympathetic philosophical community. For instance, he declined to speak to what he expected to be a hostile audience. His reluctance to publish (probably comparable to Newton's) and his preference for thinking through problems in private seem to be very different from Einstein, who appears to have often carried out his pursuits in public, notably in developing his general theory (from 1907 to 1915; see Pais, pp. 177–257). Kant's record of extensive publication over the last decades of his life contrasts sharply with G's failure to conclude his projects. (In 1798 Kant was impatient with the delay in publishing an essay of his, saying that he was not in the habit of working for nothing and throwing away what he had done.)

Of some famous people, a youthful statement of future plans is preserved and recorded. I do not know whether there exists such a document from G. There is one by Einstein (written about 1895) in which he mentioned his intention to go to Zurich to study mathematics and physics (for four years): 'I imagine myself becoming a teacher in those branches of the natural sciences, choosing the theoretical part of them.... Above all, it is [my] disposition for abstract and mathematical thought, [my] lack of imagination and practical ability. My desires have also inspired in me the same resolve' (Pais, p. 40.)

It may be of some interest to contrast this with a statement by Marx, who did fundamental theoretical work of a very different type. In 1835, at the age of seventeen, he wrote an essay 'Reflections of a young man on the choice of a profession' (*Karl Marx Frederick Engels Collected Works*, vol. 1, 1975, pp. 3–9). These wide-ranging and exalted reflections consider the abstract question of freely choosing a profession and say that 'if the conditions of our life permit us to choose any profession we like, we may adopt the one that assures us the greatest worth.' According to Marx, every profession is but a means for approaching closer to the general aim of perfection. More specifically, he said,

> But the chief guide which must direct us in the choice of a profession is the welfare of mankind and our own perfection. It should not be thought that these two interests could be in conflict, that one would have to destroy the other; on the contrary, man's nature is so constituted that he can attain his own perfection only by working for the perfection, for the good, of his fellow men.
>
> If he works only for himself, he may perhaps become a famous man of learning, a great sage, an excellent poet, but he can never be a perfect, truly great man.

1.5 The friendship between Gödel and Einstein

Both of them grew up and did their best known work in Central Europe, using German as their first language. In 1905, the 'miraculous year,' Einstein completed his articles on (special) relativity, the light quantum, and Brownian motion, as well as his doctoral dissertation (Pais, p. 89). G had proved the completeness of elementary logic and the incompletability of mathematics two years before reaching the corresponding age. Einstein's extended and successful effort, from 1907 to 1915, to formulate general relativity might also be seen as having a sort of counterpart in G's endeavor to settle the continuum hypothesis, on which, however, G's work from 1930 to 1938 brought him only a partial success (namely, a proof that it is not refutable by the known axioms).

Since G specialized in theoretical physics for his first two or three years as a university student, he undoubtedly familiarized himself with the major aspects of Einstein's work at that time. It is quite likely that he attended Einstein's lecture in 1931 at the Physical Institute of the University of Vienna. They became acquainted in autumn 1933 when both of them were in Princeton for the first time. Close contacts between them began in 1942. Either Oswald Veblen (1880–1960) or Paul Oppenheim (1885–1977) or both are said to have been instrumental in bringing G and Einstein together. They saw and talked with each other 'almost daily' from then to Einstein's death in 1955.

In a letter to Bruno Kreisky (Bundesminister für Auswärtige Angelegenheiten of Austria), dated 25 October 1965, Oskar Morgenstern wrote,

> Einstein has often told me that in the late years of his life he has continually sought Gödel's company, in order to have discussions with him. Once he said to me that his own work no longer meant much, that he came to the Institute [building] merely "um das Privilege zu haben, mit Gödel zu Fuss nach Hause gehen zu dürfen" ["to have the privilege to be able to walk home with Gödel"].

In his *Albert Einstein* (1960), Carl Seelig draws from a letter by G (autumn 1955) to give G's version of his discussions with Einstein: 'Einstein has talked with Gödel particularly on philosophy, physics, and politics, often also on his own unified field theory, although or just because he knew that his partner of conversation stood very sceptically opposed to him' (p. 421). [G's letter seems to suggest the conjecture that E enjoyed his company because G held different views in many areas from E and did not hesitate to express his own ideas. The implication appears to be E's disappointment in others who either agreed with him too readily or concealed their disagreement. Surely the more important reason was the feeling of equality, the shared clarity of thought, as well as the attractiveness of both G's ideas and the way they were expressed.] Ernst Gabor Straus (1922–1986), who was Einstein's assistant from 1944 to 1947, has mentioned the relation between G and Einstein on several occasions. The following quotation includes also his formulation of G's special form of a sort of universal 'rationalism' (Woolf, p. 485):

> No story of Einstein in Princeton would be complete without mentioning his really warm and very close friendship with Kurt Gödel. They were very, very dissimilar people, but for some reason they understood each other well and appreciated each other enormously. Einstein often mentioned that he felt that he should not become a mathematician because the wealth of interesting and attractive problems was so great that you could get lost in it without ever coming up with anything of genuine importance. In physics, he could see what the important problems were and could, by strength of charac-

ter and stubbornness, pursue them. But he told me once, "Now that I've met Gödel, I know that the same thing does exist in mathematics." Of course, Gödel had an interesting axiom by which he looked at the world; namely, that nothing that happens in it is due to accident or stupidity. If you really take that axiom seriously all the strange theories that Gödel believed in become absolutely necessary. I tried several times to challenge him, but there was no out. I mean, from Gödel's axioms they all followed. Einstein did not really mind it, in fact thought it quite amusing. Except the last time we saw him in 1953, he said, "You know, Gödel has really gone completely crazy." And so I said, "Well, what worse could he have done?" And Einstein said, "He voted for Eisenhower."

Elsewhere Straus also notices the special respect E had for G. It is highly probable that E, who valued above all in mathematics and physics the exploration of the foundations, admired in G the master who 'has shaken the foundations of logic more forcefully than anybody since Aristotle' (Seelig, op. cit., p. 417).

While the friendship between G and Einstein has often been mentioned, there is little record of a more detailed sort. It was probably in the summer of 1946 that G's mother Marianne first heard about his close association with Einstein and began to introduce Einstein into their correspondence, undoubtedly a topic congenial to both of them. Subsequently, we encounter Einstein frequently in G's letters to Marianne (LM), especially from July 1946 to May 1956. On several occasions G said, 'I see Einstein almost daily.' There are comments on Einstein's state of health, discussions of articles or books about Einstein, etc. The passages in LM that relate to Einstein not only create a concrete image of G's friendship with him, but also illustrate G's intimacy with his mother and throw some new light on Einstein's last decade.

In a letter to C. Seelig, Helen Dukas, Einstein's secretary, described Einstein's daily life during this period in the following words (as reformulated in Pais, p. 473):

Einstein's mind continued to be intensely active and fully alert until the very end of his life. During the last ten years, however, his age, the state of his health, his never-ending urge to do physics, and the multitude of his extra-scientific involvements called for economy in the use of his energies and time. He kept to simple routines as much as possible. He would come down for breakfast at about nine o'clock, then read the morning papers. At about ten-thirty he would walk to The Institute for Advanced Study, stay there until one o'clock, then walk home. I know of one occasion when a car hit a tree after its driver suddenly recognized the face of the beautiful old man walking along the street, his black woollen knit cap firmly planted on his long white hair. After lunch he would go to bed for a few hours. Then he would have a cup of tea, work some more or attend to his mail or receive people for discussions of nonpersonal matters. He took his evening meal between six-thirty and seven. Thereafter he would work again or listen to the radio (there was no television in his home) or occasionally receive a friend. He normally retired between eleven and twelve. Every Sunday at noon he listened to a news analysis broadcast by Howard K. Smith. Guests were never invited at that hour. On Sunday afternoons there would be walks or drives in some friend's car. Only seldom would he go out to a play or a concert, very rarely to a movie. He would occasionally attend a physics seminar at Palmer Laboratory, causing the awed hush I mentioned before. In those last years, he no longer played the violin but improvised daily on the piano. He also had stopped smoking his beloved pipes.

In his letter to Marianne, dated 21 July 1946, G reported,

Einstein now lives only with his sister and his secretary. He and his first wife were divorced and his second wife died ca. 1936. I have so far only been to his house two or three times, all for scientific discussions. I believe it rarely happens that he invites anybody to his house. Yes, he does enjoy going on the sailboat, but that also appears to be a sport not entirely without its danger. For instance, once last year everyone in the boat fell in the water (I was not there).

A supplement was added on 15 August: 'When I recently wrote about Einstein, I completely forgot that he has also a daughter who mostly, if not all the time, lives in his house. His sister and daughter both appear to be quite sick. Einstein was moreover born in the same year as you. Did you know that?'

After Einstein's death on 18 April 1955 G wrote to his mother on the 25th,

The death of Einstein was of course a great shock to me, since I had not expected it at all. Exactly. in the last weeks Einstein gave the impression of being completely robust. When he walked with me for half an hour to the Institute while conversing at the same time, he showed no signs of fatigue, as had been the case on many earlier occasions. Certainly I have purely personally lost very much through his death, especially since in his last days he became even nicer to me than he had already been earlier all along, and I had the feeling that he wished to be more outgoing than before. He had admittedly kept pretty much to himself with respect to personal questions. Naturally my state of health turned worse again during last week, especially in regard to sleep and appetite. But I took a strong sleeping remedy a couple of times and am now somewhat under control again.

Two months later (on 21 June) G observed, 'That people never mention me in connection with Einstein is very satisfactory to me (and would certainly be to him, too, since he was of the opinion that even a famous man is entitled to a private life). After his death I have already been invited twice to say something about him, but naturally I declined. My health now is good. I have definitely regained my strength during the last two months.'

On 24 February 1956, G commented on a certain negative attitude toward Einstein: 'The antagonism toward Einstein is, moreover, not altogether for political reasons only. What is generally acknowledged today is really only the material which Einstein wrote in the first half of his life. What he did in the last 20 or 25 years has on the contrary not been established as true at all, and is declined as a wrong way by the vast majority of the physicists, including the Jewish.'

According to G, he generally discussed with Einstein physics, philosophy, and politics. But he rarely mentions the contents of their conversations. For example, even though it is widely reported that they often discussed their different attitudes toward Eisenhower and G frequently spoke of him in *LM*, Einstein's disagreements on this subject were never reported in these letters. It was an exception when G wrote on 11 December 1946 to report what Einstein told him of the project of a rocket ship: 'People will build a rocket ship which can fly so fast (7 km per sec.) and go up so high, that it then stays up all by itself and circles the earth like a moon (hence it is also called 'artificial moon'). From such a flying apparatus one can then oversee all parts of the earth as on a map.'

1.5.1 G on Einstein's health

Not surprisingly, G wrote a good deal about the state of health of himself, Einstein, and Marianne. On the whole, G's tendency was to believe and report that Einstein was basically very healthy. That was why he was so surprised and shocked when Einstein died (suddenly for G) in 1955. G was not aware that after around the summer of 1950 Einstein was knowingly living under the shadow of death (see Pais, p. 476): 'We around him knew,' said Helen Dukas after Einstein's death, 'of the sword of Damocles hanging over us. He knew it, too, and waited for it, calmly and smilingly.' Since G's observations on Einstein's state of health are stated in the context of their mutual regard, let me give an extended account.

Judging from G's letters, Einstein stayed home (mostly lying down) from early November to the end of 1946. G's account of Einstein's state then and his recovery was quite detailed. 22 November 1946: 'Apparently there is, however, nothing seriously wrong with him. When I visited him recently, he was as lively and merry as ever. He also continues his work as usual but says merely that he feels weak in the feet.' 11 December: 'Einstein still never comes out, but already feels stronger, as can also be noticed from his voice.' 5 January 1947: 'Einstein has for a week been coming to the Institute again and is also otherwise entirely his old self. When I visited him at home, however, he often gave an impression of being rather feeble, so that I was already worried about him.' 16 March: 'Einstein's health is now again in very good order. His weak condition some time ago was apparently less a result of illness than of' preparations for a medical examination.

Einstein had to rest at home again in the summer of 1947. But from the autumn of 1947 to the autumn of 1948 Einstein appeared well to G. On 4 July 1947, G reported that Einstein was taking a rest cure recommended by the physician, 'although he feels entirely fine. So I am now quite lonesome and speak scarcely with anybody in private.' 31 July: 'I visit Einstein every week, he looks well and continues his work as usual, but not so intensively this year.' 28 September: 'Einstein is now again completely his former self and comes daily to the Institute as before.' 17 February 1948: 'I keep on wondering over Einstein's walking to the Institute in such weather. But he appears to be in this respect quite a match of you in unreasonableness.' 12 July: 'I see Einstein almost daily. He is very robust for his age. One does not see that he is already nearly seventy and he now appears also to feel completely well in terms of his health.' 22 August: 'Einstein is also already spending his second summer in Princeton.'

For a number of years Einstein had attacks of pain in the upper abdomen. In the autumn of 1948 the surgeon Rudolf Nissen diagnosed an abdominal growth and suggested an exploratory laparotomy. Einstein consented and entered the Jewish Hospital in Brooklyn on 12 December 1948. He was operated on and left the hospital on 13 January 1949. The 'sword of Damocles' mentioned by Helen Dukas was the discovery around the summer of 1950 that the aneurysm was growing. (For details and references, see Pais, pp. 475–476.)

This was the context of the following reports by G to his mother in 1949. 17 January: 'Einstein is apparently doing very well. At least one of the attending doctors tells me so. He has returned home for a few days, must of course still take good care of himself and receive no visits yet. After all, the operation took place only 17 days ago and one cannot reasonably ask for more. It must not have been a very difficult operation (not a gall-bladder operation, as is reported in the papers).' 26 February: 'I visited Einstein in the 4th week after his operation. Scarcely anything more was noticeable, except that he was paler than usual. He was then about to leave for Florida and should visibly recover there.' 28 July: 'I am, as usual, together with Einstein almost daily. He looks distinctly better since the operation and' has kept himself fully active.

During Einstein's remaining years, G apparently felt that he was basically in good health and, therefore, commented less frequently on this matter. 12 April 1952: 'I see Einstein almost daily. He is very robust and has in the last few years become younger rather than older than before. The operation of Dec. 1949 [should be 1948] has apparently worked out favorably.' 31 October: 'Einstein was ill for a couple of weeks (a light vein-inflammation), but now he is already walking home from the Institute again.' 21 September 1953: 'Einstein is very well; he felt especially fine just this summer. In any case it is now too much for him to walk both to and from the Institute, a journey lasting altogether about one hour. Therefore he now walks only one way.' 19 March 1954: 'I continue to see Einstein almost daily, only the weather in the winter is often too bad for walking.' (G was himself sick in the autumn of 1954.) 5 January 1955: 'I am also not at all so lonely as you think. I often visit Einstein and get also visits from Morgenstern and others.' 14 March: 'Einstein has again completely recovered and walks daily to the Institute as usual. Today is also his 76th birthday. Naturally his house and the Institute were besieged by reporters. But to no avail, since he took no notice at all.' 10 April: 'Einstein remains fine.'

On Wednesday, 13 April, Einstein collapsed at home. During the next few days he refused all suggestions for an operation. He said, according to Helen Dukas, 'I want to go when *I* want. It is tasteless to prolong life artificially. I have done my share, it is time to go. I will do it elegantly' (see Pais, p. 477).

1.5.2 G on Einstein's public life

Occasionally G commented on Einstein's public image. For example, he wrote on 15 August 1946 that there is again a cult of Einstein, 'because he has (indirectly through his early work) also contributed much to the invention of the atom bomb.' 'Einstein has already appeared in a film and one also sees many pictures of him in illustrated magazines, but he takes most of them very negatively' (27 April 1947). On 16 March 1948, G wrote about Einstein's receiving the prize of the 'undivided world' and his idea of a 'world government.' He also said, 'I also believe that his fame does not rest solely on his scientific work.' The goal of a world government with military power was mentioned again on 12 July in connection with Einstein's role in the Emergency Committee of Atomic Scientists [incorporated August 1946; became inactive January 1949]. On 3 April 1950, G said that he also heard on the 'television program' what Einstein said on the balance of arms in the world.

In the autumn of 1950 G said in two letters that Einstein ceased to appear in public because he was disappointed by the fruitlessness of his efforts. Einstein, according to G, warned against the arms race, but things developed in a way opposite to his wishes. There are also some scattered comments. 'Einstein meant that an anxiety because of the communists would be unfounded' (29 January 1952). 'The Einstein statement on America, of which you wrote, is interesting, but I have some doubt whether it really corresponds to the fact' (20 February 1953). G did not believe that Einstein's stand on the 'loyalty investigation' hurt his popularity (19 March 1954). There was no celebration in Princeton [for Einstein's 75th birthday] since he hated such things—only a political gathering to honor him in his absence, with written answers to questions (4 April 1954).

1.5.3 Some nonconversational interactions

G mentioned in *LM* also some of his external contacts with Einstein. In 1946 G accepted an invitation to contribute a paper to a volume (Schilpp, 1949) honoring Einstein on his 70th birthday. Around the end of 1947 Einstein served as a witness for G at his citizenship examination (for details, see chapter 4 under *1948*). In 1949 there were gifts (in both directions) for Einstein's birthday and G's housewarming. On 14 March 1951, G received the Einstein Prize. On 17 December 1955, G attended a symphony concert in remembrance of Einstein.

G wrote on 26 February 1949, 'March 14 is Einstein's seventieth birthday and I don't know what I should give him. So far as I know him, he is not at all fond of such things. Adele knit for him a wool vest (handstitched things are very hard to get here), but then gave up the idea of giving it for the birthday, and sent it to him in Florida instead. He wrote from there a charming note of thanks.' 'After long searches I finally sent him an etching for his birthday' (16 April).

G and Adele moved into their first (and only) house (129 Linden Lane) around 1 September 1949. 'We had today [12 September] a special surprise. Einstein sent a wonderful flower vase as a greeting for the new home. We had not expected anything like this at all.' 18 October: 'Recently the Einstein family visited us. He has also a daughter, who strikes me as being very nice.' Probably in response to a question of Marianne, G said on 18 January 1950, 'Einstein liked our house extraordinarily.'

G was ill around February 1951 and wrote in his letter of 17 March to say he had recovered and received the Einstein Prize: 'During my sickness Einstein was of course extraordinarily nice to me and visited me many times both in the hospital and at home. You have probably already read in the Viennese papers about the prize which I (together with another scientist) received on his birthday. It came as a complete surprise to me.'

There are many references to the volume Schilpp 1949 and G's contribution to it in the letters. The longest and most informative passage on (an early version of) G's paper is contained in his letter of 7 November 1947:

> This time it is more a philosophical than a mathematical thing, name-
> ly the relation of Kant to the Einsteinian relativity theory, and every-
> thing is naturally not so clear and unambiguous as in pure mathe-
> matics. I have chosen this theme myself when I was asked to write a
> paper for a volume on the philosophical meaning of Einstein and his
> theory; of course I could not very well refuse. I am also not sorry that
> I have accepted and chosen just this theme, because the problem has
> always interested me and its fundamental investigation has in addi-
> tion led to purely mathematical results, which I will publish after-
> wards; or perhaps in advance, since the date of publication of the
> Einstein volume depends on the editor.

18 December 1955: 'There was yesterday a symphony concert here in
remembrance of Einstein. It was the first time I let Bach, Haydn, etc. befall
me for 2 hours long. Nonetheless, the pianist on the occasion was really
fabulous.'

1.5.4 G on articles and books about Einstein

Marianne tried to read books on Einstein and often sent G articles on him.
Apparently she asked G to recommend a book and G wrote on 3 December 1950: 'You buy an arbitrary book x on Einstein, it will probably be
a bad one. There is a very good biography by Philipp Frank [probably
Einstein: His Life and Times, 1948], but it has probably not yet been translated into German. (Added footnote: have just heard that it appeared in
German a couple of months ago.)' In a postscript G added, 'I hear that the
book by Barnett on Einstein [probably Lincoln Barnett, *The Universe and
Dr. Einstein*, 1949] is very good. However, it includes nothing personal, but
only a generally understandable exposition of his physical discoveries.'
    In the next letter (8 January 1951) G offered some advice:

> Is the book on Einstein [presumably Frank's] really so hard to under-
> stand? The prejudice against and the anxiety before all that is
> "abstract," I believe, also play a part in this. If you would attempt to
> read it like a novel (without wishing to understand everything in the
> first reading), then it would, I believe, perhaps not appear so un-
> understandable to you. Yes, I am now working on cosmology, and
> cosmology and physics are natural science.

Of the articles on Einstein that Marianne sent to G, the first was con-
fiscated by the censor with a note inserted: 'forbidden enclosure removed.'
'It is completely puzzling to me what could have been the cause,' said G in
his letter of 28 July 1949. On 18 January 1950, G commented on an article
with the familiar theme of calling Einstein's theory 'the key to the universe'

by observing that such sensational reports are 'very much against Einstein's own will.' He added, 'The present position of his work does not (in my opinion) justify such reports at all, even if results obtained in the future on the basis of his ideas might conceivably justify them perhaps. But so far everything is unfinished and uncertain.' On an article dealing with the history of quantum theory, G observed (3 December 1950) that the article was completely objective in considering fairly the work of Einstein as well as of Bohr and de Broglie, who are not German.

Twice G commented on the familiar suggestion that Einstein's work has something to do with his being 'religious.' 'He is undoubtedly in some sense religious, but certainly not in the sense of the church' (27 July 1951). G remarked (29 February 1950) that he was familiar with the claim 'that the religious instructions he received underlay the endeavor to find a unified theory for the whole world. Those must in any case have been very good and interesting religious instructions. It would scarcely have been possible at all with the sort [of religious instructions] we had.' [A familiar saying of Einstein's is, 'I believe in Spinoza's God who reveals himself in the orderly harmony of what exists' (see, e.g., Clark, p. 502). It appears very unlikely that anybody would obtain such a concept of God from 'religious instructions.']

'The article on Einstein takes great pains to hold the exact middle between the left and the right, which is, however, completely unreasonable in itself' (10 February 1954). G went on to say that when it came to the details, it attributed to Einstein things that evidently he did not mean at all. On 25 August 1955, G wrote, 'The article on Einstein is being very dilettante. For example, the statement was attributed to him, that God doesn't play dice with us. But what he said was, that God doesn't play dice with the world, i.e., that nothing in the world is left to blind chance, which has nothing to do with the interpretation given by the author of the article.'

In the same letter G said, 'I don't know the biography by Antonina Vallentin. What does it contain about his psychical focus in life and about having had little luck in his private life?' Undoubtedly Marianne had been reading Vallentin's *Einstein: A Biography* (1954) and asked G about it. Some themes from this book, which was equally accessible to G and Marianne, became the subject of an extended discussion between them. In his next letter (28 September 1955), G wrote,

> If you send me the Einstein biography, then please, if possible, [do so] in the original text. Or is it neither German nor English? In that case an English version would be preferable because translations in English are mostly much better than translations in German, as I have already often remarked. It is true that Einstein was in many respects a pessimist. In particular, he didn't have a very good opinion of human-

ity in general. Among other things he based this on the fact that those who wished to do some good, like Christ, Moses, Mohammed, etc. either died a violent death or had to use violence against his own followers (like, e.g., Mohammed). Einstein was also very skeptical with regard to the value of technical developments for mankind.

G returned to the biography in several letters (from February to May 1956). He must have received a copy meanwhile. He spoke of it (on 24 February) as being 'very interesting in places. E.g., it appears to be the only biography that says something (if also not much) about his younger (sometimes mentally disturbed) son. Other biographies simply remain silent on this and Einstein has also never spoken of this. It would be of interest to know how this Antonina V. is actually related to Einstein. I will ask Einstein's daughter next time, with whom I have been invited to have tea next week.' In the next letter (29 March) he said that he forgot to ask Margot Einstein, and 'I cannot find that Einstein as a young man was exceptionally handsome. But once I saw a picture of him as a child of about 12 years old, there he appears really delightful and charming. I believe it at that time still displayed most distinctly his true nature, which then passed over more into the background later in consequence of the experiences in life.' On 6 May G elaborated his remark: 'I meant by it that his good heart and his serene nature were later, as a result of the experience he had in human relations, no longer so evidently visible.' Also in the same letter: 'About Antonina Vallentin I have learned that she was a friend of the wife of Einstein. Therefore, you see, she has got everything, so to speak, from first hand.' [Apparently Vallentin was 'a great friend of Einstein's second wife' and knew Einstein well during the Berlin days (Clark, pp. 51–52 and 388).]

Chapter 2
Some facts about Kurt Gödel

Just before his retirement, G arranged to have me visit the Institute for Advanced Study (for 1975−76). In the spring of 1976, the idea occurred to me to find out more about G's intellectual development, and he was quite willing to talk about it. We agreed that I should write up what he said and send the results to him for further comments. This went on intermittently for about a year. But in its essentials, the text was written in June 1976. He proposed to call the account 'Some facts about Kurt Gödel' and said that I could publish it after his death. Since he presumably did not consult his records, some of the dates are questionable. The text is reproduced below, with added notes* to consider some dates and insert some relevant details.

To supplement this concise account, I shall give some details of G's interactions with the Schlick Circle and consider his relation to the Hilbert program. A longish digression contrasting him with Wittgenstein is also included.

2.1 The 1976 text

Gödel was born on April 28, 1906 at Brno (or Brünn in German), Czechoslovakia (at that time part of the Austro-Hungarian Monarchy). After completing secondary school there, he went, in 1924, to Vienna to study [theoretical] physics at the University. His interest in precision led him from physics to mathematics and to mathematical logic. He enjoyed much the lectures by P. Furtwängler [cousin of the famous conductor] on number theory and developed an interest in this subject which was, for example, relevant to his application of the Chinese remainder theorem in expressing primitive recursive functions in terms of addition and multiplication. In 1926 he transferred to mathematics and coincidentally became a member of the M. Schlick Circle. However, he has never been a positivist, but only accepted some of their theses even at that time.[1] Later on, he moved further and further away from them. He completed his formal studies at the

---

* Notes to sections will be found immediately following the sections.

University before the summer of 1929. He also attended during this period philosophical lectures by Heinrich Gomperz whose father was famous in Greek philosophy.[2]

At about this time he read the first edition of Hilbert-Ackermann (1928) in which completeness of the (restricted) predicate calculus was formulated and posed as an open problem. Gödel settled this problem and wrote the result up as his doctoral dissertation which was finished and approved in the autumn of 1929. The degree was granted on February 6, 1930. A somewhat revised version of the dissertation was published in 1930 in the *Monatshefte*. It contains an acknowledgment that 'I am indebted to Professor H. Hahn for several valuable suggestions that were of help to me in the execution (Dürchführung) of this paper.' Gödel tells me[3] that 'in the execution' should be replaced by 'regarding the formulation for the publication.'

In the summer of 1930, Gödel began to study the problem of proving the consistency of analysis. He found it mysterious that Hilbert wanted to prove directly the consistency of analysis by finitist method. He believes generally that one should divide the difficulties so that each part can be overcome more easily. In this particular case, his idea was to prove the consistency of number theory by finitist number theory, and prove the consistency of analysis by number theory, where one can assume the truth of number theory, not only the consistency. The problem he set for himself at that time was the relative consistency of analysis to number theory; this problem is independent of the somewhat indefinite concept of finitist number theory.

He represented real numbers by formulas (or sentences)[4] of number theory and found he had to use the concept of truth for sentences in number theory in order to verify the comprehension axiom for analysis. He quickly ran into the paradoxes (in particular, the Liar and Richard's) connected with truth and definability. He realized that truth in number theory cannot be defined in number theory and therefore his plan of proving the relative consistency of analysis did not work. He went on to draw the conclusion that in suitably strong systems such as that of *Principia Mathematica* (type theory) and that of set theory (say ZF, 'Zermelo-Fraenkel'), there are undecidable propositions. (See section 7 of the notes on Gödel's 1934 lectures, M. Davis, pp. 63–65.)

At this time, Gödel represented symbols by natural numbers, sentences by sequences of numbers, and proofs by sequences of sequences of numbers. All these notions and also the substitution function are easily expressible even in small finitary subsystems of type theory or set theory. Hence there are undecidable propositions in every system containing such a system. The undecidable propositions are finitary combinatorial in nature.

In September 1930, Gödel attended a meeting at Königsberg (reported in the second volume of *Erkenntnis*) and announced his result. R. Carnap, A. Heyting, and J. v. Neumann were at the meeting.[5] v. Neumann was very enthusiastic about the result and had a private discussion with Gödel. In this discussion, v. Neumann asked whether number-theoretical undecidable propositions could also be constructed in view of the fact that the combinatorial objects can be mapped onto the integers and expressed the belief that it could be done. In reply, Gödel said, 'Of course undecidable propositions about integers could be so constructed, but they would contain concepts quite different from those occurring in number theory like addition and multiplication.' Shortly afterward Gödel, to his own astonishment, succeeded in turning the undecidable proposition into a polynomial form preceded by quantifiers (over natural numbers). At the same time but independently of this result, Gödel also discovered his second theorem to the effect that no consistency proof of a reasonably rich system can be formalized in the system itself.

An abstract stating these results was presented on October 23, 1930 to the Vienna Academy of Sciences by Hans Hahn. Shortly afterwards Gödel received a letter from v. Neumann suggesting the theorem on consistency proofs as a consequence of Gödel's original result.[6] The full celebrated paper was received for publication by the *Monatshefte* on November 17, 1930 and published early in 1931. In a note dated January 22, 1931 (K. Menger *Kolloquium*, vol. 3, pp. 12–13), Gödel gave a more general presentation of his theorems using Peano arithmetic rather than type theory as the basic system. The major paper was also Gödel's Habilitationsschrift.

Gödel served as Privatdozent at the University of Vienna for 1933–1938. He visited the Institute for Advanced Study in 1933–34, lecturing on his incompleteness results in the spring of 1934 (compare *The Undecidable*, op. cit. for the notes from these lectures). (Hans Hahn died in 1934.) He visited the Institute again in the autumn of 1935. During 1936 he was sick and very weak.

From autumn of 1938 until spring of 1947 [should be 1946], he received annual appointments at the Institute and stayed there all the time except for the spring term of 1939 when he lectured at Notre Dame and the autumn term of 1939 when he was back in Vienna.[7] He became a permanent member of the Institute in 1947 [1946] and a professor in 1953. He received the Einstein Award in 1951 and the Science Medal in 1975. He has received honorary degrees from Yale (1951), Harvard (1952), Amherst (1967), and Rockefeller (1972). He is a Fellow of the American Academy of Arts and Sciences, American Philosophical Society, and the National Academy of Sciences. He is a Foreign Fellow of the British Academy and the Royal Society [of London].

During 1930–33, Gödel continued his study of logic and mathematics (including the foundations of geometry and the beautiful subject of functions of complex variables). He read the proof sheets of the book by Hahn on real functions and learned the subject [*Reelle Funktionen (Erster Teil: Punktfunktionen)*, Leipzig, 1932; preface dated August 1932]. He attended Hahn's seminar on set theory and took part in Menger's colloquium. A number of Gödel's results from this period were reported in the proceedings of this colloquium. He also wrote a fairly large number of reviews for the *Zentralblatt*.

Gödel visited Göttingen in 1932 and saw Siegel, Gentzen, Noether, and probably also Zermelo there. He never met Herbrand, but only corresponded with him. His second letter did not reach Herbrand, who had died in the meantime. [The letter was sent 25 July 1931, and Herbrand died 27 July.] In the earlier years at Princeton, he met with Church and Kleene more often than with Rosser.

Gödel's health is generally poor and for certain periods has prevented him from serious work. He had rheumatic fever when he was eight or nine years old and this has had a bad effect on his heart.[8] He has had serious trouble with his digestion during almost all his adult years. Since 1947 he has had an infection of the kidneys which makes him very sensitive to colds and he does not recover from colds without using antibiotics. In particular, his health was exceptionally poor in 1936, in 1961 and in 1970.

It must have been in 1930 when Gödel first heard about Hilbert's proposed outline of a proof of the continuum hypothesis in axiomatic set theory (say ZF). This was the time when Gödel began to think about the continuum problem. He felt that one should not build up the hierarchy in a constructive way and it is not necessary to do so for a proof of consistency of CH, and, therefore, one does not have to construct the ordinals except for a prejudice against the objectivist point of view. The ramified hierarchy came to Gödel's mind.[9] Gödel observes that Hilbert did not believe CH to be decidable in ZF, since Hilbert adds a tacit axiom stating that every set can be defined and speaks of his proposed proof as a great triumph of his proof theory. Moreover, according to Hilbert's claim, he did much more than proving CH, he also proved the consistency of ZF on the way. To prove so much, one must expect a very difficult proof.

It must have been in 1935 when Gödel first came up with his consistency proof of the axiom of choice, with a ramified hierarchy.

He was then sick in 1936. It was either in the autumn of 1937 or in the spring of 1938 when Gödel lectured on this result in Vienna; the series of lectures was entitled Axiomatik der Mengenlehre.[10] In the summer of 1938, Gödel extended his result to the extent familiar today.[11] He introduced the axiom of constructibility and proved the relative consistency of GCH. An announcement of these and related results was submitted to *Proc. Natl. Acad.* and published before the end of 1938. At the same time, viz., in the autumn term of 1938–39, Gödel lectured in detail on the main proofs at the Institute, resulting in the monograph that appeared in 1940. A rather detailed and more intuitive outline was communicated to *Proc. Natl. Acad.* on Feb. 14, 1939 and published shortly afterwards.[12]

Gödel's health was relatively good during 1940–43. He worked mostly in logic.[13] In 1941 [or 1942] he obtained a general consistency proof of the axiom of choice by metamathematical considerations. Gödel has agreed recently to reconstruct this proof when his health is better. Gödel believes it highly likely that the proof goes through even when large cardinals are present. After so much development in set theory, it will indeed be a remarkable event to see a result obtained thirty-five years ago open up large new horizons.

Gödel's famous interpretation of intuitionistic number theory by primitive recursive functionals was obtained in 1942 [should be 1941]. Shortly afterwards he lectured on these results at Princeton and Yale [cf. note 13]. E. Artin was present at the Yale lecture. The result was published in German in 1958 on the occasion of Bernay's seventieth birthday. An English translation was completed before 1970 by Gödel himself with a note explaining why the proof is not circular but uses something more evident to interpret intuitionist number theory. The paper was already in proofs when Gödel fell ill [around January 1970]. He is now willing to have it published.

It was in 1943 [should be 1942] when Gödel arrived at a proof of the independence of the axiom of choice in the framework of (finite) type theory. The idea of the proof makes it clear why the proof works. For that reason alone, it would be of interest to reconstruct the proof. It uses intensional considerations. The interpretation of the logical connectives is changed. A special topology has to be chosen.

The method looked promising toward getting also the independence of CH. But Gödel developed a distaste for the work and did not enjoy continuing it. In the first place, it seemed at that time he could do everything in twenty different ways and it was not visible which was better. In the second place, he was at that time more interested in philosophy. Looking back with the results of Paul J. Cohen (1963) it becomes clear that the method can also establish the independence of the continuum hypothesis. He now regrets that he did not continue the work. If he had continued with it, he would probably have got the independence of CH by 1950, and the development of set theory would have progressed faster.[14]

He was interested in Leibniz, particularly the universal characteristic, and in the relation between Kant's philosophy and relativity theory.[15]

Gödel used to reside near Einstein and for many years they went home together almost every day. But Gödel's interest in relativity theory came from his interest in Kant's philosophy of space and time rather than his talks with Einstein.[16]

Gödel worked on GTR during 1947 to 1950 or 1951. He then spent one year working on his Gibbs Lecture.[17]

It caused Gödel a good deal of trouble to have agreed to write a paper on Carnap to prove that mathematics is not syntax. He went through many versions during 1953 to 1955 or 1956. Finally he did not publish the paper, because he thinks that a more convincing refutation could be found.[18]

Gödel started to read Husserl in 1959.

In philosophy Gödel has never arrived at what he looked for: to arrive at a new view of the world, its basic constituents and the rules of their composition. Several philosophers, in particular Plato and Descartes, claim to have had at certain moments in their lives an intuitive view of this kind totally different from the everyday view of the world.[19]

Notes

1. On 4 November 1976, G mentioned some details on this point. At that time (1926 and soon after), he agreed with them that the existing state of philosophy was poor (not necessary but just a historical accident) and, in substance, only agreed with their method of analysis of philosophical and scientific concepts (using mathematical logic). He disagreed with their negation of objective reality and their thesis that metaphysical problems are meaningless. In discussions with them, G took the nonpositivistic position.

   In one of their publications before 1930 (*Wissenschaftliche Weltanschauung: der Wiener Kreis*, 1929, edited by O. Neurath with the assistance of H. Hahn and R. Carnap), G was listed as a member. Of Carnap's *Logische Aufbau*, G said that it only treats the relation between sense perception and physical objects logically and leaves out psychological aspects. I do not know whether he meant to contrast this with Husserl's writings, of which he certainly thought well in the 1970s.

2. Theodore Gomperz was famous for his *Griechische Denker*, Vienna, 1897 (translated by L. Magnus, *Greek Thinkers*, London and New York, 1900). Heinrich also specialized in Greek philosophy.

3. G had completed his dissertation before showing it to Hahn. This was longer than the published paper and accepted for the degree in its original form. It was in preparing the shorter version for publication that G made use of Hahn's suggestions.

4. Or 'propositional functions' according to a prominent tradition at that time. I have tried to reconstruct a few details of G's initial approach in my *Popular Lectures on Mathematical Logic*, 1981 (pp. 21–23). Incidentally, as we know now, even assuming truth for number theory, we can represent only a fragment of all the real numbers (viz., only those definable by 'arithmetical sets').

5. For more details, see chapter 3, under *1930*.

6. The letter from v. Neumann was sent on 20 November 1930.

7. G married Adele Pockert on 20 September 1938. He asked me to delete this information from an early draft on the ground that his wife had no direct influence on his work.

8. As a result, he came to believe, contrary to evidence, that permanent heart damage resulted; compare RG in section 1.1. He also told me once that his teeth had been bad since his early adulthood.

9. A more extended evaluation by G of Hilbert's approach is given in *MP* (pp. 11–12). I have tried to elaborate G's intuitive ideas on the constructible sets in my *Popular Lectures* (pp. 127–134).

10. Actually the course was given in 1937 from May to midsummer.

11. There is an ambiguity with regard to the time of G's discovery of his consistency result on the (generalized) continuum problem. It appears that G must have obtained some proof of the result during or not long after his course in the summer of 1937 (for more details, see chapter 3, under *1937*). However, the fact that he did not announce his result in public until the autumn of 1938 would seem to indicate a dissatisfaction with his proof in 1937, either because it was inconclusive or because it did not yield the full result (say, of a finitist relative consistency).

12. For an accidental reason, G elaborated the history of these results in May and June of 1977 and I was asked to write up his observations. The result follows:

> In this connection his main achievement really is that he first introduced the concept of constructible sets into set theory defining it as in his *Proceedings* paper of 1939, proved that the axioms of set theory (including the axiom of choice) hold for it, and conjectured that the continuum hypothesis also will hold. He told these things to v. Neumann during his stay at Princeton in the autumn of 1935. The discovery of the proof of this conjecture on the basis of his definition is not too difficult. G gave the proof (also for the GCH) not until three years later because he had fallen ill in the meantime. This proof was using a submodel of the constructible sets in the lowest case countable, similar to the one commonly given today.

13. Judging from the Nachlass, G must have misremembered the dates of the three major discoveries reported here: they should be 1941 (or 1942), 1941, 1942 rather than 1941, 1942, 1943. For example, it was on 15 April 1941 that he gave his lecture: In what sense is intuitionistic logic constructive? (According to one of the notebooks, the idea of the proof apparently occurred to him on 1 January 1941.) Here again, there is the ambiguity over the question of when an evolving proof is thought to be secured.

14. Apparently G did not continue to work on trying to apply his method to the continuum hypothesis for very long. It seems likely that his philosophical paper on the continuum problem (solicited in 1945 and published toward the end of 1947) was meant in part as a sort of conclusion of his own mathematical work on this problem. It could be interpreted as a summary of his thoughts on this problem and an invitation to others to continue where he left off. At any rate, the data available now seem to indicate that around the end of 1942 there was a transition from G's concentration on mathematical logic to other theoretical, primarily philosophical, interests.

15. On 9 June 1976, G recalled that in 1942 or 1943 he wrote his paper on Russell's mathematical logic. He described the paper as a history of logic with special reference to the work of Russell.

   Judging from Russell's reply to his critics (dated July 1943), it seems likely that G wrote the paper mainly in 1942 to 1943. The note says in part, 'Dr. Gödel's most interesting paper on my mathematical logic came into my hands after my replies had been completed, and at a time when I had no leisure to work on it.... His great ability, as shown by his previous work, makes me think it highly probable that many of his criticisms of me are justified.'

16. In fact, G wrote several drafts of an article entitled 'Some observations about the relationship between theory of relativity and Kantian philosophy.' The paper published in the volume honoring Einstein was completed in 1949 but says much less about Kantian philosophy. It seems likely the longer paper was written from 1947 to 1950.

17. The lecture was given at Alumnae Hall, Pembroke College in Brown University, 26 December 1951, 8 P.M. I remember G reading from a manuscript at high speed, including quotations in French from Hermite. G told me of some of the ideas of the lecture, which are reported in *MP* (p. 324).

18. The original invitation from P. A. Schilpp is dated 15 May 1953. For more details, see chapter 4, under *1954*.

19. G thought that Husserl probably had a similar experience of revelation at some time between 1906 and 1910.

   In June 1976 G said that his work at the institute had been split in three ways: institute work, mathematics, and philosophy. He was very conscientious about his work at the institute, especially with regard to the evaluation of applicants. Hassler Whitney reported on this in his lecture on 3 March 1978.

2.2 Relation to the Schlick Circle

In G's papers, there is the draft of a reply dated 12 April 1972 [in folder 01/105] to a letter from Karl Menger of 17 January 1972, asking about some of G's connections with the 'Vienna Circle' and including two specific questions on G's relations to Wittgenstein. [The date of G's draft is also interesting because I was sending Moore's notes on Wittgenstein's lectures 1930–1933 to G in the early part of 1972 and G talked about Wittgenstein's work in the session of 5 April 1972 with me (see the record of the conversations in *CG* under that date).] It appears that G never did send the reply (at least in the form as drafted). A copy of some parts of this preliminary draft follows.

[Recently I saw from Menger's memoir that G did send a reply on 20 May 1972. In particular, Menger quotes from it a passage that is essentially (2) below. I have, therefore, revised the draft of (2) slightly to conform to Menger's version.

Menger also gives helpful information on G's continued occupation with philosophy, particularly in the 1930s. Writing about the period from 1929 to 1933, Menger reports, 'In addition, Gödel studied much philosophy in those years, among other topics post-Kantian German metaphysics.... But Gödel already then began to concentrate on Leibniz, for whom he entertained a boundless admiration.' In the context of G's 1939 visit to Notre Dame, Menger reports, 'Gödel tended more and more to Platonism. . . . Meanwhile, Gödel was ever more preoccupied with Leibniz.']

In conseq[uence] of frequent tiredness I hardly ever answer letters before a week's time. But in this case there was moreover a sp[ecial] reason, namely that I always have inhibitions in writing about my relationship to the Vienna Circle *because* I never was a logical pos[itivist] in which this term is commonly understood and explained in [the manifesto of] 1929. On the other hand by some publ[ications] (probably in part through my own fault) the impr(ession) is created that I was.

I am sure I did not enter the Circle before the ac[ademic] year 1925–26 and very probably not before the calendar year 1926. Moreover I practically never attended it after the spring term of 1933. I attended the meetings regularly in 26, 27. I don't remember how frequently I did in 28–33. . . . I remember only very few talks given in the Circle. There were not many that really interested me.

1) I was never introduced to Wittg[enstein] and have never spoken a word with him. I only saw him once in my life when he attended a lecture in Vienna. I think it was Brouwer's. [Probably G is referring to the one entitled 'Mathematik, Wissenschaft, und Sprache,' given 10 March 1928.]

2) As far as my theorem about undecidable propositions is concerned, it is indeed clear from the passages you cite [pp. 50–55 and 176ff.] that Wittgenstein did *not* understand it (or pretended not to understand it). He interprets it as a kind of logical paradox, while in fact it is just the opposite, namely a mathematical theorem within an absolutely uncontroversial part of mathematics (finitary number theory or combinatorics). Incidentally, the whole passage you cite seems nonsense to me. See, e.g. the 'superstitious fear of mathematicians of contradictions.' [Compare note 8 in section 2.4.]

From these paragraphs, it appears that G was led to read Wittgenstein's remarks on his incompleteness theorem by Menger's letter. They also give some details about G's relation to the Circle. Some of G's contacts with Hahn, Menger, Natkin, and Feigl are reported in chapter 3. It so happens that Carnap had kept some records of his interactions with G, which are preserved at the University of Pittsburgh (under the charge of Dr. Richard Nollan) with the Carnap papers (*CP*). I have been kindly granted permission to quote from them, and would like to review these records to give an illustration of G's relation to some members of the Circle.

The records in *CP* consist of about 50 pages, of which 37 pages came from the period between March 1931 and July 1933, largely concerned with Carnap's manuscripts for his *Logical Syntax*. In addition, there are 3 pages from 14 December 1928, 2 pages from Monday 23 December 1929, 1 page from 29 June 1935, 3 pages from 13 and 14 November 1940, and 2 pages from 26 March 1948. Most of the pages are notes on what G said, except for three handwritten letters by G (totaling 8 pages) and 3 pages of responses by Carnap, all written in 1932.

1928.   Carnap asks whether in mathematics only that part is to be developed that will actually be applied in physics (while allowing for a possibility of extending it for simplicity and unity). In reply G says one should permit also parts having nothing to do with applications, for, he observes, we never know whether something might sometimes be needed in physics. On another topic: if, G says, I wish to follow the constructivistic viewpoint thoroughly, I must either remove the law of excluded middle (because it is not always the case that either p or its negation is provable) or else presume a 'complete' (decidable) logic.

1929.   Carnap's diary for 23 December records his encounters at Arkadencafé from 1 P.M. to 9 P.M. From 5:45 P.M. to 8:30 P.M., Gödel. 'On the inexhaustibility of mathematics (see separate sheet).' (For more details, see chapter 3 under *1929*.) The separate sheet gives an extended record of what G said:

> We admit as legitimate mathematics certain reflections on the grammar of a language that concerns the empirical. If one seeks to formalize such a mathematics, then with each formalization there are problems, which one can understand and express in ordinary language, but cannot express in the given formalized language. It follows (Brouwer) that mathematics is inexhaustible: one must always again draw afresh from the 'fountain of intuition.' There is, therefore, no characteristica universalis for the *whole* mathematics, and no decision procedure for the whole mathematics. In each and every *closed language* there are only countably many expressions. The *continuum* appears only in 'the whole of mathematics.' ... If we have *only one language*, and can only make 'elucidations' about it, then these elucidations are inexhaustible, they always require some new intuition again. [In contrast with these remarks, G's incompleteness theorem achieves the additional task of refining some of the ideas expressed here to get propositions *within* the given formal system, which go beyond it relative to *provability*.]

Of the material from 1931 to 1933 (and also the one page from 1935) I shall omit detailed comments on specific texts (mostly related to Carnap's work toward his *Logical Syntax*), which are undoubtedly of interest to scholars of Carnap's work. I shall select only a few items that are less dependent on special contexts.

1931.   On 10 June, G made some observations similar to what he told me in the 1970s. It is arbitrary where one wishes to put the limit: (1) only concrete propositions, (2) number variables and mathematical induction, (3) Hilbert (in metamathematics), (4) Brouwer, (5) classical mathematics. Which formulas and rules (in mathematics) to admit as 'meaningful' in the first place, because certain ideas are associated with them: this is entirely a matter of free resolution. So one can equally acknowledge all of classical mathematics. There is no plausible boundary (Unterschied), even though a well-defined limit can be indicated at different places.

On 2 July 1931, G proved 'in the circle' that arithmetic truth is not definable (in arithmetic). 'There are in arithmetized metalogic ordinary concepts which are not definable. This is proved by deriving a contradiction (after Richard) from supposing the concept available; in the argument we have to grant the consistency of arithmetic. True Zahlformel (without variable) is not definable.' G went on to give details of the proof, which are similar to those given in his letter of 21 September 1931 to Zermelo (for details, see chapter 3, under *1931*). Indeed, *CP* includes an extended quotation from this letter, followed by Carnap's note that G told him on 26 March 1932 that the antinomy does not arise, because 'true' cannot be defined. [Perhaps Carnap forgot (or did not understand) his earlier notes and asked G about it, who then showed Carnap a copy of the letter.]

1932.   In a letter dated 11 April G returned Carnap's manuscript 'Metalogik I' and a manuscript by L. Chwistek, which G had found to be 'in so vague a form' that he could not evaluate it. G's long letter of 11 September is mostly devoted to comments on Carnap's manuscript 'Semantik,' pointing out errors in his definition of 'analytic' and in his exposition of the proof of incompleteness. G said that the difficulty of defining 'analytic' can only be avoided by using a language that already contains the concepts of set (and relation), and that he intended to give in part II of his famous paper a definition for 'true' along such a line. Carnap wrote back on 25 and 27 September to propose a correction. G replied on 28 November to say that Carnap had understood his suggestion and that the interest of such a definition lies not in a clarification of the concept of 'analytic' (because in it the same problematic concepts of 'arbitrary set,' etc., are used), but in showing that the undecidable propositions in a system of the type hierarchy are decidable by going to a higher type. G said also that he was occupied with the 'Bericht über die Grundlagungforschung' [presumably the projected joint book with A. Heyting]. Also something about the Circle: 'The Schlick Circle has been meeting again, not, however, to continue the discussion with Waismann, but to report on Ramsey, etc.' Carnap came to Vienna in December and met with G on the 8th and the 13th. The notes contain the following statement. 'Gödel: Ja; *er* hat mir vor einigen Jahren betont, dass nicht-konstituierbare Begriffe nötig sind.' [I take this to be a suggestion that Carnap often failed to understand what G told him.]

1933 and 1935.   There are six pages from July 1933 and one page from 29 June 1935. I list some of G's observations as formulated by Carnap. (1) Theology begins with indefinite concepts: man bei gegenseitiger Verständigung immer vom definiten aufgehen muss; aber auch er will selbstverständlich indefinite Begriffe verwenden. (2) The natural laws and the recognized concrete (general) propositions belong together. There is *no* formal demarcation between laws like 'all ravens are black' and laws like Maxwell's. (3) Synonymy holds only when sentence parts with equal content can always be interchanged; this is satisfied in extensional languages, but not always in an intensional language. (4) 'Gehalt' kann f-Begriff sein da diser Begriff etwas *objektives* an sich hat. Der Unterschied ist eben der: die a-Begriffe sind *subjektive*, d. h. bei diesen besteht die Möglichkeit der Feststellung, bei den f-Begriffen nicht. [The last two sentences refer, I believe, to Carnap's distinction between d-terms and c-terms in section 34a of his *Logical Syntax*.]

1940.   On 13 November, G discussed with Carnap his favorite idea of a metaphysical theory dealing with such concepts as God, soul, 'Ideen'; these notes are considered in section 8.1. On 14 November, G gave a lecture on the continuum hypothesis and Carnap afterward wrote down some of his own thoughts.

1948.   G saw a strong analogy between theoretical physics and set theory. Physics is confirmed by sense perceptions; set theory by its consequences in elementary arithmetic. The fundamental insights in arithmetic, which cannot be reduced to anything simpler, are analogous to sense perceptions. G also considered some ideas of Leibniz; this part is discussed in section 6.2.

I am not aware of further interactions between G and Carnap, even though Carnap was at the I.A.S. from 1952 to 1954, and G began to work on his Carnap paper in 1953.

2.3 The dramatic response to Hilbert

Hilbert's development from 1900 on culminated in four basic problems, which he explained in September 1928 to an international audience. Within about two years G settled all of them in a definitive and surprising manner. In many ways this was probably a unique occurrence in the history of science. This section is given to a recounting of this dramatic story.

2.3.1 Historical background: Hilbert and proof theory

In 1900 Hilbert turned his attention from the foundations of geometry to offer an axiom system for analysis, departing from the usual genetic approach to the study of the concept of (real) number (in 'Über den Zahlenbegriff'). Indeed the consistency of some such system is listed as the second problem in the list of his Paris lecture of the same year. Hilbert's axioms characterize the real numbers as forming a real Archimedean field that permits no further extension to any field of the same kind.

The requirement of nonextendibility is given in a pregnant axiom of completeness, which, however, has a complex logical structure and is indeed somewhat ambiguous. As we now know, this matter of closing-off or completeness calls for going beyond formal systems even when we consider the simpler case of integers. In current terminology, only the second-order Peano axioms are complete; first-order axioms for the integers are incompletable. It is interesting to see that Hilbert soon came to relate the question of axiomatically closing-off the theory of integers to that of the indeterminate range of what makes up logic.

In 1901 he gave a lecture to the Göttingen Mathematical Society on the problems of completeness and decision (of true or false by the axioms). In E. Husserl's formulation, Hilbert asked (*Philosophie der Arithmetik*, Husserlina, 1970, p. 445), 'Would I have the right to say that every proposition dealing only with the positive integers must be either true or false on the basis of the axioms for positive integers?' 'When we assert that a proposition is decided on the basis of the axioms of a domain, what may we use for this apart from the axioms? The whole of logic. What is that? All theorems, which are free from every particularity of a domain of knowledge, what holds independently of all "special axioms," of all material of knowledge. —But we come thus to a neat fix: in the domain of algorithmic logic? in that of finite cardinals? in the theory of combinations? in the general theory of ordinal numbers? And finally isn't the richest set theory itself purely logical?'

I have quoted this passage in full because it is relevant to certain current debates, particularly with regard to the range of logic. I tend to agree with Dedekind and Hilbert (and G) that logic includes set theory. If we use this concept of logic, then we are justified in accepting the familiar argument for proving Peano's axioms categorical. Hence, each proposition is 'decided' by the axioms (i.e., either true or false). But this decidability or determination is different from the more strict requirement of an algorithm to carry out the decision in each case. The stricter decidability is the concept that is familiar nowadays and most likely also what Hilbert wanted. But Hilbert's foremost concern was consistency proofs; next came completeness, which for him was probably a weaker requirement in general than decidability.

In his 1904 Heidelberg lecture on the foundations of logic and arithmetic

Hilbert for the first time observed that, while one can prove the consistency of geometry by an arithmetic interpretation, for the consistency of arithmetic (meaning number theory and analysis) 'the appeal to another fundamental discipline seems unreasonable.' He suggested a plan of building up logic and arithmetic simultaneously, as well as the thought of translating proofs into the language of formulas (of symbolic logic), thereby turning the proof of consistency (the proof of the 'existence of the infinite') into a problem of elementary arithmetic. Probably for lack of good ideas and due to interest in other matters (particularly integral equations and physics), Hilbert did not return to this area until his 1917 Zurich lecture on axiomatic thinking, in which he praised the 'axiomatization of logic' by Whitehead and Russell as 'the crowning of all the work of axiomatization.' Of course there remained for Hilbert the matter of proving consistency, and he proposed that the concept of specific mathematical proof itself be made the object of study.

It was only after 1920 that Hilbert, in collaboration with Paul Bernays and provoked by the opposition from Weyl and Brouwer, began to concentrate on proof theory. The fruits of this labor were reported in the first Hamburg lecture of 1922, the 1922 Leipzig lecture, the 1925 Münster lecture on the continuum, and the second Hamburg lecture of 1927. Meanwhile, apart from Bernays, other young mathematicians, notably M. Schönfinkel, W. Ackermann, and J. v. Neumann, also joined in the exciting enterprise. By 1928 it was believed that the consistency of number theory had been achieved by the finitist method envisaged by Hilbert (and Bernays), and that even a similar proof of the consistency of analysis had been essentially completed; only 'the proof of a purely arithmetical elementary theorem of finiteness' was wanting.

2.3.2 Hilbert's list of problems

On 3 September 1928, Hilbert delivered the address 'Problems der Grundlegung der Mathematik' and 'received a stormy applause at the beginning as well as after the end of the address' [*Atti del Congresso Internationale dei Mathematici, Bologna 3–10 September 1928*, Bologna, 1929, vol. I, pp. 135–141; *Math. Annalen*, vol. 102 (1930), pp. 1–9; *Grundlagen der Geometrie*, seventh edition, 1930, Anhang X; K. Reidemeister, *Hilbert Gedenkband*, 1971, pp. 9–19].

Hilbert began his address by reviewing general advances in mathematics over the ten-year period to 1928 and then announced that the work of Ackermann and v. Neumann had carried out a (finitist) consistency proof of number theory. Then he listed four yet unresolved problems.

Problem 1. (Finitist) consistency proof of the basic part of analysis (or second-order functional calculus). Hilbert stated that Ackermann had already worked out the main part of such a proof; only an elementary finiteness condition remained to be established. He remarked that the proof would justify the theory of real numbers with the Dedekind cuts, the second-order Peano axioms, and the theory of Cantor's second number class.

Problem 2. Extension of the proof to higher-order functional calculi (or the part of the simple theory of types to three or four or five levels). Hilbert mentioned in this connection the additional problem of proving the consistency of a stronger axiom of choice, because his formulation contains a certain form of the axiom of choice as an integral part of the basic system. It is interesting that Hilbert did not mention explicitly full set theory, but confined himself to what we would now consider small fragments of set theory adequate to the development of standard mathematics (of 1928).

Problem 3. Completeness of the axiom systems for number theory and analysis. Hilbert remarked on the familiar fact that second-order theories are indeed complete in both cases on the basis of the usual proofs that they are categorical. The problem is to render the proofs of categoricalness 'finitely rigorous.' For number theory, Hilbert explained his idea by requiring that the proof of isomorphism of two models be 'finitely recast' to show that whenever a proposition A can be shown to be consistent with the axioms, the opposite of A cannot be shown to be so. In other words, whenever A is consistent with the axioms, it is provable. This seems to be more specific than the familiar idea of so rendering the second-order axioms more explicit that we do have 'formal' axiomatic systems. In any case, Hilbert appears to believe at that time that such complete formal systems exist.

Hilbert did not mention the question of decidability of number theory and analysis. We are now familiar with Turing's observation that if a formal system is complete in the sense just mentioned, it is also decidable. If Hilbert had been aware of this connection at that time, he would probably have been more skeptical about the existence of complete formal systems in the two cases, since presumably he would have more doubt about these theories being decidable. But I am merely conjecturing and have not looked into the historical evidence about Hilbert's beliefs at that time on these questions of completeness and decidability. (See, however, *1930* in chapter 3 for a published statement by Bernays in 1930 to the effect that decidability is stronger than completeness.)

Problem 4. The problem of completeness of the system of logical rules (i.e., the first-order logic) in the sense that all (universally) valid sentences are provable. Hilbert offered this as an example of purely logical problems which fall under his proof theory. This same problem was also mentioned in the first edition of the Hilbert-Ackermann textbook of 1928.

Hilbert did not list the Entscheidungsproblem (for the first-order logic), which was of course a central problem in his school, except to mention that for monadic quantification theory the known method of solving the Entscheidungsproblem (Schröder's elimination problem) also yielded a proof of completeness of the rules in the subdomain. Perhaps Hilbert did not include this or the decision problem for number theory because he did not regard them as belonging to his proof theory.

2.3.3 Gödel's response

G settled problem 4 in the summer of 1929, by proving the completeness of the first-order logic. In 1930 his attempt to prove the (relative) consistency of analysis (to number theory) led surprisingly to the discovery of undecidable propositions. After another month or two he realized that his result also implied a negative reply to the initial problem of proving consistency (not only of analysis but even of number theory). This unexpected, gratifying succession of steps illustrates a remarkable phenomenon in scientific discoveries, which, for lack of a suitable term, I propose to call 'problem transmutation.' More explicitly, there are five steps in the particular succession. (1) G divided the difficult problem of proving the consistency of analysis by finitist methods into two. (2) He chose to tackle first the more definite problem of relative consistency. (3) He noticed that truth in number theory is not definable in number theory. (4) He found the undecidable propositions by considering (formal) provability in place of truth. (5) Finally, he realized that the statement of consistency is itself also an undecidable proposition. Astonishingly, his attack on half of problem 1 led him rather painlessly to settling all three problems (1, 2, and 3), but with answers opposite to Hilbert's expectations. (For detailed considerations of G's results and papers in connection with Hilbert's problems, see chapters 6 and 10.)

I am under the impression that according to the consensus today, finitist number theory as originally envisaged by Hilbert consists basically of the quantifier-free theory of primitive recursive functions. It is on the basis of an identification more or less like this that we can speak of G's results as settling Hilbert's problems unambiguously.

G quickly found that truth in number theory cannot be defined in number theory, quite apart from particular formal axiom systems for number theory. He was then able to formulate propositions in elementary segments of type theory or set theory that are not decidable in them. After announcing the result in the September meeting at Königsberg, he improved the result to obtain elegant arithmetic propositions that are undecidable in the given formal system, and also discovered that for the familiar systems of number theory and set theory, there can be no consistency proof of any of these systems formalizable in the system itself. Hence, since the finitist method as explained by Hilbert should be formalizable in these systems, G had not only settled Hilbert's problems 1 and 2 negatively, but also refuted Hilbert's belief that a finitist consistency proof of number theory had already been found. Moreover, he had also settled Hilbert's problem 3 negatively. In all these cases, G proved that the finitist proofs and complete formal systems asked for in these questions simply cannot exist.

In the spring of 1961 I had the opportunity to go with a friend to visit L. E. J. Brouwer at his house (uninvited, as was the custom with him). He did most of the speaking and discoursed on diverse topics apparently at random. I remember his mentioning, for totally different reasons in each case, Huygens, Hadamard, Heyting, and Gödel. Of G's incompleteness results, he expressed astonishment that so much had been made of them, saying that the conclusions had been evident to him for a long time before 1931. Of course a major difference is the feat of strengthening the idea of incompleteness by constructing undecidable propositions within the given formal system. G's precise formulations were convincing to people with widely different beliefs, while Brouwer's convictions were based on a motley of much less explicitly or homogeneously expressed interesting ideas. Moreover, the wide implications of G's results can only be negated from a highly special point of view that to most mathematicians and philosophers must appear highly arbitrary and one-sided.

Even though it seems fair to say that G had destroyed Hilbert's original program, G continued to be interested in the underlying problem of mathematical evidence and to look for natural broadenings of Hilbert's stringent requirements. In 1932 G gave a report to establish that classical number theory is as consistent as intuitionistic number theory (an observation also made independently by Bernays and by G. Gentzen). In 1941 G found an interpretation of intuitionistic number theory by primitive recursive functionals, which were regarded by him as an extension of Hilbert's finitist method.

Another 'transmutation' of problems and ideas is in connection with the continuum problem. In 1976 G thought that it was in 1930 that he began to think about the continuum problem and heard about Hilbert's proposed outline of a proof of the continuum hypothesis in axiomatic set theory as presented in the 1925 lecture 'On the infinite.' Hilbert's idea was just to construct (recursive) ordinals and use recursively defined sets and functions of orders indexed by such ordinals. Consistent with his belief that finitist consistency proofs exist for strong systems, Hilbert believed and thought he could prove that these exhausted all the ordinals and all the sets of integers. Hence, since it is easy to see and prove in set theory that the cardinalities of these ordinals and these sets are the same, he thought that he had (the outline of) a proof of the continuum hypothesis in set theory. In addition, Hilbert thought that the axioms of set theory are also true in his constructive interpretation along the same line. That is why he thought he also had (the outline of) a finitist consistency proof of the axioms of set theory (as known then).

G used the idea of analyzing sets (of integers) into orders indexed by ordinals. Instead of using recursively defined sets, he soon thought of the first-order definable sets in the ramified hierarchy. He experimented for some time with different ways of introducing (countable) ordinals. Finally the idea of using all ordinals occurred to him. This implies that instead of proving the continuum hypothesis, one could only hope for a relative consistency proof, unless one could get all ordinals in some suitably explicit way. In 1976 G thought that it was in 1935 that he verified that all the axioms of set theory at the time, including the axiom of choice, are satisfied by the constructible sets, i.e., the ramified theory over all ordinals. In 1937 or 1938 (see note 11 to section 2.1) he proved that the (generalized) continuum hypothesis also holds in this model.

2.4 Some comparisons with Wittgenstein

Wittgenstein (1889–1951) was seventeen years G's senior. In terms of their chief work, Wittgenstein had two periods: from 1908 or 1912 to 1918 and from 1929 to 1951. A similar division for G would be mathematical logic from 1929 to 1939 or 1942 and philosophy from 1943 to 1972 or 1978. The latter period can be subdivided into philosophy of mathematics and physics (1943–1958) and general philosophy (1959–1978). Earlier, Wittgenstein went through a stage of seeking (1906–1912) and G had a stage of preparation (1924–1929).

'In Wittgenstein's life the years from 1906 to 1912 were a time of painful seeking and of final awakening to clarity about his vocation.' He read Schopenhauer's *Die Welt als Wille und Vorstellung* in his youth, and studied engineering from 1906 to 1911.[1] At the beginning of 1912, he went to Cambridge. 'At the end of his first term at Cambridge he came to me and said,' according to Bertrand Russell, 'if I am a complete idiot, I shall become an aeronaut; but, if not, I shall become a philosopher.' It is impossible to determine whether the exaggeration originated with Wittgenstein or Russell. One thing is clear: the mundane question of making a living played no part in Wittgenstein's deliberations about a proper vocation. Family wealth must have contributed to this situation. 'One Sunday morning in Manchester in 1910, for example, he decided he would like to go to Blackpool.' After being dissuaded by his friend W. Eccles from hiring a special train, they 'took a taxi to Liverpool, a distance of nearly forty miles, and had a trip on the Mersey ferry before returning to Manchester.' Later on in life, he chose to live very simply and frugally.[2]

Wittgenstein's philosophical career has been retold many times. The period beginning with 1908 (see *BA*, p. 237) or 1912 culminated in the completion in August 1918 of the *Tractatus*, which appeared in book form in 1922. 'The author of the *Tractatus* thought he had solved all philosophical problems. It was consistent with this view that he should give up philosophy' (*S*, p. 24). It is rumored that after hearing Brouwer lecture in March 1928, he was stirred to take up philosophy again. In January 1929 he returned to Cambridge and started developing his later philosophy, which seems to have occupied him more or less continuously until his death in 1951. The only other book that he seriously planned to publish was completed in January 1945 and published in 1953 as part I of his *Philosophical Investigations*.

Neither G nor Wittgenstein published much during their lifetimes. What they did publish was brief and full of content as well as implications. Since Wittgenstein's death in 1951, there has grown up a forest of publications both of his manuscripts and lecture notes and of discussions about him. Of course G's published results are included conspicuously in all logic textbooks. It is too early to tell what will happen to G's Nachlass over the years. A crucial difference is that G did not give nearly as many lectures, and most of his unpublished writings are only in the form of rough notes (and much in Gabelsberger shorthand).

Both G and Wittgenstein had acquired early on a high standard of intellectual work and were meticulous in preparing their writings for publication. Unlike the majority of practicing philosophers and mathematicians, each strove only for basic advances. Yet what they achieved is very different. In their early work, the contrast is easy to see, since G's achievement is definite and definitive, while the *Tractatus* is sweeping, suggestive, and subject to drastic revisions. More generally G aimed at new knowledge, not merely at 'What is possible before all new discoveries and inventions' (*Investigations*, §126). G was preoccupied with conceptual precision (often disregarding literary elegance) and with eliminating the multiplicity of meanings, even though readers of his philosophical writings often see alternative interpretations. Contrary to this emphasis, v. Wright in commenting on Wittgenstein's work offers the opinion that 'what makes a man's work a *classic* is often just this multiplicity, which invites and at the same time resists our craving for a clear understanding' (*S*, p. 34). A cruder mind would be inclined to consider the 'inviting and resisting' a form of deception. Or is the 'craving' misplaced and to be blamed? Perhaps the idea is rather that in dealing with perennial concerns a serious treatment inevitably contains this multiplicity that accompanies a classic but does not make it one.

G considered what he told me in his discussions with me from 1971 to 1972 to be *applications* of his philosophy. At a later stage I asked him to give me a general account of his philosophy perhaps more or less in the form of private lectures. In reply, he said that he had only developed his philosophy to the extent of being able to apply it, but that he had not reached the stage of giving it a direct statement. The distinction between stating and applying his philosophy suggests to me a connection with later Wittgenstein. Compared with familiar books in philosophy, Wittgenstein's later writings appear to be at best applications of a philosophy that calls for a more straightforward statement. On the other hand, if one agrees with Wittgenstein, it could be said that G should have been content with expounding his philosophy by giving typical applications of it. I take it that, according to Wittgenstein, such is the appropriate exposition of a philosophy.

Both G and Wittgenstein were closely associated with Vienna, and each had a second center of activity, Princeton in the one case and Cambridge (England) in the other. From 1924 to 1939, G lived mostly in Vienna. Over this period Wittgenstein also spent much time in Vienna and elsewhere in Austria. On the whole, Wittgenstein traveled a good deal, to Norway, to Ireland, to Russia[3] (in 1935), to America (in 1949), and of course between Cambridge and Vienna. In contrast, from January 1940 to his death 38 years later, G resided and worked at Princeton for the entire period (except for very brief trips).

This common association with Vienna and their common interest in philosophy (and, in particular, in the philosophy of logic and mathematics) provide some coordinate system for contrasting their different outlooks and types of work. In addition, both of them reacted toward the work of Cantor, Frege, Hilbert, Russell, and Brouwer, but in totally different ways. Direct confrontations between their work are rather limited. The only ones I know are Wittgenstein's discussion of G's incompleteness theorem and G's private remarks on Wittgenstein's work. More substantial mediated confrontations are perhaps their contacts with and views about the Vienna Circle, as well as the reactions to the *Tractatus* of F. P. Ramsey, whose interests overlap with both of them. A. M. Turing is less suitable, even though there is record of his discussions with Wittgenstein and he and G much appreciate each other's work. The reason is that he never took Wittgenstein's work as seriously as did Ramsey.

In terms of authors and friends who are said to have influenced Wittgenstein positively and negatively, we now have a long list,[4] including St. Augustine, Dr. Samuel Johnson, Pascal, G. C. Lichtenberg, Kant, Kierkegaard, Schopenhauer, Dostoevsky, Tolstoy, Otto Weininger, Karl Kraus, Adolf Loos, Heinrich Hertz, Fritz Mauthner, Ludwig Boltzmann, Frege, Russell, G. E. Moore, Cantor, Hilbert, Brouwer, Ramsey, P. Sraffa, and so on. It is of course hard to determine with any exactness how these contacts, his family background, and the 'Kakania' society of the decaying Habsburg Vienna[4] combined to condition his work and general outlook. But one thing seems clear: general artistic and intellectual culture in Vienna exerted much more influence on Wittgenstein's work than on G's.

Like Kant, Wittgenstein tries to draw a line between sense and nonsense. In the *Tractatus*, a sharp distinction is made between the world as idea (the sayable and its fringe) and the world as will (the rest, or the unsayable, including the 'higher'). The preoccupation with language and its purity is shared with F. Mauthner and K. Kraus. When the corruption of language plays an important role in the prevalence of dishonesty, it is natural to attempt to find a castle of security, however much it may shut out. But when the 'higher' is left out, one is led to the paradoxical conclusion that nonsense is more important than sense. 'Language, according to Mauthner, is a defective tool for acquiring knowledge, a ladder one must throw away after use.' A more consistent way of proceeding would seem to be to throw away the nonsense (as the Vienna Circle did) or try to build a larger castle (as G did). The logical apparatus developed by Frege and Russell is used in the *Tractatus* chiefly to argue a priori that there must be Elementarsätze (atomic propositions).[5]

His changing view after 1929 puts Ramsey's 'pragmatist tendency' in the foreground and shares Moore's questioning the question. Contrary to Moore, however, Wittgenstein is not content to silence his opponents by an appeal to common sense (usage), but probes the 'grammar' to 'dissolve' the confused problems.

The *Investigations* uses the suggestive terms 'language-games,' 'family resemblances,' and 'forms of life.' It also considers, particularly in connection with the role of new definitions, the phenomenon of 'seeing as' so much emphasized by the Gestalt psychologists. 'Forms of life' was a familiar term. There was a very popular book, *Lebensformen* (1914), by W. Spranger, and the theologian H. Scholz (later a symbolic logician) related forms of life to differentiations of the religious consciousness in his *Religionsphilosophie* (1921). To the question how mathematics is possible, Wittgenstein rejects crude 'conventionalism' and accounts for agreement in mathematics by agreement in forms of life. 'What has to be accepted, the given, is—so one could say—*forms of life*' (*Investigations*, p. 226).

Wittgenstein emphasizes the use of language in the 'stream of life.' There is, however, a slight ambiguity that leaves room for partiality. 'When philosophers use a word,' he says, 'and try to grasp the *essence* of the thing, one must always ask oneself: is the word ever used in this way in the language-game which is its original home?—What *we* do is to bring words back from their metaphysical to everyday use' (*Investigations*, §116). For example, 'infinity' is often used by mathematicians; is this part of everyday use? Or, can we deny that their 'language-game' is the original home of words like 'infinity'? If we cannot deny this, then much of what Wittgenstein says about mathematics violates his own injunction.

Some of our everyday concepts are the most basic. G sympathizes with Husserl's program of looking for a deeper foundation of science by contemplating such concepts. From this approach the concepts of the mathematicians are not thrown away, but will somehow be reconstructed. Hence, the disagreement is not over the importance of everyday concepts, but over Wittgenstein's taking clear concepts, such as arithmetical truth, for nonsense.

When it comes to reacting to the same mathematicians, the contrast between G and Wittgenstein is striking indeed. Wittgenstein regards Cantor's work in set theory and especially how it is interpreted as hocus pocus. For example, according to him, the diagonal procedure does not show that the real numbers are uncountable because there is no such thing as the *set* of real numbers. G in contrast enriches and clarifies Cantor's concept of set; he also shows that it is consistent to say that the real numbers are the smallest uncountable set. In fact, by extending set theory, G arrives at a broad domain of logic that transforms significantly the issue about the place of logic in thought as it is treated in the *Tractatus*.

Hilbert introduced a program of securing transfinite arguments by proving that they can lead to no contradictions. From 1929 onward, Wittgenstein repeatedly discusses the matter of contradictions and consistency proofs, but I find it hard to acquire a coherent picture of much of what he says. G, on the other hand, shows that the kind of consistency proof Hilbert looks for does not exist.

The reactions to L. E. J. Brouwer's ideas are less one-sided. G demonstrated that classical logic can be reinterpreted in Brouwer's logic when applied to natural numbers, and Brouwer's logic can be interpreted in turn by certain more transparent constructions. Wittgenstein, on the other hand, agrees with Brouwer on a constructive reading of logic connectives, but in addition introduces a sort of anthropomorphism that requires proofs to be surveyable or perspicuous.[6] This deals with the discovery and the communication of a proof. It sounds plausible that unless a proof is taken in, it has not been understood and the theorem has not been established. But the matter is not so simple. For example, a 'proof' of the four-color theorem has recently been obtained with the help of computers. It is so long that nobody has checked it; yet it is generally agreed that the theorem is established.[7]

An extreme view on the change and stability of concepts is proposed. For example, Wittgenstein says at various places that a proof creates a new concept. From Hegel we are familiar with the idea that concepts change and that contradictions are the driving force for the development of concepts. In fact, if one has anything new to say, quite often one is using old words in new ways. In all these cases we are faced with the ancient problem that in the way language is commonly used, when change takes place, there is a need for some unchanging stratum. G has quite a different view of the matter. According to him, it is not the concepts that change, but rather our perceptions of them. 'If there is nothing sharp to begin with, it is hard to understand how, in many cases, a vague concept can uniquely determine a sharp one without the *slightest* freedom of choice.' 'Trying to see (i.e., understand) a concept more clearly' is the correct way of expressing the phenomenon vaguely described as 'examining what we mean by a word' (*MP*, p. 85).

In his later writings, Wittgenstein is less explicit than in the *Tractatus* about what he takes to be the range of logic and mathematics. On the whole, the eagerness to escape from confusion is exhibited in the demand of direct connections with pictorial images and applications in terms of action or behavior. For example, the proofs considered by him are either numerical calculations or something functioning like a picture, or formal-ized artificial proofs, of which he is highly critical. The kind of sustained conceptual thinking in significant mathematical proofs is left out perhaps for the purpose of avoiding myth-making. In particular, only the poten-tially infinite is acceptable, so that the proposition 'There is no greatest positive integer' is highly special for him and indeed lies at the limit of our thinking. To illustrate his general outlook, let us examine his discussion of G's theorem more closely.[8]

For each of a wide class of formal systems S (such as first-order Peano arithmetic), G constructs a sentence P that is true but not provable in the system S. For numerical formulas such as $2 + 3 = 5$, $2 \times 3 > 5$, we have a clear idea of which are true and which are false. Wittgenstein does not question this. The sentence P goes beyond such simple statements $F(n)$ by one generalization, being essentially of the form 'For all positive integers n, $F(n)$.' G shows that each of $F(1)$, $F(2)$, etc., is provable in S and therefore true, but P itself is not provable in S. It now seems clear that, since $F(1)$, $F(2)$, all are true, then P is true by the meaning of 'all n.' This, however, is the main step with which Wittgenstein is not willing to go along. The objection is presumably that we are taking the infinite collection of positive integers or $F(1)$, $F(2)$, etc., as a completed (rather than a potential) whole. The proof assumes the consistency of the system S, an assumption that is generally taken for granted and that in particular nobody questions when S is the Peano arithmetic. But surprisingly for this context Wittgenstein brings in his favorite disdain: 'the superstitious fear and awe of mathema-ticians in face of contradictions' (*Remarks*, p. 53).

Wittgenstein seems to have little appreciation of the autonomy of math-ematics, which he discards all too easily as empty constructions because they are not connected directly with everyday applications. His treatment of mathematics illustrates a general tendency to assimilate mathematics and science directly to everyday discourse. To quote Bernays, 'Our entire analysis with its applications in physics and technology rests on the infinity of the series of numbers. The theory of probability and statistics make continually implicit use of this infinity. Wittgenstein argues as though mathematics existed almost solely for the purposes of housekeeping' (BP, p. 522). Certainly beliefs in daily life are full of contradictions, not only between those of different individuals and groups but even within individuals. Moreover, bridges would not collapse because set theory contained hidden contradictions.[9] But mathematics is different from (or is a very special kind of) daily discourse, and the requirement of freedom from contradiction is one of its distinct features. Many mathematicians are not interested in totally explicit formalization, but that does not mean they are not bothered by contradictions.

Neither G nor Wittgenstein says much about moral, social, and political problems in their philosophy, but for different reasons. While Wittgenstein believes that nothing general can be said about such problems, G seems to believe that once the right basic theory is found, the rest will follow as applications, comparable to those of physics to engineering.

In 1972 G commented on Carnap and Wittgenstein. He said that the later work of Wittgenstein was, compared with his early work, a step backward. Through the years G continued to believe that mathematical logic is useful for philosophy because it makes philosophy more precise and easier for those not specially gifted. Carnap, he thought, misused symbolic language, wanted to discredit mathematical logic as a tool, and wanted to destroy philosophy. In particular, G emphasized the importance of mathematical logic to the axiomatic method, which is his favorite method for characterizing concepts in science and philosophy.

It is clear that as the range of logic is expanded, more can be done with logic. Traditionally axiom systems for branches of science generally leave out the logic part because it is thought to be included implicitly. Hence, as we change the range of logic, representationally the same axiom system becomes richer with a richer underlying logic. Could it be that Carnap's misuse of logic (such as too much formal rigidity) is partly a result of his having too narrow a notion of logic?

More than in other subjects, it is especially difficult to find the right 'beginning' in philosophy. In simpler situations, one is accustomed to thinking that given enough perseverance, a territory can be traveled wherever the trip is started. We see as a fact that in philosophy this process is, to a considerable extent, irreversible. For instance, G and Wittgenstein chose different beginnings and covered different grounds. In fact, each person is born into certain specific circumstances so that the choice or the sequence of choices that can be made is severely constrained. G repeatedly emphasizes the importance of overcoming prejudices, and he thinks that a major task is to get rid of the bad effects of a largely negative education. For example, for the generations grown up with television, it is a very arduous task indeed to shake off the vast quantity of prejudices acquired in the process.

Both G and Wittgenstein stress (conceptual) analysis, although they perform it in radically different ways. Moreover, they both agree with Ramsey that 'philosophy must be of some use and we must take it seriously,' yet the kind of use envisaged by Wittgenstein probably would not satisfy Ramsey, who would, though impressed by the actual use of philosophy G says he has made, also be impatient to wait for the doubtful realization of philosophy as a rigorous science.

It is well known that Ramsey was for several years very much impressed by the *Tractatus*. From Ramsey's writings we can see that he gradually moved away from the *Tractatus* position. In a paper of 1927, he suggests[10] that atomic propositions (Elementarsätze) may be relative to a language and that a gap in the *Tractatus* needs to be filled up by a sort of 'pragmatism': 'The essence of pragmatism I take to be this, that the meaning of a sentence is to be defined by reference to the actions to which asserting it would lead, or, more vaguely still, by its possible causes and effects.'

By the summer of 1929, Ramsey's disagreement with Wittgenstein became very strong. In his reflections on the nature of philosophy written down at this time, he makes three different criticisms of Wittgenstein's approach to philosophy.[11] (1) Wittgenstein equivocates with his notion of 'given.' (2) Scholasticism treats what is vague as if it were precise and tries to fit it to an exact logical category. 'A typical piece of scholasticism is Wittgenstein's view that all our everyday propositions are completely in order and that it is impossible to think illogically.' (3) Ramsey believes that philosophy must be of some use, and that it must clear our thoughts and so our actions. Otherwise it is a disposition we have to check and philosophy is nonsense. 'And again we must then take seriously that it is nonsense, and not pretend, as Wittgenstein does, that it is important nonsense.' This was at a time when Wittgenstein was beginning the transition to his later views. It is not clear how much of these comments Ramsey would take to be applicable also to these views.

It is clear that G had more interests in common with Ramsey. For example, in a collection of letters from Wittgenstein to C. K. Ogden, 1973, ed. G. H. v. Wright, there are included also several interesting letters by Ramsey. Two items indicate some common interests with G. In the letter of December 1923, Ramsey reports that he has been trying a lot to decide the continuum hypothesis, but has had no success. In the letter of February 1924, he comments negatively on Russell's new stuff for the second edition of *PM*, saying that all there is is but a clever new proof of mathematical induction. In fact, as G points out (*BP*, p. 226), the proof is mistaken. Moreover, we now know that it is demonstrably impossible to prove the conclusion from those axioms.

Notes

1. The authoritative biography is G. H. v. Wright's *Sketch*, first published in 1954 and reprinted in his *Wittgenstein* (1982). Unless otherwise indicated, biographical details will be drawn from this sketch (briefly, *S*); the quotation here is from pp. 17–18.
2. K. T. Fann (editor), *Wittgenstein: The Man and His Philosophy*, 1967, pp. 31–32 and 86.
3. On the question of Wittgenstein and Russia, there is a piece by John Moran in *New Left Review*, no. 73, 1972, pp. 83–96. In Wittgenstein's letters to Paul Engelmann (published 1967), we find a letter of September 1922 in which he says, 'The idea of a possible flight to Russia which we talked about keeps on haunting me' (p. 53). Again, in June 1937, 'I am now in England for a short stay; perhaps I shall go to Russia. God knows what will become of me' (p. 59). It is widely reported that in 1935 Wittgenstein 'had plans for settling in the Soviet Union.' In any case, it is well known that he had an intense distaste for private property as well as a strong belief in the dignity of manual labor.
4. See, e.g., Engelmann's *Memoir*, 1967; C. A. van Peursen, *Wittgenstein*, 1963 and 1969; K. T. Fann, *Wittgenstein's Conception of Philosophy*, 1969; A. Janik and S. Toulmin, *Wittgenstein's Vienna*, 1973; R. Rhees (editor), *Recollections of Wittgenstein*, 1984. For the term 'Kakania,' see Janik and Toulmin. Other books on Wittgenstein include N. Malcolm, *A Memoir*, 1958 and 1984; B. McGuinness (editor), *Wittgenstein and His Times*, 1982.
5. The comparison with Kant is elaborated in D. Pears, *Wittgenstein*, 1971. The influence of Mauthner and Kraus is discussed at length in Janik and Toulmin. The quoted sentence on Mauthner is from v. Peursen, p. 26. There are various books on the *Tractatus*, including E. Stenius, 1960 and G. E. M. Anscombe, 1959 and 1963.
6. E.g., *Remarks on Foundations of Mathematics*, 1956, II 11, 'To say of an unending series that it does *not* contain a particular pattern makes sense only under quite special conditions,' etc.; II 2, 'I want to say: if you have a proof-pattern that cannot be taken in and by a change in notation you turn it into one that can, then you are producing a proof, where there was none before.' Compare also *Survey*, pp. 39–41, and *MP*, chapter 7.
7. An extended discussion of some of the issues involved is given by T. Tymoczko, *Journal of Philosophy*, vol. 76 (1979), pp. 57–83.
8. *Remarks on Foundations of Mathematics*, 1956, and expanded edition, 1978. The part on G's theorem is included in the original edition as appendix I to part I (pp. 49–54, written around 1937–38), plus V 18–19 (pp. 176–177, written in 1941) and as appendix III to part I (pp. 116–123) plus VII 21–22 (pp. 385–389) in the revised edition. A long letter of July 1935 to Schlick about G's theorem has been preserved. For criticisms of the 1956 edition, compare the articles by P. Bernays and by A. R. Anderson in *BP*. According to R. L. Goodstein, Wittgenstein had in 1935 a better understanding of G's theorem and made the following correct observation about it: it shows 'that the notion of a finite cardinal could not be expressed in an axiomatic system and that formal number variables must necessarily take values other than natural numbers' (*Mind*, vol. 66, 1957, pp. 549–553). References to the remarks will be to the 1956 edition. For his view of the special place of the proposition 'there is no greatest integer,' see middle of p. 57.

9. For an extended discussion of this question with Turing in 1939, see *Wittgenstein's Lectures on the Foundations of Mathematics*, ed. C. Diamond, 1976, pp. 211–220.

10. Reprinted in his *Foundations of Mathematics*, 1931; see p. 155.

11. Ibid., pp. 269 and 263.

Chapter 3
A chronological account: Central Europe
(1906–1939)

In the last few years a good deal about Gödel's life has been reported in the literature. Undoubtedly substantially more material will appear within the next few years. I would like to put together a selection of facts based on what is available to me. In general, I shall give sources only in the case of quotations and items not directly available otherwise.

1906
Kurt Friedrich Gödel was born on 28 April 1906 at 5 Bäckergasse (now Pekarska) and baptized in the German Lutheran congregation of Brünn in Moravia [see his Taufschein (baptismal certificate)]. Brünn was (and Brno is) the most important city of Moravia and had been for a long time a major textile center. Gregor Mendel (1822–1884) spent most of his active years there. Its population was predominantly Czech, with a substantial German-speaking minority, to which G's parents belonged.

According to WS, other famous people from Brünn include Ernst Mach, Tomas Masaryk, the inventor Viktor Kaplan, the writer Ernst Weisz, the architects Adolf Loos and Josef Hoffmann, Bruno Kreisky (chancellor of Austria from 1970 to 1983), the tenor Leo Slezak, and the cabaretist Fritz Grünbaum.

His father Rudolf (28 February 1874 to 23 February 1929), whose (Old Catholic) family had come from Vienna, was an energetic, inventive (in the textile field), and self-made man. He was director and part owner of the Friedrich Redlich textile factory. (Redlich was G's godfather, from whom G's middle name was presumably taken. G did not use his middle name in his publications and officially dropped it when he became a US citizen in 1948. But the initial F. survives on his tombstone.) Later (before the beginning of World War I) he built for the family a beautiful villa at 8A Spilberggasse (now Pellikova), where G grew up. In 1929, not quite 55, Rudolf died unexpectedly from a painful abscess of the prostate. He left his family in comfortable financial circumstances; also before his death, the 'close to wealthy' family had been little affected by World War I and the subsequent inflation.

G's mother Marianne (31 August 1879 to 23 July 1966) was Lutheran, received a broad literary education (partly in the French school in Brünn), and had multiple cultural interests. (Her father Gustav Handschuh had been a poor weaver in the Rhineland before moving to Brünn to work as 'Einzelprokurist der Firma Schoeller.') She was also a competent and imaginative housewife, to whom both of her children were very much attached. After the death of her husband in 1929, she moved to Vienna to live with her sons. By that time her other son, Rudolf (born 1902), was already an established radiologist (who survives G and has never married). She remained in Vienna till 1937, when she returned to the villa in Brno. In 1944 she joined her elder son in Vienna again (and stayed there the rest of her life). Afterward she, together with Rudolf, visited G and his wife several times in Princeton. (By coincidence, she was born in the same year as Einstein.)

G's father was only formally Catholic, and G is said to have had a lifelong dislike of the Catholic Church. G's family cultivated its German national heritage. G was never a member of any religious congregation, although he was a believer: 'theistic, not pantheistic (following Leibniz rather than Spinoza)'(GQ). In January 1978, G's wife told me that G read his Bible in bed on Sundays.

1911

According to G's brother Rudolf (see RG), 'My brother was a cheerful child. He had, it is true, at about the age of five a light anxiety neurosis, which later completely disappeared.

'We (my brother and I) lived with our parents in Brünn in a villa with a beautiful garden. [This refers to the residence at 8A Spilberggasse, acquired by G's father when G was quite young.] ... He had little interest in our beautiful garden, while I enjoyed working there.'

1914

G attended elementary school (the Evangelische Volkschule in Brünn) for four years (1912−1916).

Some time during this period he had a painful bout of rheumatic fever. In 1976, G told me that it was when he was eight or nine years old. He also said that, as a result, he had a weak heart. His school report cards record a number of excused absences, including exemptions from participation in physical education during the years 1915−16 and 1917−18. The first of the two periods would seem to support the conjecture that the important illness occurred at the age of nine. His brother believes this episode to have been a source of G's lifelong preoccupation with his health, bordering on hypochondria.

G is remembered as a generally happy but rather timid and touchy child, unusually troubled when he lost a game or when his mother left the house; also a very inquisitive child, called *der Herr Warum* (Mr. Why) by the family (Kreisel, pp. 152–153).

RG: 'At about the age of eight my brother had a severe joint-rheumatism with high fever and thereafter he was somewhat hypochondriacal and fancied himself to have a heart problem, a claim that was, however, never established medically.'

1916

G attended secondary school during 1916–1924 (*Staatsrealgymnasium in Brünn mit deutscher Unterrichtssprache*).

At school he had the reputation never to have made a mistake in Latin grammar; some of his meticulous homework in geometry is preserved. His geometric drawings display an immaculate draftsmanship. Report cards from both elementary and secondary schools are in his Nachlass. Only once did he receive less than the highest mark, and that in mathematics! The curriculum of the time laid heavy emphasis on science and the languages. Latin and French were required. G chose shorthand and English as his two elective subjects (and did not choose Czech). [The library in his estate contains dictionaries of many languages (and also a book on Chinese grammar). There are vocabulary and exercise notebooks not only for English and Latin but also for Italian and Dutch.] Besides mathematics and Latin, he also excelled in theology; in his later life he recorded many theological ideas and details of church history in his notebooks.

G did a good deal of outside reading, probably using the library of the technical institute (at Elisabethplatz in Brünn) and, in cultural education, his mother's private library.

According to some reports, he had, while still in school, a romantic interest in a family friend ten years older than he, and his parents objected strongly and successfully (WS and Kreisel, p. 153).

RG: 'From about the age of ten he enjoyed playing chess and was very eager to win and very wretched or vexed when he lost, which rarely happened.'

From 1919 to 1921 G took courses in stenography in which he learned the Gabelsberger shorthand used in many of his notebooks.

[The shorthand system was devised by Franz Xaver Gabelsberger. It, together with the Stolze-Schrey script, were the two competing German shorthand systems in widespread use during the early decades of this century. Eventually the two systems merged to form the Einheitskurzschrift, and there are now few people who are familiar with the two older systems. Other Gabelsberger users include E. Husserl, E. Schrödinger, and E. Zermelo (see Dawson 1984).]

1920
G's brother Rudolf went to the University of Vienna to study medicine. Of G's early life, he wrote in RG,

It was a harmonious family life. There was very good understanding between my brother and me, and likewise between our parents and both of us.

We played mostly with one another and had few friends; our play was tranquil: with building blocks, train set, and in World War I naturally also tin soldiers.

My brother was an outstanding pupil at first in the languages, later in history and later again was interested in mathematics. In Latin lessons he *always* had the highest mark. At sixteen to seventeen, he was far ahead of his classmates in mathematics and had already mastered the university material.

He had an especially good rapport with his mother, who often played for him his favorite melodies (light music) on the piano. When I went with my parents for walks he often preferred to stay home with a book.

1921
Around 1975 G noted (in GQ) that his interest in mathematics began at about age 15 (or 14), stimulated by an introductory calculus textbook in the Göschen collection.

In this connection, it may be of interest to compare G with Einstein (1879–1955). According to his brother, G had learned a good deal of mathematics by himself before entering the university. More data are available about Einstein's self-study and extracurricular stimuli. His uncle Jakob Einstein would pose mathematical problems. From 1889 to 1894 Max Talmud (later changed to Talmey), then a young medical student, was a regular visitor to the family home (in Munich) and took great interest in Einstein's intellectual development. His impressions of and interactions with Einstein are reported in his book *The Relativity Theory Simplified and the Formative Years of Its Inventor* (1932).

He noticed Einstein's particular inclination toward physics and gave him appropriate reading matter. A. Bernstein's *Popular Books on Physical Science* 'especially, which describes physical phenomena lucidly and engagingly, had a great influence on Albert, and enhanced considerably his interest in physical science.' Soon afterward Einstein began to show keenness for mathematics and Talmud gave him a textbook of geometry, which he worked through in a few months. 'He thereupon devoted himself to higher mathematics, studying all by himself' and soon reached a height that Talmud 'could no longer follow.' 'Thereafter philosophy was often a subject of our conversations' and the reading of Kant was recommended, who 'became Albert's favorite philosopher after he had read through his *Critique of Pure Reason* and the works of other philosophers.' (For more details, compare Clark, pp. 33–34, and Pais, pp. 37–38.)

G apparently did not have a comparable early interest and advanced knowledge in physics; probably G studied more history, languages, and theology instead. While Einstein did well in school, G was nearly perfect in the required work. Clearly both had a great deal of energy and ability over and above what was needed to be good students. Since mathematics is more self-sufficient than physics, it is easier to study by oneself. While both were unusually brilliant and inquisitive, the happy combination of external stimuli and Einstein's audacity must have helped in strengthening his inclination toward physics and in bringing about a good command of the subject so early in his life.

'I came,' says Einstein in his autobiography, 'to a deep religiosity, which, however, found an abrupt ending at the age of twelve. Through the reading of popular scientific books I soon reached the conviction that much in the stories of the Bible could not be true.' I do not know whether G went through anything similar. In any case, thoughtful Europeans of their time usually did grapple with religion in their youth. As Freud observes, 'Is it not true that the two main points in the program for the education of children today are retardation of sexual development and premature religious influence?' (*The Future of an Illusion*, 1927). For example, Russell (1872–1970), according to himself, 'began thinking about philosophical questions at the age of fifteen,' discarding first free will, then immortality, and finally God (compare *BA*, p. 59). Husserl (1859–1938) 'said that at the age of 13 or 14 he had been deeply concerned with religious questions,' such as the existence of God (Karl Schuhmann, *Husserl-Chronik*, 1977, p. 3). While I do not have a clear idea of what G means by calling himself a theist, I believe that he differs from the four interesting (also to him) thinkers mentioned, who are regarded as atheists of one type or another.

G read Chamberlain's Goethe book in Marienbad, according to G's letter of 26 August 1946 ('now exactly 25 years,' see *LM*). 'This Goethe book was also the beginning of my occupation with Goethe's Farbenlehre and his dispute with Newton, which indirectly also contributed to my choice of vocation. This is the way remarkable threads spin through one's life, which are discovered only when one gets older.' On 11 August 1986 G's brother Rudolf told me that G had concluded from his study in favor of Newton's position (over Goethe's).

1922

G read (some of) Kant's work for the first time. G also said in *GQ* that of the authors in Grandjean's list, only Kant's work was important for his own development.

G told me that the three philosophers he found most congenial were
Plato, Leibniz, and Husserl. He also said that he had begun to read Husserl
in 1959. According to GQ, he studied Leibniz closely from 1943 to 1946.
He also said in GQ that Leibniz had the greatest influence on him, but not
on what he wrote. According to Menger, he was already much interested
in Leibniz through the 1930s.

Both G and Einstein have made scientific contributions that are of much
philosophical interest. While both possessed interest and knowledge in
philosophy, G, unlike Einstein, who always put physics at the center of his
research activity, concentrated on philosophy over extended periods of his
life. One reason may be that Einstein saw a sharper distinction between
science and philosophy, and was less sanguine of anyone achieving sufficiently definite results in philosophy. For example, Maurice Solovine reports, in his 14 April 1952 letter to C. Seelig, on his first visit to Einstein (in
the spring of 1902), 'He confided to me that he also, when he was younger,
had a strong taste for philosophy, but the vagueness and arbitrariness
which reigned there had turned him against it, and that he was now
concerned solely with physics' (Clark, p. 79).

In her *Reality and Scientific Truth* (1980), Ilse Rosenthal-Schneider quotes
a number of Einstein's comments on philosophy. 'Is not the whole of
philosophy as if written in honey? It looks wonderful at first sight. But
when you look again it is all gone. Only mush remains' (p. 90). 'Kant's
much praised view on time reminds me of Andersen's tale of the emperor's
new clothes, only that the form of intuition takes the place of the emperor's
clothes!' (p. 84). 'Kant is a sort of highway with lots and lots of milestones.
Then all the little dogs come and each deposits his bit at the milestones.'
Responding to her pretended indignation, Einstein, laughing loudly, remarked, 'But what will you have? Your Kant is after all the highway, that
is to stay' (p. 90). On 3 February 1947, Einstein wrote, 'My friend here, the
well-known mathematical logician Kurt Gödel, has, after much effort, at
last secured and studied your book on the relations of Kant's work to the
theory of relativity' [*Das Raum-Zeit-Problem bei Kant und Einstein*, 1921]
(p. 86). It was probably about this time that G began to write his paper
'Some observations about the relationship between [the] theory of relativity and Kantian philosophy' (folders 04/129–134 in the Nachlass).

1924
Following his graduation from the Gymnasium in Brno, G went to Vienna
to study theoretical physics at the university, which was outstanding then.
As a gifted young man from a well-situated family, he was in an excellent
position to benefit fully from the rich offerings. Among the courses he took
at the university he only mentioned to me Furtwängler's lectures on number theory, which he much enjoyed, and philosophical lectures by Heinrich

Gomperz. The lectures by Gomperz were on the history of European philosophy. Philip Furtwängler was paralyzed from the neck down, a cousin of the famous conductor Wilhelm Furtwängler, and one of the founders of class field theory. Other teachers of G include Hans Hahn, M. Schlick, and Hans Thirring.

G said in GQ that prior to his enrollment at the University of Vienna he had little contact with Vienna's intellectual or cultural life, except through the newspaper *Die neue freie Presse*.

RG: 'At eighteen he went to study at the University of Vienna where I had already been studying medicine for four years. We lived together as students each in his own room, but spent little time together since he went to the university and I went to the hospital; he seldom spoke to me about his profession. Later when he was already in Princeton, I became aware by reputation(!) that he was an important man in his field.

'Our parents often came to visit us in Vienna and then we often went to the theater [Max Reinhardt's Josefstädter Theater] in which my brother had great interest.'

From 8 October 1924 to 8 April 1927, G lived at Florianigasse 42/II/16, according to the Vienna city record (as told me by E. Köhler).

1925

G said in GQ that he had been 'a conceptual and mathematical realist since about 1925.' It appears most likely that philosophy has occupied a great deal of G's attention ever since his student days. Presumably this interest was held somewhat in abeyance over the period from 1928 to 1939 or 1942, when he concentrated on mathematical logic. According to Menger, however, G studied much philosophy also through the 1930s. He also wrote a good deal in his philosophical notebooks from 1940 through 1942.

There are in G's Nachlass two notebooks (03/72.5 and 03/72.6) on the course 'History of European philosophy' by Gomperz, marked 'Winter 1925' and '1926.' Hence, G must have studied philosophy in 1925, and the study may have helped him to crystallize his 'realist' position in about 1925.

Olga Taussky[-Todd] (1906–) entered the University of Vienna in 1925 and became acquainted with G in her first year of study. She has written some remembrances, mostly covering the period from 1925 to 1934 (see her 'Remembrances of Kurt Gödel'). In 1925–26, she and G were both in Schlick's seminar on philosophy of mathematics in which Russell's *Introduction to Mathematical Philosophy* was studied. At the end of the second meeting, Schlick asked twice for some student to report next time, and then G volunteered.

According to her, G 'had a liking for members of the opposite sex, and he made no secret of this fact.' She reports on seeing G with a very young girl, who later 'complained about Kurt being so spoilt, having to sleep long in the morning and so on. Apparently she was interested in him and wanted him to give up his prima donna habits.'

G 'was well trained in all branches of mathematics and you could talk to him about any problem and receive an excellent response.... He spoke slowly and very calmly and his mind was very clear. But you could talk to him about other things too and his clear mind made this a rare pleasure. I understand that Einstein had many conversations with him.'

On one occasion, G 'remarked that I [Taussky] counted him among the *minores gentium*. This is a medical term for doctors of not the highest standing, who of course could not command the highest fees.'

'Kurt had a friendly attitude toward people of the Jewish faith. And once he said out of the blue that it was a miracle (Wunder) how, without a country, they were able to survive for thousands of years, almost like a nation, merely by their faith.'

In 1933, after several colleagues, including Taussky, had seen him off at the Westbahnhof on his way to Princeton, he fell ill before reaching the boat and returned home. His family persuaded him to try again, and the second departure was successful. (G confided this to Taussky later on.)

After G's Gibbs Lecture in 1951, Taussky-Todd heard Mrs. Gödel say to him, 'Kurtele, if I compare your lecture with the others, there is no comparison!'

On 26 January, G requested from the library Kant's *Metaphysical Foundations of Natural Science*. This indicates an early interest in the philosophy of physics. From 1924 to 1926 G chiefly requested books in physics.

1926

In G's own words (see section 2.1), in the autumn he transferred to mathematics and coincidentally became a member of the Schlick Circle [commonly known as the Vienna Circle]. However, he was never a positivist, but accepted only some of their theses even at that time. His interest in precision led him from physics to mathematics and to mathematical logic. In GQ, G said, 'This group [the Vienna Circle] aroused my interest in the foundations.' He also said (see section 1.2.2) that the interest of some members of the group in the foundations of mathematics had begun long before its exposure to Wittgenstein's *Tractatus*. G attended the meetings of the Circle regularly from 1926 to 1928, but then gradually moved away from it.

Carnap came to Vienna as a Dozent in the autumn, and, at his suggestion, Schlick decided to devote 'as many consecutive meetings as necessary to a renewed analysis of the *Tractatus*, reading the book aloud, sentence by sentence. This filled that entire academic year. Since G began to attend the meetings of the Circle at about this time, it seems plausible that he studied the book within that year. This is clearly related to his statement (in *GQ*) that he first studied Wittgenstein in 1927 (but never read any of his work thoroughly). Judging from what he told me in 1972, he did not like the *Tractatus* because it proposes to show that philosophy is not possible.

Carnap's diary indicates that he began to talk with G in 1927 and that he preserved records of some of his discussions with G from May 1928 to 1933 (compare section 2.2). It appears that quite early (probably in 1928) the roles of teacher and student were essentially reversed. Carnap stayed in Vienna till the summer of 1931, but continued afterward to visit Vienna (from Prague) for several years.

Arthur Burks once told me two stories he had heard from Carnap. Carnap asked G, when still a student, to write some articles for an encyclopedia to make himself known. G declined and said that he did not have to depend on that to become known. The other story is, after G had got his incompleteness results, he was concerned that somebody else might get his results independently[, presumably because he thought the proofs were so simple and transparent].

At the time of G's transfer to mathematics, the (ordentliche) professors in mathematics were Furtwängler, Hans Hahn, and Wilhelm Wirtinger (whose subject was analysis and who was an expert on Abelian functions). There were also four or more Privatdozenten (unpaid but tenured lecturers), including Walther Mayer (1887–1948), who later collaborated with Einstein from December 1929 to 1934 (see Taussky, op. cit.)

By the end of 1926, G seems to have attended courses by Gomperz, Furtwängler, Schlick, Hans Thirring (on relativity theory), and Hahn. G's exceptional talents were widely recognized in the community. He undoubtedly felt very comfortable with the attractive personalities of Schlick and Hahn, who in turn had great appreciation of him. Frequent contacts with Kal Menger and Carnap began later (probably in 1927 and 1928).

According to Feigl, 'On the personal side, I should mention that Gödel, together with another student member of the Circle, Marcel Natkin (originally from Lodz, Poland), and myself became close friends. We met frequently for walks through the parks of Vienna, and of course in cafés had endless discussions about logical, mathematical, epistemological, and philosophy-of-science issues—sometimes deep into the hours of the night.' This probably refers to the years from 1925 to either 1928 or 1929, since Natkin had gone to Paris by 1929. Later in 1957, Natkin, Gödel, and Feigl 'had a most enjoyable reunion in New York' (*The Intellectual Migration*, ed. D. Fleming and B. Bailyn, 1969, p. 640).

On the whole, it appears that G's student days in Vienna were both enjoyable and fruitful.

Hahn, G's principal teacher and spokesman, was an expert in the modern theory of functions of real variables and in descriptive set theory, as well as an enthusiast of mathematical logic. Apart from being a good mathematician, he was politically active for the socialist party and much interested in extrasensory perception, to the extent of giving public lectures on the subject. Earlier he had studied at Göttingen from 1902 to 1904, after graduating from Vienna. He was active in bringing Schlick to Vienna in 1922 and Carnap in 1926. The political situation in Vienna became difficult for him in 1933, and he died unexpectedly on 24 July 1934, after a short illness.

1927

Karl Menger, one of Hahn's favorite students, returned to Vienna in the autumn as an ausserordentlicher (associate) professor, after two years spent in Amsterdam with Brouwer. He accepted Hahn's invitation to join the Schlick Circle, which met every other Thursday evening on the ground floor of a building on the Boltzmanngasse that housed the institutes of mathematics and physics. According to his paper on Schlick (*Rationality and Science*, ed. E. T. Gadol, 1982), Menger set up in 1928 his mathematical colloquium with the Circle as its model, except that records of his meetings (from 1928 to 1936) were published (in eight issues). These records are of value particularly for (the thirteen) contributions by G, many of which G would otherwise probably not have taken the initiative to get published. Indeed, G assisted in editing most of the issues (all except 6 and 8). Later Menger invited G to Notre Dame for the spring of 1939 and tried to persuade G to stay in America then.

'In the fall of 1927,' according to Menger (p. 88), 'the *Tractatus* as such was no longer. on the agenda. But it loomed over the discussions and especially over all that Schlick said and thought.' In 1929 O. Neurath, chiefly with the assistance of Carnap, wrote the pamphlet *Wissenschaftliche Weltanschauung: Der Wiener Kreis*. Menger believes that neither Hahn, even though he consented to sign as the principal author, nor Schlick, for whom the manifesto was written, liked it. It certainly estranged Menger from the Circle. 'The booklet produced an even greater disaffection in Gödel' (p. 92).

The tendency to develop a more flexible and vaguer position into a more definite and restrictive one appears to be at work when, for example, one passes from Locke to Hume. In the case of the Schlick Circle, the transition from Schlick's early views to the doctrines of Carnap seems to me to yield a result less stable and coherent than Hume's. In addition, the adoration of Wittgenstein appears to have harmed rather than helped a sound development. Apart from the attractive personalities of Schlick and Hahn, G's sympathies with the Circle were probably in the quest for precision, the undogmatic and open-minded discussions, and the close attention to fundamental science. G objected to the restrictive empiricist view of science and believed that 'theories' can also be developed about philosophical concepts.

Moritz Schlick (1882–1936), like Hahn, was refined and very sincere. (I am following here Menger's account, which agrees well with reports by others.) He was unassuming almost to the point of diffidence, especially toward the younger and the weaker (such as the students). 'Empty phrases from his lips or the slightest trace of pompousness were unthinkable.' He had a special talent for conducting stimulating discussions. He began regular discussions with his colleagues almost immediately after taking up his Vienna position in 1922. Probably by 1924, these discussions evolved into the meetings that gave rise to the name 'Schlick Circle.' For a few years, his interest in logic and mathematics had been quite strong, but after his first personal contacts with Wittgenstein in 1927, he apparently developed gradually 'a bias against formal logic and mathematics.' (This incidentally illustrates his difference from Carnap.)

'His political views can probably best be described as those of a British-style liberal.' In 1933, with Hitler coming to power in Germany, the political situation in Austria turned harsh. 'Schlick's position at the university became precarious.' Jewish and more leftist members of the Circle were generally in a worse position. In particular, O. Neurath, a socialist and one of the most active members, who was in Moscow early in 1934, could no longer return to Austria. The theoretical discussions in the Circle also reached an impasse' in 'the months before Hahn's death.' On 22 June 1936, a paranoid former student shot and killed Schlick, and the (group) activities of the Vienna Circle came to a complete stop in Vienna.

A special trait of Schlick was his single-minded admiration of a single hero or authority at each stage of his development. In the early years of the century, it was Max Planck, with whom he studied physics in Berlin. This was followed successively by Einstein and the theory of relativity, Hilbert and the axiomatic method (with special emphasis on 'implicit definitions'), Russell and mathematical logic, and finally, for the last ten years of his life, Wittgenstein. Particularly during the last stage, he was willing to credit his own ideas to his hero or give them up for no better reason than some sign of disapproval from his hero.

G gave his address in his library slips as Frankgasse 10/II/11 on 28 June and as Währingerstr. 33/IV/22 on 5 September and 12 October. The books requested in this year are mainly in number theory. More exactly, according to the city record, G used the former address from 8 April to 20 July 1927 and the latter from 6 October 1927 to 1 July 1928.

Menger wrote in 1981 a memoir, 'Recollections of Kurt Gödel' (forthcoming in *Kurt Gödel. Leben und Werk*, ed. W. Schimanovich, E. Köhler, and P. Weibel; to be referred to as Menger or Menger's memoir). In it he says that in the autumn of 1927 he gave a course on dimension theory. 'One of the students who had signed up was named Kurt Gödel. He was a slim, unusually quiet young man. I do not recall having spoken with him then. Later I saw him again in the Schlick Circle; however, I never heard him take the floor or participate in a discussion in the Circle. He indicated interest solely by slight motions of the head—in agreement, skeptically, or in disagreement.'

1928

It was around this year that G met Adele Nimbursky Porkert (1899–1981), who was working at *Der Nachtfalter*, a Viennese nightspot. She was six years older than he. She had little formal education, had worked as a dancer, or singer, or attendant and was slightly disfigured by a facial birthmark. G's parents, especially the father, objected to this romantic involvement. In fact, they did not marry until 1938.

It appears that this was the beginning of a close relationship, which lasted some 50 years (till G's death). They had no children, while Einstein, who was a widower for almost 20 years (1936–1955), had two sons by his first wife, Mileva (1875–1948, married 6 January 1903) and two step-daughters from his second wife, Elsa (1876–1936, married 2 June 1919).

G lived at Langegasse 72/II/14 from 4 July 1928 to 5 November 1929 (so that his doctoral dissertation was written there); according to WS, Adele, still married to the photographer Nimbursky, lived then at Langegasse 65, almost directly across the street. The residence was shared with G's brother and consisted of three rooms, being half of a large apartment. Their father also stayed with them when visiting Vienna.

This was the year when G became more deeply concerned with mathematical logic, stimulated both by Carnap's lectures (on the philosophical foundations of arithmetic, winter semester 1928/29) and by the first edition of the famous text of Hilbert and Ackermann (HA, 1928), in which both the completeness and the decidability of elementary logic (the restricted functional calculus) were posed as open problems. (The latter problem is called simply the Entscheidungsproblem.) [G also ordered and received *Principia Mathematica* in July.]

Brouwer gave two lectures in Vienna: 'Mathematik, Wissenschaft, und Sprache,' on 10 March (published in *Monatshefte*, vol. 36, 1929, pp. 153–164), and 'Die Struktur des Continuums,' on 14 March (published by Gistel, Vienna, 1930). Of the two lectures, the first was probably the influential one. It is said to have caused Wittgenstein to return to philosophy. It appears certain that G must have heard the two lectures. Indeed, in a draft of a letter (dated 12 April 1972) G says that he only saw Wittgenstein once at a lecture, probably Brouwer's (see section 2.2). Carnap also stated that G had been influenced by the (first) lecture. In the introductory part of

G's dissertation (1929, see section 10.1), there are some observations on Brouwer's views.

According to Feigl (op. cit., p. 639), when 'Brouwer was scheduled to lecture on intuitionism in mathematics in Vienna, Waismann and I managed to coax Wittgenstein, after much resistance, to join us in attending the lecture. When, afterwards, Wittgenstein went to a café with us, a great event took place. Suddenly and very volubly Wittgenstein began talking philosophy—at great length. Perhaps this was the turning point,' for not long after he returned to philosophy.

Hilbert led a delegation of sixty-seven German mathematicians to attend the official International Congress (the first since 1912) at Bologna, 3–10 September. At the opening session Hilbert gave the address 'Probleme der Grundlegung der Mathematik.'

Under the false impression that the consistency of number theory had been proved (finitistically), Hilbert listed four (areas of) problems. Roughly speaking they are (1) finitist consistency proof of analysis, (2) that of set theory, (3) completeness of first-order number theory and analysis, (4) completeness of first-order logic. Given the lively concern with foundational questions in Vienna, it is most likely that G learned about the content of the lecture soon after. In any case, G certainly knew this lecture before 1930, as is seen from his reference to it in footnote 48 of his incompleteness paper. It is extremely remarkable indeed that G essentially answered all four questions within about two years after the lecture. [For a more extended consideration of this matter, see section 2.3.]

The books requested by G (beginning 1 October) in this year are mainly in logic.

1929

On 23 February, G's father, born on 28 February 1874, died unexpectedly. G was granted release from Czechloslovakian citizenship on 26 February and acquired Austrian citizenship on 6 June.

After her husband's death G's mother moved to Vienna, took a large apartment, and shared it with her two sons until 1937 when she returned to their villa in Brno. In 1944 she joined her elder son Rudolf in Vienna again. The family apartment was at Josefstädterstrasse 43, from 5 November 1929 to 16 November 1937; G stayed there during this period when he was in Vienna. He lived at Himmelstrasse 43 from 11 November 1937 to September 1938 (when he married Adele) and, after his trip to America, from June to 9 November 1939. He and Adele were at Hegelstrasse 5 from 9 November 1939 to January 1940 (when they left Vienna for Princeton), but officially the address was listed under their name until 14 February 1948 (when they relinquished it).

According to G (in 1976), he had 'completed his formal studies at the university before the summer of 1929.' I am not clear about the exact meaning of this. For example, was there a large final examination comparable to what Einstein had to suffer through in the summer of 1900, after which 'I [Einstein] found the consideration of any scientific problems distasteful to me for an entire year'? My impression is that G would not have minded such an examination nearly as much. However that may be, G seems to have lost no time in doing important research immediately after 'the completion of his formal studies.' Indeed, his dissertation proving the completeness of elementary logic was approved by Hahn and Furtwängler on 6 July, and it was submitted to the dean of the philosophical faculty on 15 October.

In 1976 G said that he had read HA in 1929. The completeness of elementary logic in the sense familiar today was formulated (agreeing in spirit with Bolzano's idea of 1837, but more definite in using a specific formal system of elementary logic) and posed as an open question in HA (on p. 68). (A vaguer sense of completeness is also mentioned, which, however, gives no clear guide as to how a complete system in such a sense might be obtainable.) More emphasis is put on the Entscheidungsproblem in HA (especially on p. 77 and pp. 73–74). 'The solution of the Entscheidungsproblem is of fundamental significance for the theories in all areas where the theorems are logically deducible from finitely many axioms.'

Of these two open problems, G settled the one of completeness (positively) in the summer and wrote up the result as his dissertation, which was finished by July. A revised version was received by the editor of *Monatshefte* on 22 October and published in 1930; a main addition was what is now known as the 'compactness theorem.' G received his doctoral degree on 6 February 1930. He presented his result in Menger's colloquium on 14 May and in Königsberg (see below) on 6 September 1930. (G received 100 offprints of his published paper only after the Königsberg meeting, on 19 September.)

Since the concept of satisfiability by a model has a fundamentally different sense for the intuitionists, the whole problem becomes a different one for them. 'It is clear that an intuitionistic completeness proof could only be carried out through the [positive] solution of the Entscheidungsproblem of mathematical logic, while the result [in G's dissertation] only transforms (reduces) it to the problem of formal deducibility [in familiar formal systems of the restricted functional calculus].' (From G's dissertation, which is, together with his published paper, discussed at length in section 10.1)

On the problem of decidability G proved, with considerations closely related to his dissertation, the decidability of the hardest decidable prefix class, known as the 'Gödel case,' with the quantifier prefix E ... EAAE ... E (for satisfiability). The undated paper giving this result is included in volume 2 (pp. 27–28) of Menger's colloquium for the year 1929–30. It seems likely the result was obtained before the summer of 1930 and perhaps at about the same time as his completeness theorem. [Indeed, according to Menger, G wrote this paper at his request (before the summer of 1930), 'which applies his [G's] completeness proof.'] In 1933 G returned to this problem and proved in addition that every satisfiable formula in the class has a finite model. In a, possibly unique, seriously mistaken statement in his published work, G asserted that his method can be applied to the case when identity is added. Eventually in 1983 Warren Goldfarb proved that the Gödel case with identity is in fact undecidable and a reduction class; he did so by expressing an axiom of infinity and then appealing to the central and hardest prefix reduction class, which uses only the simple quantifier prefix AEA (a result dating from 1961) (see *Bulletin AMS*, vol. 10, 1984, pp. 113–115, and *JSL*, vol. 49, 1984, pp. 1237–1252).

The obstacle to a general (negative) solution of the decision problem at the time was the lack of a clear concept of decidability (or computability). In his incompleteness paper, written in 1930, G gave partial results (in theorems IX and X) that, as it turned out later, contained the essential mathematical steps for a negative solution. What was missing was a definition of computable functions that convincingly captures the intuitive concept and is expressible in an elementary manner. One such definition was given by G himself (refining a suggestion by Herbrand) in his 1934 lectures, in which he also considered tentatively the adequacy of his definition to the intuitive concept. (This important issue is considered more fully in sections 6.2 and 10.2)

G said in *GQ* that this was the year when he first studied *Principia Mathematica*. [By the way, in view of the impact of Russell's early work on Wittgenstein and G, it might be amusing to note that R was seventeen years older than W and W was seventeen years older than G.]

The first recorded meeting of the Menger colloquium, which had been meeting irregularly and without protocol since the autumn of 1928, took place on 24 October. Menger: 'Toward the end of 1929 I also invited Gödel to the colloquium and from then on he was a regular participant as long as he was in Vienna and in good health. In these gatherings he appeared from the beginning to feel quite well and spoke even outside of them with participants, particularly G. Nöbeling and a few foreign visitors, and later on frequently with A. Wald. He participated with enthusiasm in diverse discussions. His expression (oral as well as written) was always of the greatest precision and at the same time exceedingly brief. In nonmathematical conversation he was very withdrawn.'

I have reported on the Carnap papers in section 2.2. Here are some more details on Carnap's diary for 23 December 1929 (as deciphered from his Stolz-Schrey shorthand by Richard Nollan, curator of the collection), which not only reports on G's view but also gives some idea of the interactions of the colleagues in Vienna at that time.

Carnap was in the Arkadencafé from 1 P.M. to 9 P.M. He was with Schlick from 1 to 3, and Schlick talked about a girl student wanting to commit suicide. From 3:30 to 5:30 Waismann gave him a novel by Conrad and reported on a meeting with Wittgenstein the previous evening. From 5:45 to 8:30 Gödel talked 'about the inexhaustibility of mathematics (see separate sheet). He was stimulated to his idea by Brouwer's Vienna lecture. Mathematics is not completely formalizable. He appears to be right.' At 9 P.M. Carnap went to the Kolosseum-Kino to see the Tonfilm 'Broadway' and considered it 'not good.' [The 'separate sheet' is quoted in section 2.2]

1930

Scientifically this may have been the most important year (particularly the half-year period preceding 17 November, when his great paper was received for publication) in G's life. According to G's recollection in 1976, it must have been in this year that he first heard about Hilbert's proposed outline of a proof of the continuum hypothesis and began to think about the continuum problem. Moreover, according to him, he began in the summer to study the problem of proving the (relative) consistency of analysis. He soon realized that truth in number theory cannot be defined in number theory and went on to prove a combinatorial form of his first incompleteness theorem.

As mentioned earlier, G sent off his revised dissertation in October 1929. Most probably he had been reflecting on the specific problems suggested in Hilbert's program since 1928. In particular, during the period between October 1929 and the summer of 1930, he undoubtedly deliberated over and experimented with alternative problems in order to choose the next one to tackle after the success with proving that elementary logic is complete. Apparently he decided at some stage that the (relative) consistency of analysis was the most promising and began intensive work on it in the summer.

So far I have not seen any reports on G's activities before the summer. One exception is that Menger invited A. Tarski to give several lectures in Vienna in February. Apparently Tarski joined G in finally convincing Carnap of the need to use a separate metalanguage, a step that G had recommended the previous year but that Carnap and other followers of Wittgenstein had been reluctant to take.

There is in G's Nachlass a draft reply to a letter dated 27 May 1970 from Yossef Balas, then a student at the University of Northern Iowa, regarding G's discovery of the incompleteness theorems. G's draft states in a different manner some of the points that he told me in 1976. He started, he says in the draft reply, by looking for a 'relative model-theoretic consistency proof of analysis in arithmetic' by means of 'an arithmetical ε-relation satisfying the comprehension axiom.' This, he observes, was a new approach at the time because people were only looking for proof-theoretic absolute consistency proofs, being uncomfortable about truth and models [in the foundational parts, in contrast to, e.g, geometry: as emphasized by Hilbert]. He considered the representation of each real number by a propositional function $\phi(x)$ in arithmetic, and noticed that if $\phi(x)$ is replaced by '$\phi(x)$ is provable,' then he could express it in terms of (recondite) arithmetic. The problem is, whether truth could be equated with provability. But 'long before, I had found the *correct* solution of the semantic paradoxes in the fact that truth in a language cannot be defined in itself,' and, therefore, truth differs from provability. (Of special interest is G's explicit statement on his discovery of the correct solution of the semantic paradoxes.) In addition, G also examines in his draft reply Finsler's alleged anticipation and shows convincingly that Finsler totally missed the crucial point of being concerned with formal systems.

A crossed-out paragraph in this draft may account for his not giving (initially) a more extensive consideration of the concept of truth. 'However in consequence of the philosophical prejudices of our time: 1. nobody was looking for a relative consistency proof because it was considered axiomatic that a consistency proof must be finitary in order to make sense, 2. a concept of mathematical truth as opposed to demonstrability was viewed with greatest suspicion and widely rejected as meaningless.'

On 26 August, G met Carnap, Feigl, and Waismann at the Café Reichsrat, where they discussed their travel plans to Königsberg. According to Carnap's 'diary,' the discussion then turned to 'Gödels Entdeckung: Unvollständigkeit des systems der PM; Schwierigkeit des Widerspruchsfreiheitsbeweises.' Three days later they met again at the same place and Carnap noted: 'Zuerst erzählt mir Gödel von seiner Entdeckungen.' Afterward they, together with Hahn and Kurt Grelling, traveled by rail to Swinemüde, and thence by ship to Königsberg, to participate in the Second Conference on Epistemology of the Exact Sciences (5–7 September).

The conference was held in conjunction with (and apparently preceded) the 91st convention of the Gesellschaft deutscher Naturforscher und Ärzte (the Society of German Scientists and Physicians) and the 6th deutsche Physiker- und Mathematikertagung. It was at the opening session of the inclusive meeting (probably on 9 September) that Hilbert was made an honorary citizen of Königsberg and delivered his address 'Natureskennen und Logik,' which G attended. This was the only time G ever saw Hilbert; they never met or corresponded.

The three-day conference began on 5 September with hour-long addresses on the philosophy of mathematics by Carnap, Heyting,

v. Neumann, and Waismann (whose lecture 'Das Wesen der Mathematik: Der Standpunkt Wittgensteins' was added belatedly). On the second day H. Reichenbach, W. Heisenberg, and O. Neugebauer gave hour-long lectures, followed by twenty-minute talks by G, Arnold Scholz, and Walter Dubislav. G's talk dealt with his completeness theorem, of which an abstract appeared on p. 1068 of *Die Naturwissenschaften*, vol. 18 (1930). The third and last day was taken up by a discussion session on the foundations of mathematics, chaired by Hahn, as an adjunct to the lectures on 5 September (except Waismann's). The participants included A. Scholz, K. Reidemeister and G, in addition to the three lecturers of the first day. [The three lectures and the discussions were published in volume 2 of *Erkenntnis*, 1931, including an invited postscript supplied after the meeting by G. The published lectures were reviewed by G and appear in English translation in BP. An annotated English translation of the discussion has recently been given by John Dawson in *History and Philosophy of Logic*, vol. 5 (1984), pp. 111–129. The reviews by G appeared in *Zentralblatt*, vol. 2 (1932), pp. 321–322; they are, together with all other reviews by G, reprinted (with English translations) in the first volume of G's *Collected Works*.]

Toward the end of the whole session, G spoke for the first time and criticized the formalist assumption that consistency of 'transfinite' axioms assures the nonderivability of any consequence that is 'contentually false.' He concluded, 'For of no formal system can one affirm with certainty that all contentual considerations are representable in it.' And then v. Neumann interjected, 'It is not a foregone conclusion whether all rules of inference that are intuitionistically permissible may be formally reproduced.' Only then did G announce his incompleteness result: 'Under the assumption of the consistency of classical mathematics, one can give examples of propositions ... that are really contentually true, but are unprovable in the formal system of classical mathematics.'

Afterward G had a very interesting private conversation with v. Neumann, who immediately understood G's proof (of his first theorem with less elegant undecidable propositions than the ones he obtained later). In his letter of 20 November, for instance, v. Neumann said, 'E. Schmidt, dem ich Ihr Resultate, wie Sie es in Königsberg vortrugen, mitteilte, war davon entzückt. Er hält es, wie ich, für die grösste logische Entdeckung seit langer Zeit.'

Shortly after the conference G improved the first theorem (by bringing the undecidable proposition to a simple arithmetic form belonging to 'Diophantine analysis') and, moreover, obtained his second theorem. An abstract stating these results was presented to the Vienna Academy on 23 October. The full famous paper was received for publication on 17 November. In a letter dated 20 November, v. Neumann independently suggested the second theorem as a 'remarkable corollary' to G's result. G responded immediately, dispatching a preprint of his paper, to which v. Neumann replied graciously. (The correspondence is preserved in G's Nachlass.)

The paper was written as a first part; G planned to give full details of the proof of his second theorem in a second part. But he never published the second part because, as he said later, his sketch of the proof was generally accepted. The first detailed treatment appeared in the second volume of Hilbert-Bernays (1939).

On 24 December, Bernays wrote to G to acknowledge receipt of G's completeness paper and to request the galleys of the incompleteness paper, which R. Courant and I. Schur had told him contained 'bedeutsamen und überraschenden Ergebnissen.' G responded immediately, and Bernays wrote a 16-page letter on 18 January 1931 describing G's results as 'ein erheblicher Schritt vorwarts in der Erforschung der Grundlagenproblem.' [This was the beginning of their correspondence (and other interactions), which lasted, intermittently, over 45 years. Apparently the last letter from G to Bernays was dated 12 January 1975 and that to G 24 January 1975.]

Bernays (1888–1977) became an assistant to Hilbert in 1917, and was appointed associate professor without tenure (nichtbeamteter ausserordent-lich Professor) in 1922. As a 'non-Aryan' he was deprived of the position in 1933 and left for Zurich. His long collaboration with Hilbert is well known and the famous HB (in two volumes) was written entirely by him.

From information derived from a letter of Bernays (3 August 1966), Hilbert's reaction to G's theorems is reported thus: 'At first he was only angry and frustrated, but then he began to try to deal constructively with the problem' (Reid, p. 198). In December Hilbert gave a talk to the Philo-sophical Society of Hamburg, which formed the basis of his paper in *Math. Annalen*, vol. 104 (1931), pp. 485–494 (reprinted in part in vol. 3 of his collected papers, pp. 192–195). An infinite rule is introduced that says that the formula $(x)A(x)$ may be taken as a premise, if $A(z)$ can be shown (finitarily) to be a correct formula for each numeral z. In his review of this paper, G merely says that the rule, 'structurally, is of an entirely new kind.' According to Carnap's 'diary,' G said on 21 May 1931 that Hilbert's program would be compromised by acceptance of this rule. Further elabo-ration of the idea was made in Hilbert's talk to the Göttingen Academy of Sciences on 17 July 1931, published as 'Beweis des Tertium non-datur' in its *Nachrichten*, pp. 120–125. According to Taussky (op. cit.), G was critical of Hilbert's claims and aims, and lashed out against the 'Tertium' paper, saying something like, 'How can he write such a paper after what I have done?'

Nowadays we are familiar with Turing's observation (Turing 1936, p. 259) that a complete formal system is decidable because we can enumer-ate alternatingly all candidates for proofs of any proposition p and its negation. Since either p or its negation is provable, the enumeration always terminates. Hence, Hilbert's belief (before G's theorems) of the completeness of formal number theory implies the less plausible (even then) belief of its decidability. This appears to be a good example of the fact that beliefs are not closed under the relation of logical consequence. In this connection it is of interest to find that Bernays actually conjectured the completeness of formal number theory and then said (in footnote 19) that completeness is a weaker requirement than decidability (on p. 59 of his *Abhundlungen zur Philosophie der Mathematik*; the original essay appeared in *Blätter für Deutsche Philosophie*, vol. 4, 1930/31, pp. 326–367, and must have been written before the last months of 1930).

In the spring of 1961 I visited Brouwer at his home. He discoursed widely on many subjects. Among other things he said that he did not think G's incompleteness results are as important as Heyting's formalization of intuitionistic reasoning, because to him G's results are obvious (obviously true). There are several things that are questionable about this assertion. It is not clear that, according to Brouwer's general position, a formalization of intuitionist logic is of much interest. Heyting's work had been anticipated to a large extent by an early paper of A. N. Kolmogorov, which, moreover, made a more definite correlation between classical and intuitionist mathematics (see *FG*, pp. 414–437). The more interesting part is that about G's theorems. It is relatively easy to see that no formal system can contain all of mathematics. Even if we do not envisage the uncountable, it is highly plausible that given any formal system, we can go beyond it by a suitable diagonal argument. This is probably what Brouwer had in mind, and, as mentioned before, G, according to Carnap, was influenced by Brouwer's lecture to assert that mathematics is inexhaustible (by any formal system). But it requires more work to construct a proposition within a formal system and show that it is not decidable in the system. This was indeed what G did, from which the unprovability of consistency in the system itself also followed. Even to this day we do not seem to have essentially different and simpler proofs than G's original ones for his theorems.

1931
Before G reached the age of twenty-five in the spring, he had completed and published two very important papers. For the next four or five years he undertook four kinds of work: (1) continued study of some branches of mathematics and physics, (2) lectures on and extensions of his famous 1931 paper, (3) reflections on the continuum hypothesis, (4) short-term research on special topics in logic (and in geometry), mostly published unofficially in connection with Menger's colloquium. He also wrote reviews and assisted Hahn in his seminar and in reading the proofs of his book. 'In addition,' according to Menger, 'Gödel studied much philosophy in those years, among other topics post-Kantian German metaphysics. But he had already begun to concentrate on Leibniz.'

During this period the only full-length publication was his ten-page paper on the Entscheidungsproblem (1933, in the *Monatshefte*). In Vienna G was fortunate in having the opportunity of easy and rapid publication of his work. Otherwise it is doubtful that he would have published nearly as much as he did before 1936. In the early 1940s he also obtained a number of results, many of which would probably have been published if he had continued to participate in some group activity comparable to Menger's colloquium. On the whole, teachers and colleagues in Vienna not only influenced G in the choice of his research area but also helped greatly in making his ideas widely known in a short time.

In a note presented 22 January, G gave a more general presentation of his theorems using Peano arithmetic rather than type theory as the basic system. (Menger, according to his memoir, received the information in February at the Rice Institute in Houston. He interrupted his regular lectures to insert 'a report on Gödel's epoch-making discovery, and so the mathematicians at Rice Institute were very likely the first people in America to be astonished by this turning point in logic and mathematics.') On 15 September, G spoke on these results at the annual meeting of the Deutsche Mathematiker-Vereinigung in Bad Elster.

G contributed two notes on the propositional calculus to Menger's colloquium, one on 24 June in answer to a question of Menger and one on 2 December in answer to a question of Hahn.

In a letter of 1963, G recollected that Herbrand had sent him a letter in 1931 making the suggestion about recursive functions, attributed to him by G in his 1934 lectures. That letter, as well as Herbrand's second letter and a draft of G's reply, are in the Nachlass. That reply, dated 25 July, to Herbrand, who died on 27 July, never reached him. Indeed, Herbrand's father sent back a funeral announcement.

Though his work was quickly recognized in Austria and abroad, at home among his family he always went out of his way to 'hide his light under a bushel,' as his brother put it (compare also RG).

G was invited to write, together with A. Heyting, a book on the foundations of mathematics. G agreed but finally withdrew from the project (after delays of several years). A fragmentary draft of his intended contribution survives in his Nachlass (in folder 04/10, together with 04/11 containing Heyting's draft).

Kleene reports that v. Neumann lectured on G's incompleteness results at Princeton in the autumn. Afterward 'we all read Gödel's paper, which to me opened up a whole new world of fascinating ideas and perspectives. The impression this made on me was so much the greater because of the conciseness and incisiveness of Gödel's treatment. If I had been introduced to the world of foundations outside of Church's system by extensive reading in other literature, the effect on me would have been less dramatic.'

(See Kleene's article, to appear in the same volume as Taussky-Todd's, op. cit.)

At the meeting on 15 September at Bad Elster, Zermelo also presented a paper; in the 1960s William Feller recalled that Zermelo had spoken emotionally against G's lecture in the discussion. Later Zermelo wrote a report on both his and G's lectures (*Jber. Deutsch. Math-Verein*, vol. 41, pt. 2, 1932, pp. 85–88), which did not show adequate appreciation of G's results. Zermelo wrote a letter to G on 21 September, both to invite G to study his paper on 'Grenzzahlen und Mengenbereiche' (*Fund. Math.*, vol. 16, 1930, pp. 29–47) and to warn G that he had discovered an 'essential flaw' in G's proof. In preparing his report, the letter said, he had come to the distinct awareness that G's proof was mistaken.

Apparently Zermelo did not bother to read the main text of G's paper but just took the introductory explanation and dropped Bew from formula (1) (on *FG*, p. 598), which connects membership in the set of theorems with unprovability in the given system S. As a result, G's 'This is not provable in S' was turned into 'This is false'; and Zermelo had an easy time deriving a contradiction. He went on to attribute G's error to the 'finitist prejudice' and to preach that only by overcoming this prejudice, which he had set himself as a special task, could a reasonable 'metamathematics' be possible. If G's proof, he said, had been done right, it would have contributed much to the task and rendered an essential service to truth. He was telling G the error early so as to give G time for reexamination.

G replied on 12 October, patiently explaining his results and even offering to comment on Zermelo's paper. Zermelo remained unconvinced of the significance of G's theorems and did not take up G's offer to comment on his paper; his response of 29 October terminated the correspondence. [The G letter and a draft of Zermelo's second letter are published in *Historia Mathematica*, vol. 6 (1979), pp. 294–304, with comments by I. Grattan-Guinness; the two Zermelo letters are in G's Nachlass and are considered by John Dawson in the same journal, vol. 12 (1985), pp. 66–70.]

The G letter is elegant and pedagogically helpful. In addition, the letter contains an exact proof that truth for a formal language is not definable in itself (p. 299), a theorem commonly attributed to Tarski, who proved it as a corollary to G's work only in 1933. Indeed, as I mentioned before, this result was what G first noticed in the summer of 1930, before going on to the more substantive conclusion of incompleteness.

G also offers in his letter an alternative proof of his first incompleteness theorem (pp. 300–301). Since W (the set of true sentences) cannot be represented (by a set sign or defining formula) in the given system S, but B (the set of propositions provable in S) can, and since B is a subset of W, B is a proper subset of W. Hence, there is some true proposition A that is not provable in S. Since A is true, its negation should not be provable in S either. G observes that this proof has the drawback of not exhibiting an undecidable proposition and of being intuitionistically objectionable [presumably on account of the explicit appeal to the set W].

He does not see, G remarks, the essential point of his result in that we cannot include the whole mathematics in a formal system (or we can go beyond any given formal system); that already follows from Cantor's diagonal procedure and does not exclude the possibility of completeness of certain subsystems of mathematics. Rather the essential point of his result is that every formal system of mathematics (which includes addition and multiplication) contains rather simple propositions that are *expressible* in it but *undecidable* by it.

Zermelo's reply (of 29 October) seems to concede the correctness of G's proof but, contrary to the hypothetical proposition in his previous letter, to assign small value to G's result. He seems to conflate G's result with Cantor's uncountability result, which G took pains to distinguish in his letter. He then claimed to have obtained a general system in which all propositions are decidable. Evidently he did not like formal systems. What is puzzling is his reluctance to reaffirm his appreciation (expressed in his previous letter) of results showing the limitations of formal systems.

My teacher Shen Yuting studied with Zermelo in 1933. In a letter of 1 July 1983 he said, 'In those days Gödel's [1931] paper was generally considered both deep and specialized. When Zermelo, I recall, spoke of mathematical logic in 1933 with an air of contempt, he added, "Among these people [those who pursue the subject] Gödel is the most advanced." Zermelo initiated a seminar exclusively devoted to discussing this article of Gödel's, apparently implying that he had himself not fully understood it.' Hence, it appears that Zermelo did come later to regard G's work as important.

Recently E. Köhler showed me pages from Carnap's diary in which a number of discussions with G are recorded. Under 10 September (1931) Carnap wrote, 'Gödel reads Lenin and Trotsky, is for planned society and socialism, and interested in the mechanism of influences in society, e.g., that of finance capital on politics.'

G's brother states, according to WS, that G had a severe psychical crisis around the end of 1931 and was inclined toward suicide. The family was greatly worried about his state.

1932

Oswald Veblen attended G's presentation on 28 June (see below) and invited him to visit the Institute for Advanced Study. This was the time when members were being recruited to prepare for the beginning of group activities of the I.A.S. in the autumn of 1933. Menger had met Veblen in America in the previous year and invited him to attend G's presentation at his colloquium. G's visit in 1933 made him one of the initial participants at the I.A.S. It appears that if G had so chosen, he could have stayed at the I.A.S. continuously, with or without additional regular arrangements at the University of Vienna. But instead G apparently wished to retain Vienna as his home base and finally decided to leave only in 1939 after personal and political circumstances in Vienna had deteriorated for him in various ways between 1933 and 1939.

It was also in 1932 that Abraham Flexner succeeded in getting Einstein to accept an appointment at the I.A.S. (originally intended for five months each year only). It was at their third meeting (in June, at Caputh) that Einstein indicated acceptance (for more details, see Pais, p. 450). In 1933 both G (at 27) and Einstein (at 54) arrived at Princeton in October, the month in which the I.A.S. began its operations. While Einstein had traveled and moved a great deal from 1909 to 1933, he stayed in Princeton, except for vacations, from 1933 to his death in 1955. On 1 October 1940, Judge Phillip Forman inducted him as a citizen of the United States; later on (in 1948) the same judge also inducted G (see below).

According to G's recollection in 1976, he 'visited Göttingen and saw C. Siegel, G. Gentzen, E. Noether, and probably also Zermelo there.' [This may be the same visit as the one mentioned in C. Christian (Leben und Wirken Kurt Gödels, *Monatshefte für Mathematik*, vol. 89, (1980), pp. 261– 273), on p. 264, line 10].

A note of G's on the intuitionistic propositional calculus was communicated by Hahn to the Vienna Academy on 25 February (also printed in Menger's series). Several contributions on geometry were presented to Menger's colloquium: on 18 February, 25 May, and 10 November.

G's contribution on 28 June shows that classical arithmetic is translatable into the intuitionistic. This shows that intuitionistic arithmetic is no more evident than the classical, in any essential way.

A note from about the same time gives axioms for the predicate B*p* ('*p* is provable') and relates the resulting system to intuitionistic and modal systems of logic.

On 25 June, submitted his famous paper to the University of Vienna as his Habilitationsschrift, to obtain his *venia legendi* (the right to teach as a Privatdozent). On this occasion G prepared the following summary of himself (Christian, p. 261):

> Ich bin im Jahre 1906 in Brünn als Sohn deutscher Eltern geboren, besuchte dort vier Klassen Volkschule und die acht Klassen des deutschen Staatsrealgymnasiums, an dem ich im Jahre 1924 die Reifeprüfung ablegte. Im Herbst desselben Jahres begab ich mich nach Wien, wo ich mich seither ohne längere Unterbrechung aufheilt und 1929 auch die österreichische Staatsbürgerschaft erwarb. Im Wintersemes-

ter 1924 inskribierte ich als ordentlicher Hörer der philosophischen Fakultät und widmete mich in der ersten Zeit physikalischen, später vorwiegend mathematischen Studien. Daneben beschäftigte ich mich, angeregt durch Prof. Schlick, dessen philosophischen Zirkel ich häufig besuchte, auch mit modernen Arbeiten über Erkenntnistheorie. Meine eigene wissenschaftlich Tätigkeit bezog sich hauptsächlich auf das Gebiet der Grundlagen der Mathematik und der symbolischen Logik. Im Jahre 1929 reichte ich eine diesem Gebiet entnommene Arbeit "Über die Vollständigkeit des Logikkalküls" als Dissertation ein und promovierte im Februar 1930. Im selben Jahre referierte ich auf der Königsberger Tagung über die eben erwähnte Arbeit, ferner auf der Tagung der deutschen Mathematikervereinigung in Bad Elster 1931 über meine als Habilitationsschrift eingereichte Arbeit. In Wien beteiligte ich mich an dem von Prof. Menger veranstalteten Kolloquium und wirkte auch bei der Herausgabe des alljährlich darüber erscheinenden Berichtes mit. Auch in dem von Prof. Hahn im Studienjahr 1931/32 abgehaltenen Seminar über mathematische Logik war ich bei der Auswahl des Stoffes und der Vorbereitung der Hörer für ihre Vorträge mittätig.

Im Jahre 1931 wurde ich von der Redaktion des Zentralblattes für Mathematik, dessen ständiger Mitarbeiter ich bin, aufgefordert, zusammen mit A. Heyting einen Bericht über die mathematische Grundlagenforschung zu schreiben, mit dessen Ausarbeitung ich beschäftigt bin.

Wien, im Juni 1932
Dr. Kurt Gödel

On 1 December, Hahn presented the following report on G's application (Christian, p. 263):

Schon die Doktordissertation hatte sehr hohen wissenschaftlichen Wert ("Die Vollständigkeit der Axiome des logischen Funktionenkalküls"). Sie löste, indem sie zeigte, dass jede allgemeingültige Formel des engeren Funktionenkalküls beweisbar ist, das wichtige und schwierige von Hilbert gestellte Problem, ob die Axiome des engeren logischen Funktionenkalküls ein vollständiges System bilden. Die Habilitationsschrift 'Über formal unentscheidbare Sätze der Principia Mathematica und verwandter Systeme' ist eine Leistung ersten Ranges, die in allen Fachkreisen das grösste Aufsehen erregte und— wie sich mit Sicherheit voraussehen lässt—ihren Platz in der Geschichte der Mathematik einnehmen wird. Es gelang Herrn Gödel zu zeigen, dass sich im logischen System der Principia Mathematica von Whitehead-Russell Probleme angeben lassen, die mit den Mitteln dieses Systems unentscheidbar sind, und dass dasselbe für jedes formallogische System gilt, in dem die Arithmetik der natürlichen Zahlen ausdrückbar ist; damit ist auch gezeigt, dass das von Hilbert aufgestellte Programm, die Widerspruchsfreiheit der Mathematik zu beweisen, undurchführbar ist.

Von einigen weiteren Arbeiten Gödels, die das Gebiet der symbolischen Logik betreffen, sei noch die Note 'Zum intuitionistischen Aussagenkalkül' hervorgehoben, in der die Sätze bewiesen werden: Es gibt keine Realisierung des Heytingschen Axiomensystems des intuitionistischen Aussagenkalküls mittels endlich vieler Wahrheitswerte, für welche die und nur die beweisbaren Formeln bei beliebiger Einsetzung ausgezeichnete Werte ergeben. Es gibt unendlich viele zwischen dem Heytingschen System und dem System des gewöhnlichen Aussagenkalküls gelegene Systeme.

Die von Dr. Gödel vorgelegten Arbeiten überragen bei weitem das Niveau, das üblicherweise bei einer Habilitation zu beanspruchen ist. Dr. Gödel gilt bereits heute als erste Autorität auf dem Gebiete der symbolischen Logik und der Forschung über die Grundlagen der Mathematik. In enger wissenschaftlicher Zusammenarbeit mit dem Referenten und mit Prof. Menger hat er sich auch auf anderen Gebieten der Mathematik aufs beste bewährt.

1933

On 11 March, G was made Privatdozent. He lectured in the Sommer-Semester (summer semester), with a relatively large enrollment of about 20 students (judging from the registration slips G kept). The announcement of the course (Grundlagen der Mathematik) was hand entered by G on a slip of paper in one official catalogue, which had been printed before G's Habilitation had gone through. The second course G announced and taught in Sommer-Semester 1935 was Ausgewählte Kapitel der Mathematischen Logik. The third and last course he taught in Vienna, Axiomatik der Mengenlehre (two hours), was actually taught in Sommer-Semester 1937, but it had been announced twice before, for Winter-Semester 1935/36 (Tag, Stunde and Ost de vorlesung wird später bekanntgegeben) and for Winter-Semester 1936/37, n. Ü. (i.e., nach Übereinkunft). The first announcement conflicts with G's brief visit to Princeton in the autumn of 1935, and his poor health in 1936 probably prevented him from acting on the second. [Fragmentary notes for the three courses are in folders 04/25, 31, and 36.]

G made a long visit to America in 1938/39. In the spring of 1939, while he was away, the unpaid position of Privatdozent was abolished and replaced by a new paid position of Dozent neuer Ordnung, which required a new application. His name was listed under Lehrbefugnis hat bis auf weiteres zu ruhen (*Personalstand der Universität Wien* as of 1 July 1939,

p. 55). For complex reasons, G did not apply for the new position until 25 September, and the approval came only belatedly on 28 June 1940 (after G had settled in Princeton; for more details see below). Ironically, G was listed in the catalogues between 1941 and 1945 as Dozent für Grundlagen der Mathematik und Logik, and under course offerings: 'wird nicht lasen.'

A joint contribution with K. Menger and A. Wald on coordinate-free differential geometry was presented on 17 May.

The second paper on the 'Gödel case' (mentioned above under *1929*) was received for publication on 22 June and appeared shortly after. This contains the mistaken statement that similar results 'may also be proved, by the same methods, for formulas that contain the $=$ sign.'

According to G in 1976, he continued his study of logic and mathematics in 1930—1933, including the foundations of geometry and 'the beautiful subject of the functions of complex variables'; he attended Hahn's seminar on set theory, read the proof sheets [probably in 1932] of Hahn's book on real functions, and learned the subject.

In the autumn G began his close association with the I.A.S. The Institute was formally established in 1930; Albert Einstein and Oswald Veblen were named as its first professors in 1932. Veblen played a principal role in inviting H. Weyl, J. v. Neumann, M. Morse, and J. Alexander to the school of mathematics. He also helped arrange for visiting mathematicians, including Gödel. Veblen had been much impressed by the lecture of G's (mentioned above) that he attended in Vienna in 1932; v. Neumann was of course in favor of inviting G.

G's visit of 1933—34 to the I.A.S. was the longest of his three visits before taking up permanent residence there in 1940. The durations of his visits can be seen from his Princeton domiciles before 1940: from October 1933 to May 1934, 32 Vandeventer Avenue; from October to November 1935, 23 Madison Street; from October 1938 to January 1939, Peacock Inn. The academic year 1933—34 was the Institute's first year of operation, without a building of its own, with the mathematicians using the former Fine Hall (now Jones Hall) of Princeton University. The official *Bulletin* for that year lists G simply as 'worker.'

G gave an address to the AMS on 30 December at Cambridge, Massachusetts. A text of the address, 'The present situation in the foundations of mathematics,' is preserved in the Nachlass.

Menger: 'In 1933 already he [G] repeatedly stressed that the *correct*—sometimes he said *right* (die richten)—*axioms of set theory have not yet been found.*' 'After one session [of the circle] in which Schlick, Hahn, Neurath, and Waismann had talked about language,' G said, according to Menger, 'The more I think about language, the more it amazes me that people ever understand each other at all.'

1934

G lectured on his incompleteness results at the I.A.S. from February to May. Notes on these lectures by Kleene and Rosser (edited by G) have been widely circulated and were published in Davis (1965) with a post-script by G, which recommends Turing's analysis of the mechanical procedure (1936) as an essential advance bringing G's incompleteness theorems to a form of completion. As a consequence of Turing's work, the theorems can be seen to hold 'for *every* consistent formal system containing a certain amount of finitary number theory.'

The most conspicuous innovation of these lectures was the introduction (in the last section) for the first time of a definite concept of general recursive functions, which he also came close to identifying with the notion of finite computation (in footnote 3). But he wrote in the 1960s to M. Davis to say that at that time he was not at all convinced that his concept of recursion comprised all possible recursions. Another addition (in section 7) is the theorem that truth in a language cannot be defined in itself, a result previously explained in his 1931 letter to Zermelo.

In April G gave lectures in New York and Washington, DC. The text of his lecture 'The existence of undecidable propositions in any formal system containing arithmetic' (to the New York Philosophical Society on 18 April) is preserved in the Nachlass.

It is known that G and A. Church discussed, probably in early 1934, the question of finding a precise definition of the intuitive concept of computability, a question that was undoubtedly of great interest to G. According to Church, G did raise specifically the question of the relation between the intuitive concept of computability and that of his recursiveness, but did not think that the two ideas could be satisfactorily identified 'except heuristically.' G suggested the idea of formulating first 'a set of axioms which would embody the generally accepted properties of' the intuitive notion (M. Davis, Why Gödel didn't have Church's thesis, *Information and Control*, vol. 54, 1982, pp. 3–24; see p. 9).

Over the years G habitually credited A. M. Turing's paper of 1936 as the definitive work in capturing the intuitive concept, and did not mention Church or E. Post in this connection. He must have felt that Turing was the only one who gave persuasive arguments to show the adequacy of the precise concept (in satisfying the implicit axioms determining the intuitive concept). In particular, he had probably been aware of the arguments offered by Church for his 'thesis' and decided that they were inadequate. It is clear that G and Turing (1912–1954) had great admiration for each other, but it so happened that G was in Vienna when Turing was in Princeton (from the autumn of 1936 to the summer of 1938).

G left Princeton for Vienna in May, traveling from 26 May to 3 June aboard the S.S. *Rex*. Upon his return to Europe he suffered a nervous breakdown and was treated by the famous psychiatrist J. von Wagner-Jauregg. In the autumn he was admitted to the well-known sanatorium in Purkersdorf bei Wien for treatment of nervous depression. A scheduled return visit to the I.A.S., for the second term of 1934/35 was postponed till the autumn of 1935.

Hahn died on 24 July after a brief illness (of about three weeks). This must have affected G quite strongly.

G remarked at the 6 November colloquium, after A. Wald's lecture, that a realistic analysis of demand in economics must take into account a firm's income, which depends on the cost of production.

Menger: 'All in all, Gödel was more withdrawn after his return from America than before; but he still spoke with visitors to the colloquium. To all members of the colloquium Gödel was generous with opinions and advice in mathematical and logical questions. He consistently perceived problematic points quickly and thoroughly, and made replies with greatest precision in a minimum of words, often opening up novel aspects for the inquirer. He expressed all this as if it were completely a matter of course, but often with a certain shyness whose charm awoke warm personal feelings for him in many a listener.'

G had trouble with his teeth this year (the 'teeth business,' mentioned several times in *LM*).

1935

His comment on Waismann's paper at the 5 June colloquium was mentioned without quotation.

He presented a note on the length of proofs on 19 June. This gave an early example of what are nowadays called 'speed-up theorems' in the theory of computational complexity.

He lectured at the University of Vienna in the summer on 'selected chapters in mathematical logic.' There are in the Nachlass nine slips from registered students for this course.

From about 1930 he had continued to think about the continuum problem, using to some extent Hilbert's proposed outline. The idea of using the ramified hierarchy occurred to him quite early. He then played with building up enough ordinals. Finally the leap of taking classical ordinals as given made things easier. It must have been in 1935, according to his recollection in 1976, when he realized that the constructible sets satisfy all the axioms of set theory (including the axiom of choice). He conjectured that the continuum hypothesis is also satisfied. In the autumn at Princeton he told v. Neumann all these ideas and results.

G began his lecture course on 4 May.

On 7 and 10 May, E. Husserl gave two lectures in Vienna on 'Die Philosophie in der Krisis der europäischen Menschkeit.' These lectures form part of Husserl's work from 1934 to 1937, in which for the first time he dealt explicitly with the relation between history and philosophy (compare his *Crisis*, discussed below in section 8.2). Presumably G did not attend these lectures, since his interest in certain aspects of Husserl's work came much later, which, in any case, apparently did not include that from the *Crisis* stage.

In September he left Vienna for Princeton, traveling aboard the Cunard Liner *Georgia* from 20 to 28 September. (Bernays was on the same ship, but, unlike G, traveled tourist class.) This visit to Princeton was the briefest of his three visits. On 17 November, he suddenly resigned, suffering from depression and overwork. O. Veblen saw him aboard the steamer *Champlain* in New York (to Le Havre, from 30 November to 7 December) and telegraphed ahead to G's family. G passed through Paris and stayed there for a few days. He telephoned his brother from Paris and returned to Vienna by train. (Menger: G 'returned to Vienna in December in quite a bad state of health and mind.') Rest and recuperation (including periods in the sanatorium) were to take a long time.

1936

Around the beginning of the year G started to spend periods in the (same) sanatorium in Purkersdorf bei Wien.

According to his own account in 1976, this was one of the three years when his health was exceptionally poor; the other two years were 1961 and 1970. He cancelled teaching a few times. In 1939 he wrote at one place that he had spent several months in a sanatorium in 1936.

Menger: 'When I saw him [G] again in 1936, he told me he was striving to prove the consistency of the continuum hypothesis in set theory.'

Schlick was assassinated on 22 June.

1937

G started lecturing on axiomatic set theory (Axiomatik der Mengenlehre) in the spring. There is only one registration slip for this course in the Nachlass, giving the name of my teacher Wang Sian-jun (spelt differently there). Professor Wang told me that there were perhaps five or six students in the class. Apparently A. Mostowski also attended the course. These lectures dealt with constructible sets and G's results from 1935.

On 13 July, v. Neumann wrote from Budapest urging G to publish the 1935 results in the *Annals of Mathematics*. They met on 17 July. On 14 September, v. Neumann wrote again from New York, this time referring instead to the consistency proof of the generalized continuum hypothesis (GCH). In 1976 and 1977 G talked to me about the matter on several occasions, saying consistently that he obtained the stronger results only in 1938. He also said more than once that getting the GCH is comparatively easy once the idea of constructible sets is there. One time he even said that v. Neumann might have obtained a proof of the consistency of GCH before himself. In view of the fact that G did not announce his results until late in 1938, it seems likely that he was not satisfied with whatever version of the proof he had in 1937. Hence he might have felt that he really got his results only in 1938.

Recently I came across several pieces of additional information in Menger's memoir. Menger began working at Notre Dame in January (1937). G wrote to Menger on 3 July and 15 December. The first letter mentions 'the partial result on the continuum hypothesis which I reported in the Colloquium' (in the spring of 1937). It also includes this statement: 'As you know, I had had bad experience in America with my health and hence do not want to bind myself in advance for a longer period.' The second letter says much about G's work on the continuum problem: 'I have continued my work on the continuum problem last summer and I finally succeeded in proving the consistency of the continuum hypothesis (even the generalized form) with respect to general set theory. But for the time being please do not tell anyone of this. So far, I have communicated this, besides to yourself, only to von Neumann, for whom I sketched the proof during his latest stay in Vienna. Right now I am trying to prove also the independence of the continuum hypothesis, but do not yet know whether I shall succeed with it.'

G's mother returned to Brno and G changed his domicile in Vienna, living, when not away in America, at Himmelstrasse 43 from 11 November 1937 to 9 November 1939.

In 1976 I was struck by the fact that G spoke of the *summers* of 1929 and 1930 as the time when he proved the completeness of elementary logic and obtained his first incompleteness result. Shortly before 1 June 1972 G had told me that he could make himself comfortably warm [presumably with the help of clothing and blankets] when the [room] temperature was 75°F or above. It is not clear how long this had been true for him, but warmer weather would seem to have suited him better. I venture to conjecture that on the whole summers tended to be the season when he was scientifically most productive. (G's preference for hot weather is also amply confirmed by his letters to his mother, in which he said several times that he loved it when it was very hot in Princeton and often did not go to the seashore with Adele.)

['Gödel was a slight, frail man. He complained of chronic stomach trouble and was sensitive to cold weather. He could be seen on a warm day trudging along a Princeton street in an overcoat. He said that he and his wife once tried the New Jersey shore for a summer vacation, but found it too cold for comfort' (Quine, *Yearbook 1978*, The American Philosophical Society, p. 84).]

There is apparently no reliable record of when in 1935 G did discover the constructible sets. Since he told v. Neumann his ideas on this in the autumn and had not informed v. Neumann earlier, it seems not unlikely that the discovery was made in that summer. At any rate, the circumstances seem to date quite exactly G's first discovery of (at least a preliminary version of) his relative consistency proof of the GCH. In addition to the dates of the two letters from v. Neumann, there are also the accounts by Mostowski and Professor Wang that nothing of the sort had been suggested in G's set theory course in the spring. Therefore, it seems reasonable to believe that the discovery occurred in the summer of 1937, prior to his meeting with v. Neumann on 17 July. Indeed, a note in one of his workbooks indicates that he got the crucial idea during the night of 14–15 June (*Arbeitsheft 1*, folder 03/13 in the Nachlass).

1938
In March the Anschluss (political and economic union) of Austria and Germany took place; Austria became a province (Ostmark) of a wider Germany.

By 1938 a number of things had happened to various teachers and friends known or conjectured to be close to G. Hahn died in 1934 (of natural causes). Schlick was assassinated on the way to his last lecture of a course in 1936, by a deranged former student. Karl Menger left around the beginning of 1937 to take a permanent position at the University of Notre Dame in Indiana. F. Waismann left for England in 1937. O. Morgenstern and A. Wald left for America in 1938. All these events must have made Vienna a less attractive place to G.

On 20 September, G married Adele Porkert after a close association for more than a decade. Based on the little evidence I have, I believe that they were much devoted to each other and completely at ease together. After they had settled in Princeton in 1940, G never returned to Europe again and, indeed, traveled very little altogether; he seems to have confined his small number of trips to the East Coast of America. In contrast Adele went back to Europe a number of times. From all accounts, Adele had few friends in Princeton and was socially isolated there. She must have had a rather lonely life in Princeton. At G's funeral I got the impression that Mrs. M. Morse was friendly with Adele. When G came to Harvard for his honorary degree in 1952, people at a reception in Quine's house (in Belmont) were urging G to move to Harvard. I remember Adele pleading with G to accept the suggestion, saying that people at Harvard were so much more friendly than those [she came across] in Princeton. Adele seems to have been forthright and unassuming; she appears to have radiated a personal warmth. They had no children. She survived G by three years and died on 4 February 1981.

Barely two weeks or so after the wedding G left Adele in Vienna to depart for America. He traveled aboard the liner *New York* from 6 to 15 October.

The first semester was spent in Princeton, and he stayed at the Peacock Inn from October till January 1939. He lectured at the I.A.S. on his relative consistency proof of the axiom of choice and the GCH. A revised version of these lectures, based on notes by George W. Brown, was later published in 1940 (with added notes in 1951 and 1966). On 9 November, he submitted an announcement, which was soon published in *PNAS*, vol. 24 (1938), pp. 556–557. He gave a talk on the same results on 28 December at the annual meeting of the American Mathematical Society (AMS) in Richmond and Williamsburg; the abstract appeared on p. 93 of *Bulletin AMS*, vol. 45 (1939). [A text of the lecture, entitled 'The consistency of the generalized continuum hypothesis,' is preserved in the Nachlass.]

1939

In January G moved to Notre Dame, where he stayed at the Morningside Hotel, till May. He lectured on his consistency results and offered a joint course with Menger on elementary logic. The Nachlass contains all these lectures, carefully written in English.

Menger gives more information on G's visit to America from 1938 to 1939. G's letter of 3 July 1937 was a response to Menger's invitation to visit Notre Dame, containing a provisional acceptance with this condition: 'It is essential for me to be obliged only for *one* semester' (for reasons of his health). In his letter of 15 December 1937, G says, 'I have decided not to come to America in the current academic year after all.' 'In spring 1938 Gödel decided to spend the year 1938–39 in America.' On 25 June 1938, G replied to Menger's letter of May, 'I have already abandoned the plan to come to Notre Dame in autumn on my own, because it would be too strenuous for me after all. So I am coming in February 1939, unless unforeseen circumstances hinder me.' G also wrote to Menger from Princeton on 19 October and 11 November 1938. From all five letters (with the exception of the one of 15 December 1937) Menger quotes G's repeated deliberations over what courses he was to teach at Notre Dame and especially his worries about the need to teach introductory logic.

G gave an elegant and concise proof of the main results of relative consistency, which was received for publication on 14 February and published on pp. 220–224 of *PNAS*, vol. 25 (1939).

G intended to return to Princeton in the autumn. [He probably did receive annual appointments at the I.A.S. from 1938 on (rather than only from 1940 on).] But political events intervened.

He left New York on 14 June aboard a German liner, landed at Bremen on 20 June, and then went by train to Vienna. Shortly afterward he was notified of an upcoming military physical. This did not come for months, and World War II began on 1 September. The physical took place after this date. Contrary to his expectation, he was 'found fit for garrison duty.' He applied for a Dozent neuer Ordnung on 25 September. The application was reviewed on 30 September and commented on by the dean on 25 October and also in a letter of 27 November from the dean to the rector of the University of Vienna. In any case, the application was not accepted until 28 June 1940, long after G had left for America.

The question about G's Dozent status is a little confusing. There are documents from July and August saying that G's Dozent status would expire on 1 October 1939 unless G took some action before that date. (But compare the somewhat different information quoted above under the year 1933.) This may be one reason why G applied on 25 September for Dozent neuer Ordnung, which, moreover, was, unlike the old status of Dozent, a position with pay. The other reasons may be the outcome of his military physical and the new obstacles blocking his planned return to Princeton. Apparently G's financial situation was also deteriorating about this time. He applied in November for leave of absence to go to America on the ground that he had no source of income. [This seems to indicate that G's application of 25 September enabled him to retain an official status at the University of Vienna. His application for a leave of absence was probably made with a view to improving the chances of getting an exit permit.] Apparently at this time G could no longer get a visitor's visa from the American Consulate, and he would have difficulty in obtaining an exit permit if he had an immigration visa. The dean's letter to the rector (of 29 November) suggested that if G got a paid position, he would have no cause to leave. However, it does not appear that the suggestion was carried out.

G wrote (or at least planned to write) to Veblen around this time seeking assistance to get him out of his difficult situation. There is a draft of the letter dated 29 November in the Nachlass. The draft contains a crossed-out sentence about looking for a position in industry as a last resort. The difficulty facing him then seems to be twofold: with his Dozent application pending, he had no job; and having no job presumably increased the probability of his being called up for military service. Somehow German exit permits (issued 19 December) and US nonquota immigration visas (issued 8 January 1940) were arranged for G and his wife; these two kinds of document were apparently both necessary for getting G to Princeton and thereby out of his difficult situation. According to some accounts, Abraham Flexner, the director of the I.A.S., successfully accomplished the feat of somehow getting these needed visas and permits. Russian transit visas were issued in Berlin on 12 January 1940.

G lectured at Göttingen on 15 December, amid his efforts to apply for visas (in Berlin) for his trip to America. (His passport, preserved in the Nachlass, indicates that he had to obtain various transit documents from consulates in Vienna and Berlin.)

According to John Dawson, G and his wife bought their residence at Hegelstrasse 5 and spent much money to improve it in November. This would suggest that they were still contemplating in November a future that would include spending a good deal of time in Vienna. As it turned out, G never set foot in Vienna again after leaving it in January 1940.

According to WS, G was attacked by ultrarightist students near Strudel-hofstiege at the beginning of November.

Menger's memoir includes some details on G in 1939, particularly during his stay in Notre Dame from January to the beginning of June. 'During his stay at Notre Dame, Gödel appeared healthy but not particularly happy.' 'Gödel esteemed some scholastic logicians as forerunners of G. Boole and A. de Morgan.' One day G asked Menger, 'all of a sudden': 'Is there actually a list of all the saints of the Catholic Church?' 'But despite all pleas and warnings by all his acquaintances at Notre Dame and then by all his acquaintances on his passage through Princeton, he [G] was determined to go to Vienna, and he went. After a while I [Menger] heard rumors that he was attacked on the street in Vienna by Nazi rowdies and that they knocked his glasses off.' G wrote to Menger on 30 August 1939; G stated that in autumn he hoped to be back in Princeton, but said not a word about political events or the social atmosphere in Vienna.

Menger also gives an account of some of G's philosophical ideas expressed in 1939. 'Important arguments for his *philosophical* thinking were the following considerations: (1) The assumption of classes [sets] and the belief in their existence are just as legitimate as the assumption of bodies and the belief in their existence. (2) Classes [sets] are just as necessary for a satisfactory system of mathematics as bodies are for a satisfactory theory of sensations and of physics.' G stated 'that adequate characterizations of the objective domain of sets in which he believed do not yet exist: characterizations adequate for deciding the fundamental problems of cardinality such as the continuum hypothesis. This conviction he expressed more and more emphatically, but I [Menger] myself never heard from him any indications about where he expected to find such axioms.'

'Meanwhile, Gödel was ever more preoccupied with Leibniz.' Menger asked G, 'Who could have an *interest* in destroying Leibniz's writings?' 'Naturally those people who do not want men to become more intelligent,' G replied. To Menger's suggestion of Voltaire being a more likely target, G answered, 'Who ever became more intelligent by reading Voltaire's writings?' Later (perhaps in or after the 1950s) Menger discussed G's ideas about the destruction of Leibniz's writings with O. Morgenstern, who described how G, to supply evidence for his belief, 'took him one day into the Princeton University Library and gathered together an abundance of really astonishing material.' The material consisted of books and articles with exact references to published writings of Leibniz on the one hand, and the very series or collections referred to on the other. Yet the cited writings are all missing in one strange manner or another. 'This material was really highly astonishing,' said Morgenstern.

Chapter 4

Account continued: the Princeton years

(1940–1978)

In several ways the year 1940 was a turning point in G's life and work. The seven or eight months preceding his arrival in Princeton must have been extremely demanding and exhausting, in a way most unpleasant to him. Moreover, the commuting between Vienna and Princeton (plus the excursion to Notre Dame) from 1933 and the unsettled life with Adele from about 1928 had both come to an end with their arrival in Princeton. From this time on G continued in a position most congenial to him at the I.A.S. No more extended travels or great changes in his external life were made, since they were no longer necessary, and G seemed temperamentally unwilling to undertake them unless forced to. However, almost all of G's major published results in mathematical logic were conceived and worked out in Vienna, the part on set theory amidst travels and poor health. Needless to say, G was younger during that period (age 23–32) and probably had more concentrated energy at his command. A more indefinite issue is the less easy evaluation of his 'unfashionable pursuit' of philosophy after 1940.

In terms of his intellectual work, G published much less after 1940. When he did publish or write with the intention of publication (in his lifetime), the papers or lectures were in most cases written in response to invitations or other external stimuli. The three papers on relativity (two published in 1949 and the third given as a lecture in 1950, published in 1952) were also occasioned by the invitation (extended in 1946) to contribute a paper honoring Einstein. Generally it appears that the scarcity of G's publications since 1940 resulted from a combination of several circumstances.

G had certainly obtained mathematical results during this period that would be publishable by even the highest standards. He refrained from writing up less fundamental results and failed to complete either his independence results in set theory or his attempt to settle the CH by new axioms. [The reason he did not complete his 'general consistency proof of the axiom of choice' (mentioned to me in 1976) is less clear.] From 1943 on, the major portion of G's work seems to have been devoted to philosophy, in which at some stage (possibly already in the 1940s) he began to aim at

an ambitious fundamental system (of metaphysics). It is of course notoriously difficult to attain in philosophy the kind of definitive formulation that
G was in the habit of requiring from his own work. In addition, he felt that
the spirit of the time was not congenial to his philosophical views. This
matter of the Zeitgeist had a strong inhibiting effect, given his tendency to
dread controversy and especially criticism that he could not conclusively
refute. As a result, he seemed willing to allow his philosophical views to
emerge 'in driblets,' generally only in contexts where he felt that he stood
on ground commonly accepted to be solid.

1940

In mid-January, G and his wife left Vienna to travel through Lithuania and
Latvia, and to board the trans-Siberian railway at Bigosovo. (Because of the
British blockade after the German-Soviet invasion of Poland, it was not
possible to leave Europe by ship at this time.) They made their way to
Yokohama and thence by ship to San Francisco, where they arrived on 4
March. They then went by train to Princeton, where G began his uninter-
rupted and tranquil married life for the following thirty-eight years (minus
about two months).

According to E. Köhler, Hans Thirring saw G immediately before G's
departure from Vienna, and asked him to 'warn Einstein of the possibility of
a German application of atomic fission to making bombs.' Early on G had
studied with Thirring, 'who had made an important early contribution to
relativity theory' and 'was a friend of Einstein's.'

Since 1940 G seems to have given only three public lectures (all before
he turned 46): the invited remarks at the Princeton Bicentennial in 1946 (17
December); the invited address to the International Congress of Mathematicians in 1950 (31 August, Cambridge, Massachusetts); and the Gibbs
Lecture in 1951 (26 December, Brown University). The texts of the first two
lectures were later published; of the third I have seen only a handwritten
manuscript (in the Nachlass). He did give three less formal lectures, two in
1941 (see below) and one on rotating universes (Princeton, May 1949), as
well as two sequences of lectures at the I.A.S. in 1940 and 1941.

The main items among his publications and nearly completed manuscripts can be summarized as follows. The Russell paper (completed in
1943), the Princeton lecture (1946), the expository and philosophical paper
on Cantor's continuum problem (published in December 1947, written
from 1946 to 1947 by invitation), the three papers on relativity and a
longer philosophical manuscript (in several versions, probably started in
1946 and completed essentially in 1950), the Gibbs Lecture (probably
written in 1951), the paper on mathematics and the syntax of language to
criticize Carnap's views (probably written mainly from 1953 to 1956, in six

drafts), the 1958 paper to honor Bernays (based on technical results obtained in 1941, probably written from 1956 to 1958), the additions to his Cantor paper (completed in 1963), a postscript to his 1934 lectures (dated 3 June 1964), added notes to his incompleteness papers (dated 28 August 1963 and 18 May 1966), his two letters to me (7 December 1967 and 7 March 1968), the expanded English version of his 1958 paper (probably mainly written from 1967 to 1969 but begun much earlier), his contributions to my *MP* (from October 1971 to June 1972), and his observations on his results about constructible sets (occasioned by serious misrepresentations in a paper describing his work, April to June 1977, quoted in note 17 to section 2.1).

G was an ordinary member at the I.A.S. from 1940 to 1946, receiving annual appointments. He became a permanent member in 1946, a professor in 1953, and retired in 1976.

At Princeton the Gs rented lodgings up to September 1949 and bought their house on Linden Lane on 3 August, 1949. The house was first numbered 129 (at least up to 1 October 1960), but later changed to 145. Once G told me that at some stage they extended their house by some additions. Their domiciles (before settling in their house) form the following sequence. They lived at 245 Nassau Street from March 1940 to July 1941, followed by a summer in Maine. Then they lived at 3 Chambers Terrace (from September 1941 to September 1942), 108 Stockton Street (from September 1942 to September 1943), and 120 Alexander Street (from September 1943 to September 1949).

According to *GQ*, G first read Brouwer in 1940. Once he told me that his idea for his independence proof (of the axiom of choice) occurred to him while reading a passage in Brouwer's work. But he did not specify the passage or its context.

He found and indicated corrections of serious mistakes in Herbrand's dissertation of 1930, probably some time in 1940–1942.

He obtained, between 1940 and 1942, a general consistency proof of the axiom of choice by metamathematical (syntactical) considerations. He believed (in 1976) it highly likely that the proof goes through even when large cardinals are present.

1941

He obtained his interpretation of intuitionistic number theory by primitive recursive functionals, a result only published in 1958 (to honor P. Bernays), as a part of a largely philosophical paper. He lectured on these results at Princeton and Yale. The Yale lecture, at which E. Artin was present, took place on 15 April. The text of this lecture (entitled 'In what sense is intuitionistic logic constructive?') is preserved in the Nachlass.

1942
G arrived at a proof of the independence of the axiom of choice in the framework of (finite) type theory. The method looked promising as a way of getting also the independence of the continuum hypothesis, but his prolonged efforts on this did not succeed. In 1976 he said that in the light of Paul J. Cohen's later work, it is clear that this can be done. Elsewhere he also said that his methods were closer to using Boolean models than forcing.

G and his wife took a summer vacation in Maine (at Blue Hill House, Hancock County). In G's index for his *Arbeitshefte*, pp. 26–57 of book 15 are headed 'Blue Hill.' These pages are devoted to extended considerations of the independence of the axiom of choice. It is conjectured that it was during his stay at Blue Hill House that he discovered the proof.

In 1976 G said that he regretted not having continued the work to arrive at a proof of the independence of the continuum hypothesis. It is tempting to compare G's lack of persistence in this case with what has been called Einstein's 'long road from the special theory to the general theory of relativity,' especially from 'the happiest thought of my [Einstein's] life' ('If a person falls freely he will not feel his own weight') of November 1907 (or from his return to gravitation theory in June 1911) to his arriving on 25 November 1915 at the general theory as we now know it (Pais, pp. 178–179, 189, 253–256). There are important differences between physics and mathematics in these two examples. One is inclined to say that Einstein was working on a much 'richer' problem, which involved more aspects and diverse ramifications. Entirely contrary to G's habit, Einstein seems to have carried out his pursuit 'in public' for several years. In a way, G's work on the relative consistency results by the constructible sets had more the feature of prolonged efforts. According to his own account, he began to think about the continuum hypothesis in 1930 and obtained the definitive proofs only in 1938.

If we assume that G gave up his work on the independence proof around the end of 1942, then it was at almost exactly the same age as Einstein was at the time Einstein obtained his 'field equations of gravitation' (a few months before reaching 37). Afterward Einstein continued with physics for the rest of his life, while G essentially ceased doing pure mathematical logic.

Compared with Einstein, much less information is available on the process of G's intellectual activities. It is clear that both were primarily interested in 'fundamental' questions. An obvious difference was between Einstein's determination to confine his research to physics and G's attempt also to attain definite results in philosophy (including metaphysics). After his multiple contributions in 1905, the two central questions for Einstein were the generalization of special relativity and the quantum problem (Pais,

p. 188). Success with the first question was followed by a decade of gradual transition toward an exclusive concentration on developing a unified field theory, which promised for him also an indirect approach to the quantum problem in a more fundamental manner than the powerful but theoretically unsatisfactory (to him) quantum mechanics. Even though Einstein is generally thought to have been, like G, engaged in an 'unfashionable pursuit' during the last two or three decades of his life, one cannot detect any comparably unified pattern in G's work after 1942.

The shaping of G's work before 1940 is more open to inspection. Given his solid training in mathematics and the influence of the Schlick Circle, it was not surprising that he became attracted to logic and the foundations of mathematics. The possibility of attaining precise results in foundational areas, where less definite observations and programmatic promises prevail, is intrinsically appealing. From 1929 to 1930 he settled most of the fundamental problems of the Hilbert school in quick succession. One of the remaining questions was to find a precise concept that would capture the intuitive notion of computability. But it was not clear at the time that the problem admitted of any definitive answer. He must have felt that the next fruitful area was set theory: 'jetzt, Mengenlehre.' He was probably surprised by Turing's solution, which was more elegant and conclusive than he had expected.

One conjecture is that his central interest after 1930 was in understanding the foundations of set theory. A natural choice of a challenging and more definite topic was the continuum problem, on which, moreover, Hilbert had made illuminating suggestions but failed in attaining anything conclusive. Since there was little prospect of proving or refuting the continuum hypothesis (CH) in a conclusive manner, G's favorite strategy of 'dividing the difficulties' led him to the sharper and weaker question of its independence or consistency relative to familiar axioms of set theory. As it turned out, an improvement of Hilbert's approach yielded not only the relative consistency result but also a highly attractive structure of constructible sets. The quest for an independence proof was the obvious next step, which had probably occupied G centrally since 1939 or even earlier. (His attempt to do this was mentioned in his letter, quoted earlier, of 15 December 1937 to Menger.)

But G undoubtedly had larger but less definite issues in mind within which the independence of the CH was to be a conspicuously impressive and noncontroversial step. Basic to the foundations of mathematics are a hierarchy of richer and richer idealizations and the problem of (relative) evidence of these idealizations. G's 1941 interpretation of intuitionist mathematics is clearly a contribution to making it more evident. The search for an independence proof for the CH was also along the direction of making more explicit the idealization of envisaging arbitrary sets (and, in particular, those of integers), or, in G's favorite language, the search for the axioms determining the concept of set. Hence, the major technical results and partial results obtained from 1940 to 1942 (or 1943) are all parts of the program of consolidating idealizations and determining the nature of their (relative) evidence.

After his arrival (with Adele) at Princeton in March 1940, G was in a good position to plan his future work with a great deal of freedom. He had several important results to his credit and was finally able to live a settled married life. There was no immediate external or internal pressure to complete any unfinished project or attain new heights quickly. He was in relatively good health and could look forward to a long period of peace and quiet, devoid of the need to travel or change employment. Apparently he undertook not only to work on a diversity of topics in mathematical logic but also to pay more attention to his philosophical interests. For example, from May 1941 to 18 November 1942 he filled five of his philosophical notebooks (books 4–8, totaling 670 pages). This fact agrees with his account that he discontinued his frustrating work on the independence of CH partly because of his interest in philosophy and, in particular, also in its relation to basic scientific concepts.

I believe that the change of direction was connected also to a disappointment in the impact of mathematical logic on other parts of mathematics. For example, his incompleteness results did not lead to any promising approach to showing the independence (or, as it so happens, also the truth) of famous conjectures by Fermat, Goldbach, Riemann, etc. G had, I think, expected from important advances in foundational studies a more conspicuous impact on mathematical practice. For example, toward the end of his paper on Russell's logic (completed in 1943), he expresses himself thus (BP, p. 231):

> Many symptoms show only too clearly, however, that the primitive concepts need further elucidation. It seems reasonable to suspect that it is this incomplete understanding of the foundations which is responsible for the fact that Mathematical Logic has up to now remained so far behind the high expectation of Peano and others who (in accordance with Leibniz's claims) had hoped that it would facilitate theoretical mathematics to the same extent as the decimal system of numbers has facilitated numerical computations. For how can one expect to solve mathematical problems by mere analysis of the concepts occurring, if our analysis so far does not even suffice to set up the axioms?

While G often expects to obtain in philosophy results as definitive as in science, he does emphasize the distinction between analyzing (or elucidating) concepts in philosophy and using concepts in science (in particular, mathematics). For example, he considers, I believe, Turing's justification of the adequacy of his precise concept to the intuitive notion of computability as a piece of philosophical work. But in some cases the desired precise concepts are more elusive; he seems to require, for example, from philosophy a more radical analysis of the concept of time than is done in physics.

Given what we know today, it appears likely that if G had discussed his ideas on the independence proofs with some able mathematician, more definite advances would have been made on the CH. Evidently it was G's habit to work by himself, and I do not know all the reasons for this practice. According to Straus, both Einstein and G believed 'that thinking, the quest for truth, is an entirely solitary occupation,' and they both thought it a miracle when, on one occasion, Einstein and Straus solved a problem by thrashing out their ideas together for half an hour (Holton and Elkana, p. 420). Conceivably one could argue that 'truly original' ideas can only be obtained by solitary work. But the whole issue of conditions for (different types of) fruitful collaboration is highly complex. For example, according to Einstein's own report, he had great difficulty in developing his special theory and went in the spring of 1905 to talk with his friend M. A. Besso: 'Trying a lot of discussions with him, I could suddenly comprehend the matter' (Pais, p. 139).

On 18 November, P. A. Schilpp wrote to invite G to contribute a paper to be entitled 'Russell's mathematical logic,' saying that Russell 'considers you the scholar *par excellence* in this field.' He apparently accepted the invitation and began to work on it soon after.

1943

G sent in the manuscript on Russell on 17 May. When a revised version was ready on 28 September, Russell had completed his replies and G wrote to him attempting unsuccessfully to change his mind about his decision not to reply. When it became clear that Russell was not going to reply, G considered withdrawing his paper, but eventually yielded to Schilpp's entreaties. Russell's reply to his critics was dated July 1943 and concludes with an apologetic note about not being able to reply to G's late contribution. (In retrospect, it seems regrettable that Schilpp had not forwarded the May version to Russell; surely he could have conducted his editorial correspondence with G concurrently. But since Russell's note was under the July 1943 date, it is not clear that Schilpp did not send him the May version. At any rate, it appears that Russell was at that time probably no longer capable of dealing with G's paper judiciously.)

The rich content and meticulous care of the paper show extensive concentrated work by G. This is likely to be the year when G's attention was turned rather decisively from (getting new results in) mathematical logic to philosophy (with special emphasis on the philosophy of mathematics and its broader implications for general philosophy).

1944

The paper for Russell was published in the Russell volume (1944) and reprinted with minor changes in 1964 and 1972. Once G described the paper to me as a history of logic with special reference to the work of Russell. It is remarkable that G's own work on incompleteness and on constructible sets fits so naturally and so centrally into the frame of the paper.

On 30 November 1936, Russell began an unsuccessful attempt to get a position at the I.A.S., and the pursuit lasted a while, with Einstein, Veblen, and Weyl all supportive. Eventually Russell spent some time in Princeton (unattached to any institution) before sailing for England in May 1944. In his *Autobiography*, Russell declared; 'While in Princeton, I came to know Einstein fairly well. I used to go to his house once a week to discuss with him and Gödel and Pauli.... all three of them were Jews and exiles, and, in intention, cosmopolitans, ... Gödel turned out to be an unadulterated Platonist, and apparently believed that an eternal "not" was laid up in heaven, where virtuous logicians might hope to meet it hereafter.'

In 1971 Kenneth Blackwell called G's attention to this paragraph and G drafted a reply (never actually sent):

> As far as the passage about me is concerned, I have to say *first* (for the sake of truth) that I am not a Jew (even though I don't think this question is of any importance), 2) that the passage gives the wrong impression that I had many discussions with Russell, which was by no means the case (I remember only one). 3) Concerning my 'unadulterated' Platonism, it is no more 'unadulterated' than Russell's own in 1921 when in the *Introduction* [to *Mathematical Philosophy*, first published in 1919, p. 169] he said '[Logic is concerned with the real world just as truly as zoology, though with its more abstract and general features].' At that time evidently Russell had met the 'not' even in this world, but later on under the influence of Wittgenstein he chose to overlook it.

I may observe incidentally that the sentence quoted by G is his favorite and corresponds pretty closely to his own view. Indeed the influence of Wittgenstein on Russell in this regard, accurately indicated by G, remains a great mystery to this day.

1945

In the 1940s, G delayed proper treatment of a bleeding duodenal ulcer until blood transfusions had to be administered. Afterward he observed a strict dietary regimen. The date of the event has not been ascertained. In view of G's known intensive work before and after 1945, I am conjecturing that the interruption occurred around 1945. One account says that 'in his final years it [the aftermath of the illness] aggravated the prostate trouble which he called "weakness of bladder," well known to be desperately depressing at best' (Kreisel, p. 153).

RG: 'Later, in Princeton, he had a duodenal ulcer with heavy bleeding. Thereafter he lived on *such a strict* diet that he lost weight continually and was under-nourished.

'I do not understand why after World War II my brother never came again to Vienna for a visit. He gave as the reason that in Vienna he could perhaps not follow the required diet(?).

'However, he did invite his mother and me several times to Princeton and we spent many happy hours with him and his wife.'

The collection *LM* begins with a letter dated 7 September from G to his mother and his brother. For a year before this G had been writing every two months or so through the Red Cross, but apparently these letters were not received. 'We are fine and we have just been back from our summer vacation at the seaside for a few days.'

On 30 November L. R. Ford invited G to write an expository paper on Cantor's continuum problem. A first draft was completed in August 1946.

1946

G began his regular and fairly frequent correspondence with his mother, which lasted till his mother's death in 1966.

In his letter of 22 January G wrote that his position at the institute had recently been made definitive. Indeed, this is the year when he became a permanent member.

'So I have now successfully reached the age of 40, already older than Papa at the break of the first world war' (letter of 28 April).

Adele was eager to visit Vienna 'at all cost' (21 July). Einstein was mentioned for the first time in *LM* (in the same letter, compare section 1.5 for an extended account of items in *LM* that have to do with Einstein).

By invitation G lectured on 17 December at the Princeton Bicentennial before the conference on problems in mathematics. A transcript of these 'remarks' was published only in Davis 1965. In analogy with (absolute) computability, he suggested studying the concepts of absolute provability and absolute definability. Concerning the first concept, he suggested the introduction of stronger and stronger axioms of infinity that are true and have 'a certain (decidable) formal structure,' and proposed a remarkable conjecture: 'It is not impossible ... that every proposition expressible in set theory is decidable from the present axioms plus some true assertion about the largeness of the universe of all sets.' Concerning the second concept, he introduced for the first time what is now known as 'ordinal definable sets' and conjectured (this time in a strong sense) that the axiom of choice is satisfied by these sets but CH is not. (These remarks are striking examples of how G managed to be quite precise on questions where most of us find it impossible to be precise at all.)

G was invited (apparently in June) by Schilpp to contribute a paper to honor Einstein; he accepted the invitation. I can only conjecture why Schilpp invited G on this occasion. One possibility is that Einstein suggested G. Another possibility is that by 1946 the close contact between G and Einstein was known to Schilpp.

G wrote in this year a letter to C. A. Baylis giving his apprehension that service in offices or on committees 'would be expected,' as 'the very reason' why he had not joined the Association for Symbolic Logic earlier. This would suggest G's reluctance to occupy positions that require administrative services. People have been puzzled by G's slow promotion at the I.A.S. There are several suggested causes that could have operated in combination. (1) It was due to the personal opposition of some unnamed colleague. (2) Some colleagues felt that G would not welcome the administrative responsibilities of being a professor. (3) Others feared that his sense of duty and legalistic habit of mind might hinder efficient decision making by the faculty. I have certainly never heard directly or indirectly that G ever expressed dissatisfaction with how the I.A.S. treated him.

1947

On 16 March (see *LM*) G wrote that he had to complete his contribution to a book in the next weeks. 'I have already for a long time done much for its preparation, but the subject of the article interests me very much.' This undoubtedly refers to his work on Kant and Einstein.

After a great deal of effort, Adele finally sailed for Europe on board the ship *Marine Flasher*. She was away for the next seven months or so (see G's letters of 12 May and 9 December in *LM*).

On 28 September G wrote that he had finally finished the manuscript of his newest article the week before and could turn to something else. This was presumably his discussion of Cantor's continuum problem, which was published in December (a revised and expanded version was later published in 1964). This (especially the expanded version) is one of G's major philosophical publications. But G's letter of 7 November seems to imply that the paper supposedly finished in September was the paper on Kant and Einstein, because he now said that much more remained to be done on the paper.

E. G. Straus continued as Einstein's assistant this year (see section 1.5). According to him, 'As was our custom, we picked up Gödel to go home for lunch,' and Einstein 'had many friends, including some extremely close friends, at least in Wolfang Pauli and, in particular, in Kurt Gödel' (Holton and Elkana, p. 420). (Pauli spent the years 1940 to 1946 at the I.A.S.) A contrast is put in these words: 'The one man who was, during the last years, certainly by far Einstein's best friend, and in some ways strangely resembled him most, was Kurt Gödel, the great logician. They were very different in almost every personal way—Einstein gregarious, happy, full of laughter and common sense, and Gödel extremely solemn, very serious, quite solitary, and distrustful of common sense as a means of arriving at the truth. But they shared a fundamental quality: both went directly and wholeheartedly to the questions at the very center of things' (ibid., p. 422).

In terms of what is known of their activities, one can note other comparisons. Einstein had a natural antipathy for gymnastics and sports—he easily became dizzy and tired; in school he earned the highest or the next-highest mark in mathematics and in Latin (Pais, p. 37). In these respects G resembled Einstein, but in later life Einstein enjoyed better health and was more rational toward his own health and in his attitude toward doctors. While in his younger days Einstein had to worry about earning a living, G was well sheltered at least up to his early 30s. It is difficult to estimate what effects the difference in early financial security had on their later life-styles. Certainly Einstein was more ready than G to interact with others and to make his ideas public.

1948
G probably worked on relativity theory and its relation to philosophy. On 10 May G wrote that he had for several weeks been so occupied with a problem that he had simply not been able to stop thinking, despite his efforts to interrupt the work. 'Even in a cinema or with a radio I could only listen with half an ear.... I have now settled the matter to such an extent that I can again sleep peacefully.' It is likely that this concentrated work was connected with his Einstein paper.

In connection with the interview for his US citizenship, he once told me that for this occasion he had studied how the Indians had come to America. Einstein and O. Morgenstern were his witnesses, and Morgenstern has told different people about aspects of the event. The following account is given by H. Zemanek and E. Köhler (see Zemanek's report, *Elektronische Rechenanlagen*, vol. 5, 1978, pp. 209–211). Even though the routine examination G was to take was an easy matter, G prepared seriously for it and studied the US Constitution carefully. On the day before the interview G told Morgenstern that he had discovered a logical-legal possibility of transforming the United States into a dictatorship. Morgenstern saw that the hypothetical possibility and its likely remedy involved a complex chain of reasoning and was clearly not suitable for consideration at the interview. He urged G to keep quiet about his discovery.

The next morning Morgenstern drove Einstein and G from Princeton to Trenton. Einstein was informed; on the way he told one tale after another, to divert G from his Constitution-theoretical explanations, apparently with success. At the office in Trenton, the official in charge was Judge Philip Forman, who had inducted Einstein in 1940 and struck up a friendship with him. He greeted them warmly and invited all three to attend the (normally private) examination of G.

The judge began, 'You have German citizenship up to now.' G interrupted him, 'Excuse me sir, Austrian.' 'Anyhow, the wicked dictator! but fortunately that is not possible in America.' 'On the contrary,' G interjected, 'I know how that can happen.' All three joined forces to restrain G so as to turn to the routine examination.

G and Adele took their citizenship oath on 2 April 1948. According to G's letter of 10 May, about 10 candidates took it together, and the officer, who was a personal friend of Einstein's, gave a long speech of about an hour. Previously, on 11 January, G wrote that he and Adele had taken their examination, with Einstein and Morgenstern as G's witnesses. Indeed, on 9 December 1947 G had already said that he would probably be a citizen in a couple of months. Hence it seems likely that the examination had taken place around the end of 1947.

1949

On 17 January G wrote that the year number 1949 suited him very well, apparently indicating a good state of mind.

G published in July novel solutions of Einstein's field equations (with 'rotating universes' that permit 'time travel' to the past), as well as a discussion (in December) of the relationship between relativity theory and idealistic philosophy in the Einstein volume. Einstein's response hails G's discovery as an important advance and acknowledges his own earlier qualms about the concept of global time.

The technical paper was undoubtedly written before the philosophical paper, which was completed in March. In his letter of 21 March G said that he had been again very busy, undoubtedly in putting the philosophical article into its final form. As he reported in his letter of 28 May, G also gave a lecture, for the first time in many (about 8) years, at the institute on relativity theory.

G and Adele bought their house on Linden Lane, and moved in around 1 September.

In February I visited v. Neumann at the I.A.S. and spoke with G by telephone. I taught G's incompleteness theorems at Harvard in the spring, the first time that these results were taught at Harvard with any degree of completeness. I visited G in his large office in Fuld Hall in July; this was the first time I saw him. [Afterward, there was a period when, apparently by his own choice, he occupied small office(s) in Fuld Hall.]

1950

G gave an invited address on 31 August to the International Congress of Mathematicians that extended his previous work on rotating universes. He mentioned the lecture and its good reception in his letters of 21 August and 29 September to his mother.

From about this time was a manuscript (with several versions), entitled 'Some observations about the relationship between theory of relativity and Kantian philosophy.' [According to David Malament, who has examined the manuscript, it was probably written before 1949, because no reference is made to G's relevant results of 1949 and 1950.]

'It is worth noting that G's interest in relativity went beyond the purely theoretical. In his essay he argues in favor of the possible relevance of his models to our own world, in the Nachlass there are two notebooks devoted to tabulations of the angular orientations of galaxies (which G hoped might exhibit a preferred direction). Freeman Dyson has remarked that even much later, G maintained a keen interest in such observational data' (Dawson, 1984).

In his letter of 1 November (and that of 8 January 1951) G answered 'yes' to his mother's question whether he was at the time working on 'cosmology.'

I was in Zurich for 1950–51 and got to know Bernays and E. Specker well.

1951

G was sick and hospitalized for a period in or around February, as reported in his letter of 17 March (in *LM*).

G received the Albert Einstein Award (shared with Julian Schwinger) on 14 March; v. Neumann paid his tribute, beginning with these words: 'Kurt Gödel's achievement in modern logic is singular and monumental—indeed it is more than monumental, it is a landmark which will remain visible far in time and space' (*New York Times*, 15 March, p. 31).

D. Litt., Yale University. (Quine had proposed G for an honorary degree at Harvard either this year or even earlier; but Harvard only took the step a year after Yale.) On 28 June, G wrote of the recipients, 'I was of course by far the youngest; all the others were 60 or even older.'

G planned to visit his mother in the autumn, but did not do so. His mother was naturally very disappointed. On 12 November G had to protest that of course he was more than glad to come to Europe to see her.

G probably worked on his Gibbs Lecture entitled 'Some basic theorems on the foundations of mathematics and their philosophical implications,' which was given on the evening of 26 December in Providence. I attended the session. Some of the ideas in this lecture are reported in my book *MP* (p. 324), in a form preferred by him in 1972.

1952

Sc.D., Harvard University. On this occasion G and his wife both came to Harvard, and I met them at dinner in Quine's house. Mrs. G collected the local newspapers, which reported on the ceremony at Harvard. In his letter of 22 July G considered with pleasure the citation calling him 'the discoverer of the most significant mathematical truth of this century.'

On 31 October G wrote, 'For the last two months I have been so much occupied with politics, that I had almost no time for anything else.'

1953

In March Adele went on a trip to Europe.

At the age of 47, G was finally made a professor at the I.A.S. In the letter of 25 March, he told his mother that he would not have any lecturing duties, though the salary was even higher than at universities. R. Bott recalled that at about this time he had happened (at a dinner) to sit next to G, who told him of the promotion with pleasure. In 1976 G told me that his work at the Institute had been split in three ways: Institute work, mathematics, and philosophy. Presumably the Institute work (or most of it) only began when he became professor. In the memorial service on 3 March 1978, H. Whitney pointed out that G was keenly interested in the affairs of the Institute. It was, Whitney said, hard to appoint a new visiting member in logic since G could not 'prove to himself that a number of candidates shouldn't be members, with the evidence at hand.'

Adele had some amusing things to say about the I.A.S. 'On one occasion she painted the I.A.S., which she usually called *Altersversorgungsheim* (home for old-age pensioners), as teeming with pretty girl students who queued up at the office doors of permanent professors.' She also 'spoke of him, affectionately, as a *strammer Bursche*' (Kreisel, pp. 154–155 and 153).

In the letter of 31 October G said that he had been occupied with a recent 14-day visit of a famous professor (of 72 years) from Holland, evidently referring to Brouwer.

1954

Carnap visited the I.A.S. from 1952 to 1954. I have seen no report on his interaction with G during this period. In fact, on the pages devoted to this extended visit in Carnap's *Intellectual Autobiography*, G's name is conspicuously absent.

On 15 May 1953, Schilpp extended G an invitation to contribute a paper, to be entitled 'Carnap and the ontology of mathematics,' to the Carnap volume. G replied on 2 July, agreeing to write a shorter paper on 'Some observations on the nominalistic view of the nature of mathematics.' The manuscripts were to be due on 2 April 1954. But G went through six versions of his paper (quite neatly preserved in the Nachlass)—retitled 'Is mathematics syntax of language?'—before finally advising Schilpp on 2 February 1959 that he was not going to submit the paper after all. His reasons for withdrawing were (1) he was still not satisfied with the result; (2) his manuscript was quite critical of Carnap's position; and (3) since it was too late for Carnap to reply, he felt it would be unfair to publish it. All of Schilpp's pleading, cajolery, and admonishment were thus to no avail.

In *LM*, work on the Carnap paper was mentioned on 19 March and again on 31 July (saying that he wanted to finish the paper before going away for the summer vacation), as well as on 14 February and 14 March 1955.

Actually the Carnap volume was published only in 1963. The undated reply to his critics might have been completed much earlier; but it seems likely that if G had submitted his paper at the beginning of 1959, Carnap would have replied. However, it is quite probable that Carnap would have honestly missed G's essential points.

According to G's own account in 1972 and 1976, it caused him a good deal of trouble to have agreed to write a paper on Carnap to prove that mathematics is not syntax; he went through many versions from 1953 on, but finally he did not publish the paper. It seems likely that G found in Carnap's work a level and type of precison different from his own and had difficulty devising a satisfactory common language to make his own arguments conclusively convincing to his opponent.

Incidentally, Schilpp also invited G (in 1964 and 1971) to contribute a paper on Karl Popper, but G declined both invitations (as well as Popper's own appeal). Hence, the four invitations (Russell, Einstein, Carnap, and Popper) had four different fates. Only in the case of Einstein were both G's paper and a reply published.

1955

G must have spent a good deal of energy working on the Carnap paper.

G was elected member of the US National Academy of Sciences.

Einstein died on 18 April (age 76). G and Bruria Kaufman, Einstein's last collaborator (with a last joint paper completed January 1955), put in order the scientific papers in Einstein's office, Room 115 in Fuld Hall.

On 7 September and 18 November G wrote two replies to Carl Seelig on his relations with Einstein. G first met Einstein in 1933, and they became close in 1942. G thought the reason why Einstein enjoyed his company may be that G held opposite views from Einstein on many questions and made no secret of his own different views. Their conversations usually had to do with philosophy, physics, and politics. (For a more extended account, see section 1.5.)

In February Adele went to Vienna, and she brought her mother with her to Princeton in March.

G planned to visit his mother in the summer. On 26 June he wrote that his physician advised him against going in the summer.

1956

In August Kreisel and I went to have tea with the Gs in their house (on Linden Lane). When the suicide of Turing was mentioned, G asked whether Turing was married. When he was given a negative answer, he said, 'Maybe he wanted to get married but could not.'

Invitations for participation in the Bernays Festschrift were extended to a number of people, including G, leading later to G's 1958 paper.

1957

On February 8 (at age 53), v. Neumann died.

G was elected fellow of the American Academy of Arts and Sciences.

At the long Logic Summer Institute in Ithaca, C. Spector was probably the only one who attended every session and paid close attention. He had published his substantive dissertation and was in quest of an exciting research problem. His contacts with Kreisel this summer were in part instrumental in his choice later on to extend G's work on primitive recursive functionals to a consistency proof of analysis by adding a new principle of definition called 'bar recursion.' He worked on the project from the summer of 1959 till his unexpected death on 29 July 1961, at the age of 30. He was at the I.A.S. during 1960–61 and discussed his work with Bernays and G. (Bernays was in Philadelphia for the spring of 1961.) The work was published in a volume dedicated to his memory, *Recursive Function Theory*, 1962 (Proceedings from a Symposium in April 1961). G wrote a postscript to this paper and changed its title from 'Provably recursive functionals in analysis: a consistency proof by an extension of intuitionistic principles' to 'Provably recursive functionals of analysis: a consistency proof of analysis by an extension of principles formulated in current intuitionistic mathematics' (compare section 11.1).

On 9 August G wrote of being occupied with an article (probably the one to honor Bernays) as well as with the reprinting of two of his earlier papers in a book.

1958

G's mother and brother visited G and Adele in May. This was the first time that G had seen them since January 1940.

G published a philosophical paper that contains his method using primitive recursive functionals (from 1941) on the occasion of the seventieth birthday of Bernays. Bernays visited the I.A.S. at the beginning of the year for a month or two. (On 11 August G wrote that he had sent off his paper three weeks before.)

This paper occupies a crucial place in the (extended Hilbert) program of justifying classical reasoning by constructive means. While G's incompleteness theorems have shown the impossibility of Hilbert's program as originally conceived, there remains the indefinite question of extending Hilbert's finitist method to include broader ranges of constructive reasoning, of which the intuitionistic conception is of course the most conspicuous example. While with Hilbert's original program, had it been successful, there would be no problem of the favored reasoning being evident, the extended program faces a twofold task: to see that the chosen constructive reasoning is evident and to ground classical reasoning on it. Indeed, from the experience accumulated since 1930, one sees that the relation between constructivity and evidence is highly complex. In my opinion this experience illustrates the sort of grounds for needing to relax absolutist appeals to intuition (and introspection), associated with Husserl's program.

G's 1932 translation (28 June, mentioned above) of classical arithmetic into the intuitionistic proved that the latter was no more evident than the former. The translation reveals that the unwinding of derivations built up by intuitionistic formal rules is of about the same order of complexity as their classical counterparts. G's 1958 paper aims at giving a more evident interpretation of the intuitionistic arithmetic (and therewith also one of the classical by his 1932 translation); this point is suggested in footnote 1 on p. 283 and extensively elaborated in his famous revised English version from the late 1960s (specifically in the longest new footnote, labeled k in the privately circulated manuscript; see section 11.1 for an extended discussion of the English version).

1959

Adele's mother died in Princeton in March (letter of 3 April).

Adele went to the White Mountains in July for three and a half weeks, and G was able to work 'again' with great concentration in her absence. The summer was the hottest in 20 years, but G did not mind, or rather enjoyed it (letter of 30 July).

Adele was in Europe (mostly in Vienna) for about two months from October to December (letters of 8 November and 6 December).

G began to study the work of Husserl; he was only interested in Husserl's later work (after 1907). According to him, he used to think that philosophy could be pursued in the same manner as, and (or) by reflecting on, fundamental science, but at some stage he decided that philosophy needs a different method, such as that proposed by Husserl. Also he considered (at least in the 1970s) everyday knowledge as more basic and more important data for philosophy. His change of view on the proper method of philosophy and his study of Husserl's work very likely went through a 'dialectic' process. He probably did not accept Husserl's emphasis on subjectivity, and he wished to use the method to arrive at a system of metaphysics that would be of comparable scope with Leibniz's monadology but more solidly founded on a sharable and disciplined intuition.

[By coincidence, Husserl was born one hundred years ago (and so were also H. Bergson and John Dewey). Indeed, the year 1859 has sometimes been called the climax of the nineteenth century. It was the year of Darwin's *On the Origin of Species*, Marx's *Critique of Political Economy*, J. S. Mill's *Essay on Liberty*, Dickens's *A Tale of Two Cities*, Wagner's *Tristan und Isolde*, Tennyson's *Idylls of the King*, George Eliot's *Adam Bede*, Thackeray's *The Virginians*, the death of Macaulay and Tocqueville, the centenary of F. Schiller's birth, etc.]

1960

Bernays and K. Schütte were both at the I.A.S. in 1959–60, and I saw them several times, as I happened to be at Bell Laboratories for the year. G had frequent discussions with Bernays (indeed, generally when Bernays visited the Institute).

G's mother and brother were in America for an extended visit, probably from March to May (letters of 6 March and 6 July).

Adele was in Vienna in November (letter of 18 November). Before Adele returned in December, G had eaten mostly only eggs (letter of 16 December).

1961

According to G in 1976, his health was exceptionally poor this year. I do not know what the health problems were.

G was elected a member of the American Philosophical Society.

To an inquiry from A. W. Burks (8 August) regarding some references to G's theorem by v. Neumann, G replied on 7 November (quoted on pp. 55–56 of *Theory of Self-Reproducing Automata*, 1966). Among other things G said in his letter, 'I think the theorem of mine which von Neumann refers to is ... the fact that a complete epistemological description of a language A cannot be given in the same language A because the concept of truth of a sentence of A cannot be defined in A. It is this theorem which is the true reason for the existence of undecidable propositions in the formal systems containing arithmetic.'

Bernays was in Philadelphia in the spring.

G had begun to go to bed and rise earlier and liked this schedule much better than his previous one (letter of 18 March).

In his letter of 30 April G offered an extended discussion of *Hamlet* and Goethe's *Faust*.

Adele visited Italy from July to September (letters of 25 June and 23 July).

G wrote to his mother the four 'theological' letters (23 July, 14 August, 12 September, and 6 October), considered in section 8.1.

In reply to his mother's inquiry G mentioned (12 September) that he would like to own good books in philosophy, including the classics, such as Kant's *Critique of Judgment* or also the *Critique of Pure Reason*, so as to be able to read in them from time to time.

1962

G published the postscript to Spector's paper (mentioned above under *1957*); this relates to one of G's enduring interests over the years, viz., constructivity and its place in mathematics.

Another enduring interest (at least since the 1930s) was of course set theory. Of the work in this area since 1950 he was interested in the study of large cardinals (compact, measurable, Ramsey, etc.), the reflection principles, and probably also Ackermann's set theory. [It is said (Kreisel, p. 159) that in the '50s he looked, without success, for logicians interested in the partition properties (to visit at the I.A.S.).]

Of his philosophical interests, it appears that for many years he kept his ideas to himself both because he had not formulated them to his own satisfaction and because he had not found a sufficiently sympathetic audience. It is likely that he discussed many of his philosophical ideas with Bernays, who shared with him a good deal of interest and knowledge (of the technical and philosophical literature, including Kant and Husserl).

G to Marianne (17 March): 'You are completely right that mankind is not improved through the moon flight. This has to do with the old conflict between "natural" and "spiritual" sciences. There would be no danger of an atomic war, if advances in history, the science of right and of state, philosophy, psychology, literature, art, etc. were as great as in physics. But instead of such progress, one is struck by significant regresses in many of the spiritual sciences.' [I consider this an informative statement of G's views on the nature and state of the realm of human studies.]

On 4 and 19 July G made observations on his 'recent discovery' of the 'modern poet' Franz Kafka.

'Adele has, for the first time in a long while, spent the whole summer here' (letter of 27 August).

Marianne and (G's brother) Rudolf visited from late September to the middle of October.

1963

Paul J. Cohen's preprint of his independence proof of the continuum hypothesis began to circulate in the spring. G corresponded with Cohen in the process of correcting errors and polishing the paper. Toward the end of the year, G communicated (on 30 September and 27 November) Cohen's article (in two parts) to the *PNAS* (1963, pp. 1143–1148; 1964, pp. 105–110).

G had completed a revision of his 1947 paper on Cantor's continuum problem with a primarily philosophical supplement, probably before the spring. A postscript was added toward the end of the year referring to Cohen's independence result. (The whole text was published next year in the collection by P. Benacerraf and H. Putnam. Apparently G was reluctant at first to have his papers included in the collection because he felt that the editors were not sympathetic toward his philosophical views. In particular, he was afraid that the editors would make unfair negative comments in their introduction. He consented to have his papers included after their assurance that they had no intention of evaluating the papers in their introduction.)

The combination of the revision and the interaction with Cohen must have stimulated G to think again about the continuum problem, both to review his previous work on the independence question and to attempt a resolution of the CH. He was very generous and conscientious about not depriving Cohen in any way of the credit for his remarkable work. In the spring of 1965, when visiting Harvard, Cohen told me that he had asked G about G's own independence proof of the axiom of choice and that G had responded, 'What proof?' [Since the late 1940s, I had heard references to G's unpublished proof in conversations.] On 30 June 1967, G wrote a letter to Wolfgang Rautenberg (published on p. 20 of *Mathematik in der Schule*, vol. 6, 1968) to deny in part a published statement by Mostowski on this matter. The statement gives an account of how he viewed in 1967 his results from 1942: 'Die Mostowskische Behauptung ist insofern unrichtig, als ich bloss in Besitze gewisse Teilresultate war, nämlich von Beweisen für die Unabhängigkeit der Konstrucktibilitäts- und Auswahlsaxioms in der Typentheorie. Auf Grunde meiner höchst unvollständign Aufzeichnungen von damals (d.h. 1942) könnte ich ohne Schwierigkeiten nur den ersten dieser beiden Beweise rekonstruieren. Meine Methode hat eine sehr nahe Verwandtschaft mit der neuerdings von [R. Solovay und] Dana Scott entwickelten, weniger mit den Cohenschen.' Moreover, G wrote a letter on 1 May 1968 to correct a description by Cohen of his own work as a 'refinement' of G's (see Kreisel, p. 201).

G's attempt to settle the CH by inventing new axioms was later communicated to others in 1970 and afterward (see below).

G added a note (dated 28 August) to his famous 1931 paper to say that due to Turing's work a completely general version of his two incompleteness results is possible (published on p. 616 of FG, 1967).

In his letter of 14 May G reported on his professional activities to explain why he had not written (to Marianne) since 24 March. At the institute, he said, this was a busy year, and, for instance, candidates had to be evaluated to decide on the stipends. 'This year applicants in my field more than doubled.' Moreover, 'Somebody has solved a very important problem in my field 14 days ago.' Since G was asked to communicate the work to the National Academy, he had to 'answer for its correctness.' Since the problem is difficult, this required much time. [This passage of course refers to Cohen's proof.]

G also remarked on the rapid growth of mathematics during the recent years as a result of the competition with Russia and the increase of federal funds. 'The number of Ph.D.s tripled in a few years.' In addition, there were more disagreements at the institute, so that much could depend on [his] one vote. But to form a well-informed opinion was time consuming.

On 7 August G wrote 'I received today the agreeable news that the translation (into English) of an article of mine, whose revision has also been costing me much time, will only appear later. I am, therefore, using the time to write you fully once more.' (The translation is evidently of G's 1931 paper, which was later published in FG.) 'I have more or less lost touch with politics, since I only very rarely read the papers nowadays.'

Adele was away at the seaside for about four weeks in August. In September, G and Adele spent three days at a resort area to celebrate the 'silver anniversary' (of their marriage).

On 20 October G said that he must read the article on the implications of his work (apparently sent by Marianne): 'It was something to be expected that sooner or later my proof will be made useful for religion, since that is doubtless also justified in a certain sense.'

1964
G wrote a postscript (dated 3 June) and added several footnotes to his 1934 lectures, to comment on some of the relevant work since 1934. These were included in the publication of the lectures in M. Davis, *The Undecidable* (1965, pp. 39–74, especially pp. 71–73). Later (before 1970) G prepared another note to be adjoined to his postscript, which was published in *MP* (pp. 325–326), in a form further revised by him in 1972.

Marianne and G's brother visited in May. Marianne suffered an accident (Unfall) or attack (Anfall) around the beginning of July.

Adele was at the seaside for three or four weeks from July to August.

1965

G not only concentrated his study on what he regarded as fundamental, and therefore deserved continued attention, but also displayed an exceptional preoccupation with precision and completeness, especially in writing for publication. The several (in fact, four) additions he wrote around this time for the republication and publication of his earlier papers and lectures (five in 1964, two in 1965, and two in 1967, with the 1931 paper in two English versions) all illustrate his interest in making (a selection from) his early work more complete. His two letters to me and the revision of his 1958 paper (see below), also harking back to his earlier work, reveal, like his (other) philosophical papers, his central concern with relating (his) technical work to (his) philosophical views.

In terms of more novel research, it appears likely that he devoted himself in the 1960s to the study of philosophy on the one hand and of the continuum problem on the other.

Marianne suffered another attack in March.

G praised the new library at the institute as well as his new office attached to it (in his letters of 14 February and 18 March). 'It is now the most beautiful and most modern part of the Institute.'

Adele had an extended summer vacation and 'cure' in Europe.

1966

G wrote a note (dated 18 May) for the English translation of his 1931 reformulation of his incompleteness results in terms of number theory (rather than set theory), to outline more general statements and more elegant proofs of his theorems (printed on pp. 616–617 of *FG*, 1967).

G's sixtieth birthday fell in this year. An ill-prepared symposium to celebrate the occasion was organized by the Ohio Academy of Sciences and took place on 21–23 April at Columbus, Ohio, to which G sent the following 'greetings': 'I wish to convey my greetings to the symposium, and in particular, to the speakers. I am sorry I cannot attend, but I am looking forward with interest and pleasure to the volume in which the lectures will be printed.' The volume appeared in 1969 and contains also greetings from J. R. Oppenheimer (director of the I.A.S. for many years) and a reproduction of v. Neumann's tribute to G (made March 1951).

Vienna, the second of G's three 'homes,' made largely unsuccessful attempts to honor G on his sixtieth birthday. He had no use for the honorary professorship of mathematics proposed by the University of Vienna on 23 February. The honorary membership of the Austrian Academy of Sciences he declined in a letter dated 6 August, using a somewhat tortured argument. Apparently it had not been possible to offer him an honorary doctorate of philosophy before the division of the philosophical faculty into two (in the 1970s). Eventually the University of Vienna was able to make G an honorary doctor of natural sciences posthumously (with the consent of Mrs. G). (For more details, see Christian, op. cit., under *1932* in chapter 3, pp. 266–267.) In addition, G was offered the Austrian medal for art and science and was sent a personal letter from the Bürgermeister.

G's mother Marianne (Handschuh), born on 31 August 1879, died in Vienna on 23 July. Marianne had wanted very much to be with G on his sixtieth birthday and was greatly disappointed that she was not able to make the trip. She telephoned G on G's birthday (28 April). G's last letter to his mother (in *LM*) was dated 4 July.

In his letter of 24 February G mentioned that Carl Kaysen had been chosen to be the new director: 'You have perhaps already heard that in the Institute a successor to Oppenheimer has now been named.'

G replied to Constance Reid (22 March) on the relation of his work to Hilbert's program.

1967

The Summer Institute on Set Theory took place at U.C.L.A. G was invited to attend. In a reply to Paul J. Cohen dated 27 April, G declined the invitation and said that he had been for years mainly concerned with basic philosophical and epistemological questions and new applications of these studies to science. But he had not reached the stage of being able to make such applications. I have the vague recollection that G sent a message commending recent advances in the study of large cardinals and independence problems.

G was awarded the Sc.D. degree at Amherst College and elected honorary member of the London Mathematical Society.

On 27 July I sent G the draft of a first section of my paper on Skolem's work in logic, asking for comments. On 14 September, I sent G a draft of the complete paper, repeating my request for comments. (The revised paper was published in *Selected Logical Works of Th. Skolem*, 1970, pp. 17–52.) [On 28 September I also wrote to G for a letter on Solovay, which, as I recall, he sent me without much delay.] He began his reply, dated 7 December, with an explanation indicating the great care he must have taken in preparing his reply: 'Thank you very much for sending me your manuscript about Skolem's work. I am sorry for the long delay in my reply. It seems to me that, in some points, you don't represent matters quite correctly. So I wanted to consider carefully what I have to say.' [There are nine pages of handwritten material for the letter in the Nachlass.]

On 19 December I sent G a long letter, including proposed revisions of my Skolem paper (to take G's comments into consideration) and general philosophical questions under six headings (finitary position, nonfinitary consistency proofs, objectivistic conception and G's work in logic, the iterative concept of set, set-theoretic paradoxes, and philosophical implications of the incompleteness results). [This letter and its envelope are preserved in G's Nachlass with marginal marks by G. On the envelope G put 'Wiss. interessante.'] Meanwhile I was also corresponding with Bernays both on my Skolem manuscript and on G's comments.

G's second letter was dated 7 March 1968; in it he supplemented his preceding letter and also incidentally replied to some of the points raised by Bernays and me. Both of G's letters were, with minor omissions, published in my *MP* (1974, pp. 8–11).

1968

G was elected a foreign member of the Royal Society of London.

G concluded his letter of 7 March to me with, 'Unfortunately I was very busy the past few weeks with rewriting one of my former papers. But I hope to be able soon to answer the other questions raised in your letter of 19 December.' I wrote back on 23 April, saying that I looked forward to his answers.

I believe that the former paper he was rewriting at this time was his 1958 paper. In 1976 he told me that the (rewritten) paper had already been in proofs before he fell ill [presumably around the beginning of 1970]. I have recently found a draft of an unsent letter of mine to Bernays dated 29 October 1976, which dealt with G's request about this paper of his. The draft reported that G was then willing to have the paper published in the form of the proofs, with two minor corrections:

1. Under the added note (c), append the sentence, 'Gödel has notified me that the axiom of disjunctive definition is derivable from the other axioms of the system T.'
2. Under 'Some remarks on the decidability result,' replace the second paragraph of section 1 by 'The theorem remains valid for much weaker systems than Z. With insignificant changes of the wording, it holds for any recursive translation of the primitive recursive equations into S.'

As I recall now, he changed his mind about the 'corrections' and also failed to send me one of his two copies of the galley proofs. At one stage he suggested that even the corrections quoted above were unnecessary and he merely wished to change two or three words, which I can now no longer remember.

About the rewritten paper he mentioned several times the added note (apparently k, elaborating the old footnote 5), which explains 'why the proof is not circular but using something more evident to interpret the intuitionistic number theory.' [I have in my file an invitation from Bernays and E. Engeler, dated October 1966, to contribute a paper to a *Dialectica* symposium on the foundations of mathematics. The papers were due 30

September 1967. It seems likely that G, who had been working on an English translation of his 1958 paper for several years, decided to rewrite it to meet an invitation to the same 'written symposium.']

1969

It is widely reported that in the late 1960s G refused recommended surgery for a prostate condition, despite urgings of concerned colleagues. More generally it is reported that G's health had been poor from the late 1960s on. Of the factors that had a negative effect on G's spirit and work over the years 1969 to 1978, one summary said, 'The events during this period would have unsettled Gödel at his best. His wife suffered two strokes and a major operation. There were—obviously interrelated—changes for the worse in America and at the I.A.S., the country and the institution to which he was so much attached. . . . But the decisive factor was his own illness' (Kreisel, p. 159).

In 1984 a letter dated 10 December 1969 from G to Professor George A. Brutian (of the International Research and Exchanges Board in New York City) was published in a Soviet journal.

> Here is one formulation of the philosophical meaning of my result, which I have given once in answer to an inquiry:
> The few immediately evident axioms from which all of contemporary mathematics can be derived do not suffice for answering all Diophantine yes or no questions of a certain well-defined simple kind. (See: M. Davis, *The Undecidable*, New York 1965, p. 73, last but one paragraph.) Rather, for answering all these questions, infinitely many new axioms are necessary, whose truth can (if at all) be apprehended only by constantly renewed appeals to a mathematical intuition, which is actualized in the course of the development of mathematics. Such an intuition appears, e.g., in the axioms of infinity of set theory.
> There are other formulations, which ought to be added, in order to make the situation completely clear. Perhaps I can send them to you at some later date through the International Research and Exchanges Board.

According to Köhler, 'Morgenstern related that, after the late 60s, Gödel confessed he could no longer understand the work of younger logicians.'

1970

According to Köhler, 'O. Morgenstern carried Gödel from his house and drove him to a hospital in 1970.' I also heard once that G had left the hospital when the operation for his prostate was to be performed. Perhaps this took place during the same hospitalization. It is my impression that G never did undergo the needed surgery.

According to G in 1976, his health was exceptionally poor this year. The early part of the year was apparently a period when he thought he was about to die and tried to wind up some aspects of his work. For instance, I received a letter dated 3 April from Dana Scott, written on behalf of G, in which G was reported to be in ill health and to wish to put some of his papers in order before it was too late, and in which a useless idea of extending the Gödel case to include identity was said to be G's recollection of his original approach. In a letter to Bernays dated 16 June, Scott reported that G's health was much better.

I wrote a letter to G on 9 January to say that I would be in Princeton on 20, 27, and 29 January and to ask whether he could see me on one of these dates. G drafted a positive reply but did not send it; he asked Carl [Peter] Hempel to locate me on the 29th, but we were able only to talk briefly on the telephone. Later on 9 July 1971 G wrote to me, saying, 'I am sorry that, in consequence of my illness, our meeting, proposed for January 1970, never materialized. I shall be very glad to see you sometime this year at your convenience.'

Atypically, early this year he sent A. Tarski a clearly unpolished manuscript (apparently for the purpose of publication) entitled, 'Some considerations leading to the probable conclusion that the true power of the continuum is aleph-two.' G listed four new axioms and claimed to derive from them the proposition included in the title. The proposed proof turned out to be mistaken and the paper was withdrawn by 19 May. According to one report, G blamed his oversight on the prescribed drugs he was taking at the time. In fact, he was later on able to derive the continuum hypothesis from his new axioms, of which axiom 4 is the strong one. (The proof was reported by Erik Ellentuck in 'Gödel's square axioms for the continuum,' *Mathematische Annalen*, vol. 216, 1975, pp. 29–33.)

1971

On 25 May I wrote G asking for permission to quote his letter of 7 December 1967 in the book I was working on (with the title *Knowledge and Logic* at the time, later published as *MP*). G first asked Stanley Tennenbaum to inform me of his positive reply and then wrote me on 9 July to request that the letter of 7 March 1968 also be published and to give detailed instructions on the parts to be included. The instructions were essentially followed in the actual publication of the letters. He said also, 'In fact I am very much in favor of these things becoming generally known.'

It was in the same letter that G expressed willingness to meet with me. I wrote back on 20 July to propose beginning our meetings in the autumn, since I would be mostly in the Boston area in the summer. I also sent him a copy of a large part of my book manuscript. He replied on 4 August, saying about my manuscript, 'Since I shall not have time to read it in the near future, I would request, in case you want any comments from me, to mention to me the passages where my name occurs.' On 11 August I sent him a selection of three parts from the manuscript that were specially related to his work. After my return to New York in September, a schedule was worked out to visit him at his office every other Wednesday from 11:00 to around 1:15. For a period Carl Kaysen, the director, also arranged an apartment for me on Einstein Drive, but I soon gave it up, since I found I made too little use of it.

In 1971 the visits took place on 13 and 17 October, 10 and 24 November, and 6 December. During the visits, up to June 1972, he would both comment on my manuscripts and answer questions as they came up. I took notes, but did not think it proper to bring a tape recorder.

1972

G was elected a Corresponding Fellow of the British Academy and Corresponding Member of the *Institut de France* (Académie des Sciences Morales et Politiques). Sc.D., The Rockefeller University (1 June).

My visits to his office continued on 5 January, 19 January, 2 February, 23 February, 15 March, 5 April, 19 April, 3 May, 24 May, 14 June, 9 August, 13 September, 4 October, 18 October, 8 November, 29 November, and 15 December. In the process of discussing my manuscripts, he made contributions that he asked me to write up and send to him. These were revised a number of times and included in my book, the manuscript of which was sent to the publisher in June. (Between the visits in June and August, I was abroad for seven weeks.) O. Morgenstern told me that G much enjoyed these sessions; one day in the spring Morgenstern came to G's office and took pictures of G with me.

At the convocation for conferring degrees on 1 June, I presented G and N. D. Zinder presented Alfred Day Hershey, the (only) other recipient of the degree of Doctor of Science Honoris Causa from The Rockefeller University that year. A few days later G mentioned his surprise at the fact that there had been no religious service and no reports in the press.

1973

G probably continued his work on the continuum hypothesis. The title of one manuscript from this period (preserved in the Nachlass) is 'A proof of Cantor's continuum hypothesis from a highly plausible axiom about orders of growth.'

I have not (yet) found the record of my talks with G during 1973 to 1974, even though I remember there were telephone calls. But some brief notes in the Nachlass seem to indicate that I did talk with G in February, June, September, and November of 1973, possibly in his office. It was probably in September that an amusing equivocation of 'character recognition' occurred in our conversation. I was for a short time interested in computer recognition of Chinese characters (words), but G thought I was interested in the task of recognizing people's characters (from external traits) and said that he was also interested in the problem.

Looking back, I believe that it was primarily my preoccupation with China and dialectical materialism from the summer of 1972 on that reduced my contacts with G during 1973 and 1974. Three postcards from me are preserved in the Nachlass: 14 July 1972 from Beijing, 28 June 1973 from Hawaii, and 17 December 1973 from Beijing. There is also a letter (23 August) on the proofs of *MP*.

1974

My book *MP* with G's varied contributions appeared in January, and he was as disappointed as I that so little attention was paid to the book. There were correspondence and telephone calls about reviews of the book. In addition, I wrote a letter in April mentioning my reading of some of Freud's books and passing on a request to read several pages by my teacher Shen Yuting. A letter of 1 July mentioned a long telephone conversation the previous day that found G in good spirits. There was a discussion (4 December) on giving permission for an Italian translation of *MP* (by Alberto Giacomelli, which eventually appeared in 1984, Editore Boringhieri).

1975

G was awarded the National Medal of Science by President Ford, but due to ill health he did not attend the ceremony on 18 September. (The award was for the year 1974.) He was awarded a Doctor of Science by Princeton University and planned but failed to attend the ceremony. As a result, the degree was withheld.

G arranged for me to visit the I.A.S. for 1975–76. I was there (part-time) from July 1975 to August 1976. During this period he rarely came to the Institute, and I visited him in his office only a few times. But we talked frequently and at length on the telephone.

A major occupation of mine during the early part of this period was to revise my paper 'Large sets' and to write up some of G's views on sets and concepts.

1976

The text of 'Some facts about Kurt Gödel,' reproduced in section 2.1, was essentially written in June.

G retired from the I.A.S. on 1 July.

Correspondence, even with his brother, virtually ceased during the last two years of G's life. G was in a hospital around the beginning of April.

From about that time on, G often mentioned the health problems of himself and his wife.

There were proposals to treat G's health problems with special attention at the University of Pennsylvania Hospital, and I discussed details with G by telephone. But nothing came of this because G did not consent to have himself brought to the hospital.

1977

From April to June there were many telephone discussions on the history of his work on constructible sets.

In July Mrs. G had a major operation and was hospitalized until a few days before Christmas. This was very hard on G. For instance, he complained about being left alone, but when the nurses came to the house, he would not open the door.

Oskar Morgenstern (1902–1977) died on 26 July. G telephoned him some days later and was informed of the bad news by Mrs. Morgenstern. G said nothing in reply, undoubtedly because he was too upset even to express his sympathy.

Paul Bernays (1888–1977) died in September. Probably G never knew that Bernays had died.

From 17 September to 16 November I was away. I called G before my departure and after my return.

I visited him in his house on 17 December exactly four weeks before his death. His mind remained nimble and he did not appear very sick. He said, 'I've lost the faculty for making positive decisions. I can only make negative decisions.' A day or two later Mrs. G came home and persuaded G to enter the Princeton Hospital.

1978

I telephoned him on 11 January. He was polite but sounded remote.

It was said that G's weight was down to sixty-five pounds before his death and that, toward the end, his paranoia conformed to a classic syndrome: fear of food poisoning leading to self-starvation.

He was sitting in a chair. He stretched and was gone. This was Saturday, 14 January, at one in the afternoon. According to the death certificate, on file in the Mercer County courthouse (Trenton, New Jersey), G died of 'Malnutrition and inanition' caused by 'personality disturbance.'

H. Whitney telephoned me in the early morning of 16 January, and in the afternoon I visited Mrs. G, who was talking with a minister.

There were only very few people at the (private) funeral on 19 January; I recognized only Mrs. G, Mrs. Morse, and Mrs. Morgenstern. G is buried beside his wife and his mother-in-law in the Princeton Cemetery.

There was a memorial meeting at the I.A.S. on 3 March, at which A. Weil presided and lectures were given by me, S. Kochen (in place of R. Solovay), and H. Whitney (see *Mathematical Intelligencer*, vol. 1, 1978, pp. 182–184). Kochen compared G's work to that of Einstein (in transforming existing problems into new ones) and Kafka (in combining a great power of imagination with a legalistic precision). Kochen also spoke of his Ph.D. oral examination in which he was asked to list G's major contributions, remarking that the list covered pretty much all aspects of mathematical logic at the time. Whitney attempted an analysis of G's psychology and reported on G's activities for the I.A.S. For many years G and Whitney had made up the committee for selecting visiting members in logic.

G's will left everything to his wife, who later gave his Nachlass to the I.A.S.

1979

The Association for Symbolic Logic organized a meeting devoted to G's work on 24 March at San Diego, with lectures by Jockusch, me, Feferman, and Kreisel.

By coincidence, a widely acclaimed long book, *Gödel, Escher, Bach*, by D. R. Hofstadter appeared, which has brought G's name and one aspect of his work to the attention of a wider public. Once I heard a publisher expressing interest in printing G's papers on account of the popularity of Hofstadter's book, and was struck by the contrast between intellectual and commercial values.

1983

Two sessions devoted to G took place at the Seventh International Congress of Logic, Methodology, and Philosophy of Science, July, Salzburg, Austria.

1985

The cataloguing of G's papers was completed in July 1984. The papers have been donated to the Firestone Library at Princeton University, where they have become available to scholars since 1 April 1985. The I.A.S., however, will retain copyright to all the Nachlass material. (A review of the Nachlass will be given in the *CG*.)

1986

This is the year of G's 80th birthday.

The *Collected Works of Kurt Gödel* has been in preparation for some time by the Association for Symbolic Logic with a committee of six editors. The first volume appeared early this year.

A meeting devoted to G was held on 28 and 29 April at the University of Vienna, at which I gave a lecture on 'Discussions with Kurt Gödel.' There are also a conference in Bulgaria and a symposium in Kirchberg (Austria).

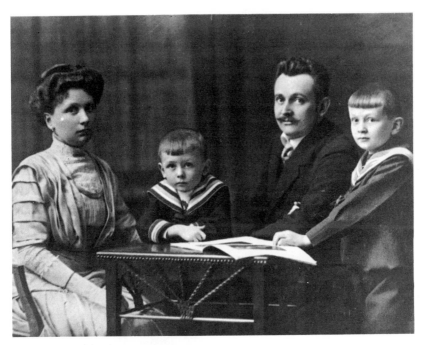

G with his parents and elder brother, Rudolf, circa 1910.

138

Adele, circa 1932. (Courtesy the I.A.S. and Princeton
University Library)

G, March 1939. (Courtesy the I.A.S. and
Princeton University Library)

Wedding portrait, Vienna, 20 September 1938. (Courtesy the I.A.S. and Princeton University Library)

140

The Gödels, June 1940, Princeton, New Jersey. (Courtesy the I.A.S. and Princeton University Library)

Home of the Gödels, 145 Linden Lane, Princeton, New Jersey, winter 1962. (Courtesy the I.A.S. and Princeton University Library)

March 1972, with Hao Wang. The photograph was taken by O. Morgenstern, near G's study. (Courtesy the I.A.S. and Princeton University Library)

1 June 1972, at the Rockefeller University; G is between A. Hershey and Hao Wang. (Courtesy The Rockefeller University)

142

August 1950, with Albert Einstein, Princeton, New Jersey. The photograph was taken by Richard Arens. (Courtesy Professor Arens)

14 March 1951, receiving the Einstein Prize, Princeton, New Jersey, with (left to right) Albert Einstein, Lewis Strauss, and Julian Schwinger. The photograph was taken by Alan Richards. (Courtesy the I.A.S. and Princeton University Library)

1964, with mother and Adele, on Einstein Drive, Princeton, New Jersey. (Courtesy the I.A.S. and Princeton University Library)

PART II

Thoughts

For most people Gödel's life and work are like a remote and esoteric landscape that is attractive but hard to reach. Only the travel is in the mind. Facts about him are more easily digestible than his thoughts, of which those having to do with the more direct responses to the concrete experience in his upbringing, education, and daily life are accessible at least to the extent that the data, if available, are of the familiar sort. It is, however, by the addition of specialized knowledge and G's penetrating private reflections that he obtained his more distinctive abstract and purely theoretical ideas. Clearly the effective approach to these thoughts is not the genetic one, but rather a conceptual exposition that considers the essential points in the context of fairly universal concerns. Indeed, there are, I believe, two ways of approaching G's work that are more capable of stirring the power of our imagination.

In the first place, it is possible to relate, largely through contrasts, some of G's fundamental thoughts to the more familiar figure of Einstein. By more or less a historical accident, G and Einstein happened to be good friends for more than a decade. They had extended discussions on physics, philosophy, and politics. In all these areas, and also in religion, they appreciated and admired each other's views, which are, however, different in basic ways. Roughly speaking Einstein's views were generally more 'realistic,' more engaged in current affairs, less optimistic with regard to the power of reason to capture the eternal, and fitted in better with the 'spirit of the time.' Their differing positions on certain fundamental issues represent two of the major alternative responses to our experience of the world we live in.

In the second place, G's thoughts include novel ideas about perennial issues that interest not only the specialists. For example: Is mind more than a machine? How exhaustible and conclusive is our knowledge in mathematics? How real are time and change? Is Darwinism adequate to giving an account of the origins of life and mind? How precise can physics become? Is there a 'next world'? Not surprisingly, G's ideas do not settle any of these questions conclusively. Indeed, to the extent that his results are definitive, the clear implications are more limited. But his precise work is remarkably relevant to some of the issues, and his speculations throw doubts on some of our fundamental beliefs that are commonly taken to be well established today.

The examples just listed are philosophical problems that have eluded scientific solutions so far. G believes some of them capable of scientific solutions. In general, he is much concerned with the connections between science and philosophy (in several different directions). It is attractive to motivate scientific work by, and apply it to, broad philosophical concerns. There is, however, a conflict between wider appeal and more definite results (such as G's exact mathematical theorems). The practitioners of a specialized area of science or philosophy (in one of its current forms) make up a community or a village, in which common understanding and purpose bind them together. But this sense of community and objective understanding is largely absent in the wider society or, in particular, between different villages. Einstein and G are exceptional in that their scientific work and philosophical ideas are, to a greater or lesser degree, fascinating also to the general public. While this fact creates a path that points to their more deliberate thoughts, an informed discussion of these inevitably requires from the reader more concentrated attention than is commonly available. Moreover, where and when they have more instructive things to say, what they say usually does not address directly to the more familiar common concerns.

In the autumn of 1955 G commented on the wide appeal of Einstein's work. 'The reason why Einstein stirs the power of imagination of so many contemporaries is surely this, that his theories interest not only the specialists. They concern also general philosophical problems, which are significant in everyday life and in science, such as for instance the problem of time. People, therefore, feel attracted to him by inclination, without penetrating into the spiritual kernel of his work' (Seelig, p. 356). In addition, it should be pointed out that sudden fame came to Einstein in 1919, when the world was sick and tired of war and longing for new ideals.

In the case of G himself his most famous theorem proves and defines the inexhaustibility of mathematics and the limitations of formal systems (or computer programs). It is, therefore, related to the familiar question whether mind surpasses machine. Hence, the continuingly broadening attention to computers and artificial intelligence lends a growing popular interest to G's work. But, as G himself recognizes, his theorem does not settle the question of mind surpassing matter. Moreover, his new solutions of Einstein's field equations are accompanied by a speculation on 'time travel' and on whether time and change are in a sense subjective and illusory. But there is serious doubt whether his solutions are a genuine candidate for a realistic description of the physical world. On the other hand, G's more articulate mathematical or conceptual realism and his ideas on the method of philosophy (with an emphasis on introspection and the pervasive power of reason as well as the auxiliary place of language) are not similarly accessible beyond the community of professional philosophers.

Chapter 5
Introductory observations

A good deal of information is available about Einstein's life, work, and (other) thoughts. His views are also more familiar than G's in the sense that what he says about religion, philosophy, politics, art, etc., departs less remarkably than G's from the contemporary outlook of (the majority of) the intellectual community. In particular, while I find G's views more challenging, I feel more comfortable with Einstein's. Hence, a comparison of some of their beliefs helps both to locate a few distinctive features of G's thoughts and to prepare the discussion of my own agreements and disagreements with G.

5.1 By way of Einstein

Einstein's love of classical music is well known; it was, however, of little interest to G. On the other hand, G's reported liking for modern abstract art was presumably not shared by Einstein. In the 1950s Einstein, like most intellectuals at that time, preferred Stevenson to Eisenhower, but G was strongly in favor of Eisenhower. Einstein wrote in 1949 an essay, 'Why socialism?' (for the first issue of *Monthly Review*, reprinted in his *Ideas and Opinions*, 1954, pp. 151–158); but I think that G, while sympathetic with the general goal, was more skeptical of the prevalent proposals on the way of attaining it.

G calls his own religion theistic and not pantheistic, following Leibniz rather than Spinoza (see *GQ*). Einstein's views on religion are much better documented (see, for instance, his autobiography in Schilpp, pp. 3–5, and the summary and references in Clark, pp. 502–504, 516–517). For example, by the age of 12 he had attained 'a deep religiosity,' as a result of 'the traditional education-machine.' But soon after he changed his mind 'through the reading of popular scientific books.' This was followed by 'a positively fanatic free-thinking' and a 'suspicion against every kind of authority.' His frequently quoted statement of 1929 says that he believed, contrary to G, 'in Spinoza's God,' and 'not in a God who concerns himself with the fate and actions of men.'

What effects did their different religious ideas have on their work? G did propose a proof of the existence of God, argue for a next world, and suggest taking God as one of the primitive concepts of metaphysics. But I am not sure whether these thoughts formed an integral part of his chief work, or even whether they affected his life in any significant way. More relevant and central to his thinking was the predominant (or even exclusive) importance that he attributed to the individual soul or person, independently of whether he was able to assign any meaningful probability to a next life. For example, when he contrasted mind with machine, he thought of mind as that of one person living forever. According to him, if you know yourself, you know everything. In particular, in order to understand society, the more effective way for him is to know yourself. He did not think that ethical problems are difficult or require serious theoretical considerations. For him issues having to do with society are irrelevant to fundamental philosophy. His conception of what might be called a rational religion also requires, I believe, a direct connection of each individual to God or the whole or what is ultimate.

As I said before, both Einstein and G were very much peace loving and cosmopolitan in their outlook. Even though Einstein was from time to time concerned with Jewish affairs, he was certainly not a fanatic, and, according to Philipp Frank (on p. 107 of his biography), 'The problem of nationality and of the relations of the Jews with the rest of the world appeared to him only as a matter of petty significance.' For over four decades, he spoke in public, from time to time, for peace and against nationalism. As early as the autumn of 1914, at the initial stage of World War I, Einstein signed a 'Manifesto to Europeans' to deplore the war (full text quoted in Clark, pp. 229–230). In 1932 he wrote an open letter (dated 30 July) proposing and asking for ways to 'deliver mankind from the menace of war.' Freud wrote a long discursive reply, and the correspondence was published next year (with the title *Why War?*). On 11 April 1955, a week before his death, Einstein signed the 'Russell-Einstein Declaration' calling for a conference to apprise the perils of war. Apart from efforts for peace, from the 1920s onward Einstein was the supporter of every good cause that could gain his ear.

I am not aware that G lent his name to any public declarations or involved himself in any public actions not strictly connected with his professional life. It is likely that Einstein viewed most of his public activities as an obligation entailed by his great fame. G was more cautious and more reluctant to make (public) commitments. Even if G had been as famous as Einstein, it is doubtful that he would have participated much more in public and other interpersonal affairs. For example, in the realm of his professional work, G was exceptionally reluctant to receive research assistance or undertake cooperative efforts, while Einstein had many (more than thirty) collaborators over the years (for an extensive account, see Pais, pp. 483–501).

In the spring of 1902 Einstein told Maurice Solovine, his first (private) pupil (who was studying philosophy), that he had also had a strong taste for philosophy when younger, but had been turned against it by the reigning vagueness and arbitrariness (for more of Einstein's comments on philosophy, see chapter 3, under *1922*). G probably agreed with Einstein that vagueness and arbitrariness reign in contemporary philosophy. But instead of abandoning the pursuit of philosophy, G had chosen to attempt to do philosophy in a better (or the right) way. Most people would probably say that Einstein had made a wiser choice. Actually it would be more accurate to say that they chose to pursue philosophy in different but overlapping ways. Corresponding to G's elaboration of the importance of his objectivism for his mathematical work (*MP*, pp. 8–11), we have Einstein's summary observation: 'Science without epistemology is—insofar as it is thinkable at all—primitive and muddled' (Schilpp, p. 684). But G's position seems more complex toward Einstein's immediately preceding assertion: 'Epistemology without contact with science becomes an empty scheme.'

In the first place, G rarely spoke of epistemology, but was more concerned with philosophy or metaphysics. This may in part be a matter of terminology, but only in part. While G recognized that science is suggestive for philosophical reflections, he appears to imply also that pure thought could penetrate into philosophy as an autonomous discipline. At any rate, G viewed philosophy (and metaphysics) as capable of arriving at a separable theory (that embodies the fundamental truth) in the end, even if familiarity with some (rudimentary) science may be a prerequisite. Moreover, G seems to view epistemology as a secondary aspect of philosophy not to be considered except as such. In terms of the differing views of Newton and Leibniz on dynamics, G was in favor of a richer concept of force (than Newton's) that belongs, as with Leibniz, to the fundamental discipline of metaphysics. According to G, while philosophy analyzes the fundamental concepts, science only uses them.

Evidently Einstein considered himself equally capable in physics and philosophy but decided that a primary concentration on physics would be more rewarding. Moreover, according to his position, I think, epistemology can be more fruitfully pursued and more effectively communicated within the context of fundamental science. For example, Einstein spoke with approval of attempts 'to treat my occasional utterances of epistemological content systematically' (Schilpp, p. 683). Hence, it would seem possible to view these treatments (ibid., pp. 357–408) as a formulation of Einstein's theory of knowledge and his conception of science. Nonetheless, the formulation involves frequently and essentially references to Einstein's thoughts in physics; it does not take the form of a direct statement (such as was done by Leibniz in his *Monadology*) of Einstein's philosophical position.

In my opinion, if one were to distill from it such a statement, the result would be less cogent and open to a great deal more misunderstanding. Also in G's published philosophical writings, we find the same intimate connection between his philosophical assertions and the relevant scientific facts that clarify and render more definite their meaning.

In other words, I am inclined to think there is a special problem of formulation and communication in philosophy that calls for a different way of presentation from science. G told me that he had not yet succeeded in formulating a direct statement of his philosophical position, but had only advanced so far as to be able to apply it in special contexts (such as commenting on the manuscript of my *MP*). I often wonder whether G was not looking for a kind of formulation that is inappropriate or even impossible in philosophy. This is related to my skepticism about G's quest for an exact theory in philosophy that is comparable to Newton's in physics. I doubt that our correct or at least reasonable thoughts on the most basic concepts can all be formulated without residue and unambiguously in a set of 'axioms,' or otherwise in terms of general statements detached from explicit connection with familiar 'gross facts' in science and everyday life (which are, I believe, the most stable and reliable communicable parts of our experience). If G's project is feasible, then it would seem to be a sort of science that is even more exciting than fruitful work in fundamental science, although it is presumably also more difficult. If it is not believed to be possible, then the distinctive attraction of philosophy, whether or not it be deceptive, has to be sought elsewhere. In the exceptional case of G and Einstein, many have said or are likely to say that both of them in their later lives pursued (along different directions) unrealistic (and therefore mistaken) goals. But one has to wait for the judgment of history to learn whether this was indeed so.

Einstein's and G's different conceptions of philosophy have much to do with their scientific work and preferences. G moved from theoretical physics to mathematical logic in quest of precision. Einstein considered it a good fortune to have, at the age of 12 to 16, familiarized himself with mathematics through 'books which were not too particular in their logical rigor, but which made up for this by permitting the main thoughts to stand out clearly and synoptically' (Schilpp, p. 15). G's scientific results are sharper and cleaner, while Einstein's may be said to be richer in content and involved in more complex contexts. Their conceptions may be seen as natural projections of their scientific work. While G apparently thought a comparable precision possible in philosophy, Einstein was presumably struck by the decreased precision and increased meaning as one moves from mathematics to physics (and analogously, from physics to philosophy).

It is (also) clear from their attitude toward quantum theory (see below) that neither G nor Einstein was in favor of positivism. G's position on this matter is familiar. Einstein did favor and influence positivism in the context of his special relativity, but he would undoubtedly agree with G that 'the fruitfulness of the positivistic point of view in this case is due to a very exceptional circumstance' (MP, p. 12). For example, according to Einstein, the aim of all physics is 'the complete description of any (individual) real situation (as it supposedly exists irrespective of any action of observation or substantiation). Whenever the positivistically inclined modern physicist hears such a formulation his reaction is that of a pitying smile' (Schilpp, p. 667). In stating their own positions, however, Einstein appears to allow the mind more room for free creation than G.

Consider the following two passages (ibid., pp. 674 and 669) in Einstein's reply to his critics:

> [My theoretical attitude] is distinct from that of Kant only by the fact that we do not conceive of the "categories" as unalterable (conditioned by the nature of the understanding) but as (in the logical sense) free conventions. They appear to be a priori only insofar as thinking without the positing of categories and of concepts in general would be as impossible as breathing in a vacuum.
>
> "Being" is always something which is mentally constructed by us, that is, something which we freely posit (in the logical sense). The justification of such constructs does not lie in their derivation from what is given by the senses. Such a type of derivation (in the sense of logical derivability) is nowhere to be had, not even in the domain of pre-scientific thinking.

I am sure that G would object to the three phrases 'free conventions,' 'mentally constructed by us,' and 'freely posit.' But I am not sure how much of the disagreement is substantive rather than terminological and somewhat extraneously psychological. An analogous distinction is G's insistence that concepts do not change; only our perceptions of them change. For instance, Einstein also said, 'To him who is a discoverer in this field [theoretical physics], the products of his imagination appear so necessary and natural that he regards them, and would like to have them regarded by others, not as creations of thought but as given realities' (Ideas and Opinions, p. 270). Presumably it makes little difference for most purposes whether we choose to speak of discovery or creation. But I believe G's definite preference of thinking in terms of discovery is connected with a strong desire for Sicherheit (certainty and security) in the sense of being assured of an ultimate court of appeal. Apart from this, I do not see, for example, that convergence of our changing perceptions (of fixed concepts) is more discernible than that of our changing concepts. But I am probably missing something substantive in the disagreement that is more subtle and could only be appreciated in a fully developed philosophy.

Of quantum physics, G says that the present 'two level' theory (with its 'quantization' of a 'classical system,' and its divergent series) is admittedly very unsatisfactory (*MP*, p. 13). There are more extensive reports on Einstein's dissatisfaction with quantum mechanics as a 'complete' theory. While it is often said that he wanted determinism, Pauli stresses that his ideas have nothing to do with determinism, but more to do with his belief in realism. (See Max Born, *The Einstein-Born Correspondence*, 1971, pp. 221– 226.) Einstein does not deny that the uncertainty principle is conclusively 'demonstrated' and expects a satisfactory theory to contain the formal relations given in quantum physics as consequences (Schilpp, pp. 666– 667). According to Pauli, he believes and requires that a macrobody always has a quasi-sharply defined position in the 'objective description of reality.' In Einstein's own words, 'In the macroscopic sphere it simply is considered certain that one must adhere to the program of a realistic description in space and time' (Schilpp, p. 671). It seems that he looks for a complete theory in which quantum theory is seen as an ensemble description, while his opponents wish to adhere to quantum theory also in its (apparently yet unobserved) consequences for macrobodies: 'A macrobody has in principle to show diffraction (interference) phenomena, and the difficulties are going to be *technical* because of the small size of the wavelength' (Pauli, quoted in Born, p. 222).

A familiar impact of general relativity on philosophy was the widely publicized idea that it disproves Kant's theory of our spatial intuition and its relation to geometry. This has often been accompanied also by an inclination to doubt or even refuse all appeals to intuition. But, as we know, the actual situation is somewhat more complex. According to G, 'In geometry, the meaning usually adopted today refers to physics rather than to mathematical intuition and that, therefore, a decision [as to whether Euclid's fifth postulate is true] falls outside the range of mathematics' (BP, p. 271). In a letter (October 1973) to M. J. Greenberg (p. 250 of his *Euclidean and non-Euclidean Geometries*, 1980, second edition), G wrote, 'Geometrical intuition, strictly speaking, is not mathematical, but rather a priori physical intuition. In its purely mathematical aspect our Euclidean space intuition is perfectly correct, namely, it represents correctly a certain structure existing in the realm of mathematical objects. Even physically it is correct "in the small."'

In the 1940s G worked on the relation between Kant's philosophy and relativity theory and suggested that both may be seen as leaning toward the idealistic view that time and change are not real. A short version of his views was given in his paper honoring Einstein (Schilpp, pp. 557–562), which mentioned also his new solutions of Einstein's field equations. In his reply (p. 687) Einstein called the work 'an important contribution to the general theory of relativity, especially to the analysis of the concept of time,' but declined altogether to discuss 'the relation of the theory of relativity to idealistic philosophy or any philosophical formulation of questions.' (For a more extended consideration of this aspect of G's work, compare section 6.5.)

In his two letters to Seelig (autumn 1955), G discussed his own work in relativity theory as well as his ideas on some directions of further development (Seelig, pp. 421–423):

> My own work on the theory of relativity relates to the pure theory of gravitation published in 1916 which, I believe, was left, not only by Einstein himself but also by the whole generation of contemporary physicists, in its state of a torso, physically, mathematically, and with respect to its application in cosmology.
>
> Regarding the further development of the pure theory of gravitation, which I spoke of in my last letter, I do not mean an extension in the sense that the theory should comprehend a broader range of facts, but a mathematical analysis of the equations which would make it possible to take hold of their solutions systematically and to recognize general properties of the solutions. So far we do not even know the analogue of the fundamental integral formulas of the Newtonian theory, which, in my opinion, must unquestionably exist. If such integral formulas as well as other mathematical formulas had a direct physical meaning, then the physical understanding of the theory would thereby be deepened as well. Conversely a more precise analysis of the physical content could lead to such mathematical theorems. Einstein did not exactly abstain from such pursuits, at least the first (of the two), but he was hardly optimistic about them.—The reason why I myself have not undertaken to pursue these problems is simply that they are very remote from my own area of work, namely that of logic and foundational studies, and on the other hand so difficult that they would demand the total working power of a mathematician. I have nevertheless for a period occupied myself, in connection with certain philosophical problems, with a less difficult complex of problems from the general theory of relativity, viz., with cosmology. The fact that here as a novice to the domain of relativity theory I could quickly produce essentially new results appears to me to prove sufficiently the unfinished state of the theory.

In reply to my inquiry about the 'integral formulas' in the above quotation, Howard Stein told me that the existence of a set of 'universal global integrals' for Newtonian mechanics is asserted in the conservation laws and closely connected with the spatial and temporal invariance of the Newtonian laws: 'The absence of universal space-time symmetries in general relativity means that no analogously derived integral theorems are there available; and what Gödel clearly hopes for is "a mathematical analysis of the equations" of Einstein's theory that would lead to *some* kind of general theorems about the structure of their solutions, in the sense in which the conservation laws are general theorems about the structure of the solutions to the Newtonian equations.'

It has often been asked whether one can get a Gödel theorem for physics. For instance, in 1979, F. Dyson said, 'Forty-eight years ago, Kurt Gödel, who afterward became one of Einstein's closest friends, proved that the world of pure mathematics is inexhaustible.... It is my hope that we may be able to prove the world of physics as inexhaustible as the world of mathematics' (Woolf, p. 379). Since physics uses enough mathematics to carry out G's proof, there is an obvious sense in which physics is incompletable. But we need a different concept of completeness to capture the idea of the (in)exhaustibility of physics. Dyson spoke of some physicists thinking 'that they are coming close to a complete understanding of the basic laws of nature.' It is clear that one first step toward proving the 'inexhaustibility' of 'physics' calls for clarifying the two concepts appearing in the problem.

Straus continued with Dyson's idea: 'One, I think was mentioned by Professor Dyson yesterday: the idea that an ultimate theory, which Einstein obviously very strongly had in mind, would be something almost as unattractive as the idea of converting all mathematicians into some kind of glorified computer using Hilbert's algorithm, which Gödel had effectively killed' (ibid., pp. 484–485). [This is not quite correct since there was no 'Hilbert's algorithm' to kill, except in the hypothetical sense that Hilbert asked for and might even have expected complete formal systems in mathematics and a decision procedure for elementary logic. It was to Hilbert's credit that he formulated the problem in fairly precise terms for G to settle.]

Straus went on to paraphrase Einstein's reply to the question what would be left for physicists to do. 'Well, if the ultimate theory is established, then physics will be in the situation in which mathematics is now. That is to say, then you start proving theorems. At the moment what the great physicists do is look for axioms. Mathematicians don't do that. They have axioms and look for theorems.' This observation leaves out the exceptional case of the search for new axioms in set theory. It also reminds one of G's project of looking for axioms in metaphysics.

G considers Newton's physics to be an exact axiomatic theory. Indeed, it had been regarded as the ultimate theory for a long time, when physicists only looked for 'theorems' in Newton's system. The continuing quest (by Einstein and others) for an ultimate theory in the sense of a unified theory reveals an awareness of essential incompletion, which had been lacking for two centuries or so with respect to Newton's theory. If Newton's theory had been mistakenly thought to be the ultimate theory for such a long time, what will prevent the repetition of such a mistake (on a higher level), if and when the community of physicists will believe that they have obtained a unified theory? G's wish to 'do to metaphysics as much as Newton did to physics' (*MP*, p. 85) suggests a distinction between 'exhausting' physics or metaphysics and discovering its 'backbone.' In other words, since Newton's physics is not the ultimate theory, G was not looking for an ultimate theory in metaphysics, but a sort of backbone. G's own philosophical position appears not to exclude the possibility that while mathematics is inexhaustible, physics may turn out to be 'exhaustible' in some appropriately significant sense. I have, however, no idea what sort of sense that might be. It seems more plausible to me that while being able to believe what one is striving for to be the ultimate theory may increase one's devotion to the pursuit, it is hardly a rational projection from empirical evidence.

In 1952 a philosophy student at Brown University wrote to Einstein to ask for a brief note of guidance. In reply (9 December) Einstein commented on the place of empirical knowledge in theoretical work: 'It is true that the grasping of truth is not possible without empirical basis. However, the deeper we penetrate and the more extensive and embracing our theories become the less empirical knowledge is needed to determine those theories' (*Albert Einstein, the Human Side*, selected and edited by H. Dukas and B. Hoffmann, 1979, p. 29). The spirit of this observation may be seen to agree with G's idea that in doing fundamental philosophy no extensive empirical knowledge is needed.

On 27 January 1921, Einstein responded to a question on the nature of Art and Science (ibid., pp. 37–38): 'Where the world ceases to be the scene of our personal hopes and wishes, where we face it as free beings admiring, asking, and observing, there we enter the realm of Art and Science. If what is seen and experienced is communicated in the language of logic, we are engaged in science. If it is communicated through forms whose connections are not accessible to the conscious mind but are recognized intuitively as meaningful, then we are engaged in art. Common to both is the loving devotion to that which transcends personal concerns and volition.'

The statement emphasizes a 'free' state that leaves behind the worries for food and shelter as well as the hopes and fears accompanying emotional entanglements in human relations; clearly such a state can only be more or less one aspect of real life. The contrast between Art and Science is sensibly characterized in terms of their different forms of communication. There is more similarity in the process of pursuing the one or the other. In both cases we implicitly obey logic, and we hover between the conscious and the unconscious, the articulate and the inarticulate (even when conscious).

But Art as a different type of communication further depends (more strongly) on intuition, as can be seen from the fact that it needs a much more
complex procedure for paraphrasing and building upon existing artistic
creations. The process of learning to appreciate Art is also quite different
from Science. To borrow a term from Russell, one may say that intuition
yields 'knowledge by acquaintance,' which occupies a more conspicuous
place in Art, both in its creation and in its appreciation. In cultivating and
applying our intuition it seems that generally it is more satisfactory to
begin with a larger whole (e.g., intuition in its manifestations in diverse
areas rather than just in knowledge). Otherwise, it will be hard to pull the
separately acquired moments (or aspects) together.

In 1937, undoubtedly with the situation of Germany in mind, Einstein
remarked, 'Politics is a pendulum whose swings between anarchy and
tyranny are fueled by perennially rejuvenated illusions' (ibid., p. 37). We
certainly cannot call this a priori truth. As an empirical generalization it
is of interest even though its 'verification' would be a complex affair. It
goes without saying that 'illusions' are an important part of human reality,
and not only in politics.

5.2 Comments on the following chapters

The remaining chapters are a preliminary attempt to sort out my agreements and disagreements with Gödel, as promised in BA (pp. 23–24, note
21). The task has turned out to be much more formidable than I had
expected before I worked out the facts (reported in part I) and the conversations (to be organized and included in CG). What I say on philosophy in
this part can only be viewed as a tentative sketch, which will, I hope and
expect, be reconsidered in the context of a more direct exposition of my
own views.

There is no question of disagreeing with G's admirable scientific work
and its immediate interaction with his philosophical views (both as a
heuristic and as consequences). It is only when a successful approach in one
domain is 'projected' beyond the domain that we have an issue of how far
and in what manner the projection is justifiable. By entering deeply into
one aspect of the experience of a culture, one penetrates, I believe (like G, I
think), a central region that enhances the understanding of all aspects of
human experience. For example, a more adequate understanding of the
nature of mathematics, by revealing more and richer common features with
other intellectual and artistic activities, sheds greater light on the roles
played in all cultural endeavors by intuitions, idealizations, metaphors, and
empirical evidence. That is why, if these features are seen from an appropriate perspective, a greater penetration into one area need not separate it
more drastically from others but rather help to combat fragmentation and

superficial conflict between different philosophical positions. Where I seem to disagree with G is my less audacious outlook of wishing to pay attention also to the specificity of different fundamental districts of our cumulative experience, contrary to his apparent belief in the overwhelming centrality of the mathematical experience.

In philosophy I find appealing G's recommendation to be selective (confining oneself to the essential), precise, unprejudiced (open-minded), tentative, and (yet) audacious. But these virtues are subject to varied interpretations. G seems to aim at the level of precision that is attained in mathematics. If achieved, the other virtues would all receive a more definite guidance, criterion, and formulation. But even *his* philosophical work is not precise in this strong sense, and I doubt that such an ideal is on the whole realistic in philosophy. A less objective and restrictive concept of precision is 'to paint only what one sees clearly.' The ability to see clearly and to paint well varies from person to person and, of the same person, from time to time. Moreover, clarity shares with precision most of its ambiguities. Nonetheless, precision in this sense is a pregnant and forceful standard well worth frequent consultations, especially when one departs from the charted courses in philosophy.

All five recommended virtues are relative to what one begins with, and they acquire greater significance from a more adequate outlook on what is central or certain. G has a highly developed sense of the different degrees of centrality and certainty (especially in mathematics). Being selective, open-minded, tentative, or audacious is governed by the idea of developing and structuring his worldview in such a way as to increase its certainty (and clarity) by weighted penetrations into and arrangements of selected points according to the interrelated degrees of centrality and certainty of all the components. I agree with this idea, but, since what I begin with is different, the incomplete picture I have and the more complete picture I look for are different from G's.

G and I agree, I think, in believing that empirical inductions are important for doing philosophy, not only in predicting the future (which is involved in G's 'rationalistic optimism' and in estimating which approaches to philosophy will turn out to be more fruitful) but also in evaluating what are (to be) taken as facts (as to their degrees of importance, certainty, etc.). But since he and I start with different bases (for reasons it would be of interest to determine), our priorities differ and we make different 'probability calculations.' The striking instances have to do with G's bidding defiance to the widely shared 'modern' skepticism toward the supernatural (which is to him a part of the 'prejudices of the time'). He says, I am not sure how seriously, that the 'spirits' were more active in antiquity than they are today. More significant and relevant is his prediction of the emergence of (religious) metaphysics as an exact theory before long (*MP*, p. 85), on the ground that past failures in this direction were caused by the less advanced state of science and the prejudices either of 'materialism' (in more recent times) or of (erroneous) theology (in earlier times).

It seems clear to me that G would essentially agree with my criticism of 'analytic empiricism' and the sketched alternative view of mathematics in *BA* (summarized on pp. 10−26). But I am not able to convince myself of the universal applicability of G's mathematical or conceptual realism. G expresses his sympathy with Plato by saying that he is, like Plato, a 'rationalist' and an 'idealist,' and his antipathy toward Aristotle by calling him an 'empiricist' and a 'materialist.' I believe that I attach more importance than G to the contingent and the unpredictable, feel a greater need to be down to earth, care more about what is this-worldly, and recognize more of the basically new human experiences (acquired after the days of Plato or Leibniz) as philosophically relevant. [It has been said that Plato represents the highest form of unity of Apollonian (intellectually centered, more in the early and late dialogues) and Dionysiac (the emotional or mystic, more in the middle dialogues) humanism. G's philosophy appears to point to a similar combination, except that it is hard to imagine Plato striving for 'philosophy as an exact theory' or G writing extended 'poetic' passages.]

If A and B are concerned with attaining different things (say C and D) in philosophy, one may still ask whether C is more significant or more likely to be attainable than D. But it is probable that A simply finds C to be more valuable than D, and we have a disagreement on a different level. Moreover, if neither C nor D is attained or attainable, then it remains possible that B will recognize what A attains by aiming at C to be more significant than what is attained by B by aiming at D. In addition, it may be that A views C (and B views D) as the best means of reaching a shared goal E. There is then the question whether A and B will contribute more toward E by pursuing C or D. Implicit in this complex of abstract alternatives is also a reference to community or communities of which A and B may be thought to be members. Their contributions may be taken as parts of cooperative efforts. The general outlooks of A or B may be congenial or unacceptable to one or another of the communities to which A and B belong. A natural and notoriously difficult question is why A and B disagree (in terms of temperament, character, upbringing, class background, wish, total experience, etc.).

This involved list of questions and possibilities shows how hard it is to evaluate a thoughtful and distinctive approach to philosophy like G's. He seems to find little that is relevant to philosophy in the historical experience since the beginning of the eighteenth century, the exception being the advances in the exact sciences and perhaps Husserl's quest for a method. Moreover, he has little faith in the basic accuracy of written history. According to him, the crucial task is to understand the individual by understanding oneself, and, for this purpose, what is needed is primarily introspection. It is a very attractive idea that each of us possesses all the necessary data and true philosophy is merely a matter of seeing things clearly by the right kind of thinking (or the proper exercise of one's own pure reason). When you understand yourself, he says, you understand everything (i.e., including society and history). Clearly solid achievements along the line of 'Know thyself' by introspection are important for oneself and, if adequately communicated, for others as well. They are also of more permanent value to the extent that they are more fundamental in the sense of being less dependent on other factors than the 'superstructures.' G recognizes that using this special mode of 'philosophical thinking' in everyday life is generally harmful. Only the fruits of such thinking are directly relevant to G's belief that good philosophy is widely helpful.

But social relations include components that are hardly graspable merely by understanding a 'typical' individual, and to understand an individual person, as a 'social animal,' much depends on seeing interrelations of different persons. Indeed, in certain respects typically others have a better knowledge of a person than he has of himself. Moreover, we are all very far from fully understanding ourselves and from being able to communicate fully the understanding. G seems to share with Leibniz the belief that every person is a windowless monad. Hence, facing the obvious separation of wish and fact in one's life, the familiar remedy of partially identifying oneself with a community or a country or mankind is less effectual for him, and he seems to have to appeal to the belief in a next life.

Perhaps I can consider G's philosophy by distinguishing several levels. There is the moderately well-developed objectivism in mathematics, which I find attractive and convincing. When the objectivism is extended to concepts that are taken to be always precise and permanently fixed, I find the 'idealization' too strong and too remote from our familiar experience with concepts. Related to his conception of concepts is the part of his views that he attributes to Husserl. He says that he does not like Husserl's complicated way of doing philosophy and that Husserl requires able followers, as talented as or more talented than Husserl. But this need of able followers would seem to throw doubt on Husserl's avowed ideal of philosophy as a rigorous science, to the extent that science can also be pursued fruitfully by less able practitioners. In addition, G looks for an exact or axiomatic theory in philosophy and thinks that it is also Husserl's aim. But G's conception of metaphysics as first philosophy includes centrally the concepts of God and soul. It appears clear that this religious component is not part of Husserl's conception of philosophy. G has the ideal of a good and rational religion that would directly and convincingly reach each individual, who, as a windowless monad, would see that reason prevails on the whole, potentialities will be realized, and good deeds will be appropriately rewarded. Nobody can deny the desirability of such a religion, but most of us would, I think, look for approximations to such an ideal by somehow merging the individual with a larger part of the universe (typically with mankind or segments thereof).

Reductionism and 'deductionism': In terms of methodology, I am sympathetic with one important aspect of G's approach. Let me call it 'deductionism,' which is an opposite of reductionism. Numerals can be replaced by (or reduced to) strings or strokes, and numerical formulas by (or to) formulas in elementary logic. But the 'conceptual gain' is accompanied by a loss in efficiency, and in our thought we continue to think of numbers in terms of the familiar notation. (For extended discussions of this matter, see *MP*, chapter 7, and Wittgenstein, *Remarks on the Foundations of Mathematics*.) A more familiar case is the reduction of mathematics to logic or rather set theory. If, as G sometimes does, we consider the nature of mathematics by using set theory as its substitute, we are adopting a mixture of reductionism and deductionism. Since the domain of sets is more comprehensive than the domain of numbers (and their functions), we are in one sense looking at a richer area that contains branches of mathematics as special cases. This kind of practice is what I call 'deductionism.' On the other hand, set theory is also poorer in the sense that in it our number-theoretic and geometrical intuitions are lost or at least concealed. If one disregards these essential components in the replaced (or eliminated) regions, I would consider it a case of practicing 'reductionism.' For example, G recommends expounding objectivism by concentrating on natural numbers (rather than sets) because we have stronger intuition of them and they are less controversial. I would, therefore, say that G is not a reductionist in this case.

My intention is to contrast the preoccupation with 'economy' (or the hasty drive toward a 'nothing but' conclusion) and the choice to begin with the richer or more comprehensive situation that includes the simpler or more specific ones as a special case. Familiar examples of reductionism include behaviorism, reductivist physicalism (rather than 'physicalism without reductionism'; see below), economic determinism (in its dogmatic form), 'scientism' (or the reduction of all types of reason to technical reason), etc. It is the exclusiveness that I find objectionable. A related idea is the belief that by achieving one thing (for instance, by getting power), the rest will take care of itself. In real life, it is of course desirable to select and focus on some important and feasible task, but at the same time one need not lose sight of the limited significance of the task. Indeed, the attempt to take a longer view is surely one of the things that distinguish philosophy from politics or journalism.

The ideal of 'deductionism' suffers the disadvantage of having to attend directly to the richer and more complex situation. One example is Leibniz's choice, endorsed by G, of endowing all monads with life and consciousness. Another example is to start with change and take the fixed as a special case. Yet another suggestive but hard-to-execute idea is to begin with 'praxis': If philosophy 'starts with the fact, it places itself inside the world of existence and of finitude and will find it hard to discover the way that leads from there to the infinite and suprasensual; if it begins from action it will stand at the point where the two worlds meet and from which they can both be seen at a glance' (Fichte, *Werke*, vol. 3, p. 52, from the second introduction to *Wissenschaftslehre*). One more illustration is to assimilate truth to metaphor. A metaphor transfers a term to something 'to which it is not properly applicable.' Since we are completely accurate only in exceptional cases, most of the time we as a matter of fact speak in terms of metaphors that, if apt, stir us to actions directed at refining and grasping (what is true in) the metaphor. Instead of viewing the metaphorical as a deviation from truth, it may be more liberating to regard truth as a limiting (special) case of the metaphorical.

What I take to be a primary instance of G's deductionism is his statement that the clear and natural concept of existence is in what is taken to be its broadest or weakest sense. Tables and chairs, nucleic acids and proteins, elementary particles and quarks, numbers and sets, concepts, minds, mythological characters: all of them exist, but not always in the physical space. 'Didn't the Moloch of the ancients hold sway? Wasn't the Delphic Apollo a real power in the life of the Greeks? In this context Kant's criticism is meaningless' (Marx, in the appendix to his doctoral dissertation).

Reduction and reductionism are commonly associated with several distinct ideas. Nobody can deny that it increases our understanding to see that numbers can be 'reduced to' sets (or that genes are certain large molecules). But, contrary to one sense of 'reductionism,' the 'reduction' does not imply that numbers do not exist, or that the meaning of numbers (our intentions regarding them) are exhausted by their corresponding sets, or that we should or would stop working with numbers. According to Engels, 'Chemical action is not possible without change of temperature and electric charges, organic life without mechanical, molecular, chemical, thermal, electric changes, etc. But the presence of these subsidiary forms does not exhaust the essence of the main form in each case. One day we shall certainly "reduce" thought experimentally to molecular and chemical motions in the brain; but does that exhaust the essence of thought?' (*Dialectic of Nature*, written between 1872 and 1882, trans. J. B. S. Haldane, 1940, pp. 174–175.) If one wishes, the position asserted by Engels may be described as 'physicalism without reductionism.' G questions the prediction in the first half of the last sentence, but undoubtedly accepts the implied negative answer to the concluding question.

Reductionism sometimes includes the belief that it is pointless to study life directly in addition to investigating its chemistry and physics (or, in the case of G, to study society directly besides striving to know oneself), because it leads to no real knowledge. This general belief can hardly be true under all circumstances, and seems to me to be a prejudiced projection from some isolated and partially digested evidence to what is largely unknown. In terms of the somewhat indefinite contrast between reductionism and deductionism, I am suggesting that I would like to be a more consistent deductionist than G. (I trust I have said enough in *BA* and in this book to distinguish this deductionist attitude from what are known in the literature as holism and gradualism.)

This attitude presupposes the condition of paying attention to the specificity of each of the major special cases of a covering scheme. In *BA* I have tried to list (pp. 37–44) some of my vague thoughts by introducing the metaphorical and barbarous term 'phenomenography.' It now seems better to me to shorten it to 'phenography' (by analogy to 'phenotype'). The task of endowing the name with some fairly definite content remains remote from accomplishment. Given the wish to be comprehensive and to shun reductionism, it is not very surprising that the enterprise of selecting and organizing the essentials tends to go in all directions. In each direction I am often impressed and overwhelmed by the richness and the depth of human experience, as well as by the attractive manner in which it is communicated. Reflecting on G's thoughts helps me to some extent to focus my attention in those areas where there is more of a shared interest. But the range of the focus is somewhat limited, since I am also centrally concerned with areas that G takes to be derivative or nonessential.

G's ambitious ideal of doing to metaphysics what Newton did to physics (by giving an 'axiomatic theory,' correct in its essentials) appears at first sight to offer a more effective focal point for directing his work. But even though the ideal sounds moderately definite, the ways to reach it, which, according to G, involve seeing things clearly and pointing out what is seen, are not nearly so definite. By his own judgment, he has not even determined what the primitive concepts are, not to say found the right 'axioms' for them. Indeed, he seems to have diligently looked for guidance or suggestions from the writings of Leibniz, Husserl, and, to a lesser extent, some other philosophers. He undoubtedly has a cultivated sense of what to disregard, so that he can make more progress than others. But even such an advantage is not of much help when the ideal is as ambitious (and unrealistic, I would conjecture) as his is. This of course does not rule out the high probability that his partial results toward the ideal may be of significance philosophically or scientifically.

Being religious (a 'theist') and believing in the possibility of developing a good and rational theology (or religious metaphysics), G has a more detached outlook and a more unified program. Through religion one has a direct connection to the universe, so that social considerations become secondary and derivative. It is when religion is given up as beyond the reach of reason that philosophy loses one of its principal unifying principles. G appears to wish to continue from where Newton and Leibniz left off and to believe that the historical course after the seventeenth century has regressed rather than progressed, except for the increase in information (but not of real understanding) in mathematics and the natural sciences (and in some other areas). While he uses Newton's physics as a model, his philosophical sympathy is with Leibniz. He is not satisfied with Newton's understanding of the physical concepts, but wishes to continue Leibniz's attempt to analyze the concepts deeper so that the physical concepts are merged with the truly primitive concepts of metaphysics. Hence, in particular, he is not satisfied with Kant's 'metaphysical foundations' of (Newtonian rather than Leibnizian) physics.

Once it is admitted that religion is beyond the reach of pure reason, philosophy becomes more ramified. Not only could cosmological and moral problems be taken as subordinate to religious metaphysics, even art and music once derived much of their inspiration from religion. Given his adherence to the spirit of the Enlightenment, Kant adds to Leibniz's investigations of the foundations of mathematics and natural science separate studies of morality, esthetics, and 'universal history.' Kant's double-talk on and lip service to religion can hardly satisfy any serious thinker, and G seems to accuse him of insincerity. (For example, at the beginning of *Religion within the Limit of Reason Alone*, Kant says, 'For its own sake morality does not need religion at all ... indeed, the man who finds it needful ... to look about him for some [ulterior] end, is, by this very fact already contemptible.')

Marx, using some of Hegel's ideas, unambiguously eliminated religion from his worldview and brought human aspirations back to the this-world by putting history in the place of religion. No philosophy of comparable power and comprehensiveness has appeared since, and Marxism has remained to this day a major force in politics and in philosophy. Unlike the philosophies of Leibniz and Gödel, community and society occupy as decisive a position as the individual in the philosophies of Kant and Marx; but Marx went beyond Kant by proposing a plausible program to use social practice to mediate between history and the individual.

G sees in Husserl's work a method of refining and consolidating Leibniz's monadology and believes that a careful reflection on one's everyday experience will lead to a metaphysics that provides both science and religion with a more dependable rational foundation. It is likely that he also finds Freud's work helpful in developing further Leibniz's psychological reflections. I would like to modify his program by leaving out religion and the quest for an 'axiomatic theory,' and adding considerations directly relevant to art, society, and history.

Chapter 6
Concepts in science and technology

Gödel's work straddles (fundamental) science and philosophy; for him both deal with basic conceptual problems and both strive for the discovery of axiomatic theories. The difference between them is, according to him, that philosophy analyzes concepts and science uses concepts, but the two kinds of activity are strongly interconnected in fundamental studies of both areas. Viewed in this light, G's fundamental contributions may be described as attempts both to develop axiomatic theories of sets and concepts as well as in metaphysics, and to examine closely the power and limit of an especially transparent species of axiomatic theories, the formal systems (or the mechanical axiomatic theories), with respect to elementary logic and arithmetic. In addition, his work on constructible sets may be taken as giving an axiomatic theory that is, though not a formal system, of a fairly definite form, and has been seen to be inadequate to capturing the full content of set theory.

In practice, G began with great successes in dealing with formal systems and moved, by what I call 'propitious projections,' to the more ambitious programs of looking for axiomatic theories in uncharted regions. There is an analogy with Hilbert's advance from successes in special areas of mathematics to his bold (and unrealistic, as shown later by G) program on the foundations of mathematics, by way of a digression into physics, particularly a serious flirtation with Einstein's impressive general relativity theory (see Pais, pp. 257−260). But G has not formulated sharp enough problems about his program on metaphysics to invite or admit any disproof comparable to what he did to Hilbert's program. (By the way, it may be of interest to contrast the different orientations of Hilbert's digression into physics with G's three decades later.)

As G fully realized in the early 1930s, the concept of formal systems is intimately connected with the concept of mechanical procedures, and he considers Turing's work of 1936 as an important completion of his work on the limits of formalization (see *MP*, pp. 84−85). It is through this avenue that G's work comes into contact with technology and appears to begin drawing public attention almost on a scale comparable to Einstein's work (as illustrated by Hofstadter's *Gödel, Escher, Bach*, 1979). Related to this is the direct or indirect influence of G's work on the areas known as computer science and artificial intelligence. In addition, G's work in this direction is seen to be evidence for (rather than against) 'mechanism' (or even 'finitism'!) by Judson C. Webb (in his *Mechanism, Mentalism and Metamathematics*, 1980).

Within the limited field of mathematical logic, G's presence is of course conspicuous. Nobody can deny that he is the greatest logician of the century, whose work is at the very center of the whole field. But, like Hilbert, his interest in the foundations of mathematics was strongly motivated by a belief that basic advances in this area should in some way revolutionize the whole field of (pure) mathematics, perhaps as Einstein's work did to physics. In this respect the outcome has been, I am afraid, rather disappointing. This may perhaps be taken as a confirmation of Einstein's early insight that (even) at the turn of the century mathematics was more fragmented than physics (Schilpp 1949, p. 15). Later Einstein spoke of G's work as a disproof of this belief of his (see, e.g., Holton and Elkana, 1982, bottom of p. 422). But most mathematicians would not accept the implied judgment that G's work occupies a place in mathematics comparable with Einstein's in physics. G's work has had little effect on the research practice and the conception of mathematics of the majority of mathematicians. Surprisingly the larger impact is more on conceptual issues having to do with computers and mechanization, which are a central concern of current technology.

Roughly speaking, G's major mathematical work, leaving aside that on intuitionist arithmetic, can be summarized under three headings: (1) CL, or the completeness of elementary logic (work done in 1929, paper published in 1930; compare section 10.1); (2) IA, or the incompleteness of arithmetic (work done in 1930, paper published in 1931; compare section 10.2); (3) CS, or constructible sets (invention and applications of constructible sets, work done by 1938, paper published in 1939). In particular, the results of (1) completeness and (2) incompleteness are of central importance to the whole idea of the axiomatic method and the entire enterprise of formalization. While (1) proves that elementary logic can be formalized, (2) shows that mathematics cannot. Since (2) demonstrates that the precise concept of formal systems cannot capture all of the attractive features of the vague intuitive (traditional) concept of axiomatic systems, it suggests a distinction between formal systems and axiomatic theories.

6.1 Computers and mechanical procedures

The most familiar mechanical procedures are household computations and the operations of simple machines. Of the physical machines, the mathematical (or 'informational' or 'software') component is especially conspicuous in devices like telephones, elevators, and, of course, computers. With regard to the contrast between numerical computations and symbol manipulations (or nonnumerical data processing), Frege's rules (of 1879) for elementary logic (or the familiar test procedures in Boolean algebra or the propositional calculus) may be taken to be an impressive basic (and early) example of the latter, comparable in significance to the place of household arithmetic in the former. For instance, in the spring of 1960 several programming languages for symbolic manipulations were presented at a conference, all using as illustration a particular algorithm for the propositional calculus (compare the special issue of *Communications of the Association for Computing Machinery*, vol. 3, April 1960).

Frege's rules were developed further in *PM* (1910) to derive nearly four hundred theorems. They were shown to be complete by G in 1929, and the question whether a proposition in the language is deducible from these rules was shown to be undecidable (see below) in 1936. In 1958 I wrote some programs by which all the consequences of these rules given in *PM* are proved quickly on a relatively primitive (by today's standard) computer (the IBM 704) (see *IBM Journal*, vol. 4, 1960, pp. 2–22; reprinted in my *Survey*, pp. 224–268). Along a different direction, elementary geometry, or rather elementary real algebra (the theory of ordered real closed fields, a natural formalized version of Dedekind's theory R) was shown (by an extension of Sturm's theorem) to be decidable (in principle) around 1930 (see Kreisel, p. 166), and undecidable in practice in the 1970s. Recently Wen-Tsun Wu introduced a feasible algorithm (which, by the way, may be viewed conveniently in the framework of Hilbert's *Grundlagen der Geometrie* of 1899) that applies to a major part of elementary geometry and proves many hard theorems (see the reports by Wu and S. C. Chou in *Automated Theorem Proving*, ed. W. W. Bledsoe and D. W. Loveland, 1984).

Regarding the concept of a mechanical procedure, G's incompleteness theorems naturally called for a precise definition by which one could say that they apply to any formal system, i.e., any system in which being a proof can be checked by a mechanical procedure. Indeed, Hilbert's program included also the Entscheidungsproblem, which asked for a procedure to decide whether a given proposition in elementary logic is derivable from Frege's rules (for elementary logic). This also requires a precise concept of mechanical procedures, if the answer is negative (as turned out to be the case). A similar situation holds for Hilbert's tenth problem (in his list of 1900) asking for a procedure to decide whether any given Diophantine equation has a solution. [This problem was investigated in G's famous paper, and his theorem VIII (*FG*, p. 612) may be viewed as the step that initiated the line of approach that led to a negative answer to the problem in 1970.]

G himself made contributions to the Entscheidungsproblem both by deciding a most interesting and natural subclass (see chapter 3, under *1929*), and by suggesting a negative answer to the general problem in theorem X of his famous paper (*FG*, p. 612). Moreover, he also introduced in 1934 the concept of general recursive functions (by modifying a suggestion of Herbrand), which turns out to capture also the intuitive concept. It is, however, according to G, only Turing's work of 1936 on computable numbers (reprinted in Davis, 1965) that for the first time presented a convincing analysis to show us the correct perspective by which to see the intuitive concept clearly. Once the precise concept only is accepted as the right one, it is a short step not only to see that G's incompleteness theorems apply to all formal systems but also to show that the Entscheidungsproblem is unsolvable.

Turing's own proof of this unsolvability showed that an unsolvable class of problems about Turing machines can be expressed by propositions in elementary logic. His proof was refined in 1961 along the direction of using much simpler propositions (of what are to be in the AEA form). Moreover, S. A. Cook was able in 1971 to relate problems about Turing machines to the propositional calculus and therewith to central questions about computational complexity (see, e.g., my *Popular Lectures*, pp. 67 and 98). Indeed, there is a wide class of interesting problems that are equivalent in the sense that if any class can be decided in polynomial time, all of them can. One of these is the 'tautology problem,' which is just that of deciding for every proposition in the propositional calculus whether it is a tautology. Accidentally related to this type of problem is the proposal that an algorithm is feasible or practicable iff (if and only if) it can be done in polynomial time. The proposal seems unreasonable, since, for example, if a problem stated with n symbols requires n^{100} steps to decide, the algorithm can hardly be thought to be 'feasible.' The problem of finding a satisfactory precise concept of feasible computation is certainly challenging. Indeed, we have here a case that suggests some doubts about G's belief that the precise concept is there all along, but that so far we have not found the right perspective by which to see it clearly.

G's short note of 1936 (see chapter 3, under *1935*) shows that theorems with long proofs in a given system can get much shorter proofs in extensions of the system. The idea has been applied in computer science to prove certain familiar decision procedures inefficient in the sense of requiring exponential time (or worse) to execute (see *CW*, pp. 394–397). This is a special case of the favorite general idea of G's: the idea that for problems arising in a given system, more can be done about them in a richer system (see, e.g., the famous footnote 48a in his famous paper, *FG*, p. 610). D. R. Hofstadter believes the constructions in G's famous proof helpful to the study of artificial intelligence and puts the idea at the center: 'Gödel's proof offers the notion that a high-level view of a system may contain certain explanatory power which simply is absent on the low levels' (op. cit., p. 707).

It should be mentioned that Turing, unlike G, also made important contributions to the actual development of computers, particularly in the 1940s. The contributions by Turing and v. Neumann are reported in Martin Davis's forthcoming 'Mathematical logic and the origin of modern computers.' (In the early 1950s I introduced a 'programming' reformulation of Turing machines that is more like the common computers and proved that 'erasing' is dispensable; see my *Survey*, chapter 6.) In fact, the operations of computers are so like some of the elementary considerations in logic that in recent years it has been common for logicians to involve themselves in the study of computers in one way or another. Apparently G himself took no interest in the actual development of computers.

Since 1936, the more striking advances in the study of theoretical mechanical procedures lie less in finding decision procedures than in proving the unsolvability of a wide range of significant decision problems; a survey of the major unsolvability results is given by M. Davis (in *Handbook of Mathematical Logic*, ed. J. Barwise, 1977). For the type of consideration in this book, the unsolvability of (the whole class of) Diophantine problems (Hilbert's tenth problem) is a typical representative, which, for instance, can take the place of the broader class of all number-theoretical questions in considering whether the human mind surpasses all machines (as is done by G on pp. 324–326 of *MP*).

6.2 Mathematical practice

The unsolvable problems and G's undecidable propositions can be viewed as a part of the surprising proofs of impossibility in the mathematical tradition: the Greek discovery that $\sqrt{2}$ is not a rational number, the nineteenth-century discoveries that it is not possible to solve an equation of the fifth degree by means of radicals, that e and π are not algebraic numbers, that it is not possible to trisect every angle by ruler and compass, that the parallel axiom is not deducible from the other axioms of Euclid, that the real numbers are not countable, etc. At the same time, the concepts of arbitrary mechanical procedures and formal systems are more general and give more a feeling of finality in the sense that we do not have definite conceptions of going beyond that are, for example, comparable with the extension of the domain of numbers from the rational to the algebraic. Indeed, the generality of these concepts reminds one of Kant's concept of all possible experience and his speculations about its limits.

In the conclusion to his *Grundlagen der Geometrie* (1899) Hilbert connects impossibility proofs with a more general recommendation of paying attention to, as he does in the book, what methods are needed for settling a given question. His observations, being also relevant to some general issues, are worth extended quotation.

> The preceding work is a critical investigation of the principles of geometry; in this investigation we have taken as a guide the following fundamental principle: to discuss each question in such a manner that we examine at the same time whether or not it is possible to answer this question along a prescribed course by employing certain limited means. This fundamental rule seems to me to contain a general and natural recipe. In fact, whenever in our mathematical investigations we encounter a problem or conjecture a theorem, our drive for knowledge is satisfied only when we either attain a complete solution of the problem and a rigorous proof of the theorem, or, see clearly the reason for the impossibility of success and, consequently, the necessity of failure. Thus, in modern mathematics, the question of the impossibility of certain solutions or problems plays an important role, and the attempts to answer such questions have often been the occasion of discovering new and fruitful fields of research.
>
> This fundamental principle, which we ought to bear in mind when considering the principles of the possibility of proofs, is also intimately connected with the requirement of the 'purity' of the methods of proof, which has increasingly been recommended by more mathematicians. This requirement is basically nothing but a subjective conception of the fundamental principle given above. In fact, the preceding geometrical study seeks in general to elucidate which axioms, hypotheses, or auxiliary means are necessary to prove an elementary geometrical truth, and it remains then to judge from a chosen viewpoint which method of proof is to be preferred.

Hilbert's description of the way his book is organized appears to agree in spirit with G's neutral manner of viewing the different ranges of mathematics recognized by finitism, intuitionism, classicism, etc. In other words, it is of interest to realize that there are these distinct ranges (of different degrees of certainty), and that there are alternative viewpoints and contexts, which determine the preference of one range or another. Also the advice of paying attention to the methods of proving a theorem or solving a problem need not conflict with the natural urge of first settling the matter by whatever methods are available. It is the recommendation of the purity of method that appears to introduce an additional requirement that is more involved.

In the first place, there is the distinction between the methods of discovery and the methods of proof actually employed in the finished product. It can hardly be the intention to object to the appeal to one's physical or geometrical or (as in the case of G) philosophical intuitions as heuristic aids to the discovery of a proof. Moreover, Hilbert certainly does not in his own mathematical practice deny himself the use of powerful methods (such as those of Cantor's set theory) in proving theorems. Nor would he deny that it is generally a more significant step to find for the first time *some* proof of an open problem than to determine the methods employed or to give a more elementary proof. Familiarly mathematicians are also interested in finding an 'elementary' proof for a theorem proved in analytic number theory, an algebraic proof for one proved by geometrical methods, etc. A more drastic example is the recent solution of the 4-color problem with the help of computers. In this case, the 'impurity' of the proof is more striking, and its dependence on a belief in the correct operations of a computer program certainly violates one's mathematical sense of beauty and elegance. Yet it is hard to deny that one solution of the problem has been obtained, and that it is a significant advance.

It might be said that a complete formal system is a complete realization of the ideal of the 'purity' of method, since it settles all the questions that can be expressed in it and a proof in it can be checked, in principle, by machines. What could be purer? In this sense, G's CL shows that elementary logic is pure. [But, as I said before, the proof of CL (or even its statement) uses nonconstructive concepts and is no longer 'pure' (acceptable) according to the finitist viewpoint.] But then his IA shows that arithmetic is no longer 'pure' in this sense, or that no mathematical system can be 'pure' in being both formal and complete. It is, for example, known that there is a complete formal system for addition alone (or for multiplication alone), but only because so little can be expressed in it that its deductive power catches up with its expressive power. In contrast, the interaction of higher- and lower-level formal systems revealed by IA may be viewed as another instance of the slogan 'Purity is not enough,' when we try to understand the richer domains of human experience.

The ideal of formalization seems to strive for a type of homogeneity (as a form of 'purity') on the very bottom level of intelligence. It is far removed from an intuitive understanding of a proof and may have something to do with the longing for an abstract sense of security that includes, for example, a protection against forgetfulness, since no steps are missing in an entirely formal proof. Even apart from the requirement of completeness, formal systems also possess this quality of 'mechanical purity,' which, however, does not help the search for more powerful methods of proving theorems.

G had a conversation with Carnap on 3 March 1948, of which a record is preserved in *CP*. According to G, Leibniz apparently had obtained a decision procedure for mathematics. [This may be compared with what G reports in his 1944 paper: About five years would be necessary for Leibniz's calculus to be developed by a few select scientists to the extent 'that humanity would have a new kind of an instrument increasing the powers of reason far more than any optical instrument has ever aided the power of vision' (BP, pp. 231−232).] There can be no general decision procedure that works like a machine. But, G conjectures, it can perhaps be something else, which is then not completely specific, yet still gives sufficient indications as to what is to be done. G then gives the idea of a transfinite iteration that adds a new axiom to say that 'the axioms so far are consistent.' The correlation of (infinite) ordinals with the natural numbers can be done many ways. G takes this as an example for a method, not for decision, but for setting new axioms, which cannot be done by a machine but tells the mathematician what he should do. (The idea bears some resemblance to Turing's 'ordinal logics' in his doctoral dissertation.)

I wonder whether G's example is as illustrative of the ideal of non-mechanical 'decision' procedures as some of the familiar advances in mathematics. For instance, the invention of calculus made the solution of many problems easier and more systematic. Many of us have had the experience of moving from (synthetic) geometry to analytic geometry and applied problems (such as finding out the ages of the father and the daughter from given relations between their ages, the number of chickens and rabbits in a cage given the total number of heads and legs, etc.) in arithmetic to algebra. In each case, haphazard guesses appear to be replaced by some kind of more controllable systematic method. Could Leibniz be looking for a general method of this sort that would apply to all of mathematics?

There has been little success in attempts to move from G's IA for specially constructed undecidable propositions to undecidable proofs of mathematical propositions of the common, garden variety. Some modest advance along this line is reported by Paris and Harrington (in *Handbook of Mathematical Logic*, ed. J. Barwise, 1977). More generally, IA has had little influence on mathematical practice on the whole. Of course, if (some formal system of) arithmetic had turned out to be complete (and therefore decidable), research in number theory would have taken on a totally different form. In the case of CL, what is applied in model theory, which has some connections with algebra, is the related compactness or finiteness theorem: An infinite set of formulas has a model if each of its finite subsets has one. (Since such applications are given in standard textbooks, they will not be considered here.) Of the few mathematical applications of CS, one example is a theorem saying that all groups satisfying a certain condition *W* have a free basis (for an exposition, see P. Erkof, *Am. Math. Monthly*, vol. 83, 1976, pp. 775−788).

6.3 Mathematical logic

The central place of G's work in mathematical logic is too obvious to require extended comments. For example, the standard treatise of Hilbert and Bernays, *Grundlagen der Mathematik* (vol. 1, 1934 and 1968; vol. 2, 1939 and 1970), may be seen largely as a detailed elaboration of G's CL, IA, and his translation of classical number theory into the intuitionist system. G's finiteness or compactness theorem occupies an important position in model theory. His IA is at the heart of proof theory. And CS makes up the fundamental part of set theory.

It appears that G spent more time (perhaps from 1931 to 1946) thinking about set theory than about other areas of mathematical logic, probably because it was conceptually more challenging. Apart from L (the constructible sets), he got also independence results and a more general consistency proof of the axiom of choice. In his Princeton lecture of 1946, he introduced ordinal definability and argued for the importance of new axioms of infinity in set theory. Along several of these lines there have been extensive developments particularly over the last twenty-five years or so. Since I have not kept up with the more recent work, I can only mention a few of the memorable advances from a limited and prejudiced perspective.

Paul J. Cohen's independence proof of the continuum hypothesis (1963) has received much attention and opened a way to the discovery of a number of independence results, such as Robert Solovay's consistency proof (with dependent choice) of the proposition that all sets of real numbers are Lebesgue measurable (*Annals of Math.*, vol. 92, 1970, pp. 1–56).

In his 1946 lecture G says, 'You can actually define sets and even sets of integers for which you cannot prove that they are constructible' (Davis, p. 86). It is likely that he also conjectured more: By using large cardinals, you can prove that there are such sets that are not constructible. Such a proposition was proved in the early 1960s by D. Scott and F. Rowbottom for measurable, Ramsey, and other cardinals (see, e.g., Rowbottom's paper in *Annals of Mathematical Logic*, vol. 3, 1971, pp. 1–44). In the late 1960s R. B. Jensen began to study the 'fine structure' of L by paying attention also to segments indexed by ordinals that are not cardinals (see *Annals of Mathematical Logic*, vol. 4, pp. 229–308). One of his remarkable results was a proof that 'Souslin's hypothesis' is false in L.

Given the fact that stronger set theory no longer admits the orderly structure L as a model, Jensen, W. Mitchell, and others started to look for 'L-like' models that preserve some of the attractive features of L. This would seem to suggest the possibility of alternative concepts of being L-like. Recently Jensen told me the following definition. A large cardinal axiom p is said to determine [admit] L-like models if, among all the transitive inner models of 'ZF plus p' that contain all the ordinals, there is one that is maximal in the sense that it contains all the real numbers that occur in any such model. From some recent results of W. Hugh Woodin, it follows that there are no L-like models if p asserts the existence of a 'super strong' cardinal, which, therefore, sets an unattainable limit (and introduces a frame of reference) to the quest for L-like models.

In the 1946 lecture G considers large cardinals in connection with the quest for some concept of absolute provability. It is a favorite observation of G's that there are propositons undecidable in a given system that can be decided in a higher system (or, specifically, at a higher rank in the hierarchy of sets). 'It is not impossible,' he says, extending it to a stronger conjecture in the lecture, 'that every proposition expressible in set theory is decidable from the present axioms plus some true assertion about the largeness of the universe of all sets' (Davis, p. 85). This suggests that new axioms of infinity are the principal vehicle for enriching set theory. In particular, truth of the conjecture would imply that 'lengthening' the hierarchy is the (only) way to 'widening' it. While the intended interpretation of set theory is a wide (fat, maximum) hierarchy, L is a narrow (lean, minimum) one; the fact that it ceases to be a model of set theory in the presence of certain strong axioms of infinity is a partial confirmation of G's conjecture. In any case, it is clear that G's proposal to search for axioms of infinity has led to a great deal of varied research over several decades. For example, A Kanamori and M. Magidor have given a summary of the evolution of large cardinal axioms in set theory (*Springer Lecture Notes in Mathematics*, vol. 669, 1978, pp. 99–275).

In his Cantor paper (1947) G elaborates and qualifies his idea about large cardinals (BP, pp. 264–265; for a detailed discussion of the paper, see section 11.2). In addition to axioms of infinity, G mentions (on p. 265, first full sentence) two other possible ways of enriching set theory: (a) by considering the concept 'property of set' (footnote 18) and (b) by formulating some maximum property, in contrast with the minimum property of L (footnote 23). It appears that (b) is along the line of directly widening the hierarchy and (a) is related to G's idea of a theory of concepts ('properties'). These ideas were all suggested in connection with looking for new ways of deciding CH (the continuum hypothesis), on the basis of his correct and well-founded conjecture that it is not decidable by the accepted axioms. Hence, it appears to be a misunderstanding to assert that G looked for the solution only in new axioms of infinity. In particular, his own work on 'scales of functions' around 1970 was along a different direction.

It is generally believed today that new axioms of infinity are not likely to settle the continuum problem. In one respect G's conjecture on CH did undergo a change between 1947 and 1975. While in 1947 he gave reasons for his belief that CH is false (BP, pp. 266–268), he believed in 1975 that CH may be true and that the cardinality of the continuum is either aleph-one or aleph-two. He still believed that the generalized CH is false. It appears that G's interest in CH was to a considerable extent based on his belief that the study of it is a useful handle to assist us in our analysis of the concept of set. In 1947 he said that 'the role of the continuum problem in set theory will be to lead to the discovery of new axioms which make it possible to disprove Cantor's conjecture' (BP, p. 268). He would probably have modified this in 1975 by substituting 'settle' for 'disprove.'

A lively area of recent research is what is known as 'the axiom of determinacy' (AD), which is highly relevant to the large cardinal axioms (CA). The idea is to determine how strong a case of AD can yield some given CA and how strong a CA can yield a given case of AD. A remarkable early example of this kind of result is Martin's proof of 'Borel determinacy,' which uses the iterative hierarchy up to rank omega-one (i.e., iterating the formation of power sets from, say, the set of natural numbers so many times) and, by an early result of H. Friedman, cannot use much less (see D. A. Martin, *Annals of Math.*, vol. 102, 1975, pp. 363–371). This proof also illustrates strikingly G's observation that the proof of lower-level propositons may require higher-level axioms. In this case, the theorem proved is about sets of real numbers and a proposition of rank 3 (if we take propositions about the natural numbers as of rank 1), yet its proof requires roughly a segment of the familiar formulation of set theory up to rank omega-one.

Within the last few years, impressive results on the relations between CA and AD have been obtained through the work of Woodin and others. Two quotable results are (1) if there are ω 'Woodin cardinals,' then AD holds for projective sets; (2) if there are $\omega + 1$ Woodin cardinals, then AD holds for $L[R]$.

6.4 The nature of mathematics

If we look at Euclid's axiomatic theory for geometry from our present perspective, we notice two things: it is not a formal system, and it is open to different interpretations. In the first respect, it is different from the (elementary or first-order) formal systems of arithmetic and set theory, familiar to logicians today, which also admit different models, although not by intention. In the second respect, Euclid's theory is satisfied by a whole spectrum of models from the full uncountable plane to its subset of points constructible from two points by ruler and compass. Even its intention appears to be indefinite; in this regard it is different from Dedekind's theory A (the 'second-order Peano arithmetic'; see section 7.3), which is also not a formal system. It may be said that the development of the axiomatic method within mathematics has, since Euclid, but particularly since the beginning of the nineteenth century, striven for the dual goal of finding mathematical systems that are both formal and categorical. G's incompleteness theorem tells us that we cannot find axiomatic theories (of much mathematical significance) that simultaneously satisfy both requirements.

The first achievement of formalization in a significantly central area appears to be Frege's formal system for elementary logic in his *Begriffsschrift* of 1879. In effect, his system makes it possible in principle to write out deductions in it more or less as in the case of numerical computations. Or, in terms of current technology, one might say that his system is like a computer program. The system is intended to yield all and only 'valid' propositions (or in Leibnizian language, propositions true in all possible worlds). G's completeness theorem (obtained exactly half a century later) proves that Frege's system indeed fulfills the original intention!

A system like Frege's or the area determined by it is commonly called elementary or first-order logic. In such systems the 'universe of discourse' and the interpretations of the predicates (properties and relations) and functions and individual constants are left indeterminate. The theorems are true in all possible worlds in the sense that, however we choose to determine these components, they remain true under the determination or interpretation. If, therefore, we use, for example, a single dyadic relation, intending it to be the membership relation, and add to elementary logic a formally precise set of axioms, then we obtain an elementary system (or theory) of set theory, one example being what is familiarly (and erroneously) referred to as the ZF (Zermelo-Fraenkel) system. In the case of elementary number theory, a standard formulation is the formal system Z given in HBI (p. 380), which is the natural formal approximation to Dedekind's nonelementary theory A. A typical application of G's incompleteness theorem is that the formal systems ZF and Z are incomplete (and incompletable).

If we jump from Euclid to the nineteenth century, we encounter the spectacular drama of the discovery of non-Euclidean geometries, and the surprising uncoverings of hidden assumptions in Euclid by M. Pasch and others. In 1899 Hilbert published an influential modern exposition of Euclid, *Grundlagen der Geometrie*, in which he proved the consistency and the completeness of the revised theory H. The completeness proof is somewhat analogous to the proof sketched in section 7.3 for Dedekind's theory A of the proposition that A has essentially a unique model, and reveals that the theory H can only be construed as a nonelementary system. The consistency proof is a relative one, showing that a contradiction in H yields one in the theory R of real numbers, by way of a translation of H into R. Hilbert also gave elsewhere a formulation of the theory R, which is easily extractable from Dedekind's *Stetigkeit und irrationale Zahlen*. Since we do not seem to have any more basic theory to reduce R to, Hilbert asked for a (nonrelative) consistency proof of R.

The nonelementary character of H and R is easily seen by looking at the central axiom of R, which says that every '(Dedekind) cut' determines a real number. In other words, it says that an *arbitrary* bounded set of real numbers determines a real number that is its least upper bound. While theory A asks for mathematical induction on arbitrary sets of natural numbers, theory R asks for real numbers determined by arbitrary (bounded) sets of real numbers; in both cases, no indication is given explicitly what these *arbitrary* sets are or could be. By the way, this idea of nonelementary systems or second-order theories appears to arise quite naturally. Zermelo's axiomatic set theory of 1908 also contains a generalization of the idea of arbitrary sets (of natural or real numbers in A and R) to what he calls 'definite properties,' which serve the purpose of pointing to arbitrary sets of any given domain of objects (rather than just the natural numbers or just the real numbers) (FG, p. 202).

Hilbert's consideration of the theory H moved closer to the goal of a formal system, and introduced the quest for proofs of consistency and completeness of such formal systems. Essentially what we have to do to H and R to get formal systems is to adjoin elementary logic to them and weaken their central axioms calling for arbitrary sets to sets with defining properties expressible in the language of each of the two theories. This is essentially how the formal system Z is related to the theory A (except that addition and multiplication have to be included among the primitive concepts of Z in order to be sure that at least the obviously arithmetic sets among the 'arbitrary sets' are present). Once such formal systems are on hand, the questions of consistency and completeness become more precise, except that it is natural to ask for consistency proofs that are in some sense more certain or more transparent than the systems to be proved consistent. This need led to Hilbert's requirement that the consistency proofs should be finitary (roughly in the sense that they should be executable in something like the formal system Z or rather some weaker system, such as primitive recursive arithmetic without quantifiers).

Cantor's work was continued by Zermelo and further developed by G. There is an analogy between Kronecker's opposition to Cantor and the criticism by Brouwer of the classical view of mathematics, but Brouwer considered himself a Kantian in his philosophy of arithmetic. Frege analyzed proofs carefully to reduce mathematics to logic, but proved only some very elementary properties of natural numbers. Peano invented a flexible symbolism and expressed in it a large collection of mathematical theorems, but without proofs. The work of Frege and Peano may be said to have received a combination and extension in PM (in 3 volumes, published from 1910 to 1913), of which the most influential first volume was primarily Russell's work.

From 1900 to 1910, Russell gradually moved away from a realist position in mathematics (see *BA*, pp. 66–70). In 1907 he read a paper (on 9 March) to consider 'The regressive method' of discovering the premises (i.e., the axioms) of mathematics (first published in *Essays in Analysis*, ed. D. Lackey, 1973, pp. 272–282). According to him, 'We tend to believe the premises [axioms] because we can see that their consequences are true, instead of believing the consequences because we know the premises to be true. But the inferring of premises from consequences is the essence of induction; thus the method in investigating the principles of mathematics is really an inductive method' (pp. 273–274).

The Peano axioms are, according to him, 'recommended not only by the fact that arithmetic follows from them, but also by their inherent obvious-ness. These two grounds together make their probability so great as to be almost certainty' (p. 276). He does not explain why it is that we find these axioms inherently obvious, while Dedekind's analysis (as reported in sec-tion 7.3) is more convincing. The mixture of conceptual analysis and the 'inductive method' in the search for axioms is also not excluded by the realist position, as can be seen from G's suggestion of a probable decision of the truth of new axioms of set theory inductively by studying its 'success' (BP, p. 265). In practice, Russell also engaged in a lot of conceptual analysis in his quest for the axioms for *PM* from 1903 to 1907. Indeed, Russell tends to emphasize the inductive side when the inherent obvious-ness is absent, as in the case of his 'axiom of reducibility' (compare his discussion in the introduction to *PM*, pp. 59–60).

Related to the inductive method is Russell's idea of the 'middle range.' 'The propositions that are easiest to apprehend are somewhere in the middle, neither very simple nor very complex' (Lackey, op. cit., p. 273). 'The most obvious and easy things in mathematics are not those that come at the beginning; they are things that, from the point of view of logical deduction, come somewhere in the middle' (*Introduction to Mathematical Philosophy*, 1919, p.2). I find this idea congenial and consider it specially relevant to the project of developing a comprehensive philosophy, because it describes, in my opinion, a central gross fact about human experience as we know it, and can serve as a guiding principle in attempting to draw a map of actual human knowledge. Indeed, if we look at the current quest for a unified theory in physics and for new axioms in set theory, Rus-sell's observation, I think, corresponds pretty well to the actual situation (namely, the situation that the more 'fundamental' is the less certain).

However, at the time when Russell wrote these observations, they were 'against the current.' For example, the spirit is different in Dedekind's analysis of the concepts of natural and real numbers, to be considered in section 7.3. In addition, both Brouwer's intuitionism (as introduced in his monograph of 1907) and Zermelo's axioms for set theory (1908) were primarily based on analyzing our intuitive concepts of number and set. The most spectacular success of high theory was Einstein's general theory, which was completed toward the end of 1915 and made headlines in London and New York in November 1919. Indeed, Hilbert himself worked closely with Einstein (Pais, pp. 257–260).

In 1900 Hilbert headed his list of mathematical problems by the continuum hypothesis and the consistency of (classical) analysis, and in 1904 he outlined (in Heidelberg) a program of making secure the foundations of mathematics. Between 1904 and 1917, he was busy first with integral equations and then with physics. In 1917 he acquired Bernays as his assistant and began to develop his proof theory and finitary viewpoint, centering on the questions of consistency and completeness of formal systems of arithmetic and analysis. In the 1920s he and his colleagues were actively engaged in the development of proof theory.

Hilbert (1862–1943) is generally taken to be the leader of formalism, as Russell (1872–1970) is of logicism, and Brouwer (1881–1966) is of intuitionism. These three 'contending schools' are often taken to be setting the stage for the development of the philosophy of mathematics in this century. For instance, the symposium on the foundations of mathematics held at Königsberg in September 1930 centered on the views of these three schools as presented by their eminent spokesmen v. Neumann, Carnap, and Heyting; and BP begins with these three papers. Related to the debates between these three schools is a more objective distinction of three areas of mathematics: finitist, intuitionist, and classical.

Both the formalists and the logicists wish to preserve classical mathematics, and Hilbert regarded Russell as a sort of comrade. Hilbert was, possibly stimulated by the successes in physics of Einstein and of the atomic theory, optimistic about high theory and expected to make classical mathematics secure by finitary consistency proofs. G proved that optimism was an illusion. The logicists wanted to reduce mathematics to logic, which was somehow to be given an account that would render it transparent. For example, I have elsewhere pointed out the confusion in Carnap's inadequate account (BA, section 2). It now appears that an adequate account of classical mathematics calls for something like a realist position. Moreover, intuitionist mathematics may be viewed as essentially a distinct part of the classical.

In his 1928 lecture at Bologna, Hilbert crystallized his program into four open problems, which are roughly (a) the consistency of (number theory and) analysis; (b) the consistency of set theory; (c) the completeness of number theory and analysis; (d) the completeness of elementary logic. G's completeness theorem gave a positive answer to (d), his first incompleteness theorem answered (c) negatively, and his second incompleteness theorem answered (a) and (b) negatively. (This quick and dramatic response on G's part and its historical background are described in detail in section

2.3.) As I have mentioned above, G stresses the importance of his objectivist position for his discoveries.

At first, it might seem that since (d) is concerned only with the sufficiency of formal deductions, it need not appeal to nonconstructive concepts. Since, however, it also requires a connection with the concept of validity (or truth in all possible worlds), the proof was missed even though the mathematical components were all available long before 1929. G agrees that the 'completeness theorem, mathematically, is indeed almost a trivial consequence of' some work of Skolem's from 1922. 'But now the aforementioned easy inference,' G adds, 'is definitely non-finitary, and so is any other completeness proof of the predicate calculus' (*MP*, pp. 8–9; for a more detailed discussion, see section 10.1).

6.5 General relativity theory and the concept of time

Schilpp visited Einstein on 29 May 1946. Either on that occasion or shortly afterward G agreed to write a paper for the volume to celebrate Einstein's seventieth birthday (14 March 1949). For the next few years (up to the beginning of 1951) G devoted much of his energy to a 'digression' into physics, paying special attention to the central philosophical problem of time. Initially the projected paper was to have the title 'The theory of relativity and Kant.' At some stage G decided to contribute only a short philosophical article, leaving the physics part and some extended philosophical considerations to be dealt with in separate papers. The article was hand delivered to Einstein a few days before his seventieth birthday.

G's relevant writings include the following:

(P) 'An example of a new type of cosmological solutions of Einstein's field equations of gravitation,' *Review of Modern Physics*, vol. 21, July 1949, pp. 447–450.

(E) 'A remark about the relationship between relativity theory and idealistic philosophy,' *Albert Einstein: Philosopher-Scientist*, ed. P. A. Schilpp, 1949 (toward the end of the year), pp. 557–562.

(L) 'Rotating universes in general relativity,' invited lecture given on 31 August 1950 at the International Congress of Mathematicians, Cambridge, Massachusetts, text published in 1952 in its *Proceedings*, vol. 1, pp. 175–181. This is a continuation of (P) that announces and briefly sketches the argument for the existence of additional solutions to Einstein's equations with rotating universes. A note by G (probably written in 1970) indicates that there is a fuller paper in the Nachlass.

(K) 'Some observations about the relationship between theory of relativity and Kantian philosophy,' unpublished manuscript.

I have read the following comments on these papers:

1. Einstein's reply to (E) in the Schilpp volume, pp. 687–688.
2. R. Penrose's comments on the three published papers in Kreisel, pp. 214–215.
3. David B. Malament, 'Time travel' in the Gödel universe, *PSA 1984*, vol. 2, copyright 1985 by the Philosophy of Science Association.
4. Howard Stein, introductory note to (E), with some reference to one version of (K), forthcoming in *CW*, vol. 2.

According to (E), relativity theory 'gave new and surprising insights into the nature of time, of that mysterious and seemingly self-contradictory being which, on the other hand, seems to form the basis of the world's and our own existence. The very starting point of special relativity theory consists in the discovery of a new and very astonishing property of time, namely the relativity of simultaneity, which to a large extent implies that of succession.' This appears to deprive 'the lapse of time' of its objective meaning. 'The existence of matter, however,' G continues, distinguishes the observers who 'follow in their motion the mean motion of matter.' And in all known cosmological solutions (before G's work) 'the local times of *these* observers fit together into one world time,' which may be taken as the 'objective time.'

G then turns to his new solutions (worlds) set forth in (P), in which there cannot be such a 'world time' and, indeed, in which time travel in one sense is possible. 'Namely, by making a round trip on a rocket ship in a sufficiently wide curve, it is possible in these worlds to travel into any region of the past, present, and future, and back again, exactly as it is possible in other worlds to travel to distant parts of space.' In these worlds 'the experienced lapse of time can exist without an objective lapse of time,' so that 'no reason can be given why an objective lapse of time should be assumed at all.'

G concludes (E) by making two observations on the physical meaning of his solutions: (a) Even though the solutions given in (P) are stationary and yield no red shift for distinct objects, there are also expanding rotating solutions [as they are sketched in (L)]. (b) 'The mere compatibility with the laws of nature of worlds in which there is no distinguished absolute time, and, therefore, no objective lapse of time exists, throws some light on the meaning of time also in those worlds in which an absolute time *can* be defined.'

In (1) Einstein says, 'The problem here involved disturbed me already at the time of the building up of the general theory of relativity, without my having succeeded in clarifying it. Entirely aside from the relation of the theory of relativity to idealistic philosophy or to any philosophical formulation of questions,' one thing is clear: the distinction of earlier and later is abandoned in G's solutions for world-points which lie far apart in a cosmological sense. 'It will be interesting to weigh whether these are not to be excluded on physical grounds.'

The distinguishing features of G's solutions of Einstein's equations are three: (a) the presence of closed timelike curves, (b) the possession of spatial homogeneity but not isotropy, (c) rotation of matter in these worlds relative to the local inertial frames (violating one version of 'Mach's principle' that denies cosmic rotation). Apparently, working cosmologists, who consider 'realistic' only solutions that are both spatially homogeneous and isotropic, exclude G's solutions on physical grounds. G seems to have thought it possible that one of his 'expanding' solutions may actually describe our universe. Penrose says in (2) that G's three published papers 'were highly original and, in the long run, quite influential'; he then describes the several ways in which they have influenced research in physics.

The complex relation between physics and a philosophical formulation of problems is well illustrated by (E) and (K). The relativity of simultaneity depends only on the location and the motion of the observer in spacetime, so that each local time is 'subjective' only in an objective sense that has nothing to do with variations determined by one's psychological states or an illusion or a form of our sense intuition. What is seen to be impossible in the G universes is to fit chosen local times into a world time. Moreover, the closed timelike curves deprive time of its unique direction and make it behave like space. Instead of an object changing from A into B, we have just two objects A and B located somewhere in a fixed frame of spacetime. As in space, we could get from any position (or world-point) to any other; together with time, change loses its meaning. In such a universe, if somebody went 'back in time' and killed himself, then we would seem to have an absurdity in disrupting the 'fixed frame,' so that he would be both alive and dead at the 'same time.' In (E) G argues that this is practically impossible (p. 561). But it seems that the reason is more intrinsic: If such a solution is true, then it follows that no such 'change' can occur. Since, however, G is leaving open the question whether such solutions are true, the argument from practical impossibility is probably relevant.

The relation to idealistic philosophy (with its numerous varieties) is ambiguous. It could, for instance, be said that the field equations and their solutions (including G's) all presuppose a realistic (or even materialistic) view of the physical world. G seems to have in mind more specifically 'the view of those philosophers who, like Parmenides, Kant, and the modern idealists, deny the objectivity of change and consider change as an illusion or an appearance due to our special mode of perception' (ibid., p. 557). He goes on to quote Kant (*Pure Reason*, A37, B54): 'Those affections which we represent to ourselves as changes, in beings with other forms of intuition, would give rise to a perception in which the idea of time, and therefore also of change, would not occur at all.'

But Kant's dualism is a very peculiar form of 'idealism,' if it is regarded as a case of idealism at all. Moreover, Kant's idealism with regard to space and time differs from relativity theory in asserting that all human beings see the same temporal properties and in denying the empirical aspect of geometry. Unlike Kant, G does not deny that we can perceive things as they are in themselves. What G sees as the common feature between Kantian philosophy and relativity theory is the conclusion that, for all we know, time and change may be only our ways of representing aspects of the world. For Kant, our faculty of representation, which is intersubjectively the same, cannot reach the things in themselves. For relativity theory, though there is no impenetrable barrier between us and things as they are, temporal relations are fully defined only by way of our cosmology, which may or may not yield an objective world time that fits together the local times of all the members of a suitably distinguished class of observers. It is, however, a little strenuous to say that in relativity theory each local time is determined by the 'sensibility' or the 'form of sense intuition' of the appropriately situated observer.

Chapter 7
Gödel and philosophy

There are two different questions: (1) What are Gödel's philosophical views? (2) To what extent are these views 'true'? For any person A, an answer to these questions of course depends very much on the data available to A and on A's own views. In practice, (2) is likely to be weakened to (2') To what extent does A agree with G? G himself distinguishes different degrees of certainty and tentativeness, which are also applicable to his own (philosophical) beliefs. Moreover, some of his views have received more definite formulations and more extensive developments than others. He also makes allowance for the fact that, as a rule, some strong beliefs are based on reasons having to do with our particular circumstances. Like most of us, G cannot give good reasons for some of his beliefs, but, unlike many of us, he is aware of this. Hence, the second question has to take into consideration the extent to which G himself considers the different parts of his views to be true and objectively justified. The varying extents are partially reflected in how willing he was to publicize one or another of his views.

The records of G's views include his own publications, reports of his sayings by others, and his unpublished writings. Of course much more was contained in his mind than these records. In working on this book I have often come upon questions that I wish I had asked him. This not being possible, one expects to find some clarifications of his views on certain particular issues in his unpublished writings. Most of these remain, however, in a form that denies easy access. There are various tantalizing directions along which future studies of them promise to reveal new things in philosophy, science, scholarship, and the history of ideas.

These writings are in different stages of completion. Much of them consists of notes and reminders for his own use, so that their purposes and relative positions may not be clear to the readers. Very likely the less articulate controlling ideas are absent, both because G must have felt that he could remember them and because there were probably large gaps in his more ambitious philosophical projects. In these respects his informal conversations may supplement in some degree his extensive (unpublished) papers. In any case, in my attempt to answer the questions about his views,

I am limiting the data primarily to the published material and a fraction of his conversations with me. All the conversations will be reported at great length in *CG*.

7.1 Conceptual realism

There are different components in G's philosophy that I am not sure I know how to fit together. The best known aspect is his objectivism (or 'objectivistic conception of mathematics,' *MP*, p. 9) and conceptual (or mathematical) realism. There is (potentially) a general agreement in accepting a mathematical proof and its conclusion. This unexceptional agreement reveals a kind of objectivity in mathematics (its universality) that accounts for and goes beyond mere intersubjective agreement. This universality is also recognized by the intuitionists, provided the proof uses only methods acceptable to them. But objectivism requires also objectivity in the sense of a concept of truth for which the law of excluded middle holds: For each proposition, either it is true or its negation is. One suggestion is to recognize this objectivity, but leave it open whether and in what sense there are mathematical objects. According to G, given objectivity, there must be (mathematical) objects. It is indeed difficult to imagine how we can think objectively without thinking about something.

The disagreement is more about the nature of these 'objects.' For example, Bernays says in a letter to me (23 February 1976), 'I am inclined to compare the world of mathematical objects and relations with the world of colors and their relations as also with the world of musical entities and their relations. In all these cases we have an objectivity which is to be distinguished from the one we have in the physical reality.' This may be construed as a comment on G's assertion that 'we do have something like a perception also of objects of set theory, ... we *form* our ideas also of those objects on the basis of something else which *is* immediately given' (BP, p. 271). However, it is not clear to me whether they do feel that they have a disagreement here. They both appear to reject the views that mathematical objects are merely names or mental constructs, views that familiarly are thought not to agree with the acceptance of classical number theory.

G admits the difference in the degrees of certainty between our intuition of small numbers and that of the totality of natural numbers. But we idealize when we move from small to large numbers and then to all of the natural numbers. He argues that without such idealizations, science (in particular, number theory) would be impossible. Given the stability, clarity, and precision of number theory, objectivism with regard to natural numbers is justified, I would like to say, on the ground of 'doing justice to what we know.' Meanwhile, it is also desirable to render proofs in number theory as evident as possible. G's own interpretation of intuitionist number theory, he believes, makes the proofs in it more evident, and, by adjoining his translation of classical number theory into it, also the classical proofs as well (compare section 11.1). This gives additional support for the belief that objectivism in number theory is very well founded.

Indeed, G recommends the strategy of concentrating attention on number theory in expounding objectivism, since mathematicians are familiar with it and it is less controversial than set theory. It is, however, he goes on to say, arbitrary to stop with number theory (or intuitionist mathematics or predicative set theory or classical analysis); the natural course is rather to accept full set theory (as it evolves). He suggests that the domains from number theory to set theory are so intimately connected that any contradiction in one area is likely to infect all of them. This seems to imply that, in his view, what are taken as the big jumps relative to the degrees of certainty, such as the use of impredicative definitions and the introduction of measurable cardinals, are small compared with the first infinite jump to the totality of natural numbers.

Even though G seems to speak of mathematical and conceptual realism interchangeably, the obvious connotations are different. He takes mathematics as the study of (pure) sets and logic as a more inclusive domain that studies (pure) concepts. This already suggests that conceptual realism is a stronger position than mathematical realism, except perhaps in the metaphorical sense of having been suggested by his mathematical experience but covering much more. At any rate, G's conceptual realism goes far beyond mathematics.

In this respect Bernays does feel that he disagrees with G. In the same letter (mentioned a moment ago), Bernays says, 'A concept on the other hand is something originally conceived (more or less instinctively) by a mental being which has impressions and sensations, conceived for the purpose of orientation and understanding. Once concepts have been introduced there result of course objective relations between them.' G does say that he is dissociating concepts from their traditional association with psychology. Hence, it may appear that the question is in part terminological. G does, however, say things about concepts that are highly distinctive and possibly contrary to what Bernays believes.

The only published account of G's views on concepts, as far as I know, is given in section 3.1 of MP (pp. 84–86, especially on p. 85). He also talked about concepts in his conversations with me. Let me try to distinguish several aspects of his views (his 'primitive theory') on concepts, which appear to occupy the central place in (the more developed part of) his philosophy.

G certainly speaks of intuition in a sense that is a vast extension of Kant's conception of Anschauung, which is tied to sense impressions. I find the extension congenial and believe it to be close to common usage. One has of course to shake off the implicit associations (widespread among philosophers) of intuition with certainty, finality, etc. (compare BA, p. 20). In addition, G makes a corresponding extension of the concept of perception. He speaks of perceiving concepts (e.g., that of mechanical procedure, from the right perspective; see MP, p. 85), and recommends, in talking about the perception of sets, 'confidence in this kind of perception, i.e., in mathematical intuition' (BP, p. 271). This extension seems to me to do some violence to common usage. G's reason for the extension appears to be his belief that concepts and sets, 'too, may represent an aspect of objective reality' (BP, p. 272). This belief I also find attractive. But, as G realizes, the dialectic of intuitions and idealizations does extend the range of what we can perceive (in his sense) very far and renders the connection of them with objective reality much less direct. In particular, there are different degrees of certainty in our perceptions and intuitions of the concepts, as well as in our beliefs about them.

G 'conjectures that some physical organ is necessary to make the handling of abstract impressions (as opposed to sense impressions) possible, because we have some weakness in the handling of abstract impressions which is remedied by viewing them in comparison with or on the occasion of sense impressions' (MP, p. 85). I discern two related components in this statement: the fact that we do handle abstract impressions moderately well, and the fact that we often do better when abstract and sense impressions are viewed together. G seems to suggest that the two facts would be mysterious if there were not some physical organ. He goes on to say, 'Such a sensory organ must be closely related to the neural center for language. But we simply do not know enough now, and the primitive theory on such questions at the present stage is likely to be comparable to the atomic theory as formulated by Democritus.' We have here an important research topic for neurophysiology, which, however, is, according to G, far beyond present capabilities. It would be interesting to know whether or what manageable research tasks can be extracted from G's conjecture.

G believes generally that, for each vague intuitive concept, 'the sharp concept is there all along, only we did not perceive it clearly at first'; he does admit 'cases where we mix two or more exact concepts in one intuitive concept.' He considers several examples (all of a mathematical character): mechanical procedure, formal system, velocity, size (e.g., of a lot), continuity, and point (MP, pp. 84–86). This is the aspect of G's views on concepts that I find most involved. His view seems to me to suggest an ideal that, though undoubtedly admirable, is unattainable in most areas outside of mathematics (at least in the foreseeable future). Take the concepts of being poor, normal, rational, good, beautiful, reasonable, etc. It is difficult to see how we can, for any one of them, find one or more sharp concepts to consitute 'solutions' that are *'unquestionably* unique,' and such 'that only they satisfy certain axioms which, on closer inspection, we find to be undeniably implied in the concept we had' (*MP*, p. 85). For the purpose of this book, the crucial issue is G's application of this ideal to his conception of the nature and methods of philosophy and, in particular, to his recommendation as to the best way of pursuing philosophy today.

G envisages eternal (unchanging), objective, and exact concepts, which we learn to perceive more and more clearly. In practice, we use words or intuitive concepts that are ambiguous or metaphorical or vague or fuzzy, etc. It is not clear at all that each such word or intuitive concept could or should be broken up into two or more exact concepts. In any case, this is an important and complex problem that has deservedly received much attention. For example, the later Wittgenstein has considered the familiar fact of one word (e.g., the word 'game') embodying a cluster of concepts connected by 'family resemblance.'

It is a fact that our intuitive concepts change. G regards the fact as changes of our perceptions of fixed concepts. It may be thought that otherwise concepts would no longer be objective, but I doubt this. For example, the concrete situations that would constitute the conditions for a family being (said to be) poor vary with countries and historical periods. But, in my opinion, all the different concepts of poverty, nonetheless, are or at least can be objective. At any rate, there is clearly a strong assumption implicit in G's recommendation that we can and should always try to locate the exact concepts in a unique manner.

In this connection and in G's related general outlooks (his 'rationalistic optimism,' his Husserlian ideal, his idea of a better monadology, etc.), I believe that G displays a tendency toward what I propose to call 'propitious projections.' The tendency is to generalize inductively, relying only on the most propitious aspect of the known cases, from a few specially happy circumstances to other situations where the conditions are different. It is certainly not denied that in cases where the 'solutions' to an important intuitive concept are found, the result is especially gratifying. What is at issue and more involved is the practical question as to when and where and to what extent it is fruitful to look for such solutions. In the special case of philosophy today, the answer depends heavily on a complex of factors, of which many vary with each individual. G's answer is certainly exceptional in the world of today; and so are his achievements. But I doubt that his answer is the right one even for himself.

What is commonly known as 'reductionism' embodies a fruitful heuristic principle in current biological research, but it is less convincing as a general position or a very long-range prediction. It is even more dubious when one puts the dialectic of stimulus and response at the center of philosophy or uses it as the main foothold to understand the richer human phenomena. In contrast, G's projection appears to have the protection of his own high standard of good work, so that there is less danger of harvesting only insignificant fruits; the issue is feasibility. In addition, he seems to look for, also in philosophy, not a cumulative development, but some major advance after which other things will take care of themselves or become 'merely a matter of engineering' (to use a phrase from some biologists).

Since G did not, by his own account, attain what he was looking for in philosophy, his own philosophical work cannot be viewed as strong evidence for the feasibility of his larger ideals. He also contrasts a satisfactory formulation of one's philosophy with its applications. In his own case, he did not, he said, have the formulation, but was applying his philosophy in his work and in his conversations with me. The applications are attractive, but, viewed impartially, they do not appear to me to support G's anticipation of 'philosophy as an exact theory,' which, according to him, 'should do to metaphysics as much as Newton did to physics.' He 'thinks it is perfectly possible that the development of such a philosophical theory will take place within the next hundred years or even sooner' (MP, p. 85).

7.2 Aspects of Gödel's philosophy

Philosophy as an exact theory may be viewed as a special application of G's conceptual realism. It is to bring about the right perspective so as to see clearly the basic metaphysical concepts. More explicitly, he says that the task is to determine the primitive concepts C of metaphysics and find the axioms A for them (such that only C satisfy A and A are implied in our original intuition of C). (He does admit that we may add new axioms from time to time, presumably just as we do modify Newton's physics.) This ideal is closely related to other aspects of G's philosophy. For instance, he says that his philosophy agrees, in its general features, with (the metaphysical system of) the monadology of Leibniz.

It is not clear what G means by metaphysics, and he says that he has not yet determined the complete list of the primitive concepts. He does mention (the concepts of) object, concept, substance, cause, and sometimes a few others. Given my lack of familiarity with (and interest in) theology, G rarely talked to me about it, but did say that, to study philosophy, I should know something about rational theology. In his discussion with Carnap (1940), he did speak of the desirability of developing a theory that deals with the concepts of God, soul, and ideas (see 8.1). I believe that for G metaphysics probably includes the concept of God (or the central monad). But he appears willing to consider also metaphysics dissociated from theology. Since more can be said about my disagreement over the matter of religion, I shall consider 'religious metaphysics' in the next chapter.

In any case, it now seems to me that some sort of monadology is the line along which G wishes to develop philosophy as an exact theory. In addition, G also says that the meaning of the world is the separation (and its overcoming) of fact and wish (more generally, force). (Of G's large suggestions, this is the one that I find most congenial and stimulating.) I now believe that this statement is an indication of his central idea for his monadology, even though the concept of fact is presumably a composite one and, therefore, not a primitive one in G's sense. Another assertion of his is that he is an idealist. I take this to mean his Leibnizian idea that all monads are minds and that matter and living things generally are lower forms of mind. In this connection he says that the important consideration is to get a better theory, apparently believing the idealist construction to be more promising according to his standard. I believe that G values Husserl's work because 'bracketing' promises for him a method of finding the right perspective to perceive concepts more clearly.

G also advocates a 'rationalistic optimism.' His justification for this view appeals to (1) 'the fact that those parts of mathematics which have been systematically and completely developed ... show an amazing degree of beauty and perfection.' Therefore, (2) it is not the case 'that human reason is utterly irrational by asking questions it cannot answer, while asserting emphatically that only reason can answer them.' It follows that (3) there exist no 'number theoretical questions undecidable for the human mind.' Hence, (4) 'The human mind surpasses all machines' (*MP*, pp. 324–325). Of course, once the superiority of the mind in this one aspect is thought to be established, one tends to presume also its superiority in other aspects. In his conversations, G endows (not quite seriously, I think) the optimism with more content by projecting directly from the developed parts of mathematics to the whole world, concluding that it is also beautiful and perfect. I find these propitious projections a strange piece of inductive generalization. In particular, the inference from (1) to (2) appears to move from accidental successes in very limited areas to an anticipation of universal success. Moreover, both (2) and (3) concern only the limited part of mind and of reason that has to do only with questions in mathematics. It is not clear to me how broadly G wishes to construe his optimism. In a broad sense it includes his belief in philosophy as an exact theory, and much more. In a narrow sense, it is limited to mathematics. Since the general concept of a rationalistic optimism can cover different alternatives, I shall return to it in the next chapter.

The basic categories of G's ontology (i.e., the 'things,' or all that which exist) are objects and concepts. (In my opinion, it is appropriate to add a basic category of *images*, which play an important part in life, and conspicuously in art and literature.) The objects consist of mathematical objects (i.e., the 'pure' sets) and others. The sets are in some sense included in the concepts because G conjectures that every set is the extension of some concept. Sets are extensions, while concepts are intensions.

According to G, a set is something obtainable from some well-defined objects by iterated application (including transfinite iteration) of the operation 'set of,' not something obtained by dividing the totality of objects into two categories (BP, pp. 262–263). The 'pure' sets are those sets that remain if all objects that are not sets are disregarded; or, in other words, a pure set is something obtainable from the empty set by iterated application of the operation 'set of.' (Compare chapter 6 of MP or the last part of BP2 for extended considerations of the concept of set.) According to G mathematics may be taken as the study of pure sets.

In contrast, logic is, for G, the study of (pure) concepts. In place of the membership relation for sets, we have the corresponding relation of 'participation' or 'falling under' or 'instantiation' or 'subsumption' for concepts. Let me say that a thing A subsumes under a concept C (or the subsumption relation holds between A and C), if C applies to A (or A is an instance of C). Since, however, we do not have nearly as fairly developed a theory of concepts as we do of sets, we do not have as definite a notion of the pure concepts as we do of the pure sets. G appears to suggest that we can formally think of a theory of pure concepts if we change the familiar language of set theory by adding the subsumption relation or perhaps by substituting it for the membership relation. This ambiguity is connected with G's conjecture, that every set is the extension of some concept. If the conjecture is true, then the two alternative ways are not so different. For definiteness, I shall assume the first alternative, so that mathematics is a proper part of logic. It is my impression that G's ideas on the theory of (pure) concepts are somewhat rudimentary. Many of his tentative observations on the subject will be reported in CG.

Clearly G wants to say that the relation between logic and concepts (or the concept of concept) is entirely analogous to the relation between mathematics and sets (or the concept of set). Presumably he wishes also to say that the relation of logic to metaphysics is entirely analogous to the relation of mathematics to physics. These suggestive analogies are undoubtedly stimulating. But given the primitive state of the theory of concepts as envisaged by G, I am not even sure what G takes its range to be; apparently the concepts of substance and cause do not belong to logic in G's sense, but I am less certain whether the concepts of possibility and necessity are taken by him as available (as primitive or definable concepts) in logic. (Following up my suggestion a moment ago, I would like to see also included in logic something that aims at being what might be called the theory of pure images or the pure theory of images.) What G calls, probably following Leibniz, positive (and negative) concepts (or properties) appear to introduce a moral element. According to G, 'Being a positive property is logical.' Hence, it would appear that the range of logic includes for G also certain basic moral considerations, even though I do not have such an impression from his conversations with me.

The positive properties are central to G's ontological proof of the existence of God, which apparently began to circulate in 1970. Independently of the question whether the arguments are in or beyond logic as G understands it, it may be of some interest to quote the structure of his reasoning.

Axiom 1.	(Dichotomy) A property is positive iff its negation is negative.
Axiom 2.	(Closure) A property is positive if it necessarily contains a positive property.
Theorem 1.	A positive property is logically consistent (i.e., possibly it has some instance).
Definition.	Something is God-like iff it possesses all positive properties.
Axiom 3.	Being God-like is a positive property.
Axiom 4.	Being a positive property is (logical, hence) necessary.
Definition.	A property P is the essence of x iff x has P and P is necessarily minimal.
Theorem 2.	If x is God-like, then being God-like is the essence of x.
Definition.	NE(x): x necessarily exists if it has an essential property.
Axiom 5.	Being NE is God-like.
Theorem 3.	Necessarily there is some x such that x is God-like.

I have seen some unpublished discussions of this proof of G's. It will undoubtedly be considered by people familiar with this area. I am only including the quotation for some measure of completeness and shall, out of ignorance, make no comments on it. According to G, he first got his idea of this proof in reading Leibniz.

As I have said before, either logic taken as being identified with set theory or G's idea of logic as a theory of concepts (or even a logic including also the theory of images) each suggests a program of trying to develop an analogue of Wittgenstein's *Tractatus* that would give the richer logic an analogously nice place in it, or, in other words, retain some of the attractive features of the place occupied by the very limited logic (of the propositional calculus) in the system of the *Tractatus*. For instance, one would like to say that set theory is true in all possible worlds in the sense that no matter what the other objects (besides the pure sets) are, the theory of (pure) sets remains the same. Also desirable would be an analogous statement about the pure concepts.

So far I have concentrated on those aspects of G's philosophy that are primarily unfinished large projects. What he is best known for is rather his solid achievements in the area where science and philosophy interact, particularly in the part known as the foundations (and the philosophy) of mathematics.

It seems to me that a schematic summary of the work of his life can be given in terms of his concern with attaining definite results on large conceptual issues. Crudely speaking, I would like to put his work into three groups. At the center of his work we see him using fruitful heuristic views derived from his philosophical position to arrive at basic mathematical results, which, in turn, clarify greatly conceptual issues related to empiricism (or rather positivism) and the prevalent foundational schemes. In addition, he developed ideas along two other directions, which I propose to call vertical projections and horizontal digressions.

His fascination in his college days with Plato's philosophy and with number theory led him to his mathematical realism, which, combined with his acute mind and the stimulus of the Schlick Circle (and therewith the Hilbert program), produced his major theorems in logic during the decade beginning with 1929 (when he was 23). These results are, first of all, of central importance for the projects of formalization and axiomatization. His results related to intuitionism are directed to the problem of evidence. Even though his incompleteness theorems reveal certain intrinsic limitations to formalization, he was more struck by the positive power of axiomatization and chose to use a more flexible notion of axiomatic theories, which takes Newton's physics as the model and may also include the Leibnizian monadology, or some refinement of it.

A vertical propitious projection led him to the quest for an axiomatic theory of metaphysics that presumably takes the form of a monadology. The goal is to determine the primitive concepts and find their axioms, probably with the help of Husserl's method of 'bracketing', so that composite concepts can be defined and true propositions about them can be derived. He also looked for (but failed to obtain) an epiphany (a revelation or sudden illumination) that would enable him to see the world in a different light. (In his conversations with me, he repeatedly said that Plato, Descartes, and Husserl all had such an experience.) The more limited and less remote project of developing a richer logic as a theory of pure concepts may be viewed either as an independent moderate projection or as a (preliminary?) part of the ambitious program.

The horizontal digressions involve more specific speculations, which are, in his mind, more directly connected with existing definite scientific results and conjectures. The published instances are his views on (1) minds and machines (*MP*, pp. 324–326), (2) the origin of life (*MP*, p. 326), and (3) time travel (and rotating universes, in his three papers of 1949 and 1950, as well as in his manuscript on Kant and Einstein). In my opinion, (3) may be viewed as an approach to the Leibnizian position of asserting the subjectivity of time and change; the emphasis on Kant is presumably for the purpose of rendering the considerations more definite because Kant makes more explicit and extended statements than Leibniz. Some comments on the papers related to (3) have been given in section 6.5.

With regard to (1), unlike certain ignorant philosophers, G realizes that his incompleteness theorem does not by itself imply that the human mind surpasses all machines (*MP*, p. 324). Some additional premise is needed. G makes three suggestions for this purpose: (a) It is sufficient to accept what he calls 'rationalistic optimism.' (b) By appealing to 'the fact that *mind, in its use, is not static, but constantly developing*,' G suggests that 'there is no reason why' the number of mind's states 'should not converge to infinity in the course of its development.' (c) He believes that there is mind separate from matter and that this will be proved 'scientifically (perhaps by the fact that there aren't enough nerve cells to perform the observable operations of the mind).' (*MP*, pp. 324–326.) In addition, G brought up in conversation another argument based on the conjecture that there is some decidable theory such that for every decision procedure of it, there is some very short proposition that requires a very long time to decide. He asserted that if the conjecture is true, then the human mind, which always had the potentiality of coming up with a new idea (to give a shorter proof), surpasses all machines. I am not able to see the force of the new argument. Why should it be impossible to absorb the new idea into a new decision procedure?

More generally, G believes that 'mechanism in biology ... will be disproved.' One disproof, he believes, will be a mathematical theorem to the effect that the probability of forming a human body within geological times (by the laws of physics, starting from a random distribution of 'matter') is vanishingly small (*MP*, p. 326). His formulation differs from (2) by substituting the human body for the more elementary and less definite whole of a living organism ('life'). But presumably he also believes that a similar theorem can be proved if 'a human body' is replaced by 'a living organism.' It is significant that, in contrast to more elaborate speculations on the origins of life, G's conjecture appeals to no specific details that would give a more definite guide to the calculations or even render the conclusion more directly plausible. This appears to be related to his preference for results covering broader ranges and his general belief that large conclusions are independent of small details. [There is of course a vast literature on the origins of life. I have happened to come across Walter M. Elsasser, *The Physical Foundation of Biology*, 1958, *Atoms and Organism*, 1966, and *The Chief Abstractions of Biology*, 1975; F. H. C. Crick and L. E. Orgel, 'Directed panspermia,' *Icarus*, vol. 19, 1973, pp. 341–346; and Richard L. Thompson, *Mechanistic and Nonmechanistic Science*, 1981 (particularly chapter 5 and appendices 1 and 2).]

There is a familiar ambiguity in the notion of 'mechanism' between being confined to the mechanical (in its precise sense of computable or recursive) and being materialist. For example, in a conversation with E. Specker (1950) the question came up whether the time instances at which an earthquake begins form a recursive sequence. It is not obvious to me that what can be observed in the physical world is always recursive (or 'mechanical'). For example, in 1971 I asked G whether a physical machine can be built such that it can produce nonrecursive sequences, as a consequence of the properties of the material. G answered negatively, but I could not understand the reason he gave for his conclusion. A less vague question is perhaps to ask whether every analog computer can be simulated by a digital one completely adequately (allowing for definite probabilities of error).

Specifically, G lists two propositions: (i) The brain functions basically like a digital computer. (ii) The physical laws, in their observable consequences, have a finite limit of precision. He thinks that (i) is very likely, and (ii) is practically certain (*MP*, p. 326). I see no convincing reason to believe that (i) is true and do not know why G thinks it very likely (except perhaps for the wish to make room for a separate mind). I am not sure that I know what (ii) means. For example, it has recently been proved that one can find computable initial conditions for the wave equation so that the unique solution, although continuous, is not computable (M. P. Pour-El and Ian Richards, 'Noncomputability in analysis and physics,' *Advances in Mathematics*, vol. 48, 1983, pp. 44–74; the quoted result is theorem 9 on p. 67). If we think of the initial conditions as the input and the solution as the output, we would appear to have something like a physical machine with some nonrecursive output; the question of 'making such a machine' would seem to be a 'practical' one. If G means by (ii) that only mechanical laws are precise, then the result just quoted would seem to refute (ii). It appears, however, that (ii) is more plausible than such an interpretation of it. Indeed, one would be inclined to think that all observations have finite limits of precision. But then (ii) seems to have nothing to do with (i), while G takes (ii) to be a weakening of (i) that preserves some of the content of (i). Maybe G is saying that there is a uniform finite limit of precision to all observable consequences of the physical laws. Such an interpretation of (ii) seems to render it compatible with the presence of nonmechanical physical laws and at the same time connect it with (i) in the sense that for all that we can observe of the functioning of the brain, it can be treated as a digital computer.

In the remainder of this chapter, I shall give a more extended account of objectivism (centered on natural numbers as objects), and its relation to logic and number theory (arithmetic truth and the concept of natural number), as well as the implications of G's work in the philosophy (and the foundations) of mathematics.

7.3 Objectivism centered on number theory

G was greatly impressed by the sharp clarity of propositions and proofs (in number theory) about all (the infinitely many) natural numbers. For example, everyone is convinced by the familiar proof that there are, among the natural numbers, infinitely many prime numbers. Even though Goldbach's or Fermat's conjecture has not yet been proved (or disproved), nearly everybody who studies number theory is firmly convinced that the proposition is either true or false. We feel we have a stable and fixed concept of arithmetic truth that makes it meaningful to ask whether a proposition in number theory is or is not true; in other words, we have objectivity in number theory and the law of excluded middle holds for arithmetic propositions, which are about the natural numbers. Natural numbers are the objects we study in number theory, and there is no doubt that they 'exist' in some sense (in particular, in the weakest and probably the most natural sense).

In 1888 R. Dedekind introduced for the first time what has been called the Peano axioms in his essay *Was Sind und Was Sollen die Zahlen*? In a letter of 27 February 1890, addressed to Headmaster Dr. H. Keferstein (of Hamburg), he explained how he had arrived at these axioms. (The letter was first published in *JSL*, vol. 22, 1957, pp. 150–151; it was reprinted in my *Survey*, pp. 73–74, and in *FG*, pp. 99–103.) Dedekind is also interested in developing arithmetic within the framework of an informal set theory; in this regard his work had been to a considerable extent anticipated by Frege's *Begriffsschrift* (1879). For our present purpose, it is better to keep this aspect in the background and consider those parts of Dedekind's analysis that give the Peano axioms.

In the letter Dedekind says about his essay that it is 'preceded by and based on an analysis of the sequence of natural numbers, just as it presents itself, in practice so to speak, to the mind. Which are the mutually independent fundamental properties of this sequence *N*, i.e., those properties which are not deducible from one another and from which all others follow?'

'When the problem is put in this manner, one is, I believe, forced to accept the following facts':

1. The number sequence *N* is a set of individuals or elements, which are called numbers.
2. The elements of *N* stand in a certain relation to one another. They are in a certain order determined, in the first place, by the fact that to each number *n* belongs again a number *n'*, the number that succeeds or is next after *n*.
3. Given distinct numbers *a*, *b*, their successors *a'*, *b'*, are also distinct.

4. Not every number is a successor n'. This and (3) constitute the infinitude of N.

5. More precisely, 1 is the only such number.

6. These facts are still far from adequate to a complete characterization of the nature of the number sequence. Indeed, all these facts also apply to every set S that, in addition to N, contains also a set T of arbitrary other elements t. What must we add to the facts above in order to exclude from S such intruders t, and to restrict ourselves to N? 'This was one of the most difficult points in my analysis and its mastery required much thought.' What one would like to get at is the thought that n belongs to N if we can reach it from 1 by a finite number of steps of moving from a number to its successor. The final result is this: N is the intersection of all sets S that possesses the two properties (i) 1 belongs to S and (ii) for any k, k' belongs to S if k does. In other words, every such S contains N.

From this summary of Dedekind's letter, it is clear that Dedekind is giving an *analysis* of N, or the concept of natural number. This seems to me a most attractive illustration of what G means by determining the axioms through an analysis of the concept. Indeed, the axioms can be stated more explicitly:

P1. 1 is a number. By (5).

P2. The successor of any number is a number. By (2).

P3. No two numbers have the same successor. By (3).

P4. 1 is not a successor. By (4) and (5).

P5. For any set S, if (i) 1 belongs to S and (ii) the successor of each element of S belongs to S, then all numbers belong to S. By (6).

It is relatively easy to check against our intuitive concept of N to see that these axioms are indeed true. How do we see that these axioms do determine N? Dedekind shows that any two sets satisfying all these axioms (any two models of the system) are 'essentially' the same (in paragraphs 71 and 132 of his essay). Intuitively the idea is quite simple. Correlate the first elements of the two sets and the successors of any correlated elements. Since both sets satisfy P5, both sets are exhausted in this way. This fact is commonly expressed by saying that the Peano axioms are 'categorical.' In this way, Dedekind has captured the 'essence' of the concept of N. What is determined by these axioms (call it A) seems to me an excellent illustration of what G means by an axiomatic theory.

It would then appear natural to expect also that all true propositions about N are derivable from the axioms. One might wish to argue this way. Suppose B is true but not provable. We can then extend the system in two ways: by adding either B or its negation as a new axiom. But the models for these two consistent extensions could no longer be essentially the same, and the original system would also have two different models. The situation is, however, complex, because we have not specified the auxiliary equipment for deriving theorems from the axioms. Indeed, we have not even specified the language of the system in a complete manner, because no indication is given of the range of the set variable S in P5 or what sorts of set are envisaged. In particular, there is the question whether the proposition B above is expressible in the language.

The axiomatic theory A is not a formal system. By embedding it into a formal system (such as G's system P in his famous paper; FG, pp. 599–601), its content becomes more explicit but less unlimited. The contrast between formal systems and the axiomatic method (as G appears to understand them) may be seen as a fundamental aspect of what might be called G's dialectic of the formal and the intuitive. The theory A is a much better analogue of Newton's physics than a precise formal system of number theory, to which G's incompleteness theorems apply. While G is best known for his definitive results on the limitations of formalization, his primary interest is not in what has been formalized but in clarifying our larger intuitions. From this perspective, theory A is a major 'philosophical' advance, which, according to G, consists in the *analysis* of our intuitive concepts. The additional work of finding formal systems, which, in one sense or another, capture, to a larger or smaller extent, the more manipulatable parts of it, is of less philosophical interest and has less of the pathbreaking character of the 'analysis.'

In particular, G would probably say that we do have an axiomatic theory of the concept of arithmetic truth (i.e., of the true propositions about N). Indeed, theory A might be accepted by him as such a theory. In any case, he believes that we have a clear enough intuitive concept of arithmetic truth, and the expositions of this section are meant to offer evidence for this belief. His incompleteness theorems are a spectacular result of his application of the dialectic between the intuitive concept of arithmetic truth and the more precise concept of formal provability as revealed by concrete instances of formal systems. (He considers Turing's analysis of the concept of computability as a completion of his work in making the concept of formal system entirely precise.) The dialectic is especially transparent in the process of G's discovery. He first saw that arithmetic truth is not definable in arithmetic. Then he noticed that provability (in a formal system) is definable, and constructed a proposition that is true and expressible in the system, but not provable in it.

In G's own words (MP, p. 9),

> finally it should be noted that the heuristic principle of my construction of undecidable number theoretical propositions in the formal

systems of mathematics is the highly transfinite concept of 'objective mathematical truth,' as *opposed* to that of 'demonstrability.' ... Again the use of this transfinite concept eventually leads to finitarily provable results, e.g., the general theorems about the existence of undecidable propositions in consistent formal systems.

The considerations so far have dealt with the objectivity of arithmetic truth. Typically the 'existence' of mathematical objects is taken also as a central topic in the philosophy of mathematics. G appears to believe that nobody who is unclouded by the prejudices of the time questions the existence of sets and numbers. He also seems to find it more harmonious to take all mathematical objects as pure sets, so that, for example, the natural numbers can be treated as certain pure finite sets. In addition, he is very fond of an observation that he attributes to Bernays: That the flower has *five* petals is as much a part of objective reality as that its color is *red*.

Dedekind does mention in his letter, under his heading (7), the question of the existence of the sequence *N* of numbers: 'Does there *exist* at all such a system in our realm of ideas? Without a logical proof of existence there would always remain a doubt, whether such a system contains internal contradictions.' The 'logical proof' is given in his essay (in paragraphs 66 and 72; compare also a similar consideration in section 13 of Bolzano's *Paradoxien des Unendlichen*, 1851). The main idea of his proof is this: 'My own realm of thoughts, i.e., the totality *S* of all things, which can be objects of my thought, is infinite. For if *s* signifies an element of *S*, then is the thought *s'*, that *s* can be an object of my thought, itself an element of *S*.' The existence of some initial elements is said to be seen from the fact that 'there are elements in *S* (e.g., my own ego) which are different from such' (reflective) thoughts *s'*. This interesting idea is to a certain extent similar to the familiar practice of taking the empty set as the number 1 and the unit set or power set (or some other suitable derived set) as the successor of the number assigned to a given set. Somehow there is a general feeling that numbers are more elusive than sets (and than thoughts, in Dedekind's case). For instance, G speaks of sets as being 'quasi-spatial'; I am not sure whether he would say the same thing of numbers.

In *BA* I have promised to say more about my proposition that what I call 'analytic empiricism' fails to do justice to what we know in logic and mathematics—in particular, about the concept of natural numbers (section 2; in particular, footnotes 2 and 21). This section is meant to fulfill in part that promise. It is hard to see how, from the perspective of analytic empiricism, one could arrive at a proper understanding of Dedekind's and G's appeal to our intuitive concepts of natural number and arithmetic truth. That perspective appears to deny the fact that we do have such powerful and dependable, though imprecise, intuitions. The concentration on natural numbers (rather than real numbers or sets) has the advantage of separating out the basic disagreements with analytic empiricism in a way that stays away from the more controversial issues surrounding additional idealizations beyond the more direct contact with the small finite things. An alternative course would be to consider our geometrical intuitions, as Plato and Bernays (and, I understand, also Frege in his later years) apparently preferred.

Another remarkable example is Turing's analysis of our intuitive concept of mechanical procedures. The concept appears elusive and hard to capture, yet surprisingly Turing was able to give a precise definition and convincing reasons why it agrees with our intuitions. He gave a definition of 'computable' numbers, i.e., 'real numbers whose expressions as a decimal are calculable by finite means.' In his words, the task of 'justifying' his definition can only appeal to our intuition: 'No attempt has yet been made to show that the "computable" numbers include all numbers which would naturally be regarded as computable. All arguments which can be given are found to be, fundamentally, appeals to intuition, and for this reason rather unsatisfactory mathematically. The real question at issue is: "What are the possible processes which can be carried out in computing a number?"'

The 'arguments' are set out in his paper of 1936 (pp. 249–254, especially pp. 249–252; reprinted in Davis, pp. 135–140); an alternative discussion is given in *MP* (pp. 90–95). In my opinion, these pages, which cannot be reproduced here, are a good illustration of what is meant by an analysis of our intuitive concepts. Turing's paragraph (just quoted) considers only the question whether his concept is sufficiently inclusive. There is a more direct appeal to our intuition in the description of his machines; the description makes it clear that these machines are indeed (included in what is taken to be) 'mechanical' according to our intuitive concept of mechanical procedures (compare also *MP*, pp. 84–85).

G contrasts intuition with proof. A proof can be explicit and conclusive because it has the support of axioms and rules. In contrast, intuitions can be communicated only by pointing things out. An elegant illustration of this distinction is Lewis Carroll's frequently quoted 'What the tortoise said to Achilles' (*Mind*, vol. 4, 1895, pp. 278–280; reprinted, for instance, in Hofstadter and in R. M. Eaton, *General Logic*, 1931, pp. 43–46). In the story, the tortoise was able to torture Achilles by leading him to an infinite regress, from the thoughtless implicit assumption that everything can be proved.

The regress begins with Euclid's 'beautiful first proposition' and continues in the following manner:

(A)   Things that are equal to the same are equal to each other.
(B)   The two sides of this triangle are things that are equal to the same.

(Z)   The two sides of this triangle are equal to each other.
(C)   If A and B are true, Z must be true.
(D)   If A and B and C are true, Z must be true.
(E)   If A and B and C and D are true, Z must be true.

And so on.

The solution to this puzzle is the observation that we stop at (C), because our logical intuition tells us that (C) is true. More explicitly, we may give (A), (B), and (Z) the following forms: (A) If p, then q; (B) p; (Z) q. The form of (C) is then the rule of modus ponens, which we do not prove but see to be true by intuition.

In considering the nature of mathematics, G's choice to pay attention primarily to sets does not mean, I believe, that he values less our remarkable intuitions in arithmetic and geometry. As I see it, his reasons are rather the wish (1) to use a more homogeneous and unified outlook and (2) to engage in reflections on basic concepts (the concept of set in this case) that are less fixed, more actively evolving, and, therefore, leave more room for promising conceptual advances. This was undoubtedly the reason why he turned his main attention to set theory after the discovery of his undecidability results. In fact, his experience was very gratifying when he was able to introduce the constructible sets by combining the highly nonconstructive (and indeterminate for our knowledge) concept of arbitrary ordinals with the avowedly anti-objectivistic ramified hierarchy. G himself is much aware of the flexibility of the use of his sincerely believed (rather than a pretended 'as if') objectivism in this combination. Let me quote from his letter of 7 December 1967 (*MP*, p. 9):

> Or how could one give a consistency proof for the contiuum hypothesis by means of my transfinite model Δ if consistency proofs have to be finitary? (Not to mention that from the finitary point of view an interpretation of set theory in terms of Δ seems preposterous from the beginning, because it is an 'interpretation' in terms of something which itself has no meaning.) The fact that such an interpretation (as well as any nonfinitary consistency proof) yields a finitary *relative* consistency proof apparently escaped notice.

In his letter of 3 March 1968 G further elaborated this paragraph. 'On rereading my letter of December 9, I find that the phrasing of the [above paragraph] is perhaps a little too drastic.' He then continued as follows (*MP*, pp. 9–10):

> It must be understood cum grano salis. Of course, the formalistic point of view did not make *impossible* consistency proofs by means of transfinite models. It only made them much harder to discover, because they are somehow not congenial to this attitude of mind.

However, as far as, in particular, the continuum hypothesis is concerned, there was a special obstacle which *really* made it *practically impossible* for constructivists to discover my consistency proof. It is the fact that the ramified hierarchy, which had been invented *expressly for constructivistic purposes*, has to be used in an *entirely nonconstructive way*. A similar remark applies to the concept of mathematical truth, where formalists considered formal demonstrability to be an *analysis* of the concept of mathematical truth and, therefore, were of course not in a position to *distinguish* the two.

There is a historical point about the constructible sets, denoted by *L*, which appears to be relevant to G's concept of the axiomatic method. Martin Davis has remarked that G, in his first announcement, called the proposition 'All sets are constructible' an axiom. Since G later believed the proposition to be false, does this mean that an axiom can be false? According to Kreisel, 'In conversation he [G] mentioned that for a while he thought of it as exhausting *all* definitions, in fact, "L" stands for "law"'' (Kreisel, p. 203). I do not know whether at that time G also thought that all sets are definable. In any case, what I see as the main point in this episode is an additional flexibility (besides the allowance for new axioms to be discovered) implicit in G's concept of the axiomatic method: What is thought to be an axiom at one time may later turn out to be a false proposition and, therefore, not really an 'axiom.'

When it is accepted that sets are a sort of object (and they are the mathematical objects), there remains what is called the 'problem of access.' Take small and simple physical sets, such as the set of the five petals of the flower in front of me or the five fingers of my left hand. The perceptions of them seem analogous to the perceptions of simple physical objects such as chairs and tables. According to G, there is a close relationship between the concept of set and the categories of pure understanding in Kant's sense. 'Namely, the function of both is "synthesis," i.e., the generating of unities out of manifolds (e.g., in Kant, of the idea of *one* object out of its various aspects).' 'It by no means follows, however, that the data of this second kind, because they cannot be associated with actions of certain things upon our sense organs, are something purely subjective. Rather they, too, may represent an aspect of objective reality, but, as opposed to the sensations, their presence in us may be due to another kind of relationship between ourselves and reality' (*BP*, p. 272). This suggestive comparison appears to include implicitly a generalization from physical sets to pure sets. For example, if we are somehow given five simple pure sets, the function of 'synthesis' can also generate a pure set consisting of them.

Once it is agreed that we can perceive simple and small (physical and pure) sets, the process of extensions gets started in mathematics. This process is parallel to what is done in physics and biology, as we move from familiar physical objects to galaxies, electrons, quarks, viruses, enzymes, nucleic acids, atoms, etc. In all these processes, we use certain forms of idealization that project beyond what have been observed, even though the details of how we gain greater command of and confidence in the idealizations are quite different. Indeed, the intimate connections between idealizations in mathematics and in physics are an important fact about our knowledge. According to Bernays, the theoretical descriptions have a 'schematic' character; their inner structures are 'idealized structures' (having a purely mathematical character) and cannot be fully identified with the constitution of physical nature. He also speaks of a reciprocity of approximation between the ample multiplicity of determinations of the natural objects and the mathematical perfection and precision of the schemata. (See his paper 'Concerning rationality,' *The Philosophy of Karl Popper*, ed. P. A. Schilpp, 1974, pp. 603 and 605.)

The first and perhaps the most decisive idealization in mathematics is the move from small pure sets (or small natural numbers) to the (potentially or actually) infinite totality of all finite pure sets (or all natural numbers). In this regard, it is of interest to review Kant's treatment of the intuition (in his restricted sense) of natural numbers and arithmetic propositions. Since he considers only small numbers, it is not clear how far his considerations also apply to large ones or to all numbers. G remarks that Kant's theory is not sufficient to deal with the infinite totality of natural numbers (even less to get near the concept of arithmetic truth), because Kant does not leave room for a strong enough idealization. I was pleased to see recently that Charles Parsons seems to express a similar view in his extended consideration of infinity and Kant's conception of the 'possibility of experience' (first published in 1964, reprinted as essay 4 in his *Mathematics in Philosophy*, 1983; see pp. 95 and 108). According to Parsons, the limits of 'possible experience,' when given a concrete meaning, 'must be narrower than what, according to Kant, is the extent of our geometrical knowledge of space.' He also questions whether mathematical induction is founded on the Kantian 'form of our intuition.'

From these observations, one may conclude that Kant's attempt failed to do justice not only to the potentiality of mathematics but even to the mathematics of his time. In other words, he answered unsatisfactorily his own attractively formulated question: How is mathematics possible? It is, therefore, clear that his philosophy leaves no room to accommodate stronger idealizations like the full domain of the real numbers (or of all the sets of natural numbers) and the further extensions in set theory. (In this regard, Wittgenstein's philosophy is close in spirit to Kant's. Is it perhaps an aspect of philosophy's drive toward an elegant unified outlook that it would inevitably wipe out some important heterogeneities in human experience?

This phenomenon may be taken as an instance of the vague maxim that 'purity is not enough in philosophy.') In a letter to Russell (see his *Autobiography*, I, p. 218), dated 19 September 1911, Cantor wrote, 'I am *quite an adversary* of *Old Kant*, who, in my eyes, has done much harm and mischief to philosophy, even to mankind.' 'I never could understand that and why' so many people, Cantor continued, 'could follow yonder *sophisticated philistine*, who was *so bad a mathematician*.' G was also unsympathetic toward Kant's philosophy (and Wittgenstein's).

As I understand it, there is for G a sort of dialectic between our idealizations, our conceptual thoughts, and our intuitions. 'In the process of idealization,' Bernays says somewhere, 'intuition suggests concepts while conceptual thought refines intuition, so that it is almost impossible to strictly separate the roles of intuition and conceptual thought in mathematics.' As we improve our intuition, by conceptual thought and by greater familiarity through use and (corrections of) misuse, of some idealizations, we are ready to introduce further idealizations suggested by them or by other factors, and the process continues. Idealization also brings the intuitive into contact with the conceptual. If we get into trouble (say, run into contradictions), we have to examine the idealizations more carefully to determine whether there are misunderstandings or the difficulties are intrinsic. G seems to believe, as an inductive generalization from the history of thought, that idealizations that have been good enough to receive some continued attention tend to be stable. A conspicuous example is the paradoxes of set theory that received so much attention at the beginning of the century. It is now widely accepted, certainly by G, that they were a result of misunderstanding the concept of set.

We are not certain that the strong idealizations will never lead to contradictions. But we should learn to distinguish between (absolute) certainty and rationality, not only in daily life and in the sciences, but also in mathematics. Familiarly, we tend to accept some scale of decreasing certainty in mathematics like this: (1) small numbers; (2) large numbers; (3) the totality of natural numbers; (4) predicative set theory; (5) impredicative definitions and the power set operation; (6) the axiom of replacements; and (7) various degrees with larger and larger cardinal numbers beyond the inaccessible numbers. It is of interest to improve the relative degree of certainty of each area; this is the problem of evidence. For example, even though G believes in classical number theory, he also considers his more transparent interpretation of intuitionist number theory important, and this, combined with his translation of the classical into the (formally narrower) intuitionist number theory, also renders classical proofs somewhat more evident. Therefore, since the two kinds of number theory are equiconsistent, the different outlooks on (3) embodied in them have to do less with the degree of certainty (as to consistency), but more with their distinct interpretations of the proofs. (Compare section 11.1.)

In recent years set theory has become more and more specialized and removed from generally accessible conceptual problems. If G were young today, he would be unlikely to choose to specialize in set theory. He wants philosophy to be 'precise but not technical' and believes that highly specialized knowledge is not relevant to basic conceptual problems. Even independently of his views, it is doubtful that set theory beyond its rudimentary framework is particularly pertinent to the philosophy of mathematics or, indirectly, to general philosophy as an example of the various heterogeneous directions along which human experience evolves.

G's work occupies a central place in the current study of the philosophy of mathematics, on account both of the implications of his mathematical results and of his own published philosophical writings, of which the appreciation has been increasing. To give an indication of this place, let me take a quick look at the contents of BP2, a drastically changed new edition (1983) of the standard collection of selected readings in the philosophy of mathematics, first published in 1964. It consists of four parts: (1) the foundations of mathematics; (2) the existence of mathematical objects; (3) mathematical truth; (4) the concept of set. The editors recognize that (4) 'thoroughly straddles this distinction' between the items in (1) on the one hand and those in (2) and (3) on the other (p. 2). G's work is crucially relevant to all four parts, but the implications of his mathematical results are of decisive importance to (1), and (4) centers pretty much on his thoughts, beginning with his two papers (on Russell and on Cantor) and concluding with chapter 6 of MP, which owes much to discussions with him and includes contributions by him. (A continuation of this concluding item of BP2 is the paper 'Large sets,' to be reprinted in CG.) I may also point out that the considerations in this section speak directly to the headings (2) and (3).

Chapter 8
Auseinandersetzungen

Rightly or wrongly I associate this German word with the idea of setting forth mutual points of agreement and disagreement. To some extent this is done in the preceding chapter (e.g., under what I call G's propitious projections) and in scattered observations on his conversations with me (to be reported in *CG*). What I would like to do in this chapter is to contrast G's philosophical views with my own, by way of comments on (religious) metaphysics, 'rationalistic optimism,' and the polysemic concept of rationality (under the heading 'truth and the spirit of the time').

The truth and importance of G's work in mathematical logic is universally acknowledged. It is also a fact that his success supports his philosophical views, to which it was in part due, and that his work has certain philosophical consequences that also support his views. In trying to evaluate G's philosophy this fact introduces an additional objective starting point that lends to G's views a more or less unique advantage of credibility. But what is directly relevant is only a somewhat indeterminate fragment of G's philosophy. The generalizations and projections from the fragment have to be examined as such and also checked against objective evidence that is more independent of G's definitive work. Varied considerations are necessary to determine how far it is reasonable to extend the fragment with confidence. For instance, G's second incompleteness theorem shows that the consistency of 'conventions' is a strong assumption. More broadly, a reasonable extension of the unquestionable fragment of G's views gives, I believe, a convincing refutation of what I call 'analytic empiricism' (as I have done in section 2 of *BA*, pp. 11–26). But, for example, it is for me an unreasonable propitious projection to extend the fragment to take it as strong objective evidence for a predisposed belief in the foreseeable realization of philosophy or (religious) metaphysics as an exact theory (as G asserts in *MP*, p. 85). In my opinion, G's lucid and profound understanding of mathematics (and fundamental physics) provides a model of attending imaginatively to both the universal aspects (such as the interplay of the formal and the intuitive) and the specific features (such as the central place of objects or concepts or images) of different basic areas of human activities. The fruits of his understanding are, however, fundamental, I think, only to one important part of human experience; philosophy, I believe, calls also for a more direct understanding of several other parts and somehow fitting the parts together.

This disagreement involves a number of different beliefs. Sometimes G speaks, perhaps with tongue in cheek, as though we were free to choose whatever beliefs (e.g., in the existence of God) agreeable to our wishes, provided that they are not demonstrable logical impossibilities. With regard to social reality G recommends concentrating on understanding oneself. There is a large grain of truth in his belief that 'if you understand yourself completely, you understand everything.' However, the self interacts with society, and a complete understanding of oneself appears to be an unattainable limit (especially if reflection is to be the only means). Basic to the disagreement are the different central concerns (in part conditioned by the difference of personal experience) and the different attitudes toward what G likes to call 'the prejudices of the time' (or, not to prejudge the issue, 'the spirit of the time').

In both respects I can of course understand better the reasons for my preferences than those for his. Moreover, his preferences are, I believe, more unusual than mine. For example, he prefers to go back to Leibniz, while I share the fairly general opinion that Kant and Marx had opened up new horizons in philosophy beyond Leibniz and that the issues raised by their views are a part of human philosophical experience not to be neglected. If the aim of philosophy is to describe things as they are, the added experience has made things different from what they were at the time of Leibniz. Or, to put it in another way, since we rarely capture directly the fine points and the multiple dimensions of how things are, new experience and perceptions magnify certain points and call our attention to certain neglected aspects. But G seems to feel that Leibniz had considered all the really fundamental things and that what is needed is to see these things more clearly. I tend to view 'the prejudices of the time' as a phenomenon more limited in time and in space than G seems to regard them.

This difference is related to the contrasting conceptions of philosophy as the quest for fundamental eternal truths and as the effort to capture the 'essence' of the Zeitgeist, as well as to G's favorite observation that the important question is truth, not influence. Put in this way, it seems clear to me that G's conception is the right one. But, as I see it, our goal can only be attainable truth rather than absolute truth, and long-term influence is an indication of the importance of what is attained, even though consciously striving for influence appears to me to be a false approach. Similarly, I believe that the more attractive and fruitful guide is a conscious endeavor, not to capture the Zeitgeist, but to look for attainable fundamental truths, which, if successful, will reveal some more universal and longer-range aspects of the Zeitgeist.

In my opinion, cumulative human experience, in its cooperation with pure thought to develop philosophy, plays a larger part than G seems to assign to it. In particular, it is important in estimating the feasibility of philosophical ideals. A rational estimate requires all the care that one has to exercise in making large and hard-to-control empirical inductions. For example, philosophy as an exact theory is certainly an overwhelmingly attractive ideal, but, even taking into consideration G's distinctive advantage of a clearer view how extraordinary things can be achieved by exceptional talents, I doubt that his optimistic estimate of its feasibility is quite rational. It is of course not in doubt that a continued pursuit of the ideal by him, especially with his unusual ability to single out the precise aspects in imprecise contexts, could yield fruits that would be significant in other ways. A crude formulation of the fundamental difference between his and my outlooks might, misleadingly in terms of familiar loaded words, be this: He is more an idealist and a rationalist (in sympathy with Plato), but I am more a materialist and an empiricist (in sympathy with Aristotle). But he agrees with me, I believe, in recognizing what may vaguely be called a dialectic of the two types of outlook.

In the last chapter I have commented on G's observations (to Carnap) on the project of a universal characteristic. In his conversations with me he commends the Leibnizian conception of science according to which the philosophical task of analyzing concepts is combined with the scientific one of using them. He also speaks of a kind of analysis that yields at the same time a method of proving theorems. It seems to me that this is related to the contrasting ideas of Newton and Leibniz on dynamics. In this connection, there is a paper by Pierre Constabel (*The Annus Mirabilis of Sir Isaac Newton 1666–1966*, ed. Robert Palter, 1970, pp. 109–116) that, I believe, G would find congenial. He points out that 'the very name [dynamics] is original with Leibniz.' According to him, in Newton's 'method of philosophy,' 'The question of knowing if force is real or not, if it is a primary notion or not, is not formally posed nor does it emerge' (p. 111). On the other hand, for Leibniz, 'Dynamics is so named only because its author claims in the name of metaphysics to enter the field by making the *dynamis* the primary idea' (p. 110).

Christian Wolff's revised Leibnizian monadology was more in line with Newton's physics, but G thinks Wolff generally regressed from Leibniz. I do not know enough to venture an opinion on the promise of the Leibnizian conception for physics. But, independently of this question, empirical evidence tends to show, it seems to me, that work toward fundamental scientific advances is, on the whole, not an integral part of one's effort to develop a comprehensive philosophy, except perhaps in the sense that a deeper understanding of any area helps to elevate the general level of one's awareness of the richer contents of human experience. On the whole, my inclination is to consider existing physics as a part of the data for philosophy, rather than to view the study of physics as a central component of philosophical activities.

It is clear that attention to the unworldly realms of the mathematical and the physical is the distinguishing characteristic of the European tradition of philosophy. But G's combination of this concern with an apparently serious interest in the other-worldly (or religious) considerations is exceptional in this century. Familiarly the Chinese tradition is preoccupied with what is this-worldly. To moderate the tedious concentration on the narrowly moral and political, Confucius assigns a large place to music (in a broad sense). The importance of poetry and painting (as well as their combination with calligraphy) plays a more important part in traditional Chinese life (at least among members of the educated elite). Even though Chuang Tzu's ideal of freedom and salvation comes close to the unworldly and the other-worldly, it is less a refined mathematical or religious perspective than an enriched artistic outlook. When Buddhism was assimilated by the Chinese, the more successful and respected sects (such as Ch'an or Chan or Zen) are more concerned with their applications in everyday life and show an affinity to Chuang Tzu's philosophy. While I retain my Chineseness in my concern with these worldly matters, G appears to relegate them to a secondary and derivative place.

Once G said to me that there is no proof of the impossibility of the transmigration of the soul. I mentioned to him the Chinese ideal of achieving immortality by living a good life or by performing some good deeds or by doing some good work (which, incidentally, seems to agree with Einstein's view, expressed in *Ideas and Opinions*, 1954, p. 56, and quoted in *BA*, p. 209). G found such types of immortality inadequate. I take him to mean that, being severed from the individual's self (or its consciousness), they are only poor substitutes for the authentic immortality. According to what I understand by being rational, I consider G's view on this question less rational than those of the Chinese tradition (and of Einstein).

8.1 Religious metaphysics

On occasion Gödel advised me to study (rational) theology as a necessary part of an adequate education in philosophy. It seems plausible to me that such a study is essential to a full understanding of the history of European philosophy. Moreover, struggling with the three metaphysical questions (of God, immortality, and free will) probably makes a difference to one's philosophy, no matter whether one answers the questions affirmatively or negatively. But, given the fact that I am not troubled by these questions, it appears to me somewhat artificial or even pointless for me to cultivate the troubled state of mind in order to deepen my philosophical sensibility, particularly since, even without this dimension, the amount of human experience that I would like to order is already too large. This opinion is undoubtedly based on my conditioned belief that these questions are not of basic importance to what I wish to do. This difference of views between G and me appears to me a clear instance of the relevance of social conditioning to philosophy. Of course this relevance is a highly complex relation that does not prove any simple form of relativity.

Indeed, the difference may have to do more with subtler differences in our outlook on the importance of cumulative historical experience and the omnipotence of philosophical analysis. Intellectuals of this century, even those who grew up in surroundings more similiar to G's than to mine, are likely to hold views on these large questions closer to mine than to G's. For instance, I do recognize the impersonal sort of 'immortality in the permanent things we create in common' (Einstein's words; see p. 209 of *BA*). I am content to take for granted and use only what Kant calls the practical free will that 'can be proved through experience' (*Pure Reason*, A802). I am not able to make sense of a personal God (or G's concept of a God that is 'more than a person'). I do not even have any clear conception of the evolving complex of my values and beliefs that might conceivably take the place of what believers construe, undoubtedly in a vast number of different ways, as their faith in the existence of God.

It is a widespread wish that doing good should be rewarded appropriately. But it involves a large jump to infer from such a wish the conclusion that, therefore, there is an agent to assure this. I was once surprised to read in Kant, after declaring that morality stands in no need of God, an argument in sophisticated language that appears to say nothing more than this. Kant speaks of 'an idea of an object which takes the formal condition of all such ends as we *ought* to have (duty) and combines it with whatever is conditioned, and in harmony with duty, in all the ends which we *do* have (happiness proportioned to obedience to duty)' as 'the idea of a highest good in the world for whose possibility we must postulate a higher, moral, most holy, and omnipotent Being which alone can unite the two elements of this good.' He then continues, 'Yet (viewed practically) this idea is not an empty one, for it does meet our natural need to conceive of some sort of final end,' etc. (see preface to *Religion within the Limits of Reason Alone*, 1793). It seems likely we have here an example of the sort of thing that made Cantor and G unsympathetic toward Kant's work.

In 1961 (a year when his health was, according to his own account, exceptionally poor) G wrote four long letters to his mother Marianne (82 at the time) to give reasons for believing in a next world. It is likely that there is an element of stressing the optimistic side in order to comfort his mother (as Lu Hsun used to send his mother her favorite reading material, of which he did not think well). But the reasoning in his letters is careful, even though one does not know what degrees of certainty G would assign to its separate components. Indeed, several of the observations supplement what he says elsewhere on theology and on his own version of monadology. The basic argument appears to consist of two steps: Science shows that the world is rationally arranged; but without a next life the potentialities of each person and the preparations in this life make no sense. There are supplements and ramifications along several directions.

The world is not chaotic and arbitrary, but, as science shows, the greatest regularity and order rule everywhere. Order is a form of rationality. Modern science shows that our world with all its stars and planets had a beginning and most probably will also have an end (i.e., will literally become 'nothing'). Why then should there be only this one world? Since we came into existence one day in this world without knowing how-so and whence, the same can happen again in the same way in another world. (This and the next paragraph are from G's first letter, 23 July.)

If the world is rationally arranged and has meaning, then there must be another life. What would be the point of bringing forth an essence (the human being) that has so wide a range of possible (individual) developments and changes in their relations but is never allowed to realize one thousandth of them? That would be like laying the foundations of a house with the greatest trouble and expenditure, and then letting the whole thing perish again (compare also G's observations in *MP*, pp. 324–325). [But if one believes that there is no next life, then the conclusion would appear to be this: The rational course is to plan a smaller house that one can probably complete, or, alternatively, to lay the foundations solidly enough with the expectation that others will continue the work or to make the construction into a cooperative effort.]

Even if the world is on the whole beautiful, people do not yet display that beauty. [This appears to be the question suggested by G's mother to which he is replying in his letters of 14 August and 12 September.] But exactly this fact could contain the solution of the riddle why there is a next world. In contrast with human beings, animals and plants have only very limited capacity to learn, and lifeless things have none. Only a person can, through learning, come to a better existence, i.e., a more meaningful life. One, and often the only, method of learning is, however, to make mistakes at first. The great part of 'learning' will take place in the next world, namely, through recalling and for the first time really understanding our experiences in this world, which, so to speak, are only the raw material for (really) learning. If it is objected that we cannot remember in another world the experiences in this world, the answer is that we could very well be born with latent memories of them. Moreover, one must naturally take for granted that our understanding there will be essentially better than here. So we can also be absolutely certain that all we remember has really been experienced.

[It seems to me (and, I believe, to most people who think about such questions today) that the task of using cumulative experience and improving the capacity to learn is a matter of the interaction between society and the individuals in the historical development of mankind. To put the whole burden on each individual as a monad, as G seems to do, would, to be sure, avoid a great deal of waste through repetition, but would have to resort to the highly implausible assumption of a next life in which the intellect is qualitatively superior. On the basis of what is believed today, it would seem to me more rational to expect that, just as human beings appeared in recent geological times, higher intelligence will appear in the (probably rather remote) future. G might attribute such beliefs to the influence of 'the prejudices of the time,' but in that case I would find it hard to distinguish between prejudices and rational beliefs.]

We do not know *what* we are (namely, in essence and seen eternally). If, however, in order to answer this question, one could for once get, with scientific methods of self-contemplation, a sufficiently deep insight into oneself, then it would probably turn out that each of us is something with completely determinate properties. I.e, everyone could say of himself or herself: Out of all possible essences 'I' am just this (thus and thus constituted) combination of properties. 'Wenn dann aber zu diesen Eigenschaften gehört, dass wir nicht alles gleich richtig machen, sondern vieles erst auf Grund von Erfahrung, so folgt, dass, wenn Gott an unserer Stelle Wesen erschaffen hätte, die nichts zu lernen brauchen, diese Wesen eben nicht *wir* wären. D.h. wir würden dann überhaupt nicht existieren.' [G is here answering the question why God has not so created people that they get things right from the very beginning. It seems to me reasonable to say directly that, if God had done so, we would have become perfect machines (having nothing to contribute), and would, therefore, not exist. Hence, I do not understand G's 'so folgt.' In any case it is natural to assume, as G points out in a footnote to the word 'brauchen,' that such or nearly such ('sound') essences also somehow exist or will exist.] The answer to the question 'what am I' in the usual sense would then be, I am a something that in itself has altogether no properties, something like a garment hanger on which one can hang any garment. On all these things one could of course say a great deal more. [I find the whole passage (from G's letter of 14 August) highly suggestive independently of its theological motivation. It is a fact that we do learn, and most of the time through making mistakes. This fact is a major component of our efforts to overcome the separation of fact and wish that, according to G, is 'the meaning of the world.' Life would, also in my opinion, lose (much of) its meaning if we always got things right.]

G attributes the prejudices against religion largely to the churches, one's early education, and also philosophy today. 'I believe that there is much more reason in religion, though not in the churches, than one commonly believes, but we (i.e., the middle layer of mankind, to which we belong, or at least most people in this layer) were brought up from early youth to a *prejudgment against it* through the school, the poor religious teaching, through books and experiences.' 'E.g. according to the Catholic dogma the most kind God has created the vast majority of mankind, namely all except the good Catholics, exclusively for the purpose of sending them to hell for all eternity.' Moreover, 'Ninety percent of philosophers today see their principal task in knocking religion out of people's head, thereby working for the same effects as the bad churches.'

G sees his letters to his mother as 'nothing but an intuitive presentation and an "adaptation" to our mode of thought today of certain theological teachings, preached for two thousand years, mixed, however, with a lot of nonsense.' He replies to his mother's suggestion that our understanding cannot penetrate into these matters (in the concluding letter of 6 October), and elaborates his analogy to atomic theory with Democritus (*MP*, p. 85):

> Who would have believed 3000 years ago that one could determine how big, how heavy, how hot and how far the farthest stars are, and that many of them are 100 times bigger than the sun. Or who would have believed that one could make telescopes? When the theory was first proposed 2500 years ago, that bodies are composed of atoms, it must have appeared at the time as fantastic and ungrounded as much of the religious teaching does today. There was at that time literally not a single observed material that could have caused the setting up of the atomic theory; rather it emerged entirely from philosophical reasons. Nothing in this has prevented this theory from its having today been splendidly established and become the foundations of a very large part of science.

[There are obvious questions about this argument by analogy. Most ancient theories have not acquired so much glory as the atomic theory. There are several plausible explanations of why religious doctrines emerged in history not primarily out of objective observations and pure thoughts. They have been around for a long time and shown no remarkable progress (at least during the last few hundred years). There has been no new evidence to induce a fresh examination of the hidden merits of these doctrines.]

> We are of course far from being able to confirm scientifically the theological world picture, but, it might, I believe, already be possible today to perceive by pure reason (without appealing to the faith in

any religion), that the theological worldview is thoroughly compatible with all known data (including the conditions which prevail on our earth). The famous philosopher and mathematician Leibniz already tried to do this 250 years ago, and this is also what I have tried to do in my previous letters. What I call the theological worldview is the idea, that the world and everything in it has meaning and reason, and in particular a good and indubitable meaning. It follows immediately that our worldly existence, since it has in itself at most a very dubious meaning, can only be means to the end of another existence. The idea that everything in the world has a meaning [reason] is an exact analogue of the principle that everything has a cause, on which rests all of science.

[Compared with the principle that everything has a reason, we have certainly applied more successfully and acquired a clearer conception of the principle that everything has a cause. G's theological worldview is, in my opinion, only one of the several major varieties of an optimistic outlook. Other things being equal, optimism would seem to be preferable to pessimism. But in practice, we speak of 'unrealistic optimism' in the private sector, and notoriously optimism in the public sector has been a tool of deception skillfully employed by secular and clerical politicians. If anyone can cultivate a clear-headed faith in some optimism, religious or otherwise, that does no harm to others, it can only be, or so it seems, a good thing. Any convincing optimism that aims at improving the human condition and has clear implications with respect to everyday activities is attractive in itself but, unfortunately, also subject to distasteful abuses. It is desirable and necessary to combine reason and faith; a rational optimism encourages rather than discourages the individual to exercise the responsibility of independent thinking, which, on the whole, should enrich rather than annihilate the optimism. While I am not able to assign a high enough probability to G's theological worldview to affect my life in any way, I am sympathetic with the idea that the quest for some rational optimism is one elevated goal of philosophy, although I have no clear idea of how to move toward such a goal.]

A record is preserved in *CP* (the Carnap papers) of a discussion between G and Carnap (13 November 1940), on the feasibility of developing a theory of religious metaphysics. G speaks of setting up an exact theory with such concepts as 'Gott,' 'Seele,' and 'Ideen,' which are ordinarily taken as metaphysical. Certain things about observations, he remarks, follow from, but do not exhaust the content of, the theory. G thinks that the theory is meaningful like theoretical physics, which is also not translatable into observational terms. Carnap considers such theories a part of mythology and asserts that our science today can explain everything, and better and more exactly than such theories. That, G replies, is an empirical question, which nobody can know in advance. Carnap accepts this but says that no scientist would regard an attempt in this direction as rewarding. G disagrees and says that any decisive advance in science (also in physics) is often only possible through changing the direction. Carnap thinks, however, that such a change of direction would certainly be fruitless and says that we know, from psychoanalysis, etc., how the idea of God and the whole of theology, etc., go back to childhood experiences and images. 'That I don't believe,' says G, 'in any case the attempt should be made.' [Presumably G did make the attempt during the next three decades or more. It appears from his own admission that he achieved no decisive success. But it is likely that one can find among his papers some records of the fruits of his labor.]

It is not clear to me how Gödel's religious opinions are connected with the other parts of his philosophical views. Even though he aims at finding the basic concepts and axioms of metaphysics, in practice he is careful to distinguish and make explicit different levels of certainty. Sometimes he says merely that the existence of God and a next world has not been disproved. Hence, it appears that he assigns a very low level of certainty to his belief in this. Indeed, most of the things that he asserts in his publications and conversations do not use (explicitly) this belief as a justification. For this reason, and for the reason of my ignorance of the interconnection, I shall generally consider his philosophical views as separate from his religious views.

8.2 On rationalistic optimism

Optimism is a positive attitude toward the future of the world. It implies an ultimate choice in the face of a total mass of evidence that yields no clear conclusions. I see in the use of 'optimism' as a self-description a concession that we have no rational (except on a 'second level') justification for the choice. In this sense, it is different from the Leibnizian optimism (satirized in Voltaire's *Candide*), which is a consequence of his rationalism. While 'the best possible world' could as well be the worst possible, a less extreme and more cautious optimism can be less vacuous and more consequential. It serves as a limit and a continuing guide that could permit a full respect for disagreeable but 'irreducible and stubborn facts.' [When William James was finishing his *Principles of Psychology*, he wrote to his brother, 'I have to forge every sentence in the teeth of irreducible and stubborn facts.']

Rationalistic optimism points to an optimism regarding the power of reason, an optimism that seems to be shared, almost by definition, by all rationalists. At the same time, a sober rationalism need not be seen to be an optimism by others; for example, I think many people would perhaps not take Spinoza's rationalism as an optimism. Nonetheless, rationalism has a tendency of implying optimism if only because reason suggests agreement rather than disagreement. (Of course there are other forms of optimism. Romantic ideal-ism would seem to be a less cautious form of optimism that attaches itself to one ideal or another. There is the 'American optimism' of progress as formulated most forcefully by John Dewey.) Since there are so many radically different conceptions of reason (and of experience), widely divergent viewpoints could all be taken as varieties of rationalistic optimism, which, for instance, would seem to include both Marxism and logical empiricism.

G's conception of rationalistic optimism is along the lines of Leibniz (particularly his *Monadology*) and Husserl (particularly his *Ideas* and *Cartesian Meditations*). He shares Husserl's belief in the possibility of founding a First Philosophy (a philosophy as rigorous science). While both of them give idealization a central place, G, in contrast to Husserl, also hopes to secure for metaphysics an axiomatic theory (not in the restricted sense of a formal system, but rather by modeling after Newtonian physics; see *MP*, p. 85). Their apparent difference over the emphasis on subjectivity (Husserl) or objectivity (G) is significant, but less sharp than a radical opposition. Both use a rich conception of experience (outer and inner) to get at the real, objective world. But G's objectivism offers a way to bypass the problem of intersubjectivity that is so difficult for Husserl.

G does not seem to sympathize with Husserl's 'Last Work' (*The Crisis of European Sciences and Transcendental Phenomenology*, written from 1934 to the summer of 1937, first published in 1954, and English translation by D. Carr, 1970), which is generally taken as adding a historical dimension and, according to Merleau-Ponty, 'broke tacitly with the philosophy of essences.' In the context of this work, Husserl offers a thesis for consideration in the beginning sentence of a fragment written in the summer of 1935 (*The Crisis*, pp. 389–395): '*Philosophy as science*, as serious, rigorous, indeed apodictically rigorous, science—*the dream is over*.' His discussion of this thesis seems to move between his own conception and what can be extracted from the history of philosophy. He asks (p. 391),

> [Is 'our goal'] one which gradually, after the experience of millennia, finally begins to bear a very great inductive probability of being unattainable? Or does what appears from the outside to be a failure, and on the whole actually is one, bring with it a certain evidence of practical possibility and necessity, as the evidence of an imperfect, one-sided, partial success, but still a success in this failure?

In reply, he says, 'Only by engrossing ourselves in the revitalized content of the traditional systems can we feel this evidence; and if we penetrate them, interrogate them, the sense of the task of philosophy can become clearer.'

It is remarkable that Husserl confines his attention to the history only of philosophy, and philosophy only according to his own conception of a universal knowledge that concerns the totality of the world and contains within itself whatever special sciences may grow out of it as its ramifications. His historical dimension presupposes an autonomy of universal philosophy that is, he says, though 'only a partial manifestation of European culture,' 'the functioning brain' (*The Crisis*, p. 290). In addition, he takes his ideal as the functioning brain not only of the European culture but also of the whole human development. Hence, he is far from taking seriously history in its full richness as a guide to philosophizing. Rather he is concentrating on what he takes to be the heart of the matter and expects other things to take care of themselves once his ideal is seen to be attainable.

Hence, the question is the inductive probability of the attainability (and by his 'methods') of his ideal of a universal knowledge that rests upon ultimate foundations and proceeds throughout in a completely evident and self-justifying fashion and in full awareness of itself. Many would find the goal beautiful, if attainable or even approachable as a not fully attainable limit. I find it congenial that both Husserl and G recognize this problem of inductive probability. But I believe I am certainly not exceptional in feeling that once this problem is recognized, one is compelled to consider first more limited goals. Moreover, experience seems to teach us that actually pursuing a project generally promises more convincing and digestible evidence than talking about it. At any rate, empirical extrapolations are notoriously elusive and ambiguous. For example, G's inductive argument for his rationalistic optimism (the paragraph in *MP* that begins at the bottom of p. 324) appears to select one generalization (a highly improbable one for me) out of many, from the experience that the theory of second-degree Diophantine equations with two unknowns shows 'an amazing degree of beauty and perfection.'

Husserl is more struck by the one-sidedness of the mathematization of nature and looks for something deeper than the 'natural attitude' of the scientists. Hence, the evident successes in physics and mathematics are not (at least explicitly) helpful inductive evidence for his quest. Even his favorite philosophers at most point toward the feasibility of his goal, which, as he stresses, has never been attained before. Compared with his audacious conviction, it is more modest to regard a few chosen philosophers as successful models for their historical periods and ask whether any comparable achievement remains possible today. For Husserl such modesty would apparently be a form of 'relativism' and an abandonment of philosophy. By excluding history in all aspects except the very limited one just specified, he strives to attain more with less. [In one important aspect both he and G use more material than the logical empiricists; they begin with a much richer concept of experience, and their concepts of logic, distinct from one another, are more inclusive. Indeed, to play with words, one might even call Husserl a logical (or transcendental) experientialist (to avoid the associations with 'empiricism').]

In the thesis quoted above, Husserl himself appears to distinguish four levels in his ideal of philosophy: (a) as science (Wissenschaft); (b) as serious science; (c) as rigorous science; (d) as apodictically rigorous science. It is not clear whether, as he often seems to do, he means here 'Either all (the levels) or none.' He speaks of a worldview as 'a sort of personal religious faith' and goes on to argue that any claim of its being 'totally valid for each human being' would mean the possibility of scientific knowledge 'about the absolute' (p. 390). He seems to say, contrary to what most people understand by philosophy, that a worldview that is not totally universal is not philosophy. It is not clear whether he is also saying something else that I take to be false, viz., if a worldview is capable of moving toward universality, then such a fact would prove also the feasibility of his [Husserl's] approach toward his ideal.

What I find hard to accept is his frequent suggestion that unless we can get everything (or at least a perfectly solid beginning), we can get nothing in philosophy. In this regard, G's more definite ideal appears to be less drastic: 'Philosophy as an exact theory should do to metaphysics as much as Newton did to physics' (MP, p. 85). First, even Newton's theory did not give us everything in physics, and we have witnessed surprising developments beyond it, expecting more to come. Second, Newton's theory was not preceded by extensive conscious preparations to find the correct 'methods' for a 'beginning.' Third, G's prediction offers a more specific target and criterion for evaluating the ideal than what I can discern from Husserl's continued reformulations. G's own interest in Husserl's work probably derives from his belief that Husserl's 'methods' will play an important role toward realizing his goal. However, I have not been able to detect Husserl's influences in G's available philosophical work.

Neither Husserl nor G did obtain what they looked for in philosophy. Nor have they given convincing arguments to prove that their ideals are the best general guide to the pursuit of philosophy. It is not even known how essential were their ideals to their getting the philosophical insights they did get. Indeed, for most of us the inductive probability based on past experience would seem to favor approaches that aim at less spectacular results and try to use more of the accumulated human experience. Husserl speaks of philosophy as being threatened by the suggestive force of the 'spirit of the time' (p. 392). G deplores the 'prejudices of the time' and considers today a historical period not favorable to the pursuit of philosophy. It is indeed clear that their ideals are not widely shared today. Hence, what is harder at present is not so much to doubt their approaches as to defend the salient features in their philosophical views.

Even my conception of philosophy, which aims at less conclusive results and strives to use more data, strikes most contemporary philosophers as too ambitious. I do not see why a worldview must be so private as to be only 'a sort of personal religious faith.' Nor do I see that objective knowledge is attainable in philosophy only if it is an 'apodictically rigorous science.' Hence, broadly shared beliefs are what we look for in philosophy, and data that are useful in constructing a worldview can also be used in developing philosophy. What is thought to be too ambitious and unattainable in my conception is the aim of being both objective and comprehensive.

8.3 Truth and the spirit of the time

In addition to his concentration on what is fundamental, G is exceptionally conscious of the distinction between influence and truth, particularly in evaluating writings on human and social affairs. Related to this distinction is the one between the 'horizontal' dimension of the breadth of appeal and the 'vertical' dimension of the length of its durability. Influence and the horizontal dimension have of course a closer connection with the spirit of the (longer or shorter) time.

There is a familiar conception of philosophy as the enterprise to capture the 'essence' of the spirit of the time. G is opposed to such a conception, and contrasts it with the equally indefinite conception of the quest for (fundamental) truth. Since his sympathies are more with ancient Greece and seventeenth-century Western Europe, he often blames what he takes to be false positions in more recent philosophy on the 'prejudices of the time.' In particular, he says (see section 1.1.3), 'I *don't* consider my work a "facet of the intellectual atmosphere of the early 20th century," but rather the opposite.'

When time is measured in terms of centuries and the concern is with really fundamental 'truth,' most of us do not possess a powerful enough criterion to distinguish philosophical 'truth' from large beliefs conditioned by the spirit of the 'time.' Indeed, I am inclined to consider it a lack of humility to regard the wealth of new experience of the last three centuries as largely irrelevant to philosophy. It is very likely that in this respect my belief is more in agreement with the spirit of the 'time' than G's. But the disagreement has a deeper source in the issues of what one wants from philosophy and what is the more promising path to reach it. It is not that others do not want the kind of religious metaphysics that G wants; only most of us do not believe it to be attainable. Consequently we go after lower goals and have difficulty in coming up with any program that is even remotely as definite and alluring as G's.

G often says that this is not a good historical period for philosophy. I am ready to assent to this assertion, which, however, means different things to him and to me, to the extent that I expect less (having a lower goal) and have more respect for the 'spirit of the time' (needing more data). Contrary to G, I agree with the spirit of the time in believing that the pursuit of religious metaphysics had (and has) more to do with influence than with truth. If a good and rational and effective religion can be found, then its influence and its truth will, I believe, be merged in such a way that, as a matter of fact, people will for a long time not be able to distinguish the one from the other. Part of the reason why this is not a good time for philosophy is the common and well-justified (I think) belief that such a religion is not forthcoming. But in addition to recognizing that we cannot find rational grounds for the belief in a next life, it is commonly believed, and with good reason, that this is not the time to expect grand and powerfully influential philosophies like those of Kant and Marx.

If we construe reason and rationality sufficiently broadly, philosophy may be taken as the enterprise of finding a rational picture (or understanding) of the world. But the concept of rationality changes with time and from community to community. After the Enlightenment and Darwin's theory, it has been widely accepted that it is not rational to believe in God and creation. Of course we have no 'conclusive' (or mathematically certain) disproof of God and creation. But this is just how rationality is understood, so that, for instance, despite Hume's famous argument, it is rational to believe (tentatively) in inductive evidence. Moreover, the 'unmasking' by Marx and Freud, even though often applied beyond its reasonable limits, reveals that much human 'rationality' is actually the deceptive covering of hidden dynamic forces in the mind. An appropriate attention to this fact undoubtedly modifies the range of what is taken to be rational.

There is a tendency to put natural science at the center (or take it as the model) of reason. But one also speaks of technical, humanistic, and revolutionary reason. The spirit of revolt against dogmas, entrenched authorities, and several forms of injustice acts together with a revolutionary reason in the Renaissance, the Enlightenment, and the socialist and (other) liberation movements. (In particular, revolutionary reason ought to have the function of restraining the characteristic tendency of people devoted to struggles against oppression to claim too much for themselves and their cause.) When revolutionary reason loses its humanistic grounding, it becomes technical reason that concentrates on calculations of means and ends, and forgets less tangible purposes and values.

Related to the contrast between humanistic and technical reason are also the contrasts between art and science, subjective and objective, as well as particular and universal. In its critical use 'scientism' indicates the inappropriate transfer of methods of inquiry from natural (or physical) science to human studies. The complementary transfer in the opposite direction might perhaps be called 'artism.' Typically in philosophy there are often two opposite approaches that would not hesitate to apply one or the other of the two terms (or what they connote) to each other. Moreover, there are also encroachments on philosophy from both sides: e.g., decision theory (and 'welfare theory') from one side and literary theory from the other. Those who fail, for one reason or another, to identify with any of the familiar camps long for some other alternative: either an appropriate or balanced mixture or a more imaginative development of a purer form. For example, in a very crude sense, I would consider G to be devoted to a philosophy of 'pure universality' (in the end product) and later Wittgenstein to one of 'pure particularity' (in the form of presentation). Each of the two kinds of work possesses in its own way a special esthetic appeal that is stronger than what one can find in most of contemporary work in philosophy.

   It is a familiar fact that some of G's actions and beliefs are not quite rational according to ordinary standards. Several examples are reported in Menger's memoir. In the 1930s G 'had quarrels with the prefect of his building for all sorts of trivial reasons' in Notre Dame and difficulties in Princeton 'because of a supposedly dangerous refrigerator.' 'He was now [in 1939] completely convinced that important writings of Leibniz had not only failed to be published, but were even destroyed in manuscript.' Concerning legal rights, G's 'minute punctiliousness knew no bounds' and no weighing of the relative importance of the practical consequences. In 1939 G was much exercised by the violation of his rights in 'the withdrawal of his Dozent position at the University of Vienna by the Nazi regime'; in the 1970s he once caused much disruption in the hospital and deprived himself of urgently needed medical care by insisting 'that he had no right to one of the benefits preferred.'

   It is natural to feel that these eccentricities have nothing to do with G's philosophy. But this is not so obviously certain, since he is exceptionally consistent and being rational is the central desideratum of his philosophical pursuit. As applications of his concept of rationality, the examples point to some strangeness in his concept, which is likely to be reflected in his philosophy, however indirectly. For instance, most of us believe that, other things being equal, eating and sleeping adequately helps one to work more effectively. Or, at the end of hours of concentrated work, one often has the feeling that one will never be able to complete the extended project one is engaged in; but, to his or her surprise, the next morning brings fresh vigor and a new optimism. Repeated experience of this succession of events teaches the lesson that one may reasonably expect a renewal of energy after an adequate rest. We would agree, I think, that these two examples, when properly understood, are rational beliefs. It is not likely that a philosophy will be developed so far and so exactly that these beliefs appear as 'theorems.' But if it can be seen that they are inconsistent with one's philosophy, then it has to be concluded that the philosophy has not captured the (particular) intuitive concept of rationality that contains these beliefs. In any case, given G's belief in the permanence and precision of concepts, what I call the changes of the concept of rationality are for him different partial perceptions of the concept, which, moreover, I would conjecture, is not for him a primitive. concept of philosophy. Indeed, the whole discussion in this section is not in the spirit of G's preference of looking for the primitive concepts and their axioms.

To be rational and reasonable are both to be agreeable to reason or be vernünftig (in German). Yet being reasonable seems to include more readily a flexibility (or even weakness) associated with being sensible, sane, moderate, or not excessive. Some of G's applications of the principle that everything has a reason appear not to be reasonable, even though they may perhaps still be termed rational. The extent of his distrust of doctors would seem to be neither reasonable nor even rational. If it could perhaps be argued that his apparent belief in the feasibility of religious metaphysics as an exact theory is rational, one is more strongly inclined to consider it not reasonable. My concern in this section is more with the rational, but I would like to add a check to it by postulating that the rational should not depart conspicuously from the reasonable. For example, I would like to include a component of appropriateness, so that being 'fanatically rational' is, for me, no longer rational. (A useful review of the usage of the word 'rational' is included in R. Williams, *Keywords*, 1983, pp. 252–256; included in his list are also other 'loaded' words, such as 'science,' 'theory,' 'materialism,' 'idealism,' 'subjective,' etc.)

Much harm has been done in the name of reason, and reason nowadays has the tendency to be associated with a desire to preserve the existing order (the status quo). In addition, large wars, a broader distribution of information, and a greater freedom to criticize have revealed more of the actual limitations of reason in this century. As a consequence of these and related factors, there has been an increasing distrust of reason and an accompanying acceptance of varied reductions of the range of what is taken to be the proper realm of the rational. An observation by Bernays speaks to an aspect of this phenomenon on which he and G are in full agreement (*Logic Colloquium 73*, ed. A. Rose and J. Shepherdson, p. 1). 'Positivism appears to many people to be a reasonable attitude of an enlightened man because it suggests a radical opposition to intellectual authority. However, from an antagonism to confessional doctrines it passes to a general antagonism to any kind of belief, whether it is our instinctive belief in the existence of exterior objects, or a more abstract belief in a frame of objectivity which we are induced to adopt in science.' Undoubtedly this negative attitude is not confined to 'positivism' (even if it is understood in a broad sense), which is often associated with some form of scientism. It is also shared by the opposite camp of those who have a distaste for science and technology, as well as for a goal-directed calculating rationality (in the sense of Max Weber), which are seen as having a monopoly of reason and the rational.

'The antagonism,' Bernays continues, 'to the belief in external things and beings is of course not practicable in real life but it seems to some philosophers that it can be maintained as a philosophical attitude.' In contrast, G seems exceptionally consistent in adhering to his philosophical attitude (of rationalism) in real life. At the same time this admirable coherence appears to me to reveal some inadequacy of his rationalism (as can be seen from what I take to be his unjustified optimism about the feasibility of an exact metaphysics in his sense). Full articulation and carrying over to all aspects of life are ideals for one's philosophical attitude that are not easy to attain. G is explicit that he has not given his philosophy a satisfactory formulation. His hardly rational distrust of doctors (and of people more generally) is perhaps also an illustration of the truth about all philosophy, that there are more things in heaven and earth than is dreamed of in our philosophy. While G's philosophy is directed to the discovery of fundamental objective truths, it is not clear how seriously he also views steps toward it as a direct guide to the way of arranging his own life.

G's preference of Leibniz over Kant gives a clue to some distinctive characters of his concept of reason: a greater attention to 'precision,' 'depth,' as well as to a concise, correct, and pregnant 'beginning' that promises more definite and independent developments. In contrast, Kant's extensively expounded comprehensive system is seen by G as a 'sloppy' putting together of pieces that are neither precise nor reaching the deeper insights of pure thought. Kant has a much less real understanding of mathematics and physics than G and Leibniz, nor has he any comparable deep penetration into those aspects of pure reason that are concretized in mathematical logic. Moreover, in his *Monadology* and related work, Leibniz considers imaginatively certain fundamental issues of more permanent interest (such as the unconscious and the subtle functioning of volition), which do not seem to be as clearly appreciated by Kant. (For example, Leibniz's theory of volition in his *Theodizee* is presented in the context of current research by Alfred Schutz on pp. 88–92 of his *Collected Papers*, I, 1962.)

On the other hand, Kant captured the spirit of the time at an exceptionally important juncture when the forceful ideals of Enlightenment and some of their limitations were ripe for a grand synthesis. In particular, Kant presented a more 'modern' outlook on religion and pays more attention to the material component of the world, as well as brings out the esthetic dimension and fits it into the whole range of human experience (in a manner pleasing to the advocates of art for art's sake). His prolific publications (in his old age), combined with an imposing array of technical jargon and contrived distinctions, give the impression of a definitive structure presented in all its fundamentals and suit very well the mentality of the emerging clan of professional philosophers. In addition, his ability to discourse sensibly on science, morality, religion, art, and even history appeals to the intelligent public and enhances the belief that his philosophy gets to the foundations of all the important aspects of human experience. [An early example of the disagreement on the relative merits of the philosophies of Leibniz and Kant (and on Kant's originality) is reported in H. E. Allison, *The Kant-Eberhard Controversy*, 1973.]

According to Kant, Leibniz intellectualized appearances, just as Locke sensualized all concepts of understanding. In contrast, he has, he says, worked out a system that recognizes 'in understanding and sensibility two sources of representations which, while quite different, can supply objectively valid judgments of things only in *conjunction* with each other' (*Pure Reason*, A271, B327). Roughly speaking, sensibility supplies the particular and understanding supplies the universal. This picture is compatible with his idea of building up physical knowledge by the work of synthetic a priori principles (of understanding) on data supplied through the senses. Moreover, according to Kant, Leibniz 'allowed sensibility no mode of intuition peculiar to itself, but sought for all representation of objects, even the empirical, in the intellect, and left to the senses nothing but the despicable task of confusing and distorting the representations of the former' (A276, B332). (An extended discussion of Kant's criticisms of Leibniz is given by G. Della Volpe, *Logic as a Positive Science*, 1980, pp. 5–9.)

On 11 May 1781 Kant wrote to his friend and former student Marcus Herz about the importance for metaphysics of his newly published *Critique of Pure Reason*: 'However, any person who is clearly aware of the present state of metaphysics will,' he said, 'find it worth. the trouble at least to disregard everything else in this sphere, until the problems treated in my book are perfectly understood' (G. Rabel, *Kant*, 1963, p. 127). He went on to suggest an alternative organization of the book that would have more of a popular appeal and probably be closer to his own thought process: 'This kind of investigation will always remain difficult, and sometimes I harbour a scheme in my mind as to how it might also gain popularity. To attempt that right at the start, when the ground had first to be cleared, would have been improper. Otherwise I should have started with the chapter on the antinomies, which might have been done in a very flourishing style and would have roused the reader's desire to investigate the sources of this conflict. But first the claims of the School must be satisfied, later one may try to please the world.'

Kant's solution of the antinomies depends crucially on his negative concept of the thing-in-itself, which gives a name to the various ways in which reality demands 'something more' beyond what is knowable according to his conception of the human faculty of cognition. The thing-in-itself represents a barrier, a limit, a residue, a substratum, or the ultimate reality. The forms with which we are able to know the world (as in mathematics and physics) reach only the part of the world that is amenable to them. In other words, we are able to see a good deal of order in the world because what we see is filtered through our own forms. The world and its order we know are 'created' by us in the sense that they are confined to those parts or images or effects of ultimate reality that can be ordered by our forms. The content of the forms (or matter in the contrast between form and matter) is a kind of 'intelligible matter,' and facticity always splits into a theoretically unknowable component and a reinterpreted image filtered through our eternally fixed forms. Moreover, since these forms set an outer limit or barrier to possible experience, the antinomies are seen as the result of confusing phenomena with noumena, rather than an invitation to move beyond what is presently known or knowable, and to see the potentiality of an open-ended expansion of our knowledge that knows no predetermined barrier between ultimate reality and what is knowable. (I shall make some more comments on Kant toward the end of the next chapter.)

One aspect of G's objectivism is to deny Kant's sharp separation between the thing-in-itself and our mind. In particular, he questions that 'syntheses' must be subjective (BP, p. 272). In this respect, I prefer G's position to Kant's. It is not entirely clear to me how much difference it makes in the end whether we speak of changing concepts or changing perceptions of fixed concepts (as G chooses to do). Even G's 'idealism' seems to me not to exclude the possibility of a monadology without the central monad ('God'). There are, I think, different possible courses of an extended development of such a monadology and different possible interpretations of each development. It is not clear to me that the result would necessarily be incompatible with some of my inarticulate basic beliefs, which are often associated with 'materialism' in some appropriate sense.

In terms of their external life, Leibniz was certainly radically different from G. Leibniz wanted a political career, he was intensely committed to the problems of his age, and he involved himself deeply in political, diplomatic, and other practical projects (including attempts to bring about a reunion of the Churches, arduous and unsuccessful activities in the Harz mines, etc.). Unlike G, Leibniz participated in all sorts of contemporary controversy. How is one to reconcile this great difference in their lives with G's adherence to Leibniz's general philosophical outlook?

One obvious reply is to say that, according to G's conception of philosophy, the concerns of philosophy are so basic as to be untouched by such contingent circumstances as one's life. Alternatively and more strongly, one could say that G has absorbed all that is philosophically relevant in Leibniz's personal experience, which, therefore, serves as a part of G's (richer) data. But I cannot believe that such an elegant solution tells the whole story. Rather I feel there is here an interesting problem to explore by those who are familiar with both G and Leibniz. For example, some helpful suggestions seem to me to be contained in *Leibnitz and the Seventeenth-Century Revolution* (by R. W. Meyer, English translation 1952).

Leibniz is said (on p. 8) to have experienced 'all the concrete, detailed controversies of the age, the direct assertions of the incompatibles: tradition against reform, myth against science, law against power, freedom against commitment, individual will against the common will—these are the antinomies he has to face. Hence the problem of peace dominates his thinking.' G also put the greatest value on peace, but he, like most contemporary intellectuals and unlike Leibniz, did not undertake any direct action or even attempt any direct elucidation of the foundations of a future order.

Leibniz carried on a sort of universal correspondence. 'Letters, in short, were spiritual forces which, like Newton's physical forces, evoked response and reaction at a distance' (ibid., p. 103). His letters 'are always perfectly in harmony with the recipients' frame of mind.' G did not write many letters, but his writings generally were also good at taking into account the recipients' situations and preconceptions. More generally, the following statement about Leibniz (p. 9) can also, I think, be said of G: 'The critical claims of his philosophy must be distinguished from its speculative claims. For as a critical thinker he conceives it as his task not merely to get to know the limits of man, but also humbly to acknowledge them; the theoretical principle of the critical account of the Self is the principle of toleration.'

What G found most congenial was probably Leibniz's conviction in his later life to have 'found a solution to the problem of relating the individual to the universal.' For example, according to Leibniz (and G), 'The observation of the essence of things is nothing else but an observation of the essence of our own spirit' (*Nouveaux Essais*, book I, §21). But such a view would seem to deprive interpersonal relation of much of its fundamental importance. 'In this doctrine of personalist absolution,' according to Meyer, 'no real community is possible. And at this point Leibniz's conception of man's sovereign spirit comes to contradict his own idea of toleration' (ibid., p. 9). Herder admired the 'reflective poetry' of the *Monadology*, and Frederick the Great spoke negatively of a '*Monadenpoeme*'; Lessing turned to Leibniz's work for its 'psychic values' (Gemüthswerte). Such reactions are quite different from G's taking the work as a model in his quest for philosophy as rigorous science. It is of course a most attractive ideal to look for exact (and universal) philosophy that at the same time satisfies our emotional needs. But it is easy also to think of the monad as the mythical symbol of an unbounded individualism, perhaps contrary to what Leibniz and G intended it to be.

Chapter 9
To fit all the parts together

If the function of reason is to find order in the chaos of human experience, then it is appropriate to construe reason and experience (and existence) in the broadest (or weakest) possible sense, while distinguishing and interrelating their principal types. All human activities, practical or intellectual or artistic, involve the interplay of reason and experience in this sense. As we envisage larger and larger complexes in the world, the effort to fit things together plays a more and more important and complex role in the confrontation of the self with the world.

Sometimes we seem to be caught reflecting on experience or life or existence as a whole, or at least on a range that goes far beyond the familiar particularity of an isolated problem or a limited aspect of experience. For example, I recall being puzzled (at about eight) by the question whether the universe is finite or infinite in space and in time. At about ten I felt it axiomatic that people should be equal at the starting point and only distinguish themselves by their own efforts. Undoubtedly such childhood experiences are fairly common. But most of us do not return to pursue the implications of such puzzles and beliefs.

A more memorable and more universal experience is thinking about what to do with (the remainder of) one's life, especially at some stage during one's adolescence. Of course, many people consider this problem periodically, sometimes casually and at other times extensively. But an earlier occasion generally envisages a broader range of possibilities. Only in exceptional cases do we come across what Dilthey calls 'life-projects.' In most cases the choice is more tentative and less definite. For example, at about seventeen I had the charming idea that since one cannot do everything, but one may be able to understand everything, I should choose understanding over doing. The particular problem of choosing a vocation for one person suggests and even involves the broader problem of who should do what. This appears to me to be one of the few vital problems that lead rather directly to the project of finding an order in the total human experience.

While most people most of the time are not explicitly concerned with life as a whole, such a concern is evident in religion and in some parts of art and philosophy. In the European tradition it is commonly accepted that the concern tends to drive one to the three main metaphysical questions important for understanding the meaning of life: (death and) immortality, freedom of the will (and natural necessity), and the existence of God. I am not able to feel any natural connection between a concern with the whole and these three questions. This fact must have much to do with the age and society in which I grew up. In any case, it seems clear to me that there is no logical connection between a concern with the whole and these three questions. If metaphysics is primarily concerned with them, then I have no interest in metaphysics. In other words, I do not, as Gödel sometimes does, view such a (religious) metaphysics as the or a fundamental part of philosophy. More, I shall not even include the three questions in their traditional sense among things to which a philosophy has to attend.

9.1 *Fitting together*

The concepts of whole and part are among the most inclusive of our concepts. Since everything can serve as a part of other things, given any group of things, we can always ask whether and how they fit together as parts of a whole. Fitting a few parts together can be important for its own sake, or as a representation of the typical situation, or as a basis for iterations either to continue in time or to form larger and larger wholes. The meshing of desire and reality (or the harmony of the pleasure principle and the reality principle) is a state that most of us strive for most of the time. It can mean an instant of consummation or a dominant state in the life of one person or even a group of persons. Similarly, ideal states are the union of the self with nature, the unity of thought and action (or theory and practice), and the 'identical subject-object.' It is familiar how complex it is for a person or a class or a nation or history or philosophy to pursue (but not attain) one or another of these ideal limits.

Fitting together is to a greater or lesser extent synonymous with consistency, coherence, harmony, and order (out of chaos). It is an essential ingredient of rationality, security, an organism, and a community. It is closely related to the more elusive concept of appropriateness. These and a host of related concepts nearly all point to (the quest for) an apparently desirable state of affairs that contrasts with separateness, isolation, atomism, specialization, an instantaneous gratification, and a point-to-point contact. The wholehearted pursuit of a single end is generally more immediate and more effective. Immediacy summons vigor more directly, and effectiveness adds its own satisfaction to that accompanying the attainment of the end. If purity of heart is, as Kierkegaard says, to will one thing, then achieving it would win half the battle by fixing the one thing that guides the selection of the parts and the process of fitting them together.

Both harmony and order may be said to mean that the parts fit together. But if the parts are not unchanging, harmony at one moment of time is precarious. That is why 'living happily ever after' rarely occurs in real life. Consummation (in particular, of a fixed harmony) also has the dictionary meaning of death. Very few people live through a life that fits all parts together at its conclusion; this fact is indeed a familiar factor in wishing and even arguing for a next life in which to complete what has begun in this life. Those who find such a wish ill founded ought to view one's life as, in addition to other things, a preparation for death in the sense of aiming at the achievement of a best possible fit of the parts before death. If they are capable of viewing themselves as integral parts of a community (a family, a profession, a class, a nation, the human species, or the world), there is more room for alternative interpretations of what are the best possible completions of one's life. That need not make the task easier, since the interpretations often depend so much on what one believes will happen in the future.

The world is full of strifes, struggles, conflicts, differences, disagreements, contradictions, and inequalities. To find harmony in such a world would seem to have to require a faith in some bold postulations or pay the price of hypocrisy, evasion, distortion, or (if one is fortunate) being a dedicated and 'successful' member of a small (part of the) world. If the desire is to see the whole world as it is, then the ideal of a picture of harmony (even including reasonable extrapolations into the future) would seem to be prejudging the matter for the benefit of uncritical human wishes. Even the familiar devices of viewing evils as instruments for the good and asking only for freedom based on a knowledge of necessity usually have to appeal to the ill-defined hypothesis of a God or a future paradise on earth, based on very inadequate evidence. Most of us would be satisfied with a local harmony in that small fragment of the world into which each of us happens to be thrown. Indeed each person goes through life planted within the boundary of a smaller or larger circle, meeting more or less of the demands in life and harvesting gratifications of more or less of one's desires. Each life closes a circle connecting the person with a part of the world, by their interactions through the duration of the life. It is more often than not a good fortune not to be aware of facts and problems that have no direct bearing on one's everyday life. It seems idle to speculate about all (the basic) aspects of the whole world with the intention of finding some order in the great chaos.

Surprisingly, more progress has been made, not in the human realm, but in understanding the physical world as a whole, and, to a lesser extent, in biology and geology. One would have expected that, as Vico says, since people 'have themselves made this world of nations,' it is easier to understand history and society than the physical world. By now we are all accustomed to the idea that we are capable of the most reliable and detailed knowledge in physics. But this is primarily the result of our historical experience for the last few hundred years. In a period or a society lacking this experience, it is usually the case that we have more knowledge about human affairs than physics. That physics should have been the subject in which more solid knowledge has been acquired was, if one may say so, a historical 'accident' and surprise. Somehow even though we have not made the physical world, by projecting back into it a few simple concepts that we have extracted from it, we were surprised to see how stable and well-behaved it is according to the principles we have made on the basis of the very partial experience of it. Indeed, a major concern of modern philosophy has been attempts to give some plausible account of this surprise and to determine the limits of the successful method.

As we come to the human world, we find it harder to attain the universality of physics. Major cultural traditions and schools of thought use different concepts and languages and orientations. There are alternative and seemingly incompatible descriptions of the human world, which both help one's understanding by pointing out important aspects and hinder it by putting up a barrier between reality and one's thinking. Texts become themselves a part of reality, at the same time enriching it and making it more complex and often more obscure.

A major aspect of general views on the human world is their relation to time and place, or how well they fit together with the Zeitgeist (of the interested larger cultural communities). In his *The Spirit of American Philosophy* (1963), John E. Smith considers Peirce, William James, Royce, Dewey, and Whitehead, but not Santayana. He feels obliged to defend his inclusion of Whitehead and exclusion of Santayana. The case for Whitehead seems somewhat weak: 'His coming to America provided the opportunity and stimulus for his most original thinking, and he in turn gave to the American intellectual world a new insight into its own foundation' (p. 163). But his observations on Santayana are illuminatingly relevant to the question of the Zeitgeist (p. x): 'His thought is not representative of the main drift of American thinking. The American mind, as Santayana himself saw, is voluntaristic and not contemplative; it is moral and moralistic rather than aesthetic; it would sooner give up religion altogether than retain it as mere poetry; it will not accept any theory of reality according to which the self is either an appearance or evanescent. The American mind, in short, has been everything but what Santayana was and stood for.'

These observations and much of Smith's whole book illustrate well both the strength and the weakness of powerful regional philosophies that speak for the spirit of the time. The contrast with Santayana seems to reveal the one-sidedness of what Smith calls 'the American mind.' Writing in 1962, Smith said, 'The golden period of American philosophy is over and has been gone for some time' (p. 197). At the same time, he himself points out some of the intrinsic shortcomings and time-dependent limitations of the main trend in the 'golden period.' 'The possibility that the ego has depths not to be apprehended by the experimental method or mastered by the instrumental intelligence was quietly passed by' (p. 196). 'Upheavals abroad and insecurities at home have served to bring into clearer focus questions about genuine values and worthwhile aims. Americans are not as sure as they once were that if questions of means can be solved, the ends will take care of themselves' (pp. 197–198). Perhaps the recent state of American philosophy, so unsatisfactory to Smith and many others, is also related to the preparatory efforts to go beyond regional philosophies.

There is not a sharp enough distinction between the two different responsibilities of describing things as they are and finding them propitious to certain preconceived human desires. It is a piece of more or less accidental good fortune if one's sincere convictions happen to coincide with the aspirations of a large segment of one's community. This is different from striving to satisfy (or being easily swayed by) the 'unphilosophical' wish to gain the favor of the crowd or, equivalently or alternatively, even just to please the authority that happens to be in power. Clearly nobody can entirely shake off all his presuppositions and wishful beliefs in painting a picture of the world.

9.1.1 The right to believe

It cannot be denied that our beliefs, whose essence is a readiness to act, are influenced by our will and desires. The will (or rather the right) to believe, popularized by William James and criticized by Santayana, has a private aspect and a public aspect, which are, though interrelated, distinguishable. In both aspects there is an ideal of appropriateness to be approached by a dialectic of facts and wishes. For example, a belief in success can help to bring about success only if the belief is reasonably realistic. In order to complete a piece of work, one often has to suspend a reasonable doubt about the importance of the project. And in this case, the private aspect of the right to believe may lead to a negative public outcome by adding one more worthless text. Generally the choice to postpone a decision or to suspend judgment on an issue may be the right or the wrong action, depending on a multitude of factors.

Judiciously exercising the right to believe may help toward the favorite Chinese ideal of 'settling and upholding oneself' (anshen liming), which is private and contains the idea of withdrawing from a public role to cultivate the self. A more ambitious application of the right to believe is its constructive public function toward the ideal of coordination or of creating a unity out of a multiplicity. An essential element in religions is the designing of beliefs that aim at combining a supply of incentives for the individuals with a conformity to the requirements suited to the advancement of public good. In the secular realm Adam Smith's 'invisible hand' promises, with serious reservations, the same sort of combination of selfish pursuits that jointly are expected to serve the public good. Sometimes Gödel says that Marxism falls short of a religion. I take him to mean that Marxism fails to provide, except under unusual circumstances, sufficient incentives for enough individuals to pursue an adequately definite and foreseeable common goal with the needed vigor.

The interest in attaining some unity in a multiplicity is of course familiar to every community or any group with shared concerns, be it a family, a profession, a class, or a nation. The interaction of the right to believe with established truths ('describing things a they are') takes place on several levels, involving in varying degrees a diversity of factors, such as the immediacy of the need to act, the range of relevance of the belief in question, the size and character of the group asked to share the belief, the appropriateness of the reduction of a shared concern to more accessible 'ends in view,' and so on. To adopt as a general policy to act ('positively') whenever in serious doubt does have a flavor of optimism, even though the crucial concepts in the maxim are rather elusive.

In the grander cases a member of a group is urged to exercise his or her right to believe a many-parted and only potentially determinate proposition that sets up (say) a long-range national goal and proposes certain types of tentative measures to attain the goal. If the program is reasonably realistic, a majority of the group choosing to believe the proposition will help to create a determination of the content of the proposition close to the original intent and to make the (offspring of the less determined) original belief true. Here we have another example of the vital concerns in real life that call for considerations of the world as a whole. Indeed, the efforts to design and find ways to realize such beliefs are widely taken to be one kind of philosophical activity. If it is identified with philosophy, then its relation to and its distance from immediate politics become an acute problem. Experience appears to prove that an insufficient distancing harms both philosophy and politics, not only in the long run but also much more directly than most political authorities are willing to admit.

9.1.2 Purpose and distancing

According to G, the meaning of the world is (the process of continually trying to overcome) the separation of wish (more generally, force) from fact. The wishes are themselves an important part of fact; changing them is a crucial and less tractable component in our effort to mesh wish and fact. As our wishes are modified and enriched, the realm of purposeful activities broadens to contain, beyond the practical, also the intellectual and the artistic activities. Moreover, drawing the line between the real and the illusory within either of the two realms of wishes and their satisfactions becomes difficult.

Nonetheless, as soon as we come upon the all-pervading concept of purpose, fundamental but elusive distinctions beg to be recognized. There are purposes and purposes. Certain things we do for their own sakes; other things we do, willingly or reluctantly, with or without pleasure, for the sake of attaining an end. (In the extreme case, most of us cultivate defensively, to a greater or lesser degree, a negative satisfaction in getting rid of certain tasks that we hate to perform but 'have to.')

According to G. E. Moore, 'Personal affection and appreciation of what is beautiful in Art or Nature, are good in themselves.' Moreover, 'If we consider strictly what things are worth having *purely for their own sakes,*' he goes on to say, nothing 'else has *nearly* so great a value as' these things (*Principia Ethica*, 1903, pp. 188−189). But surely, for instance, food, clothing, shelter, sex, or a job well done can each be viewed as an experience (or an activity?) or a thing that has as great an (intrinsic) value? Immediately we notice here a basic ambiguity in the concept of preferring one value or another that depends on whether we have both things or have to choose between them.

Moore distinguishes between goodness as an attribute of states of mind and rightness as an attribute of actions. Hence, the pursuit of goodness can only be activities directed toward the attainment of certain states of mind. He also discusses carefully the relative importance of mental qualities and beauty, both of them essential to the value, in the object of one's personal affection (pp. 203−204). Thirty-five years later J. M. Keynes looked back to 'My early beliefs,' which were embodied in Moore's book (see *Two Memoirs*, written 1938 and published 1949, pp. 94−95, 92, and 99). The fundamental intuitions of the book, says Keynes, 'are much too few and too narrow to fit actual experience which provides a richer and more various content.' 'It is remarkable how wholly oblivious he [Moore] managed to be of the qualities of the life of action and also of the patterns of life as a whole.' 'We lacked reverence . . . for everything and everyone.'

Most of us most of the time do not look carefully at our states of mind and find it more congenial to think, in the first place, in terms of actions and purposes rather than their accompanying states of mind. We often get tired of purposeful activities and wish to rest, to play, or to have recreations and esthetic experiences. Much of our esthetic experience is connected with the basic needs of sex and other social interactions and, to a lesser extent, with food, clothing, and shelter. We create continually new needs and new purposes. By choice or by the force of circumstances, work itself often turns into a basic need, and a generally pleasant state of mind accompanying work becomes one of the main blessings to strive for in life. For example, the main feature of G's concept of paradise is that everyone has a happy marriage and a happy job.

An obviously useful and fundamental bifurcation of each person's activities in society is between his (or her) work and his (or her) 'free time' doings. When we look at the social roles of different kinds of work, we are struck by the varying distances from the social practices directly related to the more obvious social needs. A typical example may be the largely unpredictable distance between much of basic biological research and its medical applications. The social role of intellectual and artistic work is, directly or indirectly, to change our wishes and other facts by changing individual and social consciousness. The two kinds of work are interrelated. For example, poetry is not a medium merely of images, but also and necessarily of ideas. The esthetic component of intellectual work is present in all the different things meant by 'not only getting something done but also doing it well' and in managing to see important connections missed by others.

Each discipline of either kind of work also has its autonomy. It is largely in terms of this autonomy that practitioners in a discipline appreciate and applaud a piece of fundamental (theoretical or otherwise) work in it. But if we go beyond the well-structured and clearly delineated disciplines, as we do in the project of connecting all parts together, then the process of doing and the criterion of recognizing some fundamental theoretical work both become more involved and less predictable. Indeed it is quite natural not to sympathize with the efforts to fit all parts together because it is thought to be either impossible or pointless or even positively harmful. A comprehensive order can be harmful because it is likely to be deceptive and misused. There is also a widespread and somewhat inarticulate idea or emotion that connects order with authority and the restriction of freedom. But while the quest for a comprehensive order may eliminate certain apparent possibilities, it may also point to new possibilities. In any case, if the aim is to describe things as they are, there can be no consciously harbored authoritarian design.

9.2 Aspects of method

How does one go about fitting things together? G sometimes says that if you know everything about yourself, you know everything: once you understand yourself, you understand human nature, and then the rest follows. The observation points to the Leibnizian idea that each monad is a mirror of the universe and what is needed is to make its perceptions clearer. This leads to the question of individual differences (in, e.g., the degrees of their 'maturity') and the relevance of the possession or lack of certain special knowledge and experiences, to the project of a 'complete' understanding of oneself. Both G and Husserl appear to preach the sufficiency of everyday experience as data for philosophy. But G's own philosophical writings presuppose a good deal of knowledge of logic, mathematics, physics, and the history of philosophy, which can hardly be expected from just 'everyday experience.' He also seems to have read widely and, in some cases at least (such as the work of Leibniz and Husserl), carefully. He may view these departures from everyday experience as tools or ladders (to be discarded afterward) to bridge the gap between one's inevitably weak power of seeing the abstract and what is necessary for a decisive advance in the analysis of everyday experience. The ideal of his philosophy is to be 'precise but not technical.'

While I also find this ideal attractive, I am not able to envisage any plausible course that would lead to G's accompanying requirement of being precise in the form of an axiomatic theory that calls for the determination of the primitive concepts and the axioms seen to be true of them by our intuition. Undoubtedly most of us have a tendency to burden ourselves with useless data, while what is essential can usually be seen clearly by a more careful reflection or analysis of much less data. But I am not able to see why the axiomatic method is specially appropriate to philosophy. Rather I am inclined to think that there are enough inviting ideas and facts that ask to be fitted together in whatever form that will be attractive to us. Moreover, I have more respect for the contingent in human experience, as a whole and of each individual. Striving for an axiomatic theory in philosophy appears to me to be a less fruitful approach than allowing the content to determine the form. Indeed, the very idea of fitting all the parts together is different in spirit from G's requirement of being 'thoroughly systematic.'

If A could select a small number of individuals each of whom has a good understanding of some important aspect of human experience and if A could read all their minds, then A could be said to possess sufficient data and there would remain for A only(!) the formidable task of fitting all the parts together. Since such a state of affairs is obviously humanly impossible, A can only look for some restricted approximate substitute. In practice the process consists of a sequence of interactions between the acts of finding parts and fitting them together.

G says that his own philosophy is in its main features a Leibnizian monadology. He seems to imply that the increase in human experience over a quarter of a millennium makes little qualitative difference to the fundamentals of philosophy, and that the whole task is to strive to see the same basic concepts more clearly. According to him, philosophy analyzes concepts, while science uses concepts. Keeping in mind this difference, he would probably see an analogy between the efforts to go beyond Plato and, for instance, the negative solution of the Greek problem of trisecting any angle by elementary means (more than two millennia later). This attractive idea of the perennial character of the basic philosophical concepts and intuitions points to the stability of certain deep human concerns and defines an area of study that enjoys continuity and tranquility. True, many of us are justifiably skeptical that the practice of following closely every twist and turn of the current fashion could be fruitful in a real way. At the same time, some major changes in human understanding do seem to affect our philosophical outlook both in shifting our major concerns and in opening up new perspectives on the traditional concerns.

For example, the majority of philosophers since Kant tend to move away from religious metaphysics and, in particular, see a prior question to be faced in Kant's criticism of the tradition represented by Leibniz. G has apparently convinced himself that no good reason has been presented by history or philosophy to warrant departing fundamentally from the Leibnizian approach. In another direction, current physics (and, for that matter, set theory), unlike Newton's physics, appear to me to show that what we are more certain of are the medium ranges rather than the 'ultimate' foundations exemplified by the quest for a unified theory in physics (or a rich set theory). This experience would seem to cast some doubt on G's belief in the centrality of his axiomatic approach for philosophy. Moreover, while the ideas of Darwin, Marx, and Freud contain many unresolved difficulties, it is hard to see how a comprehensive philosophy can avoid taking some of their basic suggestions into consideration.

G seems to say that, once we are clear about the fundamentals, the rest will take care of itself. I tend to think of this sort of projection as another form of 'reductionism.' Like the more familiar varieties of reductionism, it is helpful when used with care and as a heuristic guide, as is undoubtedly the case with G, but its questionable promise for the future does not disprove the feasibility and desirability of alternative approaches. I would like to think that the disagreement between G and me lies not in the details but in that we are each interested in a different aspect of philosophy, which, moreover, is thought to be the more promising direction to look for a greater advance of general philosophy. Given the many differences in the way we grew up, this sort of disagreement is perhaps to be expected.

Let A be a person trying to fit all the parts together or to contrive a moderately transparent summary of cumulative human experience that is more accessible to what might be called the 'universal' private experience of each individual. The summary will inevitably depend, to a greater or lesser extent, on the special pattern of A's experience. To arrive at a summary, there is the obvious task of broadening A's limited perspective to obtain a clearer view of those parts of human experience with which A is less familiar. Since A's special experience must be lopsided in one way or another, it appears desirable to suppress its specificity for the sake of objectivity. At the same time it is this specificity that lends to A's thoughts a measure of 'depth,' and for the project of attaining a comprehensive view, what A is conscious of is all A has got at each moment. In my opinion, A should try to make full use of A's special experience, cautiously and critically. Indeed, the whole project may be seen in part as a reaction to the discomfort with the fact that most of our intellectual efforts do not aim at using and finding a place for the varied components of the motley of one's experience.

There are familiar obstacles on the road toward a broadening of one's perspective. Historical and fictional writings are more directly accessible, but they are written from highly diversified viewpoints and are subject to varied interpretations. Of the more structured types of writing, the mass of technical jargon and details is overwhelming. This obstacle is more obvious in the natural sciences and in mathematics, but there is the compensating advantage of a greater stability, dependability, and distinguishability (of the more fundamental from the rest, etc.). In writings of a broadly philosophical nature, there are often impenetrable boundaries of special vocabularies, which, when acquired, appear to increase one's power of expressing nebulous thoughts by entering a sort of coherent circle that is somewhat insulated from both the real situation and one's scattered clearer perceptions of it. The dual character of an apparent power and the deprivation of a sharper focus appears specially conspicuously in much of the general writings in the German tradition.

A needs some evolving foothold to select and digest the good parts of the reports on the various aspects of human experience, with the view of fitting them together. The foothold evolves with the structure of A's own consciousness as well as with the driving force derived from its anticipated courses of improving this structure to approach a comprehensive picture. It undoubtedly includes central concepts such as purpose, work, value, fact, etc., A's intuitions about them, and central facts such as the pervading force of the interaction between fact and wish. A more delicate component of the foothold is A's criterion or standard for selecting and rejecting, from the multitudinous candidates and for the purpose of constituting a whole, the parts to be accepted as facts and indeed (digestible and communicable) important facts for A's project. A kind of boundary or threshold or censor is necessary to separate the more assured from the less assured beliefs and to restrict the domain of what is to be considered more closely. For example, even though Kant's writings deal with a wide range of topics, one gets the impression that he limits them to thoughts on (what he takes to be) more universal and more permanent issues. Within the range of A's more assured beliefs, a moderately closely knit web of slowly shifting 'resting places' would lend some stability to the precarious quest for an order and help to find a middle course between skepticism and credulity. Such a web implies also a movable threshold to separate what needs to be considered or retained and what can be discarded.

The 'resting places' can be taken to include both certain pockets of greater certainty or clarity and changing boundaries set up by one's critical sense to limit what is accepted as justifiable assertions. One way to characterize these boundaries is to associate them with the injunction to say only what is 'precise.' For example, G's published philosophical statements are terse and appear to invite varied interpretations and extrapolations, even though they are thought to be precise, a quality that is greatly valued by G and decisively important in poetry (which is typically more concise than prose). To be precise is to be 'strictly expressed,' to be 'exactly defined.' I would like to think in terms of the command, Make sure you really do paint only what you see! This implies the additional requirement that you paint only what you are capable of 'expressing strictly,' because otherwise you are not *painting*, but only trying to paint, what you see. But it is enormously difficult to discern or depict one's own limitations clearly, or 'to invent a style of painting capable of depicting what is, in this way, fuzzy.' (I am connecting the general question of precision with Wittgenstein's observations on Bacon; see his *Culture and Value*, p. 68e, written in 1948.)

There are several issues mixed up in the concept of precision. It has no general correlation with being easy to read, being detailed or explicit, or being technical. For example, G wants philosophy to be precise but not technical. His mathematical writings are concise but no less precise than longer expositions of his ideas by others. The crucial point is that the qualified reader, perhaps with effort, can attain a correct grasp of the essential ideas. Indeed, the concept of an 'ideal reader' receives much attention in literary theory. But in philosophy the fundamental words and their usage are often 'loaded,' elusive, and corrupted. There is in addition the question of depicting the fuzzy. G finds the concepts of existence, creation (BP, bottom of p. 271), perception (of concepts, *MP*, p. 85), etc., perfectly clear, even though they are often thought to be ambiguous. He uses phrases like 'due to another kind of relationship between ourselves and reality' and 'give meaning to the question' (BP, p. 272) to paint what he sees when they are not more specific. He also makes predictions without indicating the justifications (e.g., about the future of philosophy, *MP*, p. 85). A striking aspect of his concept of precision is its intimate association with brevity (being concise). For instance, a familiar experience is that a rambling long letter often fails to communicate as much and as well of what one wishes to say as a carefully composed short one. At the same time, we often wish the author, G being a typical example, would write less concisely. It is desirable to express exactly what is seen in terms of concepts one sees clearly. But more is needed to communicate what is seen to others who do not understand these concepts so clearly. G does speak of teaching others to see the conceptual aspects of the world, but that apparently calls for a form of communication different from the one used in his published writings.

The metaphor of fitting parts together readily suggests the concrete image of solving a picture puzzle that, like examinations, sets up an artificially restricted goal but, unlike them, is off the actual main streams of life. If we begin with this concrete image, we can detect in the search for a comprehensive order some levels of difference from it. The pieces are not given in an exact enough form. There are many redundancies, and many not easily available pieces are necessary. The sizes of the pieces vary widely. There are many alternative (all imperfect) solutions of the main puzzle, each of which is to be contrived out of provisional solutions of (hierarchies of) smaller puzzles that do not quite fit together.

If A chooses to solve this formidable and indefinite puzzle, then he has to pick the material, forge the pieces, and look for guidance from all the available sources. What happens to strike A's fancy undoubtedly changes with time and with each particular A. But it is expected that A should reflect on his changing fancies to aim at a point of stable convergence that will also appear plausible and attractive to others. To give an illustration of some of the preliminary steps, I shall list ideas that I find suggestive and appear likely to play some part in looking for comprehensive outlooks. A more helpful guide is probably to be found by interpreting and reflecting on subjective reformulations of selected aspects of some existing solutions that are impressive in one way or another. Indeed, I view my reflections on G's thoughts in this light, and this is probably also the purpose of his study of the work of Leibniz and Husserl. More in conformity with the spirit of the time (extending over one or two centuries), my preference is to take the work of Kant and Marx as models and to try to discuss certain ideas suggested by some aspects of their work, with a view to examining also what I take to be yet unresolved difficulties.

The quest for a comprehensive view by one person A individually supplies a unifying purpose for A, but is undesirably restrictive in several ways. Many things are of interest that may or may not form parts of the eventual formulation of A's comprehensive view, if there is to be one. Since there are alternative comprehensive views, ideas that will not fit explicitly into A's frame can be useful for other solutions. Moreover, for A to will just this one thing is neither natural nor healthy. Generally A is likely to be accustomed to the study of less comprehensive issues for their own sakes, and such studies by A are indeed necessary even just for moving toward the attainment of this unifying goal. A more weighty consideration is the attractive prospect of cooperation with others, whether they are more interested in relatively isolated issues or in developing their own comprehensive views.

A broader and more fruitful perspective is to cultivate one's intellectual taste and use its current form to reflect on different things that are thought to be of relatively general and stable significance. The interaction of this perspective with the unifying preoccupation can be seen as an instance of the dialectic between the pursuit of purity and the continuing realization that (each fixation of) purity is not enough. In this way the range of meaningful purposes (or anticipated resting places) is extended, beyond the construction of the one mansion, to include also the baking of bricks, the fabrication of building blocks, and the sharpening of pointers toward blueprints and heuristics. The varieties of these indefinite categories may include comments on suggestive observations, attractive broad concepts and principles, ill-defined gross facts and tasks, and seemingly promising research programs. Allow me to list a few examples to illustrate what I mean and to give some shape, at least for my own benefit, to certain alluring (perhaps deceptively) but elusive images in my mind.

9.3 Bricks, blocks, and pointers

I have come to believe that a small number of suitably chosen broad concepts, together with certain almost vacuous principles ('semi-tautologies') suggested by them, can play an important part in the formulation of a comprehensive outlook. This is related to the traditional interest in the search for a list of fundamental categories (for instance, by Aristotle and Kant) and for a few large principles (such as the Leibnizian ones of contradiction, sufficient reason, continuity, etc.). Only I cannot foresee any neat complete list or any possibility of assigning to the principles the more rigid status of being necessary, analytic, or a priori.

Elsewhere I have remarked on what I call the principles of necessary reason and precarious sufficiency (BA, pp. 43–44, 57–58). I now prefer to call the second principle that of minimal existence, both to suggest the large gap between mere subsistence and a moderately bearable life, and to contrast it with what I would like to call the principle of maximal indulgence, which says that power tends to test its own limits. The last principle generalizes the oft-quoted saying that power tends to corrupt, absolute power tends to corrupt absolutely. It applies also to the palatial tombs of kings and emperors, the arrogance of powerful classes and countries, as well as to the tendency of activists to claim too much for themselves and their (just) cause. In these principles the broad concepts of sameness (and difference), equality, existence (or survival), and power are involved.

The concept of appropriateness, almost vacuously approving, gives a standard and an ideal of the widest range of applicability. A corresponding principle may be, Under all circumstances one should look for and try to bring about what is appropriate. It contains the doctrines of (the golden) mean of Aristotle (in his *Ethics*) and Confucianism (in the *Four Books*). More broadly, it suggests both the idea of giving everything its due and the effort to see how given parts fit together, as well as to find ways to make them fit together. The principle is elusive and open-ended because what is appropriate depends on what are taken as the parts, which generally change with time for various subjective and objective reasons.

The concept of a dialectic deals with the changing aspect of what is appropriate in the objective world and in human activities. For example, as A continues with a piece of work, what is (seen to be) appropriate changes with the current state of the work. In the pursuit of knowledge, both subject and object are in a continuing process of mutual adaptation, and the process of trying to know the world is never fully completed. If we call the interaction of subject and object (or of any B and any C) *negotiation*, the attempt to see or to intervene in the interaction (to interpret or to understand or to change the world) may be called *arbitration*.

Since interactions usually involve more than two factors, the idea of negotiation is to pay special attention to two of the factors, say B and C, and to take the action of the remaining factors as one of arbitration between B and C. Typically when a person A observes, studies, controls, or so forth the interaction between B and C, he or she may be said to be arbitrating their negotiation. For instance, the formal and the intuitive interact in scientific research, which values an appropriate mixture or interaction of them. I have elsewhere considered this instance of 'arbitration' with respect to biology (*Perspectives in Biology and Medicine*, vol. 27, 1984, pp. 525–542). One example is, 'We might say that C. F. v. Gärtner misused the formal in not supplementing it with enough of the intuitive, whereas C. Nägeli overindulged in the intuitive. Mendel was able to get the right blend of the two and discover the basic laws of heredity' (p. 530).

It is a striking and significant fact that a wide range of our basic conceptual contrasts is related or analogous to or has the flavor of the contrast between the formal and the intuitive. I have compiled a long list (ibid., pp. 540–541), but have not reflected on the significance of the fact or the interrelations of the various pairs. With regard to these pairs we may metaphorically speak of the need to arbitrate the negotiation between the two sides of each pair. Here is the list: (1) form and content, following the rule and making a leap, method and judgment, public and private, verification and discovery, explicit and implicit, repetitive and unique, outer and inner, mediate and immediate; (2) objective and subjective, universal and particular (one and many), abstract and concrete, essential and existential, analysis and synthesis, conscious and unconscious (ego and id), sayable and unsayable, quantitative and qualitative, analytic and descriptive, timeless and culture-bound, argumentative and contemplative; (3) concept and imagination, theory and experience, logic and mysticism, science and art, structuralism and hermeneutics, reductionism and organicism, materialistic and vitalistic, formal logic and dialectics, form and matter, knowledge and faith, local and global, scientism and humanism (or 'artism'), left hemisphere and right hemisphere (of the brain); (4) sense and sensibility, dry and wet, fairness and love, necessity and freedom (or chance), tough-minded and tender-minded, yang and yin, simple-minded and muddle-headed.

The consideration of the biologist's arbitration of the negotiation between the formal and the intuitive is vaguely thought to be illustrative of one way to give some more tangible content to the evidently related philosophical abstractions. I am presently not clear how this study fits into the comprehensive frame I am looking for. But it does appear to me to be of value to a general investigation of the varied types of negotiation between the formal and the intuitive, which may be viewed as the central concern of logic.

A closer examination of some of the fundamental concepts in some major area, which typically also have applications outside of the area, helps us to get a more concrete understanding of these broad (and potentially broader) concepts. For example, the lessons from biology center on the widely relevant contrasts between selection and instruction, the actual and the possible, tolerance and precision, crowdedness and adaptation, whole and part, etc. By a familiarity with how they function in biology we acquire a surer grasp of these pairs.

When a dualism (say of mind and matter) gives rise to unresolvable difficulties, the dialectic approach breaks the impasse, not by a full solution of the difficulties but by showing them to be 'unreal' and transforming them into less rigid (more fluid) difficulties. Generally the dialectic of lumping and splitting serves to make certain things clearer and clearer, by twists and turns that can often be disconcerting and may also bring to light new complexities and unclarities. In each situation, many factors are involved in considering whether it is more appropriate to lump or to split. A suggestive contrast between the Chinese and the European traditions is their respective preferences of lumping and splitting. While people generally prefer harmony to conflict, it is at the same time a familiar fact that an appearance of harmony usually conceals much conflict. It is often hard to judge judiciously whether and how much of the concealed conflict it is appropriate to bring out into the open.

When culture A decides to borrow from culture B, one looks for an appropriate way to do this. It is true but somewhat vacuous to say that A should borrow only what is good in B and retain only what is good in A. Though we often have a pretty good idea of what is good in A and B, we have less knowledge of effective measures to get rid of the bad in A and acquire the good in B, and we are especially ignorant of the connections between the good and the bad in A or in B. Undoubtedly a certain amount of trial-and-error experiment is necessary, but, in order to be effective and to reduce the costs, a good deal of knowledge and reflection over a wide range of things is clearly needed. Here we come upon a type of widespread vital concern that may be thought to be pointing to a motive to see the world as a whole. But the motive tends to exclude a sufficient detachment or distancing or patience to find out things as they are. Indeed, the place of philosophy in such projects is often seen to be the application of some good practical sense based on a broad perspective, or a flexible command of some tattered and malleable authoritative ideology, rather than the anticipation of longer-range needs by a more extended study of some continually relevant and more stable (or universal) philosophical topic.

I have elsewhere (*BA*, pp. 209–211) made some observations on the matter of selecting good philosophical topics (in the world of today). There are undoubtedly many good topics in the more specialized study of the philosophy of particular philosophers and particular disciplines. But I am concerned with them only to the extent that they can be seen to be relevant to the projects of formulating comprehensive views aimed at finding a picture of the world today. This standard is subjective, and indefinite in other ways as well. For instance, G's interest in Leibniz induced me to look at some books of Leibniz, among which his extended discussion of Locke's *Human Understanding* is seen to be of some special interest in displaying explicitly his famous power for seeing what is attractive in different views and fitting them together. Hence, it might be suggested that the book is helpful in learning to fit parts together.

G's concept of the axiomatic method certainly goes beyond the concept of formal systems, since he regards Newton's physics, for instance, as an axiomatic system (or theory). I do not fully understand his concept, which is also central to his recommended method of doing philosophy. It may, therefore, be desirable to know it better. In any case, the 'method' has, in comparison with explicit definitions, the advantage of a greater flexibility in determining and communicating the meaning of concepts (or words). But G does not take an axiomatic system as an 'implicit definition' of the concept(s) in it, because it is supposed to be a report of our (generally incomplete) intuitions of the concept and can be revised and expanded. It does not define (and fix completely) the concept, but rather invites improvements by comparison with the changing intuition. This situation is clear with the incomplete formal systems, which are of course (particularly explicit) special cases of axiomatic systems.

One natural avenue for me to approach philosophy is to compare Chinese with Western thought, and reflect on their interactions, which undoubtedly involve issues of philosophical significance. The interactions have not been symmetric. Like the rest of the world, China has felt acutely the impact of a unique development that began in Western Europe, spread to North America, and then moved around the globe. The intertwined development over several centuries includes, on the intellectual side, a new kind of rationality based on modern science and the Enlightenment, and, on the social side, the new life-styles, the institutions of parliamentary democracy and capitalist economics, as well as the doctrines of liberalism and socialism, all decisively conditioned by the political and industrial revolutions.

This predominance of the Western culture makes it hard to undertake a realistic comparison of what might be called the relative 'intrinsic' merits of Chinese and Western modes of thought, that could perhaps take the form of estimating the respective future achievements if the two cultures were allowed to live their separate lives for another thousand years. As it is, if any of its components are to survive, the Chinese culture has first to come to some terms with the Western.

For example, the era or movement symbolized by the demonstration on 4 May 1919 singled out science and democracy as the central sources of the difference between Chinese and Western societies. This pair was supplemented by the idea of socialism and the urgent task of resisting imperialism. In addition, there has been the question of bypassing capitalism to go directly to a socialist society. These issues are relevant to the larger divisions of the world today between developed and developing, capitalist and socialist countries, as well as to the history of the West over the last few centuries (particularly with regard to colonialism and its technological base).

Traditionally the issue of the goodness of human nature is important in Chinese thought. Indeed, the conflict of the two answers to this question occupies almost as central a place as that of rationalism and empiricism, or idealism and materialism, in the West. The question is important politically because it is related to the choice between persuasion and coercion. Writing in 1950 C. Brinton said that the liberal is 'faced with a real question: Do I or don't I trust the wisdom and good will of the common man? He can't be sure. His hesitation [is important for contemporary politics and] has deep historical roots, at least as far back as the Enlightenment' (*The Shaping of the Modern Mind*, 1953, p. 137).

China lacks any full development corresponding to either the 'unworldly' aspect of Greek philosophy or the other-worldly system of Christian theology. Both appear to play an important part in the emergence of modern science. The idea of a direct contact with God and reason may even be viewed as a primary impetus to the ideas of equality and democracy. Once a direct contact with God is favored, the individual and his direct appeal to reason are seen to be essential. One asks, therefore, to understand the relation of the individual not only to his social groups but also to the universe. Moreover, science and religion both seem to contribute more to direct reflections on the universe than the attempt to round off a worldview in the Confucian tradition that is conditioned basically by the (existing) hierarchy of social groups.

The central place of politics in Chinese philosophy appears to use the emperor as both a messenger for God and a substitute for a combination of the pope with Charlemagne. The importance of family relations is reflected in calling the emperor the *son* of heaven; when Hong Hsiu-chuan decided to use a form of the Christian religion for his political ambition, he claimed to be the younger *brother* of Christ. (The emperor is also the dragon, the agent that brings forth rain, reflecting the crucial role of rain in an agricultural society with rather unfortunate climatic conditions.)

The two basic questions about Chinese thought are what it can contribute to the world today and how it is going to assimilate Western (or modern) thought. One fashionable doctrine is that the acknowledged current superiority of Japanese business management owes a good deal to Confucianism. Since I am ignorant of the relevant facts, I cannot tell whether there is some truth in this belief. On a more universal level, what is usually recommended includes primarily Confucianism on the one hand and Chuang Tzu combined with Ch'anism (or Zen, the influential Chinese version of Buddhism) on the other. Some would stress their more subtle ideas, perhaps to suggest that Chinese thought is no less refined and profound. The more conspicuous aspect is of course the nearly exclusive concern with the 'this-worldly.' It seems reasonable to expect helpful lessons about human relations from Confucius and about cultivating a 'free spirit' from Chuang Tzu. Particularly notable is the importance of the esthetic component both in Chuang Tzu's writings and in his recommendations on how to live one's life. Confucius puts great emphasis on music in a broad sense. In fact, music and pleasure are so closely connected that the Chinese words for them use the same character but with different pronunciations (yüeh and lo).

According to M. Foucault, in sexual behavior the Greek formula underscores 'acts,' the modern formula is 'desire' ('since you have to liberate your own desire'), while the Chinese formula underscores 'pleasure': 'Acts are put aside because you have to restrain acts in order to get the maximum duration and intensity of pleasure' (*The Foucault Reader*, ed. P. Rabinow, 1984, p. 359). These suggestive, indeed sensational, empirical generalizations are hard to prove or disprove, since their meaning is not all that definite. Different readers will think of different fragments of the 'relevant' data and interpret them differently, assuming that they are 'true' in some significant sense.

I am inclined to select a reading that has the following property. If Foucault is right, then the Chinese formula would be the most civilized according to Kant's interpretation of the fig leaf in the book of Genesis: 'In the case of animals, sexual attraction is merely a matter of transient, mostly periodic impulse. But man soon discovered that for him this attraction can be prolonged and even increased by means of the imagination—a power which carries on its business, to be sure, the more moderately, but at once also the more constantly and uniformly, the more its object is removed from the senses' (*On History*, ed. L. W. Beck, 1963, p. 57).

This example, like the familiar superiority of Chinese cooking, seems to point to the wide range of sense and sensibility that potentially the Chinese culture could contribute to the world, except that, unlike cooking, the less concrete refinements are likely to be swept away by the world's tendency to identify progress with modernization, which is in turn identified with Westernization. In addition, there is the elusive task of balancing these refinements with the costs, either of retaining them or of acquiring them. Since these refinements form an integral part of a culture that has so far not been able to meet the Western challenge entirely successfully, one is inclined to adopt the negative attitude of viewing them as something that has to be given up for the sake of 'progress.' But undoubtedly this type of issue could only be considered meaningfully in a much more concrete context.

The Chinese are eager to acquire science and democracy, as well as the philosophical thoughts associated with them. In the realm of thought, two outstanding scholars have both expressed doubts that foreign thoughts can continue to live in China without drastic reformulation, and both use the authentic but noninfluential work of Tripitaka (Hsüan-tsang) to illustrate the point (Wang Kuo-wei around 1904, in his 'On the world of learning in recent times,' and his younger friend Tschen Yinko in his 1934 referee's report on Fung Yu-lan's *History of Chinese Philosophy*, II). Tschen says more explicitly that 'even if the thoughts of North America or Eastern Europe can be faithfully imported,' they will not survive for long; he expects that only something corresponding to the taoist religion and neo-Confucianism, developed in the Middle Ages, which absorbed something from Buddhism but remained essentially in the older Chinese tradition, could really become important in China. I am, however, inclined to disagree with them to the extent that I expect a greater departure in philosophy from the Chinese tradition, because the economic and political changes are and will be qualitatively different from the more or less cyclic changes between 221 B.C. and 1840 A.D.

9.3.1 The possible and the actual

According to G, the concept of existence in its weakest (widest) sense is one of the clearest of our primitive concepts; stronger senses require additional qualities, such as action. Correspondingly we have different senses of the actual and the possible. Mathematics, as Bernays says, studies possible idealized structures, which may or may not exist (be realized) in the physical world. In this sense of existence, set theory cannot be true in all possible worlds because only certain sets (in particular, structures) are realized or at least taken seriously as 'models' of (parts of) the concrete world. But sets are seen to exist in the wide sense of existence, and possible worlds can be contrasted with actual or existent worlds according to a stronger sense of existence. It is this interplay of wider and narrower concepts of the actual and the possible that allows us to look for some appropriate sense in which one may say that set theory (and also the theory of pure concepts yet to be developed) is true in all possible worlds. This is related to the familiar idea that arithmetic remain true even when it is no longer applicable in certain imagined worlds.

In a different sense, much of art and literature also studies possible idealized structures. It is a major problem to determine what this different sense is. But this suggestive analogy does include certain familiar ideas. A main function of imagination may be thought to be the capturing of idealized possibilities. By definition, fiction is not directed toward reporting literally the actual, yet there is little interest in the blatantly impossible. An ordinary reader of a novel usually sees it as playing out certain imagined possibilities. Even though much of art may be said to aim at communicating an actual inner experience, the inner experience itself may be taken as a view of some possible idealized structure, and one may feel more comfortable in saying that the structure, rather than the experience, is the object to be communicated.

The concern with the possible and its limits plays a central role in every aspect of human activities. In trying to understand the world, we aim at narrowing down the limits of the conceptually possible in order to approach a unique determination of the actual (identifying it with the necessary), speculatively as the 'best possible' world or less hastily as a 'complete' physics that eliminates all possible idealized structures but the one that will be seen to be the actual structure of the world. (If there were such a physics, the interplay of fact and force in nature would then be seen to be following a completely 'material' course, and we would have to recognize a realm of mind separate from the realm of matter or concede that our felt freedom of will is entirely an illusion.) On the other hand, human history or an individual's biography or the dialectic of wish and fact, while constantly being frustrated by (the recognition of) the limits of the possible, strives at all times also to expand the range of the possible.

In the world of living things, even though there exist a great number of species (several million) and individual variations, they make up only a small fraction of what, according to current knowledge, constitutes the range of possibilities. The idea of struggle for survival introduces a partial substitute for the postulation of some unfathomable cosmic purpose and adds a historical factor that eliminates a number of possibilities that would otherwise be actualizable according to the (internal) rules of reproduction. Generally in the world simpler objects combine to form more complex ones, but only a small part of the mathematically possible combinations are actualized (for instance, in going from atoms to molecules, thence to cells and to animal species). To understand the wide gap between the possible and the actual, one looks for *constraints* imposed by physicochemical and biological factors as well as by historical circumstances (compare F. Jacob, *The Possible and the Actual*, 1982, pp. 30–32).

Jacob expresses the importance of the limits of the possible in social life in these words (ibid., p. vii): 'Whether in a social group or in an individual, human life always involves a continuous dialogue between the possible and the actual. A subtle mixture of belief, knowledge, and imagination builds before us an ever changing picture of the possible. It is on this image that we mold our desires and fears.' He also stresses the relevance of history 'even in physics' and more centrally for biological objects. 'As complexity increases, history plays a greater part' (p. 31). Indeed, history means in the first place human history. Traditionally history as a study of the actual tends to pay more attention to a small number of exceptional particular individuals and spectacular events. But the way ordinary people live in a historical period gives more information about the period by revealing how unexceptional possibilities were actualized under unexceptional circumstances of the time. The exceptional events and individuals may be said to be more accidental because they are harder to predict, depending more on uncommon or atypical combinations of factors.

F. Braudel begins his study of civilization and capitalism (fifteenth century to eighteenth century) with a volume entitled *The Structure of Everyday Life: The Limits of the Possible* (1979, English translation 1981). In it he considers a number of '*parahistoric* languages' of the period: demography, food, costume, lodging, transport, technology, money, and towns. He speaks of a border that in every age separates the possible from the impossible. One of the limits of the preindustrial world is the enormous place occupied by 'material life': inadequate food supplies, a population too big or too small for its resources, low productivity of labor, lack of means to control nature, and slowness in qualitatively changing these constraints.

Certainly everyday life is not the only indicator of the limits of the possible. For example, Kant's idea of the limits of possible experience may be taken as an abstract aspect of the richer and more concrete idea of the limits of the possible, an idea that suggests a systematic study to determine as far as one can all that is humanly possible to achieve, including the possibilities of better societies and better life forms. As we recognize more of the constraints, we get a clearer picture of the limits of the possible. But too many alternatives remain that are not seen to be impossible, and probability calculations are notoriously slippery in the human realm. In practice, we generally are concerned with the limits of the possible under quite concrete situations with a view to helping us to make decisions and set up goals. For theoretical studies, the attractive idea of the limits suggests an unlimited range of directions, which call for varied methods of investigation and promise results of vastly different degrees of definiteness. For example, the limits of elementary geometrical constructions and of theoretical computation have been conclusively determined, but the limits of feasible computations or of definability or of provability are much more elusive. Set theory may also be taken to be a study of the limits of possible idealized structures. Braudel's historical study of the limits of the pre-industrial world reminds one of the more formidable Marxian project of determining the limits of capitalism. In philosophy, apart from Kant's notion of possible experience, there is the notion of the sayable in the *Tractatus*; it appears, however, that philosophers no longer look for such broad unifying concepts.

I have considered the limitations (and hinted at possible extensions) of the enormously simplified model of the world depicted in the *Tractatus*, which, in particular, places logic elegantly at a central place (*BA*, pp. 75–100). Typically as we replace the simplifying assumptions in a model by more realistic approximations to our richer intuitive picture of the world, we encounter models that are more complex and less transparent. The more fruitful models are to be appropriate in the sense that they capture and give order to our larger intuitions, as well as retain a manageable degree of complexity. When we look at the interrelated idealizations in the *Tractatus*, we see that they make room for value by relegating it to the realm of the 'unsayable,' as Kant makes room for faith by putting it beyond the reach of pure theoretical reason.

Once fact and value are sharply separated and value is left out as beyond theory, it becomes easier to adopt drastic postulates that, however, are unreasonable even for the restricted realm of value-free facts. If we do more justice to this restricted realm, we are inclined to question these postulates adopted in the *Tractatus*: the complete representability of thought by language and the world by thought, the adequacy of only one kind of thing, the exclusion of intensions and intentions, the homogeneity of the finite and the infinite, and the independence of the elementary propositions. For example, instead of only one kind of thing, we seem to need both objects and concepts. For a more adequate philosophy, we may also wish to take images as a basic category. Once we think about concepts, we are led to the question whether clusters of concepts and changes of concepts can all be dealt with adequately as mere appearances or as derivatives of precise concepts. In particular, we may also ask whether the study of clusters and changes is part of logic if we adopt G's suggestion that logic is the theory of concepts.

To begin with a less complex model, we may seek to liberate the *Tractatus* by trying to develop an analogous theory in which logic turns out to be set theory, which is a moderately well-developed area and, therefore, offers a more definite guide than yet broader conceptions of logic (such as G's or even Hegel's). For example, it would be gratifying to find an appealing concept of possible worlds so that set theory is seen to be true in all possible worlds. The explicitly recognized part of the furniture of the world has to be expanded beyond that in the *Tractatus*. The incompletability of set theory (or even of number theory) calls for a more complex conception of the relation between language and thought. And so on. (For more on the *Tractatus*, see *BA*, chapter 2.)

9.4 Additional notes and remarks

The quest for and the presentation of a comprehensive view can be understood in many different ways. It aims at a statement, in one form or another, of either what A actually believes or what A takes to be rational to believe. The statement may be well organized or not, brief or extended, pedestrian or stimulating, etc.; the beliefs may be familiar or novel, lukewarm or powerful, pale or persuasive, etc.

There are collections of summaries or quotations that go under titles like *What I Believe* and *The Wisdom of the West*. (One example is *The Viking Book of Aphorisms*, selected by W. H. Auden and L. Kronenberger, 1962.) While such collections can be informative, they can hardly reveal a coherent comprehensive view. G is known to have found perceptive quotations from his preferred reading (Kant, Husserl, Fichte, Schelling, Hegel, etc.). For example, in the early 1930s he, says Menger, 'showed me a passage [in a book of Hegel] which appeared to completely anticipate general relativity theory' (see Menger's memoir). He may have kept a record of such passages. 'The publication of such an anthology is likely to produce a minor revolution in philosophy' (Kreisel, p. 218). It is conceivable that a well-organized collection of aptly selected quotations with appropriate comments can be a reasonably effective way to express one's comprehensive view, but I am not aware of any serious attempts to do so. What is more commonly done is to rewrite others' work from one's own perspective; for example, W. Windelband's *A History of Philosophy* may be viewed as an account of his own philosophy. In contrast, Montaigne presents informally a comprehensive view in his *Essays* by recording reflections on his readings and personal experience.

Herbert Spencer, Oswald Spengler, and Arnold Toynbee are known for their efforts to synthesize human experience. But their work is thought to lack sufficient 'precision' to be regarded as philosophy or serious philosophy. I have considered in *BA* (pp. 53–56) Bacon's program of an *instauratio magna*, which is hard to execute and hard to evaluate before execution. Descartes and Husserl aimed at thorough reconstructions of human knowledge that would transform philosophy into a science. The 'beginnings' presented by them have received much attention in the development of philosophy. Kant, Hegel, and Marx are more systematic, so that their work goes beyond the concentration on methods and foundations.

If philosophy is taken to be the study of what is rational, then the vague categories of technical (or instrumental), humanistic, and revolutionary reason all ask to be considered. Owing to the prevalent mood of restricting attention to the more definite and the surprising advances in computer technology, the perspective of seeing reason in terms of the capabilities of machines has received attention in recent decades. It is known as the study of artificial intelligence (briefly, AI), which is of course relevant to G's wish to separate minds from machines.

Since AI is primarily interested in what is feasibly computable, the mathematical aspect of it involves only a very small part of mathematics (and logic). What is under consideration is, however, not the objective domain of mathematical objects, but the human power to deal with them (and other things). Hence, the limitations of AI cannot be demonstrated by this easy observation about its severely restricted subject matter in the idealized sense. The focus is rather on what is practically possible. For example, it is more relevant to point out that people have a better sense of the 'order of magnitude,' even though they are more likely to make mistakes in complex details than computers. There is the idea and practice of delegating the handling of details to others (and to computers).

Once I asked a colleague, 'How are we to introduce the unconscious into the computers?' 'I would say,' he answered, after a pause, 'computers are (entirely) unconscious.' As an unconscious appendage to our consciousness, computers differ radically from the human unconsciousness in that we understand how the computers work much better than how our consciousness works, which we understand better than how our unconsciousness works. Hence, my question is premature, since we do not yet know how to introduce consciousness into the computers. The importance of the unconscious for creativity is a familiar fact. (For example, J. Hadamard, in his *Psychology of Invention in the Mathematical Field*, 1945, discusses striking examples by referring to Mozart, Helmholtz, Poincaré, P. Valéry, etc., and to related studies, such as *Art of Thought* by Graham Wallas, 1925.) What goes on may be said to be a negotiation between the ego and the id that often takes a relaxed form depending more on a general readiness of the mind than the conscious exertion of the will.

Freud formulated the concept of id in his *The Ego and the Id* (1923). It has the flavor of the Will in Schopenhauer's philosophy (as a development of Kant's noumenon), as well as the Dionysiac of early Nietzsche and even Locke's material substratum. While the contents (of the ultimate instincts of Eros and Thanatos) of the id are in themselves entirely unconscious, the unconscious parts of the ego and the superego are also included in the realm of the unconscious. 'The ego,' says Freud in the same work, 'is first and foremost a bodily ego.' These pregnant suggestions all point to the complexity of our thinking process, which implies, for instance, major long-range difficulties for the more ambitious goals of AI.

According to Leibniz, there are present in the mind insensible, minute, and confused perceptions, as well as natural or acquired habits and aptitudes. The discussion in his *Nouveaux Essais* (1704, published in 1765, partly translated in R. Latta, *The Monadology and Other Philosophical Writings*, 1898) includes the following observations. 'There is at every moment an infinity of *perceptions* in us, but without apperception and without reflexion; that is to say, changes in the soul itself of which we are not conscious [s'apercevoir]' (Latta, p. 370); it is in consequence of these unconscious perceptions that 'the present is big with the future and laden with the past, that there is a conspiration of all things.' and they 'also indicate and constitute the identity of the individual' (p. 373). 'In a word, unconscious perceptions are of as great use in pneumatics [philosophy of mind] as imperceptible corpuscles [elementary particles] are in physics; and it is unreasonable to reject the one as the other on the ground that they are beyond the reach of our senses' (p. 376).

G clearly favors Plato over Aristotle, and Leibniz over Kant. In both cases the later philosophers are more explicit (or articulate) and systematic, but less suggestive and, I believe G would also say, less (near to what is) true. Kant separated the human intellect, will, and feeling, superimposed on them a tenuous unity, and gave a structured formulation of the 'modern' worldview. The formulation claims to reconcile necessity (in nature) with (human) freedom, and reveals in a sharper form the implicit dualism in the view thus made more explicit by him. God, the final purpose (or cause), immortality, the universe as a whole and in its finest detail, etc., all lie in the realm of the thing-in-itself, which is not knowable by the human intellect, but reveals itself, though only extremely dimly and partially, to our will and feeling.

Kant saw what unites all individuals in their thoughts and actions (to constitute their imperfect community) in what is common to them in their intellect (the pure intuition of time and space and the categories of the understanding), will (the categorical imperative), and feeling (the *sensus communis*). But they are separated by contingent factors that differ from individual to individual and make them 'unsocial social animals': sensations, inclinations, selfish interests. In his 'Idea for a Universal History' (1784) Kant did speak of 'Nature's secret plan' to bring forth a perfect community or a kingdom of freedom (or kingdom of God on earth) and assert that 'the Idea can help, though only from afar, to bring the millennium to pass.' Moreover, 'On the fundamental premise of the systematic structure of the cosmos and from the little that has been observed, we can confidently infer the reality of such a revolution,' and 'It seems that our own intelligent action may hasten this happy time for our posterity' (*On History*, ed. L. W. Beck, 1963, p. 22). But Kant gave no more indication of why or how the imperfect community will eventually give rise to or approach the perfect one. According to Lucien Goldmann (*Immanuel Kant*, 1971, p. 224), perfect community was, for Kant, one of the 'suprasensible ideas which man can never realize here on earth through his will and his action. Because he *must* strive towards them, towards the only real spiritual values, without ever being able to attain them, man's existence is tragic.' This statement of impossibility seems, however, to contradict the assertion by Kant that I just quoted.

The kingdom of freedom is an ideal that is to some extent present in everyone's mind. It is, therefore, not surprising that the proposal by Marx, which promised not only the emancipation of the working class but also an approach to this highest ideal, had and has a wide appeal. The proposal includes a plausible general view of history and an acute analysis of the capitalist society. The crucial and most speculative point is probably the identification of the dynamic force of humane history with the proletariat, which is taken to be a more or less homogeneous class of individuals who share a number of special properties, ideally suitable for the grand role. The situation is analogous to proposing a solution to a very complex set of equations.

An idealized characterization of the proletariat seems to include the following features. The class makes the greatest contribution to society but is oppressed and exploited. It makes up a majority of the labor force. Its members are permitted to live only on the subsistence level, and they 'have nothing to lose but their chains.' At the same time they basically are or can be educated to become enlightened, comradely, and unselfish; their sentiments are international. The wish of the class coincides with the aspirations of humanity on the whole, and it has the power to overcome the separation of wish and fact. It is the 'identical subject-object of history.'

For many years Marx and his followers believed that the working class in several Western European countries actually or potentially satisfied these conditions to a large extent. Historical experience has shown that this was not quite the case and we do not possess a simple set of equations for the (unknown) dynamic force that admits a presently determinable group of actual individuals as its solution. It is familiar today that nationalism remains a strong force and the working class has become less homogeneous and less uniformly impoverished. In philosophical terms G. Lukacs gave an extended discussion in his famous essay 'Reification and the consciousness of the proletariat' (first published as the central paper in his *History and Class Consciousness*, 1923). In the 1967 preface to a new edition, he criticized its idea of the proletariat (by its class consciousness) 'becoming the identical subject-object of history': 'But is the identical subject-object here anything more in truth than a purely metaphysical construct? Can a genuinely identical subject-object be created by self-knowledge, however adequate, and however truly based on an adequate knowledge of society, i.e., however perfect that self-knowledge is?'

Though we have no clear idea how to approach the unattainable kingdom of freedom, the rather indefinite ideal somehow retains its impact on historical development. As one aspect of it becomes a demand and an expectation for us at a particular time, particular tasks are suggested by it that require more of our attention because of their believed connection with it. Moreover, the ideal somehow serves as a norm by which to judge a given form of society and to point to a coming one.

Apart from the inequality of different classes, we are today much aware of the major inequalities of different countries, different races, as well as of men and women. Tocqueville believed that the world does and ought to move toward equality, even though he seemed to view the process and the prospect with some misgivings in calling it one of 'levelling down.' According to what I call 'the principle of necessary reason,' it does seem to say there is a natural tendency to move toward 'equality' (in the long run). After all, every inequality demands an explanation, and when differences have really satisfactory explanations, they are no longer inequalities. As it is, the glaring major inequalities have no convincing, not to say conclusive, explanations.

The unification of heaven (*t'ien*) and person (*jen*) is a central theme in Chinese philosophy. An analogue or instance of the vague idea would be the theme of unifying naturalism and humanism. For example, Marx says in the Paris *Manuscripts*, 'Here we see how consistent naturalism or humanism distinguishes itself both from idealism and materialism, constituting at the same time the unifying truth of both' (*The Economic and Philosophic Manuscripts of 1844*, ed. D. J. Struik, 1964, p. 181). Of course, we see the world through the human senses and build up our picture of the world with the help of the mind. From accumulated experience we believe that we get more or less adequate pictures, which will be continually improved. In language characteristic of his time, Marx further points out that Hegel's process of thought superseding thought 'must have a bearer, a subject' (p. 188): 'Abstraction comprehending itself as abstraction knows itself to be nothing: it must abandon itself—abandon abstraction—and so it arrives at an entity which is its exact opposite—at *nature*' (p. 189). Hence, denying nature leads to its affirmation. 'But *nature* too, taken abstractly, for itself— nature fixed in isolation from man—is *nothing* for man' (p. 191).

'*Sense-perception* (see Feuerbach) must be the basis of all science. Only when it proceeds from sense-perception in the twofold form both of *sensuous* consciousness and of *sensuous* need—that is, only when science proceeds from nature—is it *true* science' (p. 143). Need brings in the practical element at the root of all inquiry. Moreover, need as a natural fact is of course also the source of all human values, both moral and esthetic. The twofold form of sense-perception from the beginning mixes the elements leading to truth, goodness, and beauty. Sense-perception in its full richness develops not only as a person grows but also with the changes of the human species. The sensuous is the basis of all knowledge and valuation. For knowledge, consciousness plays a more conspicuous role; for valuation, need.

Two large types of motivation in the study of philosophy are predominant: universality of knowledge and a better life. Since neither quest admits of any final and complete solution and since theory is, by definition, distinct from practice, there is usually a utopian element in the sense of a preparation for some future ideal. The two types are bound together through the interplay of agreement and disagreement. The resolution of disagreement both removes one obstacle toward universality and increases the likelihood of harmony, which is an essential ingredient of a better life. To some extent it is true that to understand is to forgive and that what is alien is the chief symptom of evil. Shared knowledge augments mutual understanding and reduces conflict. In practice, mutual understanding is rarely a conscious goal, but usually the result of interactions and other circumstances. If we know much more and everyone shares this common knowledge, the power of mutual understanding undoubtedly increases universally.

As it is, knowledge is more conspicuously associated with the power to control. For Bacon, knowledge is power, primarily to give mankind mastery over the forces of nature by means of scientific discoveries and inventions. It is tacitly assumed that knowledge is universally shared. In the human sphere, we are more struck by the refusal to share knowledge and by one person or one group using it to control or resist another person or another group. Typically there are secrets, deceptions, and outright lies, which in their subtlest form determine the 'constitution of the subject' (compare Foucault, 'The subject and power,' in *Michel Foucault*, H. Dreyfus and P. Rabinow, 1982, e.g., p. 208). This phenomenon adds a new dimension to the interplay of knowledge and power for those who look for universally shared knowledge. Increasing such knowledge will unmask the deceptions and reduce the power of those who consciously or unconsciously benefit from them. This response to the fact of deception and ignorance enriches the interaction between knowledge and emancipation.

The quest for a better life contains two related parts: for the individual and for the collective (a community, a country, the oppressed in one grouping or another, or the whole human species). There are different conceptions and degrees of the mutual conditioning of the emancipation of one and the emancipation of all; there are different mixtures of acceptance and revolt in the proposed measures for emancipation. On the highest level, objectivity and solidarity converge because universality (*universalitas*) in knowledge and emancipation of the totality (*universitas*) are the mutal conditions for each other. This is by definition the highest ideal, which is one idea of the 'kingdom of freedom.' Undoubtedly G's aim in philosophy is to secure universality in knowledge. But the major task of philosophy is, I believe, the determination of the very concept of universality so that it will be the key to emancipation and be attainable by human efforts. I certainly do not believe that the concept being sought is wholly captured by our experience with mathematics, which, after all, is only a very special aspect of our lives.

PART III

Texts (a supplement)

In this part I shall make some comments on the texts of Gödel's publications. The two chapters deal, respectively, with G's mathematical and philosophical papers.

Like Leibniz, G wrote a great deal more than was published in his lifetime, and left a number of projects in an unfinished state. Indeed, G's major results and projects can be viewed as developments of Leibniz's conceptions along several directions. I have mentioned before G's sympathy with the main lines of Leibniz's monadology and his interest in realizing some modified form of a universal characteristic (which is, largely through G's work, seen to be impossible in the strong sense of requiring a decision procedure). Both of them had faith in the power of the axiomatic method and the possibility of a fruitful logic of discovery (or science of method). Logic occupies a central place in their conceptions of philosophy. G's respect for Leibniz is comparable to Leibniz's for Aristotle (in logic) and Plato (in philosophy).

William and Martha Kneale, in their *The Development of Logic* (1963, pp. 320–336), give an extended consideration of the many different facets of Leibniz's thought about logic, which 'seemed to him [Leibniz] like a jewel that can throw light in many different directions.' The interrelated components include (1) the coordination of knowledge in an encyclopedia, (2) a universal ideal language, (3) a procedure for the rapid enlargement of knowledge (a possibility also envisaged by Bacon and Descartes before him), (4) the arrangment of all true propositions in an axiomatic system, (5) decision procedures. Of course Leibniz could not realize the whole program and he had only limited successes. From G's and related work, we know that (5) is not possible for moderately rich theories and (4) is impossible if axiomatic systems are limited to *formal* systems in the currently accepted sense. Similarly, (3) has to be understood liberally in terms of procedures that are not strictly *algorithmic*. G's modified program retains the main features of Leibniz's ideal in their essentials. G continued to look for a fundamental axiomatic theory (for metaphysics) from which he hoped to deduce (or at least to get a foundation for) all knowledge. Moreover, as a way of realizing (3), he looked for an analysis of concepts that would give us also methods of proving new results. Leibniz said, 'My metaphysics is so to say all mathematics, or could become so' (Kneale, p. 336). In a sense G's approach gives a similar impression.

Leibniz's 'interest in the making of an encyclopaedia was due in large part to his realization of a growing tendency to the fragmentation of knowledge.' When Leibniz was about twenty, he thought of the project as a series of extracts from the best writers on all the various subjects, to be presented in a logical order of development. Later he gave mathematics a bigger place in his scheme and, in addition, wished for an axiomatic theory that was, at one stage, to include even the knowledge of nature accumulated by craftsmen. At a still later date he proposed to include only the first principles of the various sciences, and in the end what he actually did was to give an outline of his worldview in his *Principes de la nature et de la grace* and *Monadologie*. (The account follows Kneale, pp. 330–331, where some specific references are given.)

I do not know whether G went through a similar process of development. G's range of knowledge was also exceptionally broad, but, certainly in his later years, he objected to collecting data and was emphatic that in philosophy one should confine oneself to what is fundamental and essential. G would, I believe, view Leibniz's changes as improvements toward a correct way to organize and ground knowledge rather than as successive lowerings of the goal. Both Leibniz and G were good at appreciating alternative viewpoints. But G spoke of analysis as the central task, while Leibniz often expressed his pride in his ability to synthesize. In practice both of them paid much attention to existing knowledge, if only to convince themselves that most of it could be disregarded in the development of their fundamental work.

With regard to the development of mathematical logic, two of Leibniz's ideas have turned out to be of central importance. His truths of reason that 'hold for all possible worlds' open up a fruitful way of characterizing logical truth. This is obvious in the account of the 'tautologies' (of the propositional calculus) as set down in Wittgenstein's *Tractatus*. It fits equally well the concept of what is valid or logically true in the framework of elementary logic. Indeed, G's completeness theorem says simply that all propositions that are true in all possible worlds are provable in the familiar formal systems for elementary logic. Moreover, as I have mentioned several times, it appears desirable to find some natural concept of possible worlds so that the true propositions of set theory are seen to be true in all possible worlds.

The other important idea is Leibniz's emphasis on 'formal arguments,' which are 'infallible.' This intuitive requirement began to receive greater attention in the nineteenth century and gradually led to the exhibition of truly formal systems for several major areas of mathematics. And G's incompleteness theorems are the decisive negative results on their capacity to be comprehensive. (For an extended discussion of this development, see my *Survey*, pp. 1–28.) As we know, it was after G's discovery that precise concepts (of mechanical procedures or algorithms) were formulated and seen to capture the essence of what Leibniz called 'formal arguments' (compare the discussion in *MP*, pp. 84–86, 90–95).

Leibniz gave one account of formal arguments in the context of explaining why he was enthusiastic about Aristotle's theory of the syllogism. 'I hold that the invention of the syllogistic form is one of the finest, and indeed one of the most important, to have been made by the human mind. It is a kind of universal mathematics whose importance is too little known. It can be said to include an art of infallibility, . . . a well drawn-up statement of accounts, an algebraic calculation, an infinitesimal analysis—I shall count all of these as formal arguments, more or less, because in each of them the form of reasoning has been demonstrated in advance so that one is sure of not going wrong with it' (*New Essays on Human Understanding*, written mainly in 1704, translated by P. Remnant and J. Bennett, 1981, pp. 478–479; compare H. Scholz, *Concise History of Logic*, 1931, English translation 1961, pp. 50–59). The examples show that Leibniz's conception included (what are nowadays called) data processing and nonnumercial symbol manipulations. Frege's *Begriffsschrift* (1879) was composed to make logical inferences explicit so as to 'attain the precision that my purpose required': 'To prevent anything intuitive from intruding here unnoticed, I had to bend every effort to make the chain of inferences free of gaps. In attempting to comply with this requirement in the strictest possible way I found the inadequacy of language to be an obstacle' (*FG*, pp. 5–6).

Corresponding to Leibniz's ideal of 'infallibility,' Frege aimed at proofs 'free of gaps' to prevent the unnoticed intrusion of intuition. The dual emphasis of (logical) *form* and of being infallible (or free of gaps) pointed to the requirement of proofs being mechanically checkable in a *formal* system. The concept of form of course indicates something that is universally true. In other words, all instances of the form are true, or a logically true proposition is true 'in virtue of its form.' An instance may be construed as a realization (or interpretation or model) of the form. When realizations of all different forms are put together in a consistent manner, we may be said to describe a 'possible world.' A true or valid form is just one that is true in all possible worlds.

In *Wissenschaftslehre* (1837, republished in 1930) Bolzano calls a proposition valid (allgemeingültig) relative to its constituents *i, j*, etc., when results obtained by varying these constituents at will are all true. If all the unchanging parts belong to logic, the proposition is said to be logically true (or 'analytic in the narrower sense'). He goes on to say, 'This distinction has of course something vague about it because the range of the concepts which belong to logic is not so sharply defined that controversies may never arise in the matter' (§148). If the concepts of logic are agreed upon, then Bolzano's definition determines the set of valid or logically true propositions. It is then natural to call a formal system complete if all logically true propositions are provable. Indeed, this is the sharper of the two definitions of completeness proposed for their system of elementary logic in Hilbert-Ackermann (1928). It is also the sense in which G proved in 1929 the completeness of (the familiar systems of) elementary logic.

Chapter 10
Mathematical papers

Roughly speaking, all G's mathematical papers were written before 1940 (more specifically, from 1929 to 1939). The only exceptions are his two technical papers in relativity theory and the technical part of his 1958 paper. Since I have made scattered comments on some of the papers in earlier parts of this book and since there are extended notes on all the papers in *CW*, I shall limit myself in this chapter to a few observations on G's work proving the completeness of elementary logic and the incompletability of mathematics. (Intuitive sketches of the steps G actually took in getting his incompleteness proof and his relative consistency proof by constructible sets are given in my *Popular Lectures*, pp. 21–23 and 128–133.)

10.1 Completeness of elementary logic

The proof was given in his dissertation (completed in July 1929) and the related paper published in 1930 (received by the editor on 22 October 1929). Both versions (and in German and in English) are included in *CW* (first volume, 1986), with an extended introductory note by B. Dreben and J. v. Heijenoort. In 1967 I discussed the proof in relation to the work of Skolem, and the discussion caused G to write his two letters to me (reprinted with minor omissions in *MP*, pp. 8–11). Afterward I revised my survey of Skolem's work to take into consideration G's comments and published it in *Selected Logical Works of Th. Skolem* (ed. E. Fenstad, 1970, pp. 17–52).

G had a good command of a good deal of theoretical physics, mathematics, and philosophy, when his interest turned to logic in 1928. For example, he requested books by Frege and Schröder in October. He attended the Carnap course on 'metalogic' (listed as 'The philosophical foundations of arithmetic') in the winter semester of 1928/29. At that time there was only a very limited literature on mathematical logic, of which the most important were *PM* and HA (Hilbert-Ackermann, 1928). G studied both of them, apparently in early 1929.

The dissertation is of special interest both as G's first extended scientific writing and as an exceptionally thoughtful essay at a time when there was a good deal of conceptual confusion about the nature of logic and its appropriate methods. Technically it added little to what was available then, yet important new results were obtained essentially just by seeing clearly what was available. The organization and the presentation shed much light on all the issues related to the work. Additional evidence of G's firmer grasp of the more or less familiar material was his application of the ideas in proving the decidability of a significant class of formulas in the prenex form, known as the 'Gödel case' (compare chapter 3, under *1929*).

The first formal system for elementary logic was introduced by Frege in his *Begriffsschrift* of 1879. It was not an entirely formal system because rules of substitution were used but not stated (and a rule of generalization is concealed in notational instructions). Nor was it a system only of elementary logic because function letters (or predicate variables) are allowed to occur in quantifiers. (For more details, see *FG*, pp. 2–4.) In both respects the system of *PM* (1910) was similar (in leaving some rules implicit and in not being entirely a separate system). The rules of inference were made explicit in the system of HA, although, as in *PM*, identity was not taken as a primitive concept. (The system of HA was due to Bernays, as acknowledged on p. 54.) In any case, all three systems were commonly and justifiably accepted as formal systems for elementary logic, and all were known to G in 1929.

Hence, fifty years elapsed between Frege's introduction of the first system and G's proof that such systems all are complete. But what took so long to realize was more the formulation of the problem (of completeness) rather than its solution (once the problem was posed). The question was for the first time formulated and asked only in 1928 (in HA, p. 68). The answer came soon afterward (from G). Indeed, G solved the problem almost immediately after he had encountered it. Hence, the puzzling part is rather the delay in formulating the question.

Both Frege and Russell took elementary logic as an integral part of a richer comprehensive logic. They were, like Wittgenstein in the *Tractatus*, convinced that one could not go outside of logic, which determines the limit of what is thinkable or 'sayable,' and talk about logic in a metalogic (or metamathematics). On the other side, Boole, Peirce, Schröder, Löwenheim, and to a considerable extent also Skolem were not concerned with formal systems. It was the Hilbert school that first asked these questions, as its members, beginning with the axioms of geometry and their completeness, consistency, and independence, moved gradually to logic and to formal systems.

The completeness of the propositional calculus was formulated and settled by Bernays in 1918 in his *Habilitationsschrift*, of which a shortened version was published in 1926. G explicitly referred to the published paper: 'For the formulas of the propositional calculus the question has been settled affirmatively; that is, it has been shown that every true formula of the propositional calculus does indeed follow from the axioms given in *Principia Mathematica*' (FG, p. 583). From a different approach, Wittgenstein's *Tractatus* (also completed in 1918) may be viewed as a formulation, though not a solution, of the problems of validity and completeness with respect to (elementary) logic. But, owing in part to his unjustified reduction of quantified propositions to conjunctions and disjunctions, all logic became the propositional calculus. His truth-table mode of analysis suggested the natural question (and solid clues to its affirmative answer) whether the analysis could all be carried out in some familiar formal system (such as the propositional calculus of Frege or *PM*), thereby establishing its (semantic) completeness.

10.1.1 Digression on Bernays

Like G, Bernays was strongly interested in both logic and philosophy. Bernays was almost eighteen years older than G (but died at about the same time). Owing in part to the age difference, their developments and successes were quite different, but they came to appreciate each other more and more in their different philosophical outlooks. The following account of some aspects of Bernays is based on E. Specker's memoir in *Logic Colloquium 78* (ed. M. Boffa, D. v. Dalen, and K. McAloon, 1979, pp. 381–389).

Bernays lived from 17 October 1888 (London) to 18 September 1977 (Zurich). He studied engineering for one semester and then switched to pure mathematics, studying also philosophy and theoretical physics. His first publication (1910) was in philosophy. In 1912 he wrote his doctoral dissertation (at Göttingen) and his Habilitationsschrift (at the University of Zurich with E. Zermelo as professor), both in analytic number theory. From 1913 to 1917 'Bernays must have passed some crisis.... He even considered giving up mathematics at this time, but did not see anything he felt he could do better.'

In 1917 Bernays went to Göttingen in reponse to Hilbert's proposal to have him as a collaborator. For his new position he wrote in short time the brilliant paper 'Beiträge zur axiomatischen Behandlungen des Logikkalküls' (briefly B, submitted in 1918). G's reference was to the shortened version, published eight years later in *Math. Zeitschrift*, vol. 25, 1926, pp. 305–320, and described more specifically as an axiomatic study of the propositional calculus of *PM*. Both the contents of B and the reason why it was not immediately published are of much historical significance.

Among the results established in B are the following items: (1) The propositional calculus of *PM* is made into a formal system by making explicit the rule of substitution. (2) Derivability and validity are defined, and it is proved that a formula is derivable in the system if and only if it is valid (in other words, the system is 'sound' and complete); a lemma is proved saying that every formula is provable if a nonderivable formula is added to the axioms. (3) One of the five axioms of the *PM* system is shown to be redundant and the other four are shown to be independent by using more than two 'truth values'; this appears to be the introduction of 'many-valued' logics for the first time. (Bernays's description of his method is given in Specker's memoir, on p. 385.) (4) Possibilities of replacing axioms by rules are demonstrated, including a system using 'if p, then p' as the only axiom and six rules.

Once Bernays explained to Specker why he did not publish B earlier (Specker, p. 382): 'To be sure, the paper was of definite mathematical character, but investigations inspired by mathematical logic were not taken quite seriously. They were thought of as amusing, a half-way part of recreational mathematics. I myself had this tendency, and did not take pains to publish it in time. It has appeared only much later, and strictly speaking not quite complete, only certain parts. Many things I had in the paper have therefore not been recorded accordingly in descriptions of the development of mathematical logic.' A number of results similar to those in B were discovered and published between 1918 and 1926 by Post and others, notably Post's 'Introduction to a general theory of elementary propositions,' *Am. J. Math.*, vol. 43, 1921, pp. 163–185.

Bernays became an 'extraordinary' professor at Göttingen in 1922, and, as a 'non-Aryan,' lost his position in 1933. He returned to Zurich in 1934, first as a Privatdozent and then as a professor, till his retirement in 1958. His best-known work includes the monumental *Grundlagen der Mathematik* (HB, in two volumes, 1934 and 1939), his system of set theory, and several of his papers in philosophy (in part collected in his *Abhandlungen zur Philosophie der Mathematik*, 1976). He published over a hundred reviews, of which some are essays both in content and in length. He corresponded with up to one thousand persons on scholarly matters and copies of about six thousand letters are preserved. He was always friendly to visiting scholars and accepted many invitations to lecture or write. He helped many authors to write their papers, from Hilbert to an obscure high school teacher. 'He was unique in his refusal to judge other people; he never spoke badly of anybody. There is every reason to assume that he did not even think badly of others.' I am certainly happy to endorse Specker's statement: 'In the name of all those who have known Bernays personally, it may certainly be said: We are grateful for the privilege to have been in contact with Bernays.'

It is somewhat surprising that the extension of the formulation (and solution) of the issue of completeness to the broader area of elementary logic had to wait ten more years. For example, Bernays did not mention the completeness of elementary logic in his 'Probleme der theoretischen Logik' of 1927 (*Unterrichtsblätter für Mathematik und Naturwissenschaften*, vol. 33, no. 12). The reason why the problem of completeness had not been formulated earlier seems to me quite similar to G's explanation why the easy solution of the problem was missed by Skolem and others (including Bernays and Herbrand). At that time, according to G, nonfinitary reasoning in mathematics was widely considered to be meaningful only to the extent to which it can be 'interpreted' or 'justified' in terms of a finitary metamathematics (*MP*, p. 8). The observation certainly applies not only to nonfinitary reasoning but also to the formation of concepts, and the very concept of completeness involves the nonfinitary component of being true in 'arbitrary domains.'

Viewed from such a perspective, what is surprising is not how late the concept was introduced, but rather that it was introduced at all. To use a fashionable term, one could say that the 'paradigm' at that time could not accommodate either the formulation of the problem or its solution. While it is plausible to say that G initiated a new paradigm, the fact that the problem was raised in HA, which belonged to the old paradigm, shows that paradigms are not as rigid or insular as many enthusiasts of 'incommensurable paradigms' have suggested. Moreover, the spirit of the old paradigm has continued to pervade the work of many logicians and the 'analytic empiricists' (compare *BA*, pp. 10−26).

At this point I would like to turn to a detailed examination of the text of G's dissertation and the related paper.

(D) *Über die Vollständigkeit des Logikkalküls,* completed in July 1929, a typescript of thirty-three pages plus a title page and a page of 'Inhaltverzeichnis.'

(C) 'Die Vollständigkeit der Axiome des logischen Funktionenkalküls,' *Monatshefte für Mathematik und Physik*, vol. 37, 1930, pp. 349−360 (completed in October 1929, reprinted in *FG*, pp. 582−591). This work is, as G says, doing to elementary logic what Bernays did to the propositional calculus in 1918. In particular, the inclusion of independence proofs of the axioms as a supplement was probably entirely suggested by Bernays's treatment.

A convenient initial frame in which to consider D and C is G's own table of contents for D. [D has just been published, together with an English translation, in *CW*, I, pp. 60−101. The inserted numbers in square brackets refer to this text.]

Section 1. Introduction (pp. 1−5 [60−65]). This was largely deleted in C. Only the beginning half-page was included in C in a revised form, with the addition of an explicit reference to Bernays's work, followed by the statement, 'The same will be done here for a wider realm of formulas' (*FG*, p. 583).

Section 2. Preparatory remarks on the underlying axiom system and the terminology employed (pp. 6–9 [65–69]). This section was shortened in C (*FG*, p. 584) by putting more material in footnotes and omitting the distinction between 'in the broader sense' and 'in the narrower sense,' according as to whether the identity sign is included or not. The system adopted is that of *PM* (*1 and *10), with the missing rules of inference made explicit. The terminology and symbolism follow HA. The following footnote (D, p. 7) was deleted in C: 'The other established axiom systems (Frege, Bernays) do not differ essentially from Russell's, so that the completeness proof carries over directly.' The reference to Bernays was probably derived from the fact (mentioned above) that the system in HA was due to Bernays.

Section 3. Summary of the theorems needed below from the functional calculus (pp. 10–12 [70–73]). These were simplified somewhat in C (*FG*, pp. 584–585, a list with seven entries). Clearly in order to prove the completeness of the system, we have to use a number of propositions provable in the system. G's idea was to make things more orderly by listing all of them at the beginning instead of introducing them as needed.

Section 4. Reduction of the completeness theorem to the corresponding one for formulas of degree 1 (pp. 12–15 [72–79]). This corresponds to theorems III and IV in C (*FG*, pp. 585–586). The formulas of degree 1 are those in Skolem normal form (i.e., with all quantifiers at the beginning and the universal ones preceding the existential ones). Skolem proved in 1920 (a paper reprinted in *FG*, pp, 252–263) that each formula *F* has a Skolem normal form *S* that is satisfiable if and only if *F* is. G referred to the paper and proved that *F* is either satisfiable or refutable if *S* is. Hence, it is only necessary to consider formulas in Skolem normal form (i.e., of degree 1).

Section 5. Proof of the completeness theorem in the narrower sense (pp. 16–22 [78–89]). This corresponds to theorems V and IV in C (*FG*, pp. 587–589), from which the completeness theorem (for elementary logic without identity) follows immediately. An argument corresponding to a proof of the 'infinity lemma' was given in D (p. 21), but replaced in C by 'It follows by familiar arguments' (*FG*, pp. 588–589). While the argument is relatively simple, it is not obvious at all. Hence, the deletion was rather unfortunate.

Section 6. Proof of the completeness theorem in the broader sense (pp. 23–25 [88–93]). This section extends the completeness theorem to include identity. It corresponds to theorems VII and VIII in C (*FG*, pp. 589–590).

Section 7. Proof of the independence of the axiom system of logic (pp. 26–29 [92–97]). This section was shortened and put at the end in C (*FG*, p. 591).

Section 8. Extension of the completeness theorem to infinite systems of logic expressions and axiomatic applications (pp. 30–33 [96–101]). The generalization says that every countable set of formulas is either satisfiable or refutable. The application says that every axiom system (first-order theory) either has a model or is inconsistent. In C the proof of the generalization (given in D) was slightly modified to prove what is known today as the 'compactness theorem': A countable set of formulas is satisfiable if and only if every finite subset is. Then the generalization was given as an immediate consequence (*FG*, pp. 590–591).

To sum up, the main changes from C to D were the addition of the compactness theorem and the deletion of the introduction and the proof of a 'lemma' in section 5. On the whole, C is shorter than D and less informal; ten theorems are numbered and displayed, more detailed references are given and put into the footnotes, and the relaxed broader considerations (in the introduction to D) are deleted. The only explicit references to the literature are a small part of *PM* (*1 and *10) and HA, Bernays 1926, and Skolem 1920. Hilbert's axiom system of geometry (without the axiom of continuity) is given as an example (D, p. 9, and C, p. 591). Brouwer and Frege are mentioned in D but not in C.

Of some historical interest is the relation of G's D and C to Skolem's lecture of 1922 (published in 1923, English translation included in *FG*, pp. 290–301). G requested the volume containing the lecture from a library in November 1928 but did not get it. He continued to ask for the volume in one or more other libraries in 1929 or 1930. I do not know when he finally saw the paper. But, in any case, G mentioned this paper in the 1960s on several occasions. On 7 December 1967, he wrote to me, 'The completeness theorem, mathematically, is indeed an almost trivial consequence of Skolem 1922' (*MP*, p. 8). In his letter to J. v. Heijenoort (4 October 1963) he gave details of his recollection at the time: 'As far as Skolem's paper is concerned, I think I first read it about the time when I published my completeness paper. That I did not quote it must be due to the fact that either the quotations were taken over from my dissertation or that I did not see the paper before the publication of my paper. At any rate I am practically sure that I did not know it when I wrote my dissertation. Otherwise I would have quoted it, since it is much closer to my work than the paper of 1920, which I did quote' (*CW*, vol. 1, p. 51).

The introduction to D considers the relation between the existence of the concept (introduced by an axiom system) and the consistency of the system. The discussion comments explicitly on Brouwer's view and implicitly on Hilbert's. The completeness theorem shows that every consistent first-order theory has a model. This is the sense in which G considers his theorem 'a theoretical completion of the usual method of proving consistency.' Against Brouwer's contrast between consistency and existence, G suggests that, since every consistent (first-order) theory has a model by his theorem, existence could perhaps be defined by consistency. However, the theorem merely proves the existence of a model; there is no assurance that we can find the appropriate structure and prove it to be a model. Of course, if all mathematical problems are solvable, then there is no difficulty because, in particular, we can solve the problem of finding the structure and proving it to be the model. This observation points out a presupposition of Hilbert's proposal (without naming Hilbert) to identify consistency with existence.

The remainder of the long first paragraph of D (*CW*, I, pp. 63 and 65) certainly suggests the possibility of finding undecidable propositions in a formal system. Consider the following three sentences:

> (1) For, if the unsolvability of some problem (in the domain of real numbers, say) were proved, then from the definition above [of existence by consistency], there would be two nonisomorphic realizations of the axiom system for the real numbers, while at the same time we can prove the isomorphism of any two realizations.
> (2) We cannot at all exclude out of hand, however, a proof of the unsolvability of a problem if we observe that what is at issue here is only unsolvability by certain *precisely stated formal* means of inference.
> (3) For, all the concepts under consideration (provable, consistent, etc.) have a precise sense only when the permitted rules of inference are exactly delineated.

Statement (3) may be taken as an implicit criticism of Brouwer's negative attitude toward formal systems. It also gives a reason why it may be possible to find undecidable propositions. G is suggesting here that the concepts under consideration have a *precise* sense only when characterized by formal systems. This would seem to imply that the concepts of absolute provability and absolute definability, considered in his Princeton lecture of 1946 (Davis, pp. 84–88), cannot have a precise sense.

The presupposition that every mathematical problem is solvable certainly refers to absolute provability (rather than provability in some particular formal system). As I see it, statement (1) also deals with absolute provability. The obvious function of this statement is of course to show that the identification of existence with consistency requires the presupposition that all mathematical problems are solvable. But in addition, it also shows that we can never exhibit a proposition (from the field of real numbers) and prove it to be absolutely undecidable. Both conclusions depend on accepting the view that we do have a categorical ('second-order') axiom system (though not a formal system, as proved later by G) for the real numbers. I see no useful way of questioning this view, which is apparently taken as a given fact in the quoted statement.

The connecting statement (2) may be construed as saying also implicitly that, since we can study the question of unsolvability only when using exact rules, what is at issue can only be unsolvability in a formal system. If we deleted 'we observe that' and 'here' from it, we would have an easier (and weaker) statement. But in that case, statement (3) would become unnecessary.

G states explicitly in D that his proof uses the law of excluded middle over infinite domains and emphasizes that the problem of completeness, unlike the problem of consistency, did not at first grow out of the foundational controversy but could be meaningfully posed within the framework of 'naive' mathematics. Hence, like any other (ordinary) mathematical problem, no restriction on the means (or method) of proof is necessary. According to the intuitionistic interpretation, he says, the law of excluded middle appears to say nothing other than the decidability of all problems; but it appears questionable whether this statement is in general meaningful. Moreover, since the concept of satisfiability by a model has a fundamentally different sense for the intuitionists, the whole problem becomes a different one for them. 'It is clear that an intuitionistic completeness proof could only be carried out through the [positive] solution of the Entscheidungsproblem of mathematical logic, while the result [D] only transforms (reduces) it to the problem of formal deducibility [in familiar formal systems of the restricted functional calculus].'

10.2 Incompletability of mathematics

According to G, he attempted to make a relative consistency proof (of classical analysis) in the summer of 1930 and was soon led to the observation that arithmetic truth cannot be defined in arithmetic. Yet provability in a given formal system S can be defined in arithmetic, and he was able to devise a proposition p in S to say of itself that it is not provable in S. Intuitively, p must be unprovable in S and therefore true. (If p were provable in S, we would have something counterintuitive because p says that p is not provable in S.) But if S is not very strange, p is also not refutable in S because p is true.

From September to October 1930, he improved and extended the result by making p into an 'arithmetical' proposition of an elegant form and by noticing that any proposition of S expressing in a natural manner the consistency of S can also serve as the undecidable (in S) proposition p.

Hence, any proof of the consistency of S cannot be fully formalized in S. An announcement of these results was submitted on 23 October, and the full paper was received for publication on 17 November. Hence the whole impressive piece of work was done in less than half a year, when G was twenty-three years old.

G's major publications in this area are

(U) 'On formally undecidable propositions of *Principia Mathematica* and related systems I,' originally in German, *Monatshefte für Mathematik und Physik*, vol. 38, pp. 173–198, reprinted in Davis (1965), pp. 5–38, and in *FG* (1967), pp. 596–616. Also included in *FG* are three additions by G: a supplement to U (from a presentation of 22 January 1931), a note (23 August 1963), and a long remark (18 May 1966) (all on pp. 616–617). The supplement makes it more explicit that the theorems apply not only to systems of set theory but also to systems of arithmetic. The remark outlines a more elegant and more general treatment of the crucial theorems. The note says that the main theorems of the paper U apply to all *formal* systems in view of the fact that we have now a precise concept of formal systems, as a result of A. M. Turing's work.

(L) 'On undecidable propositions of formal mathematical systems,' notes from G's lectures of the spring of 1934, first published in Davis, pp. 41–74, with emendations and a postscript by G (3 June 1964, pp. 71–73).

Following G's initial approach, let us enumerate the primitive symbols, the formulas, and the proofs of a given formal system S. In particular, we assume an enumeration of those formulas that are proposition forms with one free variable (call them properties). Suppose we are able to find in S a proposition form $B(x, y, z)$ that has this meaning: proof number x is a proof in S of the proposition obtained from property y by putting the numeral of the number z at all occurrences of the free variable (of the property y). Since S is a formal system, $B(x, y, z)$ is a 'decidable' (or transparent) relation such that for given values of x, y, and z, we can verify (and prove in S) whether it is true or false. Consider now the property $(x) - B(x, y, y)$ and let it be property number b. For no x can $B(x, b, b)$ be true, because if it were true, proof number x would be a proof of the proposition obtained from property b by putting the numeral of b for y, which is equivalent to $(x) - B(x, b, b)$. In that case, we would have proofs in S for both $B(x, b, b)$ and its negation. Hence, for each given x, $- B(x, b, b)$ is true and provable in S. Let Con(S) say that the system S is consistent. If we formalize the above argument in S, we can derive in S, from the hypothesis Con(S), the conclusion $- B(x, b, b)$ (with x a variable), and therefore also $(x) - B(x, b, b)$. On the other hand, $(x) - B(x, b, b)$ is not provable in S, because if proof number c were its proof,

$B(c, b, b)$ would be true and provable in S, and we would again have a contradiction in S. Therefore, if S is consistent, Con(S) cannot be proved in S.

Moreover, we have shown that if S is consistent, $(x) - B(x, b, b)$ is not provable in S, although for each given number a, $- B(a, b, b)$ is provable in S. The system S would be very strange if $(x) - B(x, b, b)$ were refutable, seeing that all its instances are provable. G excludes this strange state of affairs by requiring that S be 'omega-consistent,' which is a stronger property than mere consistency. (In 1936 J. B. Rosser was able to remove this stronger condition by using a more complex proposition.) Hence, if S is a reasonable system, $(x) - B(x, b, b)$ is undecidable in S (compare G's corresponding discussion in Davis, pp. 60–61).

The property form $B(x, y, z)$ appears to be quite remote from ordinary arithmetic operations like addition and multiplication. G was surprised when he succeeded in showing it to be an 'arithmetical' predicate, i.e., one that can be expressed in terms of addition and multiplication with the help of quantifiers. What is actually done in U is to show that B is primitive recursive and that all primitive recursive predicates are arithmetical. In addition, it is proved that every primitive recursive predicate is *decidable* (entscheidungsdefinit) or verifiable (according to HB) in the sense that every given instance [for example, $B(a, b, c)$ for constants a, b, c] is provable if true and refutable if false in any moderately strong system S. In fact, since this property is crucial in the argument sketched above, G suggests in U a generalization of his theorem VI to say that any class of formulas that is omega-consistent and decidable contains undecidable propositions (Davis, p. 26, and *FG*, p. 609).

[This concept of decidable predicates corresponds to G's *computable in* a system S, introduced later in his 'On the length of proofs' (1936), where he remarks that the concept is in a certain definite sense 'absolute,' because any function computable in a higher system S_i is already computable in the rudimentary system S_1, which may be taken as the first-order arithmetic (Davis, p. 83). The computable functions in any S_i (in particular, S_1) are indeed, as G pointed out explicitly in his Princeton lecture of 1946, exactly the (general) recursive or Turing computable functions. Hence, it is justifiable to say that G had thereby introduced a precise concept of computability (or mechanical procedures) before any of the other alternative concepts were proposed.]

It is no exaggeration to regard U as the greatest single piece of work in the whole history of mathematical logic. In many ways it pulled together, consolidated, and raised previous work to a much higher level in nearly all major directions, proving surprising central results, making old concepts precise, introducing new concepts, and opening up wholly new horizons. What is less conspicuously remarkable is that, in the process of proving his spectacular theorems, he was able to work out quite thoroughly all the many relevant known aspects and new directions in such a leisurely way that others could continue his work on a richer and more solidly structured foundation.

For example, Dedekind, Skolem, Hilbert, and Ackermann all had worked on primitive recursive functions before, but G gave the first precise definition of this class of functions, which has since been accepted as the standard one (Davis, pp. 14–15, and FG, p. 602). Furthermore, he introduced primitive recursive predicates and extended them to decidable predicates, thereby anticipating to some extent the comprehensive 'absolute' class of recursive or computable functions. He gave a systematic treatment of the intuitive idea that decidable functions or predicates are verifiable (or 'numeralwise representable') in the sense that, for example, all numerical instances of Fermat's conjecture can be checked (proved or disproved) in any reasonably strong formal system. Even his system P, as a precise formulation of the system of PM, was a great advance over familiar formulations of systems of set theory at that time (Davis, pp. 9–13, and FG, pp. 599–601). Both Leibniz and Hilbert had suggested the idea of representing concepts or expressions by numbers, but G was the first to develop the idea systematically and apply 'Gödel numbering' impressively in the 'arithmetization of syntax' (Davis, pp. 13–14, and FG, p. 601). The surprising results in section 3 of U (Davis, pp. 29–35, 65–69, and FG, pp. 610–614) both refined the main theorems (by giving the undecidable propositions a precisely arithmetic form) and anticipated and initiated major later developments. I shall say more about this when I give a consecutive summary of U below.

Of course the central and conspicuous results of U are the two famous theorems that show the limitations of formalization, settle most of the major problems posed by the Hilbert school, and refute the conjectures of the Hilbert program as originally formulated. Since the concern with forms, the formal, and formalization is central to the enterprise of mathematical logic, the two theorems raised the subject to a new level by impressing on the practitioners the central importance of the interplay of the formal and the intuitive, even though the area is devoted to the study of the formal. G's two theorems also brought a unity to the field as far as they apply to all the major domains of interest: number theory, analysis, set theory (and even elementary logic, by way of theorem X; see below).

The theorems were important in different ways for all three 'schools' of the philosophy of mathematics: formalism, logicism, and intuitionism. They destroyed the expectations of the formalists to find complete mathematical formal systems and finitary consistency proofs, as well as those of the logicists to find a (transparent) comprehensive formal system of (grand) logic. The theorems were less surprising to the intuitionists, but they and their proofs are constructive and therefore acceptable to them; moreover, the work demonstrated to them how appropriate uses of the formal method could yield precise major conclusions that they could only see in part and imprecisely. As I have observed before (in chapter 3, at the end of the entry *1930*), Brouwer's belief in the inexhaustibility of mathematics by any formal system apparently did not include the surprising fact discovered by G that an undecidable proposition can be found *in the given system*. Brouwer's lack of interest in consistency proofs was part of his belief that being consistent need not exist, or be true or right. As far as I know, Brouwer did not assert or conjecture that consistency of a system could not be proved in the system. Moreover, if there were finitary consistency proofs of fairly inclusive formal mathematical systems, one would expect to see things that would make some of Brouwer's views much less convincing. Hence, G's results on consistency proofs settled a question that was at least indirectly important for the intuitionists.

The paper U consists of four sections, of which section 2 is by far the longest and contains several parts.

Section 1. Let P be the system of *PM* as reformulated by G. Natural numbers are assigned to the primitive signs. It is noted that one can find a formula in P that says, 'I am not provable in P.' By arguments like those sketched above, G shows informally that it is undecidable in P. 'The analogy of this argument with the Richard antinomy leaps to the eye.' Richard's antinomy (1905, *FG*, pp. 142−144) is a variant of Cantor's diagonal argument, and the analogy is to enumerate all provable formulas and construct one that is different from all of them, with the additional property of being like a provable formula (corresponding to Richard's 'definable by finitely many words'). A comparison with the 'Liar' is made and stated: 'Any epistemological antinomy could be used for a similar proof of the existence of undecidable propositions' (footnote 14).

It is strange and unfortunate that G did not elaborate in this context the comparison with the 'Liar,' especially since one of the first things he noticed in the summer of 1930 was that arithmetic truth is not definable in arithmetic. The fact that he did not even put the 'Liar' in the form 'I am not true' must have been a consequence of his caution, because the concept of arithmetic truth was widely regarded as obscure at that time. It is not really surprising that Zermelo was misled by the all too brief comparison. It was only in his letter of 12 October 1931 that G explained the distinction fully and proved that truth is not definable in the language itself. (For details, see *1931* in chapter 3.) Later in L (the Princeton lectures) G did reveal what he wrote to Zermelo and devoted the whole section 7 to it ('relation of the foregoing arguments to the paradoxes,' Davis, pp. 63–65).

Section 2. The long section includes the full proof of the first incompleteness theorem and consists of several parts.

2.1 The formal system P. This is a reformulation of the system of type theory in *PM*. In L a similar system is used (section 3), but it is restricted to the first two types.

2.2 Primitive recursive functions and relations. These are defined precisely, and four basic theorems are proved. This part corresponds to section 2 of L, which includes an observation in footnote 3 (Davis, p. 44) suggesting that every function computable by a finite procedure is recursive. Davis had assumed that by 'recursive' is meant 'general recursive' as defined in section 9 of L (pp. 69–71). But G wrote in a letter to Davis (15 February 1965) that at the time he was 'not at all convinced that my concept of recursion comprises all possible recursions' (see Davis, p. 40). In any case, G always attributed to Turing the introduction of the first precise concept of mechanical or finite procedures, because he felt that Turing was the first to give a convincing reason why the precise concept agrees with the intuitive one.

2.3 This part gives a representation of the system P by a system of positive integers. It includes the assignment of 'Gödel numbers' and the proof that forty-six functions and predicates, mostly of a metamathematical nature, are all, except the last, primitive recursive. The last entry is the nonrecursive property of being 'provable in P.' In L this part makes up section 4, which, however, includes only seventeen (rather than sixty-four) entries and refers to U for details.

2.4 Primitive recursive functions and relations are shown to be verifiable (or numeralwise representable) in system P. This corresponds to the first part of section 5 of L (which contains, in addition, less formal proofs of the two main theorems).

2.5 A proof of the first incompleteness is given quite formally.

2.6 This considers the conditions that a formal system must satisfy in order to carry out the proof (of 2.5). It corresponds to section 6 of L.

At the end of section 2, the famous footnote 48a appears (Davis, pp. 28–29, and *FG*, p. 610):

> The true reason for the incompleteness inherent in all formal systems of mathematics is, as will be shown in Part II of this paper, that the formation of ever higher types can be continued into the transfinite (cf. D. Hilbert, 'Über das Unendliche,' *Math. Ann.*, 95, p. 184 [*FG*, p. 387]), while in any formal system at most countably many of them are available. For it can be shown

that the undecidable propositions constructed here always become decidable when appropriate higher types are added (e.g., the type ω to the system P). An analogous situation prevails for the axiom system of set theory.

Section 3. The concept of arithmetical relations is introduced to cover relations definable in terms of addition and multiplication with the help of logical constants (including quantifiers ranging over natural numbers). A clever application of the Chinese remainder theorem shows that all primitive recursive relations are arithmetical. It follows that the undecidable propositions are arithmetical. This part of section 3 is considered in section 8 of L under 'Diophantine' propositions that have the form $(Q)(F = 0)$, where (Q) stands for a sequence of quantifiers and F stands for a polynomial (so that $F = 0$ is a Diophantine equation). The reduction of arithmetic propositions to Diophantine ones is done by eliminating negation and disjunction. G's proof that all primitive recursive predicates are arithmetical gives an elegant representation of recursively enumerable sets. The representation played a central part in the study of Hilbert's tenth problem by Martin Davis, Julia Robinson, and Yuri Matijasevic, which led eventually in 1970 to the result that there is no algorithm to solve all Diophantine equations.

Two comments are made in the postscript (of L) on section 8. (1) On the basis of Turing's definition of mechanical procedures, the two incompleteness results (stated in section 8 with the qualification 'on the basis of the principles of proof used in mathematics today') 'can now be proved in the definitive form': There exists no *formalized theory* that answers all Diophantine questions of the form $(A)(F = 0)$, and: There is no *algorithm* for deciding relations in which both addition and multiplication occur. (2) An unpublished result is announced. The methods in section 8 can be strengthened to bring the undecidable proposition into the form $A \ldots AE \ldots E$, followed by an equation in which the polynomial is of degree 4 (Davis, pp. 72 and 73).

The other half of section 3 (of U) is omitted in L. It proves two theorems about elementary logic: X. For every formula $(x)F(x)$, F primitive recursive, one can exhibit a formula E of elementary logic such that E is satisfiable if and only if $(x)f(x)$ (is true). IX. In system P (or any system satisfying the conditions G set down), there are formulas of elementary logic whose validity is undecidable. As Davis points out, X yields directly the conclusion that the decision problem for elementary logic ('The Entscheidungsproblem') is unsolvable (Davis, p. 109).

After the work of Turing and others in the 1930s, the interest shifted from undecidable propositions to unsolvable problems. But, as

far as I know, G did little work in this area, probably because the problems are mostly technical and involve little conceptual analysis.
Section 4. A sketch of the proof of the second incompleteness theorem (listed as XI) is given. The section (and the whole U) concludes with a promise (which was never fully realized):

> In the present paper we have on the whole restricted ourselves to the system P, and we have only indicated the applications to other systems. The results will be stated and proved in full generality in a sequel to be published soon. In that paper, also, the proof of Theorem XI, only sketched here, will be given in detail.

In the 1960s, G inserted after the word 'soon' a new footnote (*FG*, p. 616, footnote 68a): 'This explains the "I" in the title of the paper. The author's intention was to publish this sequel in the next volume of the *Monatshefte*. The prompt acceptance of his results was one of the reasons that made him change his plan.' I believe another reason must have been G's reluctance to carry out laborious details that were no longer novel to him and did not represent decisive advances of the subject.

In the above summary of U, I have mentioned the contents of seven of the nine sections of L. The introduction to L explains the concepts involved in specifying a formal mathematical system. The concluding section introduces G's definition of general recursive functions, using in part a suggestion from Herbrand (in a 1931 letter to G).

Earlier in section 2.3 I have somewhat dramatized G's response to Hilbert's four problems, presented in his Bologna lecture (September 1928). In footnote 48 of U, G did indicate that his first incompleteness theorem settles Hilbert's third problem. Even though his second theorem could be viewed, as I suggested in section 2.3, as settling Hilbert's first two problems in their intended meaning, G stressed toward the end of U (Davis, p. 37, and *FG*, p. 615) that the range of finitary proofs was not known definitely: 'I wish to note expressly that theorem XI (and the corresponding results for M [formalized set theory] and A [formalized classical mathematics or number theory]) do not contradict Hilbert's formalistic viewpoint. For this viewpoint presupposes only the existence of a consistency proof in which nothing but finitary means of proof is needed, and it is conceivable that there exist finitary proofs that cannot be represented in P (or in M or A).' [As we now know, finitary proofs in Hilbert's sense can be represented in each of these systems.] Of course the theorem is useful in checking proposed consistency proofs; indeed, both Herbrand (see *FG*, p. 626) and Gentzen did this explicitly.

G continued to be interested in consistency proofs (such as those of

G. Gentzen's), and his own work on intuitionist number theory had also an aspect that can be thought of as giving consistent proofs. But what is clear from G's work is the implausibility of Hilbert's idea that somehow the foundations of mathematics can be secured once for all by consistency proofs using certain particularly transparent methods. Instead, G successfully looked for *relative* consistency proofs (interpretations, translations, and inner models). Generally the informative aspect of consistency proofs is less the concluding statement of consistency than it is the relation between the concepts used in the consistency proofs and the concepts embodied in the formal system proved to be consistent. It is less misleading and closer to the real situation to say that all consistency proofs are proofs of relative consistency. When this proposition is kept in mind, we get both a broader range of significant problems and a better guide to the extraction of the informative elements from given proofs.

Related to the idea of relative consistency proofs is the first incompleteness theorem's suggestion of the broader perspective of the more general problem of determining the limitations of given methods of proofs (not necessarily codified or codifiable fully in formal systems). For example, there is work in the literature on the minimum rank in set theory necessary for proving certain theorems and on the needed strength of methods to prove the existence of fast-growing functions.

Chapter 11
Philosophical papers

The center of interest in G's published philosophical papers is the philosophy of mathematics. (The Einstein paper of 1949, briefly discussed in section 6.5, was, in G's own words, a 'digression,' which will not be considered in this chapter.) Traditionally one speaks of three positions: nominalism, conceptualism, and realism. G calls himself a 'realist' and is generally so regarded. But there are familiar ambiguities with these labels. For one thing G chooses to think of concepts as an aspect of objective reality and dissociates them from the underlying idea of conceptualism that concepts are made by us. The chief ambiguity of nominalism is, in my opinion, its relation to infinity. If a position either excludes infinite domains altogether or 'disregards the difference between finite and infinite' (BP, p. 225, where G discusses Ramsey's view), as Wittgenstein does in his *Tractatus*, then it has little to say about mathematics (compare BA, pp. 97–99, 70–72, 149–151). If the idealization of infinitely many symbols is accepted, then we arrive at either Hilbert's finitism or, with more idealization, 'predicativism.' G appears to associate nominalism more with predicativism restricted to the 'no class theory' (BP, bottom of p. 215 and middle of p. 220), and to believe that nominalism (in this form) cannot provide an infinite domain. In view of the unclear relation between nominalism and infinity, I shall consider nominalism only in the context of the 'no class theory.' The main contrast is between realism and constructivism, commonly identified with intuitionism and taken to include Hilbert's finitary reasoning as a proper part. Predicativism may also be seen as forming a part of conceptualism, but is somewhat incoherent or rather 'opportunistic' as a self-contained philosophical position (see below). For example, inductive definitions are constructive but not predicative, while the law of excluded middle is accepted by predicativism but not by intuitionism.

In view of G's wish to extend his realism beyond mathematics, it may appear more grand to contrast it with 'idea-lism' (instead of 'constructivism'). But in his general philosophy G calls himself an 'idea-list' (apparently with respect to ontology rather than epistemology). Since the main concern of this chapter is with mathematics (and logic), I find it better to adhere to the more restrictive notion of constructivism, which is associated with some forms of 'idea-list' philosophies, much as 'conventionalism' is associated with 'positivist' philosophies. G is opposed to constructivism only if it is adopted as an intolerant position that excludes nonconstructive reasoning. He appreciates the value of making a clearer separation of constructive from nonconstructive reasoning in the problem of evidence or the study of different degrees of certainty. He is a realist with regard to the things considered in mathematics, but gives constructive reasoning (itself divisible into types of different degrees of certainty) a privileged place in the process of acquiring knowledge about mathematical objects (and even in considering the process itself).

G's flexible and inclusive perspective shows his exceptional talent for learning from historical experience by a perceptive appreciation and an imaginative synthesis, as Leibniz did in his day, of what is good and essential in the insights of his eminent predecessors. Hilbert's program supplied the sharper formulation of intuitively basic but rather indefinite problems. G answered most of these sharpened problems by his results on completeness and consistency proofs, for which he made use of the formal systems developed primarily by Frege and Russell. The constructible sets combined Cantor's ordinal numbers with Frege's elementary logic (which gives 'first-order definability') and Russell's ramified type theory. Both the constructible sets and G's ordinal definability may also be taken to be in part inspired by Poincaré's emphasis of definitions (in contrast to proofs, stressed by Hilbert and Brouwer). G's translation of classical number theory into the Brouwer-Heyting system and especially his interpretation of the latter not only reveal definite relations between the two different perspectives but also contain an improvement (in intuitive evidence) of the interpretation of constructive reasoning as proposed by Brouwer and Heyting.

It is notable that Zermelo, a realist unable or unwilling to appreciate the constructive mode of thinking, was less persuasive than G in bringing out the strength of the realist position. Indeed, as is seen from his correspondence with G (in 1931) and his later comments (*Jahrbericht Deutsche Mathematische Vereinigung*, vol. 41, 1932, pp. 85–88), he failed to understand G's incompleteness proof and regarded it as pointless to study the adequacy of *formal* systems at all (which were, he thought, obviously inadequate).

G has no sympathy with conventionalism in mathematics. It is clear that conventionalism in the sense of requiring the theoretical dispensability of concepts introduced by conventions is unsatisfactory as an account of mathematics (see, for instance, *BA*, pp. 13–16). Later Wittgenstein may be thought to be introducing a more subtle form of conventionalism, when agreement in mathematics is traced back to agreement in the 'form of life.' This view may or may not be taken as a case of conventionalism, but it differs from G's position by leaving out the connection between intersubjective agreement and objective reality or perhaps even substituting the former for the latter. In practice intersubjective agreement also plays, according to G's position, an important part in verifying the correct intuitions and eliminating the incorrect ones.

G says explicitly that we do not have any absolutely certain knowledge. This would seem to imply that even in quite simple matters we are not absolutely certain that we have fully captured what objective reality as the final court of appeal pronounces. Hence, G offers as evidence for realism what he calls 'the argument from success,' which is an empirical inference from the fact that realism has been the most fruitful outlook up to now. After all, ultimately, fruitfulness is probably the most important thing we ask from a philosophical position. I am not disturbed by the 'pragmatic' flavor of the argument, because realism is clearly not pragmatism, and the argument can be applied ad hominem in favor of realism: even from the position of pragmatism, it is the true view. If a correspondence theory of truth gives the most coherent account (in particular, more than coherence theories), such a fact is certainly evidence in favor of the correspondence theory.

G sometimes calls his position 'objectivism' instead of 'realism.' We are, he says, more certain that we have objectivity than that we have found the right objects. For example, we are certain that there are infinitely many prime numbers and that Fermat's conjecture is either true or false. G infers from this fact that there must be objects, but we are, he seems to say, less certain that the natural numbers are the 'right' objects. He says that we choose what to take as objects and there might be better choices, which we have not found yet (especially in physics).

I have myself an ambivalent feeling toward considerations in terms of loaded large words such as 'realism,' 'idealism,' 'foundationalism,' 'materialism,' etc. On the one hand, they seem to summarize and bring together interrelated components to give the sense of being occupied with major issues. On the other hand, different individuals have different associations, and a preoccupation with these words usually overlooks the more refined parts of a given philosopher's actual position. As a result, a larger than usual portion of discussions in such terms are at cross purposes (because of different terminological associations) and not substantive. It seems to me that reasonable alternative (or even opposing) positions, as they get more and more refined, tend to converge to something more adequate to the facts.

G published five philosophical papers in his lifetime. In this chapter I shall not consider the Einstein essay (1949), which was discussed briefly in section 6.5. The Princeton lecture of 1946 (first published in 1965, and reprinted in 1968 with minor changes in wording), summarized in chapter 4 (under *1946*), overlaps with the Cantor paper and the discussion of 'mechanical procedures' in *MP*. It will not be considered in this chapter.

The communicated part of G's views on the philosophy of mathematics and logic is contained chiefly in his three papers (discussing Russell, Cantor, and Bernays) and the material in my *MP* and in his conversations. The Bernays paper (in German 1958, with a much expanded English version in galley proofs 1970, to be published soon in the second volume of *CW*) illustrates G's exceptional combination of realism with a strong interest in and an incisive command of the constructive mode of thought. It studies the problem of evidence in connection with Hilbert's finitism and Brouwer's intuitionism (primarily in the realm of natural numbers as explicated by Heyting) and their relation to classical mathematics. The Cantor paper (1947, with a revised and expanded version in 1964) concentrates on set theory (centering on the continuum problem), but gives also a brief and pregnant statement of G's position of mathematical realism. The Russell paper (1944), G's first philosophical essay, is the most wide ranging. It includes observations on the nature and history of mathematical logic, the theory of descriptions, the vicious circle principle and predicativity, set theory, the theory of concepts, analyticity, and Leibniz's idea of a universal characteristic.

More of G's thoughts on the nature of logic, the theory of concepts, set theory, and his realism or objectivism are reported in *MP* and elsewhere in this book. For example, it is clear from G's conversations, but not from his publications, that logic is for him broader than mathematics (or set theory). G's apparently conflicting attitudes toward the paradoxes in the Russell and the Cantor papers are explained by him in *MP* (pp. 187–188). 'The difference in emphasis, as Gödel explains, is due to a difference in the subject matter, because the whole paper on Russell is concerned with logic rather than mathematics. The full concept of class (truth, concept, being, etc.) is not used in mathematics, and the iterative concept, which is sufficient for mathematics, may or may not be the full concept of class.' Yet G's concept of class seems to have changed somewhat over the years. In his later conversations (to be reported in *CG*), he took classes only as a subsidiary derivative of concepts. He proposed also to delete from the Russell paper the sentence, 'It might even be that the axiom of extensionality or at least something near to it holds for concepts' (BP, p. 220). In 1975 he believed that the axiom of extensionality holds only for concepts in exceptional cases and that, therefore, classes are of no central importance for the theory of concepts.

In terms of objects (or things) we know less and less as we move from small numbers to all integers, the continuum, sets, and concepts. In terms of reasoning, we have the most intuitive grasp when operating with small numbers. The degree of certainty decreases as we go from finitist to intuitionist and to classical mathematics. And (a higher) degree of uncertainty comes in as we go from classical mathematics to set theory—only as mathematics is developed more and more, the overall certainty goes up, but the relative degrees remain the same. (These observations were mostly made by G on 5 February 1976; compare *CG*.) From this perspective, contending schools give way to distinctive components of a comprehensive outlook in which their relations and relative merits are given appropriate places. The subject matter of the three papers can then be seen in a natural order. The Bernays paper relates strong intuitive evidence to constructive and to classical reasoning. The Cantor paper relates classical mathematics to set theory. And the Russell paper hovers between set theory and the theory of concepts (together with a comparison of their nominalist and realist interpretations, stimulated by Russell's ambiguous attitude toward the two opposing outlooks).

11.1 The problem of evidence

It is appropriate to begin with the Bernays paper, 'On an extension of a finitary mathematics which has not yet been used.' The German version was published in 1958, *Dialectica*, vol. 12, pp. 280–287. In the late 1960s G wrote an expanded English version, which was in galley proofs in 1970 when G decided to hold it for revisions. Both versions will appear in the second volume of *CW*. I shall use the (privately circulated) English version in this section. The content of the paper was summarized in the abstract appended to the German version:

> P. Bernays has pointed out that, in order to prove the consistency of classical number theory, it is necessary to extend Hilbert's finitary standpoint by admitting certain abstract concepts in addition to the combinatorial concepts referring to symbols. The abstract concepts that so far have been used for this purpose are those of the constructive theory of ordinals and those of intuitionistic logic. It is shown [here] that the concept of a computable function of finite simple type over the integers can be used instead, where no other procedures of constructing such functions are necessary except simple recursion by an integer variable and substitution of functions in one another (starting with trivial functions).

The first sentence disproves G's 1930 statement that 'it is conceivable that there exist finitary proofs which *cannot* be expressed in the formalism of' classical number theory (call the systen N), etc. (quoted above, *CW*, I, p. 195), if we use Hilbert's original conception. In particular, Bernays has pointed out this consequence of G's second theorem at several places (as indicated in footnote [1] of the paper under consideration). G considers in his paper alternative ways of going beyond (Hilbert's) finitary mathematics to arrive at a consistency proof of N, and proposes a new and more evident way of doing this. G's method is known as an interpretation by means of 'primitive recursive functionals' of the intuitionistic number theory, as formulated in Heyting's sytem H. For this purpose G sets up a formal system T and gives an interpretation of the formulas of H in T so that all theorems of H become theorems of T in their interpreted form. Using his 1932 reduction of N to H (Davis, pp. 75−81), the consistency of N is reduced to that of T, whose axioms 'are formally almost the same as those of primitive recursive number theory.' 'The system T has the same deductive power as a system of number theory in which complete induction is permitted for all ordinal numbers less than ε_0.'

11.1.1 Hilbert's finitary mathematics

G bases his consideration on Hilbert's 1925 exposition (*Math. Ann.*, vol. 95, pp. 170−173; English translation in *FG*, pp. 377−379). According to G, the exposition defines finitary mathematics as 'the mathematics of *concrete intuition*,' and G contrasts concrete with abstract evidence. In this context, 'intuitive' is understood in a restricted sense so that, correspondingly, much of what is taken to be 'intuitive' elsewhere (certainly in set theory) becomes 'abstract,' i.e., going beyond concrete intuition. Let me quote G's note (h) in full:

> 'Concrete intuition,' 'concretely intuitive' are used as translations of 'Anschauung,' 'anschaulich.' The simple terms 'concrete' or 'intuitive' are also used in this sense in the present paper. What Hilbert means by 'Anschauung' is substantially Kant's space-time intuition confined, however, to configurations of a finite number of discrete objects. Note that it is Hilbert's insistence on *concrete* knowledge that makes finitary mathematics so surprisingly weak and excludes many things that are just as incontrovertibly evident to everybody as finitary number theory. E.g., while any primitive recursive definition is finitary, the general principle of primitive recursive definition is not a finitary proposition, because it contains the abstract concept of function. There is nothing in the term 'finitary' which would suggest a restriction to concrete knowledge. Only Hilbert's special interpretation of it introduces this restriction.

The contrast between Hilbert's and Kant's conceptions does not, I believe, suggest that Kant's conception is broader in the case of number theory. Rather it points out that Hilbert is concerned (here) only with one aspect of Kant's conception (leaving out, for instance, certain parts that only relate to geometry). In other words, G is asserting, rightly I think, that Kant and Hilbert share a restricted concept of finitary mathematics, which is the only part of discrete mathematics that is intuitively evident to them. This is why G considers Kant's philosophy of mathematics highly inadequate (as I have reported elsewhere in this book). In particular, even though Brouwer claims to adhere to Kant's notion, he uses a broader notion of intuition than Kant.

Hilbert's finitary mathematics serves to illustrate two aspects of G's approach to philosophy. On the one hand, once something is recognized or accepted as evident, it invites further extensions (as G shows by the example of primitive recursive functions). On the other hand, as G stresses in other contexts, fairly well-defined regions such as Hilbert's are useful tools for the study of the functioning and the expansion of our intuition and what can be taken as evident. G's use of finitary mathematics in his paper gives to his comparison of alternative ways of clarifying the system N a frame of reference that increases the clarity of his whole consideration.

According to G, Bernays teaches us (see BP, pp. 280–282, 285–286) to 'distinguish two component parts in the concept of finitary mathematics.' The constructivistic element requires the restriction to mathematical objects or facts that 'can be exhibited, or obtained by construction of proof.' The specifically finitistic element 'requires in addition that the objects and facts considered should be given in concrete mathematical intuition'; the objects 'must be finite space-time configurations of elements whose nature is irrelevant except for equality or difference.' 'It is the second requirement which must be dropped.' The existing ways of doing this to arrive at N are by a reduction to H, by transfinite induction to ε_0, and G's new reduction of H to T. G examines carefully the second alternative of using constructive ordinals and the related question of 'accessibility' in his notes [3], [4], (i), (j), and the parts of his text to which these notes are attached. The examination, he says, makes 'abundantly clear' that the consistency of N cannot be proved by Hilbert's methods, even though we lack 'a precise definition of either concrete or abstract evidence.'

In contrast with the mathematics of concrete intuition, abstract concepts 'do not have as their content properties or relations of *concrete objects* (such as combinations of symbols), but rather of *thought structures* or *thought contents* (e.g., proofs, meaningful propositions, and so on).' In 'the propositions about these mental objects insights are needed which are not derived from a reflection upon the combinatorial (space-time) properties of the symbols representing them, but rather from a reflection upon the *meanings* involved.' G gives in note (a) as an example the reading of 'p implies q' as 'From a convincing proof of p a convincing proof q can be obtained.'

We have here the symbols (and their combinations), their combinatorial properties, their meanings (or our intentions), our reflections on the one or the other, and the insights derived from such reflections. Concrete objects are contrasted with thought contents. If one insists on adhering to traditional distinctions, the restriction to the combinatorial properties may be said to be a nominalist position, while stopping the extension at the thought contents may be said to be the conceptualist position, which is more inclusive. G's realist position certainly does not exclude reflections on the combinatorial properties and the thought contents, but it goes on to admit additional idealizations and to attribute the ultimate content of our reflection to (general) features of objective reality.

Since I am primarily concerned with the philosophical aspect of G's paper, I am not going to consider the technical details of T and the reduction of H to T. G centers T on the concept 'computable function of (any finite) type t' and observes in note (b) that Turing's functions 'also satisfy the axioms of the system T.' Related to this is G's observation in note [6] on Turing's definition:

> This definition most certainly was not superfluous. However, if the term 'mechanically computable' had not had a clear, although un-analyzed, meaning before, the question as to whether Turing's defini-tion is adequate would be meaningless, while it undoubtedly has an affirmative answer.

This note is related to G's thoughts about our perception of concepts (compare *MP*, pp. 84–86). In note (k), G observes in connection with the conceptual advance of T over H: 'The same method for avoiding the use of Heyting's logic or the general concept of proof probably can be applied also to the interpretation of T in terms of Turing functions, see note (b).' A possible advantage of using Turing's functions instead is also mentioned at the end of note (k).

The paper concludes by observing that much stronger systems than T can be constructed, starting with the same basic ideas. As examples, G suggests extensions by admitting transfinite types or (otherwise) Brouwer's methods of deduction (or his principle) in proving his 'fan theorem' (Heyt-ing, *Intuitionism*, 1956, p. 42). The latter alternative has been pursued by C. Spector after 1958 to derive the consistency of classical analysis from an abstractive form of Brouwer's principle. G mentions in his new note (m) Spector's work and says, 'Unfortunately, however, no satisfactory con-structivistic proof is known for either one of the two principles [namely, Brouwer's and Spector's variant].' In conclusion, G says in the note, 'Per-haps the most promising extension of the system T is that obtained by introducing *higher type computable functions of constructive ordinals*.'

The main concern of G's expanded version of the paper is to explain why T is more evident than H. The long new note (k) elaborates note [5] by pointing out that G's interpretation of intuitive logic uses an 'incomparably narrower' concept of proof than Heyting's and avoids quantification over 'any' proof. The axioms and rules of T can be proved, G observes, by using what he calls the narrower concept of 'reductive proof,' which is 'an unbroken chain of immediate evidences.' Once or twice G remarked, I seem to recall, that in note (k) his ideas are only sketched, because the proofs of his assertions are highly complex and lengthy.

As we move beyond number theory, the continuum (and classical analysis) is undoubtedly the bridge, both conceptually and historically, that leads us to set theory. Moreover, given Cantor's development of infinite numbers, the cardinal number of the continuum (i.e., the continuum problem) was one of the first natural questions to ask. Indeed, Cantor conjectured in 1878 that it is the smallest uncountable cardinal number (*Gesammelte Abhandlungen*, 1932, p. 132). It remains unknown today whether the conjecture (the 'continuum hypothesis') is true or false. G undoubtedly devoted more energy to this problem, in both its mathematical and philosophical aspects, than any other problem (certainly any one of a mathematical character).

11.2 Cantor and set theory

G's philosophical paper on this subject is 'What is Cantor's continuum problem?' It was first published in *Am. Math. Monthy* (*AMM*), vol. 54 (1947), pp. 515–525; a revised and expanded version appears in BP, 1964, pp. 258–273 (reprinted in BP2, 1983, pp. 470–485). G refers to the two versions as the first edition and the second edition. In this section I shall make page references to BP, and also to *AMM* when comparing the two versions.

The expanded version has seven parts:

1. The concept of cardinal number (pp. 258–259).
2. The continuum problem, the continuum hypothesis, and the partial results concerning its truth obtained so far (pp. 260–261).
3. Restatement of the problem on the basis of an analysis of the foundations of set theory and results obtained along these lines (pp. 261–265).
4. Some observations about the question, In what sense and in which direction may a solution of the continuum problem be expected (pp. 265–268)?
5. Definitions of some of the technical terms (pp. 268–269).
6. Supplement to the second edition (pp. 269–272).
7. Postscript (p. 273).

In the 1970s G said that he had written this paper to change the reluctance among mathematicians to work in set theory, on account of the widespread distrust of the subject associated with the paradoxes. Section (1) shows that the continuum problem is indeed a well-defined problem, and (2) reviews the 'scarcity of results.' The iterative concept of set is considered in (3), after suggesting the need for 'a more profound analysis (than mathematics is accustomed to giving) of the meanings of the terms occurring in' the most fundamental questions in this field. Two reasons are given in (4) to support G's belief that the continuum problem is unsolvable by the accepted axioms. The supplement (6) begins with a summary of relevant results obtained between 1947 and 1963, and goes on to elaborate the reasons, given in the first edition, why the truth of the continuum problem would not lose its meaning, even if it 'should turn out to be undecidable from the accepted axioms of set theory.' The postscript (7) was added in 1963 to note that Paul J. Cohen had proved the independence of the continuum hypothesis 'shortly after the completion of the manuscript of this paper.' It is noteworthy that Cohen's result did not affect the content of the paper in any substantive way.

According to G, the major portion of (3) and (6), together with his contributions to *MP*, constitutes the principal published statement of his mathematical realism. The analysis of mathematical concepts is stressed both in (3) and in (1). Indeed, the considerations in (1) offer an illustration of G's favorite idea that (mathematical) concepts, in this case the infinite numbers, have the 'character of uniqueness.' Not surprisingly the constructible sets play a central part in G's deliberations, particularly in (4). The program of looking for new axioms, in particular for strong axioms of infinity (asserting the existence of very great cardinal numbers), is proposed in (3).

The paper begins with two equivalent simple formulations of Cantor's continuum problem: How many points are there on a straight line in Euclidean space? How many different sets of integers do there exist? The question presupposes an extension of the concept of number to infinite sets. A basic requirement (or 'axiom') for the concept is this: 'The number of objects belonging to some class does not change if, leaving the objects the same, one changes in any way whatsoever their properties or mutual relations (e.g., their colors or their distribution in space).' Hence, 'Two sets,' G continues, 'will have the same cardinal number if their elements can be brought into a one-to-one correspondence.' In this context G uses one of his favorite modes of reasoning: 'Such considerations, it is true, apply directly only to physical objects, but a definition ... which would depend on the kind of objects that are numbered could hardly be considered to be satisfactory.'

Cantor's definition of equality between numbers can be extended '(again without any arbitrariness)' to the greater-less relation and the familiar arithmetical operations. In particular, Cantor's diagonal proof established that the number of the subsets of a set is always greater than the number of its elements. In addition, the problem of identifying the cardinal number of an individual set requires 'some systematic representation of the infinite cardinal numbers.' This depends on Cantor's theorem that there is exactly one next cardinal for each (set of) cardinal(s), as well as on the 'well-ordering theorem,' which was only proved by Zermelo in 1904 by introducing the axiom of choice, when Cantor had essentially stopped his work in set theory. Here G leaves out the historical development and points out that the axiom (of choice) is as well founded as the other axioms, referring also to his proof of its consistency.

Cantor wrote in 1883, 'It is always possible to bring any *well-defined* set into the form of a *well-ordered* set. I will return to this law in a later memoir' (*Abhandlungen*, p. 169). Even though the well-ordering theorem was central to Cantor's whole theory of infinite numbers and seen by him to be intuitively true, he never obtained a fully satisfactory proof (even to himself). A much discussed approximation to a proof was contained in one of his letters of 1899 to Dedekind (ibid., p. 447). [The extensive literature related to Cantor's life and work includes Jean Cavaillés, *Philosophie Mathématique*, 1962 (consisting of three parts all completed by 1941); H. Meschkowski, *Probleme des Unendlichen: Werk und Leben Georg Cantors*, 1967; J. Dauben, *Georg Cantor*, 1979; and M. Hallett, *Cantorian Set Theory and Limitation of Size*, 1984.]

In (2) G states Cantor's continuum hypothesis in its usual form and gives it also the alternative formulation: 'Any infinite subset of the continuum has the power either of the set of integers or of the whole continuum.' He stresses the scarcity of results, and remarks that the problem is only a question from the 'multiplication table' of cardinal numbers. This surprising situation brings him to the suggestion of looking for a more profound analysis of concepts, which is a philosophical task according to G's conception. I shall return later to G's development of this suggestion in (3).

In (4) G gives two reasons for his conjecture (of 1947) that the continuum problem is unsolvable by the accepted axioms. First, two differently defined classes of objects both satisfy these axioms: the constructible sets and 'the sets in the sense of arbitrary multitudes, regardless of if, or how, they can be defined.' [In view of the fact that certain (large) multitudes are not sets, G may wish to change the word 'multitudes,' perhaps to 'extensions.'] 'Now, before it has been settled what objects are to be numbered, and on the basis of what one-to-one correspondence, one can hardly expect to be able to determine their number, except perhaps in the case of some fortunate coincidence. If, however, one believes that it is meaningless to speak of sets except in the sense of extensions of definable properties, then, too, he can hardly expect more than a small fraction of the problems of set theory to be solvable without making use of this, in his opinion essential, characteristic of sets, namely, that they are extensions of definable properties.' So from either point of view, the continuum problem 'may be solvable with the help of some new axiom which would state or imply something about the definability of sets.'

At this juncture G mentions the concept of definability in the sense of his constructible sets and the 'axiom' (called 'A') that every set is constructible. And he refers to his result that the (generalized) continuum hypothesis follows from A. He states (in footnote 22, p. 522 of AMM) that 'from an axiom in some sense [directly] opposite to this one the negation of Cantor's conjecture could perhaps be derived.' This footnote is elaborated in the second edition by adding (BP, p. 266, footnote 23), 'I am thinking of an axiom which (similar to Hilbert's completeness axiom in geometry) would state some maximum property of the system of all sets, whereas axiom A states a minimum property. Note that only a maximum property would seem to harmonize with the [iterative] concept of set explained in footnote 14.'

G gives no indication of any possible ways to formulate a reasonably precise maximum axiom. Indeed, as is well known, Hilbert's 'completeness axiom' (in geometry) is no more than a statement of intention from which no precise deductions can be made. Another puzzling feature is G's use of the term 'axiom.' He appears to recognize that A and the 'maximum axiom' cannot both be true, and says explicitly that only the latter 'would seem to harmonize with' the intended concept of set. Hence, according to his usage, either an axiom (in particular, A) can be a false proposition, or at least it can be a proposition not yet known conclusively to be false. For example, he mentions in footnote 20 (BP, p. 264, an expanded version of footnote 19 on p. 520 of AMM) that A is contradicted by one of several new axioms of infinity [the one asserting the existence of a measurable cardinal] and goes on to say, 'However, that these axioms are implied by the general concept of set in the same sense as Mahlo's has not been made clear yet.' This sentence was written around 1962. G's attitude in the 1970s appears to me to indicate a stronger inclination toward believing that A is indeed false.

G's 'second argument in favor of the unsolvability of the continuum problem on the basis of the usual axioms' depends on his intuitive interpretation (which has been widely questioned) of a number of mathematical results ('facts') as indicating that Cantor's conjecture will turn out to be wrong. Since, however, it follows from his consistency result that the conjecture cannot be disproved by the usual axioms, the truth that it is false cannot be proved. Therefore, the conjecture must be independent of the usual axioms. (G's own conjecture here again implies the falsity of A.) G concludes his discussion in the first edition by asserting 'that the role of the continuum problem in set theory will be to lead to the discovery of new axioms which will make it possible to disprove Cantor's conjecture.' [This statement was included in both editions (1947 and 1964). But in 1976 he told me that the conjecture could be true and that he then believed the power of the continuum to be either aleph-one or aleph-two.]

The most extensive revisions from the first to the second edition were made in (4). One long deletion was G's suggestion of an alternative axiomatization of set theory in terms of ordinal numbers, its ordering relation, and the notion of 'recursively defined function of ordinals' (*AMM*, p. 522, the bottom twelve lines and footnote 24). Possibly the deletion was made partly because some logician published such a system in the 1950s, apparently without reference to this passage. Another long deletion was G's first publication of his results on 'ordinal definability' (*AMM*, p. 523, lines 6–7 and the long footnote 26), which was rediscovered by several people in the 1960s. (There are some misprints in the first edition, resulting from G's habit of elaborate cross references. In footnote 20, 'footnotes 13 and 19' should be 'footnotes 15 and 23.' In footnote 23, 'footnote 13' should be 'footnote 15.' By the way, the observation on the implausible results in point set theory, in the last paragraph of the section, is elaborated in *MP*, p. 86.)

The primarily philosophical parts of G's paper are sections (3) and (6). Many philosophers have scrutinized and discussed this or that aspect of these two sections, in which several intricately connected facets of G's views are presented. G's realist position is contrasted with the positions of Brouwer, Poincaré, and H. Weyl. The iterative (or extensional) concept of set is briefly described and contrasted with what might be called the 'bifurcation' (or perhaps intensional) concept of set. Logic (and epistemology) and mathematics are distinguished. Both the advantages and the inadequacies of considering formal deducibility are stressed. Much attention is paid to looking beyond the (conjectured) undecidability of the continuum hypothesis on the basis of accepted axioms of set theory; the question of its truth remains meaningful and the task is to find new axioms. More is said in the second edition about mathematical intuition (in a sense extended beyond the one used in the preceding section) and the objective existence of its objects.

11.2.1 Constructionism and realism

Brouwer's intuitionism and the semiintuitionistic standpoint of Poincaré and Weyl do not preserve much of set theory. 'However, this negative attitude toward Cantor's set theory, and toward classical mathematics, of which it is a natural generalization, is by no means a necessary outcome of a closer examination of their foundations, but only the result of a certain philosophical conception of the nature of mathematics, which admits mathematical objects only to the extent to which they are interpretable as our own constructions or, at least, can be completely given in mathematical intuition' (*BP*, p. 262). The conception thus characterized succinctly by G is what is commonly called the position of a conceptualist or a constructivist. The characterization concentrates on 'mathematical objects,' and appears to be stated from a realist perspective in using the phrase 'only to the extent.' It seems to suggest that there are other mathematical objects, which the constructivist does not admit because they do not satisfy his criterion. The phrase 'completely given in mathematical intuition' has different meanings for different outlooks. For example, as mentioned in section 11.1, intuition in Hilbert's sense is more restricted than in Brouwer's sense, and G's interpretation of the intuitionistic system H is more intuitive than Heyting's. From G's own accounts, it seems clear that he has not only a broader concept of intuition than the intuitionist, but recognizes the continuing expansion of our intuition. These differences are, I think, related to his realist position.

A (mathematical) 'realist' is, according to G, 'someone who considers mathematical objects to exist independently of our constructions and of our having an intuition of them individually, and who requires only that the general mathematical concepts must be sufficiently clear for us to be able to recognize their soundness and the truth of the axioms concerning them.' Consider first the part about independent existence. This makes it possible to recognize and 'have intuition' of mathematical objects as well as their generating principles, even when they are not 'completely given in mathematical intuition.' Hence, the realist position gives a broader range of mathematical objects and a broader concept of intuition.

It is not entirely clear how the part about the concepts and their axioms is related to the part about objective existence. If the general concept is the concept of set, then the considerations in MP (pp. 181–187) may be viewed as an illustration of how we see new sets (mathematical objects) by recognizing the 'soundness' of the concept of set and the truth of the axioms concerning it. In this case, the use of 'intuitive ranges' involves a special case of 'intuition,' which goes far beyond Kant's and Hilbert's (concrete) intuition, but does not cover all the ways of forming sets. (As pointed out by Charles Parsons, the word 'only' in the middle line of p. 182 of MP should be deleted.) G lists also 'abstract' principles that no longer use intuitive ranges (MP, pp. 189–190). But once we are convinced by some such principle that a certain set (which is not an 'intuitive range of variability') exists, we can say that we have an intuition it exists. It seems to me possible that, as our intuition improves, such a set may also at some stage be seen to be making up an 'intuitive range.' This is related to the interaction of intuitions and idealizations.

In any case, G goes on to say (BP, p. 262) that from this (realist) position 'there exists a satisfactory foundation of Cantor's set theory in its whole original extent and meaning,' namely, the iterative concept of set. A sketch of this 'foundation' is followed by comments on the restricted mathematical problem of deciding Cantor's conjecture from the existing partial list of precisely formulated axioms, which form a subset of 'the axioms underlying the unrestricted use of this concept of set' (p. 263). According to G, 'The question of whether some given proposition follows from them can be transformed, by means of mathematical logic, into a purely combinatorial problem concerning the meaningful manipulation of symbols which even the most radical intuitionist must acknowledge as meaningful.' This is an example of G's practice of paying attention to and bringing out the significance of his problems and results for not only his own views but also alternative philosophical standpoints. In this case the word 'meaningful' is ambiguous; the question of deducing the continuum hypothesis is meaningful to the intuitionist only in the very limited sense that it admits a definite answer, not in the sense of being of importance.

Of the four a priori possibilities, G first separates out (in footnote 17) the most drastic alternative: 'In case the axioms were inconsistent' Cantor's conjecture would be both demonstrable and disprovable. Of the three remaining alternatives, G's own result had shown that the conjecture is not disprovable. The possible alternatives (in 1947 and up to the latter part of 1963) were either demonstrable or undecidable. 'The third alternative [viz., being undecidable] (which is only a precise formulation of the foregoing conjecture, that the difficulties of the problem are probably not purely mathematical), is the most likely. To seek a proof for it is, at present, perhaps the most promising way of attacking the problem.' As is well known, Paul J. Cohen did follow this 'most promising way' successfully to prove the independence of the conjecture in 1963; combining this with G's early result, the undecidability conjectured by G was thus confirmed in 1963. But G's philosophical idea is that the problem (of the conjecture's being true or false) remains meaningful (and open), serving as a stimulus to the search for new axioms. I shall return to this topic later.

11.2.2 The iterative concept of set

G packs several things into his one-paragraph sketch of the concept (pp. 262–263). The paradoxes 'are a very serious problem, not for mathematics, however, but rather for logic and epistemology.' As I have said before, G distinguishes mathematics (set theory), which deals with extensions, from logic (the theory of concepts), which deals with intensions. In particular, a set can never belong to itself and there is no universal set, but a concept may apply to itself and there is the universal concept (the concept of concept, which applies to itself). We do not (yet) have a concept of concept that is nearly as clear as the (iterative) concept of set, and we do not have a good intuitive understanding of the intensional paradoxes (such as the concept of all concepts that do not apply to themselves).

'This concept of set, however, according to which a set is something obtainable from the integers (or some other well-defined objects) by iterated application of the operation "set of," not something obtained by dividing the totality of all existing things into two categories, has never led to any antinomy whatsoever; that is, the perfectly "naive" and uncritical working with this concept of set has so far proved completely self-consistent.' [A footnote is attached to 'the operation "set of,"'' which, in the first edition, concludes with 'but as opposed to the concept of set in general (if considered as primitive) we have a clear notion of this operation.' This clause (and thereby the contrast) was deleted in the second edition.] In contrasting the iterative with the 'bifurcation' concept of set (which is known in the literature as 'naive' set theory), G apparently has Frege in mind. G's own use of the word 'naive' points to a criterion of the correctness of a concept. If the intuitive concept is captured, then one expects to be able to work with it fruitfully in a naive and uncritical manner. G would, I think, consider the 'bifurcation' idea appropriate for concepts and intensions (in opposition to sets and extensions).

'As far as sets occur in mathematics,' G says, 'they can always be interpreted without any difficulty' according to this iterative concept of set. In the second edition G adds a footnote (12, on p. 262) on the theory of categories (such as the self-applicability of categories): 'It does not seem, however, that anything is lost from the mathematical content of the theory if categories of different levels are distinguished. If there existed mathematically interesting proofs that would not go through under this interpretation, then the paradoxes of set theory would become a serious problem for mathematics.' The counterfactual conditional in G's statement of course indicates his belief that there are no such proofs. A broader and different issue is perhaps the place of intensional considerations in mathematics. For instance, G seems to suggest that as the theory of concepts gets a relatively adequate development, it will be helpful also to mathematics.

According to G, the very concept of set suggests further iterations and new axioms. In this connection, he adds a footnote (18, p. 264) that I do not fully understand:

> Similarly the concept 'property of set' (the second of the primitive terms of set theory) suggests continued extensions of the axioms referring to it. Furthermore, concepts of 'property of property of set' etc. can be introduced. The new axioms thus obtained, however, as to their consequences for propositions referring to limited domains of sets (such as the continuum hypothesis), are contained (as far as they are known today) in the axioms about sets.

The text differs from the first edition (footnote 17, *AMM*, p. 520) in several ways. But the main difference is the addition of '(as far as they are known today).' In G's 1940 monograph (*The Consistency of the Continuum*

Hypothesis, p. 2), he says that classes are what appear in Zermelo's formulation as 'definite Eigenschaften.' This would seem to suggest that the properties of sets correspond to the classes in his monograph, which are, however, known to play a subsidiary role and easily dispensable. In other words, there is no essential difference between the system in G's monograph and the familiar formulation (commonly known as ZF) in which classes do not occur. In this sense it is hard to see why G calls the concept 'property of set' the second of the primitive terms of set theory, and, moreover, 'property of property of set,' etc. (thus construed), are known to be inessential ('conservative') extensions. Hence, the addition of '(as far as they are known today)' would seem to make this interpretation of 'property of set' questionable.

Another question is the relation between G's idea of the theory of concepts and what he calls here the concept 'property of set.' A property of sets is presumably a concept concerned with sets. A theory dealing with the concepts 'property of set,' 'property of property of set,' etc., is presumably a part of the theory of concepts, but can apparently only be a small fragment of the latter, since it clearly cannot reach the universal concept of concept and, according to G, a hierarchy analogous to that in set theory cannot be the principal part of the theory of concepts. In short, it is not clear to me how G construes the concept 'property of set' or what special significance it has in his conceptual framework.

Another puzzling feature about this footnote is the later reference to it: 'the axioms mentioned in footnote 18' (on p. 265). In the first edition (*AMM*, p. 521) the corresponding reference is to footnote 14 (which remains the same in the second edition but becomes footnote 15): A set of all sets or other sets of a similar extension cannot exist, since every set obtained in this way immediately gives rise to further applications of 'set of' and, therefore, to the existence of larger sets. Since G speaks of 'the axioms mentioned in' this footnote, it should perhaps be interpreted as something like what is known in the literature as the 'reflection principle' (for G's formulation of this principle in 1972, see *MP*, p. 189), which is implicitly mentioned in footnote 20 of the second edition as one of the advances (since 1947). There are three possibilities: the two different references both accord with G's intentions, the number 14 in the first edition should be 17, or the number 18 in the second edition should be 15.

11.2.3 *New axioms (and the continuum problem)*

In a letter G wrote to Menger in December 1937, he said, 'Right now I am trying to prove also the independence of the continuum hypothesis.' Moreover, reporting on his conversations with G in the spring of 1939, Menger refers to G's 'early conviction that the right or correct axioms of set theory had not yet been discovered,' and goes on to say, 'This conviction he expressed more and more emphatically.' (For details, see chapter 3, under the years *1937* and *1939*.) Hence, G clearly had conjectured the independence of Cantor's conjecture and felt the need of new axioms long before writing his Cantor paper of 1947.

According to the iterative concept of set, he says, 'The set-theoretical concepts and theorems describe some well-determined reality, in which Cantor's conjecture must be either true or false' (pp. 263–264). Undecidability of the conjecture from accepted axioms, unlike the proof of the transcendence of π, does not, he points out, settle the problem (p. 263). It is also very different from the situation with Euclid's fifth postulate, 'both from the mathematical and from the epistemological point of view' (pp. 270–271).

G mentions three types of axioms beyond the usual axioms (such as those of ZF): 'the [strong] axioms of infinity,' 'the axioms mentioned in footnote 18' (compare the discussion above), and 'other (hitherto unknown) axioms of set theory which a more profound understanding of the concepts underlying logic and mathematics would enable us to recognize as implied by these concepts (see, e.g., footnote 23 [i.e., the 'maximum axiom' mentioned above])' (p. 265). The last category means essentially 'all other acceptable axioms,' but it seems to suggest also his idea that logic as the theory of concepts, when better understood, will help the discovery of new axioms.

Of the axioms of infinity, G uses the inaccessible numbers and P. Mahlo's principles as clear examples 'which only unfold the content of the concept of set explained above.' Axioms introduced between 1947 and 1962 are mentioned in the second edition with this observation: 'However, that these axioms are implied by the general concept of set in the same sense as Mahlo's has not been made clear yet' (footnote 20). In recent years, the most interesting new axioms of set theory are the 'axioms of determinacy,' which interact with and suggest new axioms of infinity. For example, axioms of infinity have been formulated by W. Hugh Woodin and others to prove 'projective determinacy' and that the axiom of determinacy holds for $L(R)$. In addition, these results also give some close upper bounds to the attempts to generalize G's constructible sets (to 'L-like structures') by R. B. Jensen and others. Indeed, it appears that the axioms of determinacy have turned out to be a more effective stimulant than the continuum problem as far as the search for new axioms of infinity is concerned (compare section 6.3).

There are different and unpredictable ways of arriving at new axioms. When new axioms are formulated, there are for G's considerations two distinct problems: how to see that they are probably true and whether they are useful for the solution of the continuum problem. With regard to the second question, the new axioms formulated so far seem to be irrelevant.

The reason for G's belief in their relevance also appears to be weak. Indeed, I am surprised that I am not able to find much in G's paper that addresses this question. The only argument appears to be a weak analogue to his discovery that his undecidable propositions, which can be put in the form of 'Diophantine propositions,' can be decided in higher systems (p. 264). But these propositions are quite different from the familiar un-solved problems in number theory, having been constructed for the special purpose of metamathematical considerations. In particular, since the continuum problem concerns, so to speak, all the individual details of the continuum, it seems rather implausible that axioms of infinity will, 'except perhaps in the case of some fortunate coincidence,' settle it. It does appear more plausible that a 'maximum axiom' will settle it, but we have no idea how the intended axiom can be given a precise form. Elsewhere G speaks of our mathematical intuitions leading to a decision or giving meaning to such problems as Cantor's (pp. 271 and 272). However, the argument seems not to be specifically relevant to the continuum problem, but more to say merely that new axioms and intuitions will decide more problems.

More of G's attention seems to be directed to the other question of eval-uating the new axioms, which is not quite relevant to the continuum problem. The 'intrinsic necessity' of a new axiom is seen if we find that it is forced on us by the iterative concept and the accepted axioms. Mahlo's axioms are the model of this category. G says more about the 'argument from success' (both on pp. 265 and 272). G speaks of fruitfulness in 'verifiable' consequences: 'Consequences demonstrable without the new axiom, whose proofs with the help of the new axiom, however, are con-siderably simpler and easier to discover, and make it possible to contract into one proof many different proofs.' Analytic number theory is given as an example. G also speaks of 'a much higher degree of verification' that sheds 'so much light on the whole field,' etc. In the supplement, G returns to this (probable) criterion of truth by observing, 'This criterion, however, though it may become decisive in the future, cannot yet be applied to the specifically set-theoretical axioms.'

11.2.4 Objective existence and mathematical intuition
This is considered primarily in (6) (more specifically, the middle of p. 271 to the middle of p. 272). [There are also some related considerations in MP (pp. 84–85).] Various attempts have been made in the literature to interpret this text of a page or so.

In contrast to geometry, the objects of transfinite set theory 'clearly do not belong to the physical world and even their indirect connection with physical experience is very loose (owing primarily to the fact that set-theoretical concepts play only a minor role in the physical theories of today).' This observation implies the possibility of a greater role in the future, and I share this seemingly farfetched belief, on the empirical ground that more and more remote but substantive regions of mathematics have gradually come to be used in physics.

In view of this remoteness from sense experience, G proceeds to consider immediate knowledge, 'something like a perception also of the objects of set theory,' mathematical intuition, and the objective existence of its objects. [The identification implied by 'in this kind of perception, i.e., in mathematical intuition' appears to me to be a mistake, and the former is only a part of the latter. G himself may also have said something like this to me.] In *MP*, G goes beyond the perceptions of mathematical objects to speak of 'the perceptions of concepts' as well, and to perceive a concept is, he also says, to see or understand it or to grasp the meaning of a word standing for it (p. 85).

Apart from the involvement with several difficult epistemological concepts, the great complexity of G's reasoning is also due to his pursuing several lines of argument at the same time. Aided by his conversations with me, the text may be seen to be including implicitly three levels: (a) objectivity as given by 'the psychological fact of the existence of an intuition which is sufficiently clear to produce' continually objectively true mathematical propositions, (b) the objects of mathematical intuition, and (c) their objective existence. G considers (a) the least debatable, and essentially agrees with Kant on level (b) (but with a richer intuition). It is on level (c) that he argues for his strong realism, which differs from Kant's dualism.

With regard to (a), G speaks of a 'criterion of truth in set theory' that is nothing but our having an intuition that a proposition is true. Its acceptance is justified by 'the fact that continued appeals of mathematical intuitions are necessary' [here we have G's favorite ultimate weapon:] 'also for the solution of problems in finitary number theory (of the type of Goldbach's conjecture) where the meaningfulness and unambiguity of the concepts entering into them can hardly be doubted.' Since our intuition assures objectivity in this least controversial case and since we have in set theory also a similar experience of reliable intuition (as seen from the agreement on the proofs, some of them highly complex, and on many of the axioms), we have every reason to believe in the objectivity of the truth or falsity of propositions, as seen by our intuition. According to G, 'This suffices to give meaning to the question of the truth or falsity of propositions like Cantor's continuum hypothesis.' In other words (from his conversations), it is not futile to ask the question. [This of course says nothing about the prospect and the promising avenues of answering the question (for example, with regard to Cantor's conjecture).]

As I have mentioned before, G says that, once we recognize certain propositions to be true (or just meaningful), they must be about something and there must be certain objects about which the propositions are saying this or that. Hence, we move from (a) objectivity to (b) objects. G compares mathematical objects (primarily sets in this context, leaving out numbers, geometrical forms, etc.) with physical objects, and 'semi-perception' ('something like a perception') of sets with sense perception of the latter. This analogy leads G to draw a parallel that, if made explicit, says, 'Semi-perception [sense perception] induces us to build up mathematical [physical] theories and to expect that future semi-perceptions [sense perceptions] will agree with them, to believe that a question not decidable now has meaning and may be decided in the future.' (I have tried to sketch a development of this idea in section 6.3.) To this context belongs G's footnote 40, which compares the concept of set with Kant's categories of pure understanding: the idea of both is 'synthesis,' namely, the generating of unities out of manifolds (of one set out of its elements, and, 'in Kant, of the idea of *one* object out of its various aspects').

The most intricate part of G's argument deals with (c) the objective existence of the objects of our (mathematical) intuition. [In connection with his reasoning for (a), he says explicitly that the question (c) 'is not decisive for the problem under discussion here.' I take this to mean simply that the criterion of truth based on the objectivity recognized by intuition is not dependent on (c).] Consider first the case of physical experience; G recognizes 'the fact that even our ideas referring to physical objects contain constituents qualitatively different from sensations or mere combinations of sensations, e.g., the idea of object itself.' To this extent G agrees with Kant. But while, according to Kant, the idea of object itself is contributed by our mind, G believes otherwise; we *form* the idea also 'on the basis of something else which *is* immediately given. Only this something else is *not*, or not primarily, the sensations.'

The reasons G gives for this conclusion are 'the fact' just quoted and 'By our thinking we cannot create any qualitatively new elements, but only reproduce and combine those that are given.' As I have mentioned before, it is questionable that G's use of the word 'create' in this context is generally accepted. However, I am in full agreement with G's conclusion and the spirit of his argument. Among other things, the conclusion eliminates Kant's Ding an sich and its transcendence. Presumably Husserl's elaborate analysis of our perception of a physical object can also be viewed as supporting G's conclusion. One way to approach this conclusion is to question Kant's stipulated insuperable barrier between objective reality (in the sense of his Ding an sich) and our recognition. It seems to me that G's argument can be modified in the following manner. We may be able to create qualitatively new elements, but what we attribute to the physical world must be derivable from and checkable against our physical experience, in such a manner that there is no insuperable barrier between the world and our experience. In particular, as G says, we *form* our ideas of physical objects on the basis of something else that *is* immediately given.

G believes that the situation is analogous in the case of our semiperception of mathematical objects. He recognizes the different status of 'given' (commonly known as the question of causation): namely, the data of this second kind 'cannot be associated with actions of certain things upon our sense organs.' 'It by no means follows, however,' he continues, that they 'are something purely subjective as Kant says. Rather they, too, may represent an aspect of objective reality, but, as opposed to the sensations, their presence in us may be due to another kind of relationship between ourselves and reality.' I am inclined to agree with G, but do not know how to elaborate his assertions. I used to be troubled by the association of objective existence with having a fixed 'residence' in spacetime. But I now feel that 'an aspect of objective reality' can exist (and be 'perceived by semiperceptions') without its occupying a location in spacetime in the way physical objects do. Perhaps Husserl's considerations of Wesenschau can be borrowed to support G's belief in the objective existence of mathematical objects. But I do not understand Husserl's apparent emphasis on subjectivity. (Husserl once called himself a 'thorough empiricist' and later was upset when he was called an empiricist. It is not clear to me whether Husserl only uses subjectivity as a tool to refine a realist position.)

G does not distinguish intuition de re from intuition de dicto. It seems to me that the distinction is secondary in the sense that the more interesting and more basic sense of intuition is prior to such a distinction. If we begin with such a distinction, I believe that we cannot recover the more primitive idea of intuition by combining the two types. G says, 'It should be noted that mathematical intuition need not be conceived of as a faculty giving an *immediate* knowledge of the objects concerned.' I take this to imply the familiar, though often deliberately overlooked (in order to discredit the appeal to intuition), fact that our intuition makes mistakes, needs cultivation, and can be corrected and extended. Of course the whole issue of different kinds of intuition (as illustrated in the last section), different degrees of certainty, and the interaction of intuitions and idealizations is highly complex and constitutes, in my opinion, the central concern of not only the philosophy of mathematics but also philosophy as a whole.

11.3 *Russell and mathematical logic*

The Russell essay occupies a special place in G's life and work. In a letter dated 18 November 1942 Schilpp invited G to contribute a paper, 'Russell's mathematical logic,' to a volume honoring Russell. 'In talking the matter over last night with Lord Russell, I learned,' says the letter, 'that he considers you the scholar *par excellence* in this field.' G agreed to write such a paper.

The invitation came at a time when G was frustrated with his attempt to extend his independence proof for the axiom of choice to one for the continuum hypothesis. It is difficult to know whether G would have continued his efforts otherwise. As it was, G apparently began to concentrate on the Russell essay and the study of Leibniz around the beginning of 1943, essentially stopping his research activities in mathematical logic (for the next twenty years or more). Evidently this wide-ranging essay marks the transition of G's main attention from the quest for definite mathematical results in logic to investigations of a more distinctly philosophical (and historical) character. Unlike his previous publications, which were all of a mathematical character, this essay uses Russell's work as a reference point to put together his own reflections on the nature and the fundamental concepts of mathematical logic, in the light of the historical course from Leibniz to himself and beyond.

Russell's work suited very well G's purpose of giving a broad review. 'Russell has produced a great number of interesting ideas,' as G says in the essay, 'concerning the analysis of the concepts and axioms underlying Mathematical Logic' (BP, p. 212). Moreover, G's own incompleteness theorems and constructible sets fit in very naturally as decisive responses to and advances beyond Russell's ideas. The incompleteness theorems set some precise limits to Russell's project of a comprehensive logic, and their proof foils Russell's vicious circle principle (BP, p. 222, around footnote 29). They also confirm some of Russell's views (middle of p. 213). The constructible sets are a fruitful use of Russell's ramified theory of types 'from a purely mathematical standpoint,' within G's own realist framework (p. 227). Even the iterative (or extensional) concept of set corresponds quite well to Russell's idea of 'the theory of limitation of size,' proposed in 1906 (BP, p. 216, the middle part and footnote 9). (It is not surprising but somewhat unfortunate that G does not consider in the essay Russell's stimulating but more imprecise *Principles of Mathematics*, 1903 and 1937.)

The essay was completed by 28 September 1943 and published not long after: 'Russell's mathematical logic,' *The Philosophy of Bertrand Russell*, ed. P. A. Schilpp, 1944, pp. 125–153. It was reprinted in BP, 1964, with an added prefatory note, which was expanded in *Bertrand Russell, a Collection of Critical Essays*, ed. D. F. Pears, 1972, pp. 192–226 (with also minor changes in footnotes 7, 17, and 45, as well as the deletion of footnote 50). In addition, G has made various notes (partly in shorthand) on some of the offprints of the essay in his Nachlass (folder 04/79), but I have not studied these notes closely.

The prefatory note of 1972 gives no indication that G had changed his views expressed in the essay in any fundamental way between 1943 and

1972. He notes, '(1) That since the original publication of this paper, advances have been made in some of the problems discussed and that the formulations given could be improved in several places.' But he did not specify the 'several places.' The terminological observation (2) about his special usage of the term 'constructivistic' to refer to the view embodied in Russell's 'no class theory' (explained in footnote 22, BP, p. 219) clarifies the distinction between nominalism and constructivism. The corrected usage follows the current one to use 'constructivistic' to mean 'intuitionistically admissible' or 'constructive' in the sense of the Hilbert school. More specifically, the accepted convenient usage identifies the constructive (or constructivistic) with the intuitionistically admissible and considers (Hilbert's) finitary methods a proper part of the constructive (compare section 11.1).

In any case, G distinguishes these two views from the one associated with the 'no class theory': 'Both these schools base their constructions on a mathematical intuition whose avoidance is exactly one of the principal aims of Russell's constructivism,' which, according to G, is 'a strictly nominalistic kind of constructivism.' Moreover, 'What, in Russell's own opinion, can be obtained by his constructivism (which might be called fictionalism) is the system of finite orders of the ramified hierarchy without the axiom of infinity for individuals.' G believes that even this much cannot be obtained without presupposing the notion of finiteness (BP, p. 226). These considerations help to clarify the relation between infinity and nominalism (as discussed in section 11.1) by using the increased precision of a more explicitly formulated version of nominalism. At the same time, 'predicativity' is a fruitful and relatively definite idea, capable of varied extensions, if we detach it from Russell's nominalism or fictionalism, and use it in combination with concepts, axioms, and methods (such as an axiom of infinity, transfinite orders, inductive definitions, and even, as is done by G, arbitrary ordinals) that are seen to be acceptable on other grounds (compare BP, p. 227).

The reference to new 'advances' in (1) (of the prefatory note) presumably includes those in both the standard literature and G's own thinking. The fact that G chose not to elaborate the matter suggests that he did not consider the possible improvements of major significance. For example, it was well known before 1960 that the theory of integers cannot be obtained in Russell's ramified theory (said by G to be an unsolved question on p. 226 of BP) and the simple theory of types is essentially a segment of axiomatic set theory (apparently taken to be more different by G on p. 231). Clearly these are not substantive issues for the major concerns of G's essay. On the other hand, some of his observations in his conversations with me may help the reader to arrive at a better understanding of the essay.

The central point is G's sharper distinction (than is clear from the essay) between logic (the theory of concepts or intensions) and mathematics (set theory or the study of extensions). In particular, 'classes,' taken as a primitive concept in the essay, paired with concepts, and vaguely identified with sets, are dispensed with and treated as a derivative term. Hence, 'classes' should be replaced by 'sets,' which are, as is not obvious in the essay, radically different from concepts. Already in his Cantor essay of 1947, G confined his attention to sets and left out general considerations about the concepts of concept and class (except for the puzzling footnote 18 discussed in the last section). Apparently G, in 1943, thought of extensions and intensions as belonging together and assigned a secondary place to intensions. For example, 'It might even be that the axiom of extensionality or at least something near to it holds for concepts' (BP, p. 220). He suggested in the 1970s deleting the quoted sentence, because he no longer believed it.

Moreover, G made later a sharper distinction between objects and other things; in particular, concepts (and classes) are not objects (contrary to his usage in the Russell essay, e.g., they may 'be conceived as real objects,' 'the assumption of such objects,' etc., p. 220). According to his later view, an extension must be an object so that (proper) classes cannot be extensions. Hence, it is strictly speaking inappropriate even to contemplate a general 'axiom of extensionality' for concepts in terms of classes. Indeed, the quoted sentence most probably implies, contrary to his later belief, that the range of nearly every concept is a set.

In light of G's later sharper distinction between sets and concepts (and classes), the discussions in the Russell essay suffer from an ambiguity when G speaks of 'classes.' Nearly all the time he is talking about sets, but when he speaks of classes as 'pluralities of things' (p. 220), the phrase agrees with his later use of the word 'class' to the extent that such pluralities form sets only if they are also unities. It seems to me nearer to G's intention to interpret G's discussion of 'classes' in the essay as actually a discussion of sets (as is commonly understood today). The main difference between his 1943 view and his later view is, I think, that in 1943 he did not think of concepts as qualitatively more comprehensive than sets. Consequently it was also not essential to distinguish classes from sets. For example, in the 1970s he conjectured that every set is the extension of some concept. Yet the sentence quoted in the last paragraph seems to suggest that in 1943 he was conjecturing something like its opposite: Every concept has a set as its extension (or is an intension determining a set) (and, in addition, no two concepts have the same extension). (I am not sure whether G also believed in 1943, as many did and do, that there are essentially more sets than concepts. He seems to suggest this implicitly on p. 223: 'only if one assumes the existence of a concept whenever one wants to construct a class.' But this is ambiguous because it refers to Russell's notions.)

G speaks of 'a class or concept' (e.g., twice on p. 216, also on p. 228) as well as 'classes and concepts' (pp. 220 and 231) and fails to emphasize, beyond occasional references to the paradoxes in their intensional form (pp. 216 and 228), his (later) sharp distinction between sets and concepts. He does emphasize concepts on p. 229 (and, in the context of considering Russell's view, on p. 228). One difficulty about G's presentation is the mixed use of the terms 'class' and 'concept,' sometimes in Russell's sense and sometimes in his own. Along the same line, the much quoted comparison between mathematics and physics (on p. 220) is what G calls an 'ad hominem' argument, couched in the language of his ('positivist') opponent. Hence, he speaks of 'assumption,' 'legitimate,' and 'data,' but only puts the last word in quotes. (By the way, in this context he suggested in 1975 the replacement of 'physical bodies' by 'physical objects,' and 'such objects' by 'such entities' or 'such things.')

The Russell essay is unique among G's published work in offering general comments, unfortunately all too brief, on the nature and history of logic, paying special attention to the important role of conceptual analysis. The analysis is done from a realist or objectivist position, and it is natural to use Russell's idea of this position to contrast it with Russell's nominalism or fictionalism. The fruitfulness (or 'cash value') of G's philosophical position, stated more explicitly later in his letters to me (*MP*, pp. 8–11), is illustrated by gently reminding the reader of his own important discoveries. On account of the limitations of Russell's interests, broad as they were, constructivity is left out and set theory is kept in the background, because they were never Russell's principal concerns. Hence, in order to get a full understanding of G's philosophy of mathematics (which is a narrower domain than logic for G), the essay is to be supplemented by his Bernays paper (considered in section 11.1) and Cantor paper (considered in section 11.2).

Instead of following slavishly the order of presentation in G's text, it seems to me better to consider the essay on the basis of G's several themes. For this purpose, I propose to use the following order: (1) the nature and history of logic, (2) realism and nominalism, (3) predicativity and the vicious circle principle, (4) some details. From a brief sketch of his ideas on (1), G singles out conceptual analysis as the most fundamental part and restricts his attention to it. But for such a study the philosophical position from which the analysis is done is of decisive importance. Hence, (2) includes not only Russell's theory and practice (as well as his earlier and later views) but also the discussions on the theory of description and on the concept of analyticity. Since the vicious circle principle is central to Russell's work in logic, G's extended discussion of it is considered separately under (3), in light of (2).

(1) The nature and history of logic (pp. 211–212, 231–232)

In a vague and broad sense, logic may be thought of as the theory and practice of finding order in the world or of putting facts in order. It is in this sense that logic can include 'dialectic logic' and, in particular, Hegel's *Logic*. More often, however, logic is identified with formal logic, which studies the 'formal' aspect of the world or of our thought. And I shall limit my attention to logic in this restricted sense. 'Mathematical logic,' according to G, 'is nothing but a precise and complete formulation of formal logic' (p. 211). Since logic (as we know it) develops in time (as G and I agree), mathematical logic tends to lag behind logic to the extent that we generally envisage and have logical ideas that have not received 'a precise and complete formulation.' Indeed, the importance of conceptual analysis is partly to help us to arrive at such a formulation.

For example, G speaks of logic as the theory of concepts and expresses doubt whether it can be fully mathematized, although some of his statements suggest that a satisfactory formulation is always attainable. At any rate we certainly do not yet have a developed theory of concepts. Indeed, as far as I know, G has never given unambiguously a full list of what he takes to be the primitive concepts of logic. For example, he mentions 'our logical intuitions (i.e., intuitions concerning such notions as: truth, concept, being, class, etc.)' (p. 215). From what I have said above, it is clear that 'class' should either be deleted or replaced by 'set.' If we disregard the suggested incompleteness of the list, there remains the question how the explicitly listed 'notions' are to function in logic as the theory of concepts. Every being is for G either a concept or an object and a set is a mathematical object. Hence, if we have the concepts of object and concept, the concept of being can be dispensed with (or taken as the range of the general variables). One may also, as a convenience, leave out (provisionally) objects that are not sets, as we do in pure set theory (see below). The concept of truth can presumably function implicitly as a part of the metatheory, although I am not sure of G's thoughts on this issue.

Hence, the theory of concepts has three primitive concepts: concept, object, and set. In developing the theory, we may disregard the concept of object and expect that the structure of the theory will not be much affected if we add objects (other than pure sets) afterward. Moreover, as I have mentioned above, G conjectures that every set is the extension of some concept. Hence, it appears possible to obtain the concept of set and the axioms about sets in a developed theory of concepts, by considering the extensions of concepts with 'small' ranges. In practice, however, if we wish to develop the theory of concepts now, it is better to assume G's conjecture and borrow from set theory, of which we have much richer experience.

To communicate what I take to be G's idea, it may be helpful to outline a rough and inadequate system for the theory of concepts, as an illustration of the sort of thing one might experiment with. Attempts to contrive systems of set theory have been made by people who took the intensional approach and were unaware of or unwilling to accept the consensus of basing such systems on the iterative concept of set. Such attempts can be revived in the context of a theory of concepts. G mentions the ideas of Church and Quine (pp. 229 and 217). Since I am more familiar with Quine's idea of 'stratification,' let me use it as an example.

Let C be the first-order symbolism obtained from ZF by substituting the relation A of application ('xAy' for 'x applies to y') for the membership relation and construing the variables as ranging over concepts. The following axioms and definitions replace the axioms of ZF (we may also begin with a system including more axioms than ZF).

1. If a formula Fx is 'stratified,' there is a (concept) y such that, for all x, yAx iff Fx.

2. Sy (y is a set) is defined by saying that y is extensional and founded. In other words, if for all x, yAx iff zAx, then $y = z$; and if y applies to something, then there is some u such that yAu but, for all z, if yAz, then there is no w, for which both zAw and uAw.

3. xBy (x belongs to y) iff Sx and Sy and yAx.

4. All the axioms of ZF, with all the quantifiers restricted to sets; i.e., they appear only in such contexts: for all x, if Sx, then Fx; or, there exists x such that Sx and Fx. Incidentally, in the axiom of replacement, we do not require restrictions on the quantifiers in the given functional relation so that one can benefit from the richer (than ZF) content of C. In other words, given an arbitrary many one relation Ruv (expressible in C) with a set x as its domain, its range forms also a set y.

The formulation of C can probably be improved and may even contain serious mistakes. But it gives, I believe, a concrete illustration of what I take to be G's idea of a theory of concepts. A more serious matter is to take care of G's suggestion of using Russell's idea of 'limited range of significance' (pp. 228–229), which is absent in C and calls for additional considerations. One way to handle 'meaningfully applicable' (and its complement) is to use a 'partial predicate calculus,' such as the one suggested by me in *Zeitschrift für mathematische Logik und Grundlagenforschung*, vol. 7 (1961), pp. 283–288. But in that case other ideas (such as Church's) may be more suitable than 'stratification.'

'Mathematical logic,' according to G, 'has two quite different aspects. On the one hand, it is a section of Mathematics, treating of classes [sets], relations, combinations of symbols, etc. instead of numbers, functions, geometric figures, etc. On the other hand, it is a science prior to all others, which contains the ideas and principles underlying all sciences. It was in the second sense that Mathematical Logic was first conceived by Leibniz in his

Characteristica universalis, of which it would have formed a central part' (p. 211).

Even though most of the research work in mathematical logic today is devoted to the first of the two aspects, G's primary interest is in the second aspect, particularly in the essay under consideration. Moreover, the essay moves quickly from Leibniz, through Frege and Peano, to Russell, and then puts aside almost all detailed considerations 'about either the formalism or the mathematical content of' *PM* to concentrate on 'Russell's work concerning the analysis of the concepts and axioms underlying Mathematical Logic' (pp. 211–212) (which, indeed, would be a more accurate title of the essay). The selection of material undoubtedly reflects G's view on what is at the center of mathematical logic as he sees it.

G returns to this task of analysis and to Leibniz at the end of the essay, after concluding the main part of the essay with a negation and an invitation: 'Many symptoms show only too clearly, however, that the primitive concepts [of logic] need further elucidation.' This is seen to be the reason why mathematical logic has so far not been able to 'facilitate theoretical mathematics ... as the decimal system of numbers has facilitated numerical computations': 'For how can one expect to solve mathematical problems systematically by mere analysis of the concepts, if our analysis so far does not suffice to set up the axioms?' G is suggesting, I think, that once we arrive at the adequate axioms, we can learn to grasp also the derived concepts and approach mathematical problems in a systematic way. But I have not been able to see his reasons for believing this. For example, the standard incomplete system of number theory is moderately adequate, as far as we know, to the solution of most of the problems in this area, but seems to offer no clue to any systematic method of problem solving. Does he think that this is because the concepts are not self-contained on account of their not being fundamental enough (perhaps as revealed by the incompletability)?

The reference to Leibniz appears to be related to G's belief that many of Leibniz's ideas and writings have been lost (compare the report in chapter 3, under *1939*). The suggestion bears a resemblance to the story of Fermat's unwritten proof of his last conjecture, of which most people would now believe that Fermat did not have a correct proof. It is tempting to speculate about G's conception of what Leibniz took to be the universal characteristic, of which, according to G, mathematical logic (in the second sense) forms a central part. It is not easy to see how mathematical logic as it is done today could be extended to yield powerful methods of (or just effective guides to) new discoveries. (I have made some suggestions about the nature of the desired extensions in section 6.2 in connection with a discussion between G and Carnap.)

G's brief review of the history of logic from Leibniz to *PM* (over a period of about two hundred years) is remarkable for his succinct character-ization of the contributions of Frege and Peano, as well as for his being able to capture not only the principal predecessors of *PM* but also its content by mentioning the relevant aspects in the work of Frege, Peano, Peirce and Schröder, and Cantor. The discussions in the main part of the text may be seen to be containing implicitly also a history of the major advances in mathematical logic (in the second sense) from 1910 to 1940. I believe this is why G spoke of the essay (in the 1970s) as a history of mathematical logic using Russell's work as a point of reference. The paragraph on the symbol-ism of *PM* points out the lack of a precise statement of its syntax and, in particular, gives an example of some unsatisfactory definitions in *PM* that yield different results by eliminating defined symbols in different orders.

(2) Realism and nominalism
According to G, Russell not only moved from realism to nominalism, but also had in practice a tendency to turn things into 'logical fictions' (prob-ably as a result of Russell's fascination with what he calls 'Occam's razor' and what is familiarly known as 'reductionism'), even when he was in theory advocating a realist position. Once G wrote that at that time (1920 or before) evidently Russell had met the 'not' even in this world, but later on under the influence of Wittgenstein he chose to overlook it (for the con-text, see chapter 4, under *1944*). It is well known that in his later years, probably after around 1920, Russell was not even a mathematical realist in theory. But his early position was more complex (compare *BA*, pp. 67–69). G remarks on 'Russell's pronouncedly realistic attitude,' mentioning, with approval, two of Russell's expressions (from 1919 and 1906) of this attitude, and deplores that Russell's practice did not follow his theory (pp. 212–213).

As I have noted above, the main contrast in G's essay is between the positions of realism and nominalism or fictionalism (erroneously called 'constructivism' in the text), with the complex middle position of construc-tivism disregarded. In terms of this contrast, the corresponding different conceptions of concepts and definitions can be distinguished quite clearly, and G makes explicit the distinction in his essay.

Two conceptions of notions   On p. 220 G speaks of two conceptions of 'notions' (a term that G apparently did not often use again later on). G uses 'concept' for the realist conception: 'I shall use the term "concept" in the sequel in this objective sense.' According to the nominalist conception, a notion is 'a symbol together with a rule for translating sentences containing the symbol into such sentences as do not contain it, so that a separate object denoted by the symbol appears as a mere fiction.' (In footnote 23 G points out that this conception of notion need not get one into an infinite regress, when it is maintained 'for all notions except the primitive terms which might be only a few.') Any two different definitions 'may be assumed to define two notions' in the nominalist sense. 'For concepts, on the contrary, this is by no means the case, since the same thing may be described in different ways.'

This distinction is relevant to G's views on analyticity, the paradoxes, and Russell's theory of descriptions. Of the two senses of analyticity (p. 230), the first uses the nominalist conception of notion (which accompanies 'conventionalism' in its familiar and clearest sense), and the second uses 'the meaning of the concepts' occurring in a proposition (compare *BA*, pp. 13−16.)

Of the logical paradoxes G says on p. 222 that the vicious circle principle does not solve them and then continues, 'Of course, all this refers only to concepts. As to notions in the constructivistic [i.e., nominalist] sense there is no doubt that the paradoxes are due to a vicious circle.' I believe this refers implicitly to G's distinction between semantic and intensional paradoxes. G regards language and the semantic paradoxes as a nominalistic affair, so that they are solved, as is familiarly done, by an appeal to the vicious circle principle.

G discusses extensively Russell's treatment of the definite article 'the,' contrasting it with Frege's view that all true sentences have the same Bedeutung (pp. 213−215). The discussion concludes with a distinction between two conceptions of definitions (analogous to those of notions): 'Closer examination, however, shows that this advantage of Russell's theory over Frege's subsists only as long as one interprets definitions as mere typographical abbreviations, not as introducing names for objects described by the definitions, a feature which is common to Frege and Russell.'

G's and Russell's (early) realism   The one page beginning at the end of p. 212 belongs together with G's analogy of mathematics with physics on p. 220. G begins with a quotation from Russell's *Introduction to Mathematical Philosophy* (*IMP*), which was probably the very first book in the philosophy of mathematics G ever read (in Schlick's seminar of autumn 1925, when G was a 'sophomore'). G quotes from p. 169 (of *IMP*) the second half of the following sentence: 'Logic, I should maintain, must no more admit a unicorn than zoology; for logic is concerned with the real world just as truly as zoology, though with its more abstract and general features.' It is not surprising that G likes this (half) sentence, since it expresses his own realist position very well. (There are two puzzling details in G's reference to *IMP*. He refers to the edition of 1920 and says in footnote 3 that the quoted sentence 'was left out in the later editions.' The book was written in 1918 when Russell was in a prison and published in 1919. It has, I believe, never been revised in later editions. In 1955 I used in a course at Harvard its 'eighth impression' of 1953, in which the quoted sentence remains, and according to which the second impression was in 1922.)

G's other reference, which is a paraphrase, indicates the source, surprisingly (given G's famous meticulousness), only by the phrase '(in one of his earlier writings).' I believe the writing in question is a paper published (in French) in 1906 (in fact, the one listed by G in footnote 31), of which the English version was first published in 1973 (*Essays in Analysis*, ed. D. Lackey, essay 9, pp. 190–214). Since the relevant passage appears to me to correspond very well to an aspect of G's thought that I like and that has not been sufficiently communicated or appreciated, I propose to quote Russell's paragraph of eloquent prose (from p. 194) in full:

> The method of logistic is fundamentally the same as that of every other science. There is the same fallibility, the same uncertainty, the same mixture of induction and deduction, and the same necessity of appealing, in confirmation of principles, to the diffused agreement of calculated results with observation. The object is not to banish 'intuition', but to test and systematise its employment, to eliminate the errors to which its ungoverned use gives rise, and to discover general laws from which, by deduction, we can obtain true results never contradicted, and in crucial instances confirmed, by intuition. In all this, logistic is exactly on a level with (say) astronomy, except that, in astronomy, verification is effected not by intuition but by the senses. The 'primitive propositions', with which the deductions of logistic begin, should, if possible, be evident to intuition; but that is not indispensable, nor is it, in any case, the whole reason for their acceptance. This reason is inductive, namely that, among their known consequences (including themselves), many appear to intuition to be true, none appear to intuition to be false, and those that appear to intuition to be true are not, so far as can be seen, deducible from any system of indemonstrable propositions inconsistent with the system in question.

G's one (long) sentence summary of the paragraph says of Russell that he compares the axioms of logic and mathematics with the laws of nature and logical evidence with sense perception, so that the axioms need not necessarily be evident in themselves, but their justification lies (exactly as in physics) in the fact that they make it possible for these 'sense perceptions' to be deduced, which of course would not exclude their also having a kind of intrinsic plausibility similar to that in physics. If we compare the summary of Russell's view with G's own analogy of mathematics to physics (the two sentences from the line 10 to line 16 on p. 220), the similarity is striking. What G does in his extension is to move from the recognition of objectivity (by both Russell and himself) to the recognition of objects (or rather things, including sets and concepts). (I have already considered this distinction between objectivity and objects in other parts of this book.) G also answers explicitly the question, often asked about his own statement, What plays the role of 'data' in mathematics? The answer is 'arithmetic, i.e., the domain of the kind of elementary indispensable evidence that may be most fittingly compared with sense perception' (p. 213).

G shows his agreement with (his summary of) Russell's view by observing that he thinks that (provided 'evidence' is understood in a sufficiently strict sense) this view has been largely justified by subsequent developments, and it is to be expected that it will be still more so in the future. He mentions his incompleteness theorem (without identifying his authorship) as (the principal) present evidence and looks to the quest for new axioms (particularly in 'abstract set theory') for future evidence. I believe his idea is that his theorem presses on us the need for 'assumptions essentially transcending arithmetic' even for solving problems in arithmetic, just as we use physical laws that transcend sense perception. G then says that, of course, under these circumstances mathematics may lose a good deal of its 'absolute certainty'; but, under the influence of the modern criticism of the foundations, this has already happened to a large extent. The first half presumably refers to the fact that we do not always see clearly whether a new 'axiom' is true. I am not sure whether the second half again refers to his incompleteness theorem, which frustrated Hilbert's hope to secure mathematics by 'absolutely certain' consistency proofs.

While G extends Russell's objectivism (or realism with respect to objectivity) to his own mathematical realism, Russell refines or retreats from his objectivism by his concern with reduction and economy (perhaps in part conditioned by the tradition of British empiricism). G's essay does not say much about the historical development of Russell's views, of which more data are available today (compare BA, pp. 236–237, 224, and 242). Briefly the discovery of the theory of descriptions in 1905 encouraged his leaning toward a 'no class theory,' which, in addition, avoids the need to set up restrictions that he found hard to delimit without arbitrariness (see the paper discussed by G on pp. 216–217 and cited in footnote 9; it was written in 1905 and published 7 March 1906). The vicious circle principle arose from the exchange between Russell and Poincaré, and it was, I think, viewed by Russell as a guide to the execution of his project of a no class theory. G treats of the vicious circle principle first because Russell formulated it as a general principle without mentioning any longer its dependence on the no class theory (p. 217).

G does not question that the principle is justified from a nominalist position, which also underlies the no class theory. Since, however, mathematics cannot be developed from a no class theory, it is necessary to go beyond it (also in *PM*), and the status of the vicious circle principle becomes highly complex when it is viewed from the realist or even any other nonnominalist perspective. That is why G's long discussion of the principle is so involved. G believes, I think rightly, that the no class theory with its underlying nominalist position cannot coherently use even all finite orders because they presuppose 'arithmetic (or something equivalent)' (p. 224) or 'the notion of finiteness' (p. 226). The principal interest of this idea of Russell's is its suggestion of the ramified hierarchy and the related notion of predicativity, which are very useful from perspectives other than the nominalist one.

(3) Predicativity and the vicious circle principle
The vicious circle principle suggests the idea of 'the theory of orders,' according to which definitions have to be 'predicative,' because properties and propositions have a higher order when they contain quantifiers of a given order. In this way the vicious circle is avoided. The power of the theory increases as we use higher and higher orders, but how do we get these orders, which are indexed by ordinal numbers? As I have just mentioned, we cannot even justify, for instance, the use of all finite orders purely from a nominalist position.

'The theory of orders proves more fruitful if considered from a purely mathematical standpoint' (p. 227). G mentions his surprising discovery of constructible sets (by using arbitrary ordinals as orders) and their applications (without identifying his authorship of the work), speaking of his collapsing of (say) all sets of integers to below the first uncountable ordinal number (as the 'order' in this vastly extended 'theory of orders') as the 'transfinite theorem of reducibility' (implicitly comparing it with Russell's 'axiom of reducibility'). In addition, G observes in connection with the extension of the orders, 'Even if one rejects impredicative definitions, there would, I think, be no objection to extend it to such transfinite ordinals as can be constructed within the framework of finite orders.'

In 1953 I noticed that if one adds an infinite order to the system of the second edition of *PM*, then the three specified difficulties (with identity, mathematical induction, and Dedekind cut) can be overcome without violating the spirit of the system. Moreover, I suggested the idea of iterated extensions of the theory of orders by using all ordinals available in each given theory as (new) orders (known later in the literature under the name of 'autonomous progression'; see my *Survey*, p. 579, and the paper appeared in *JSL*, vol. 19, 1954, pp. 241–266). I can now see that this proposal may be viewed as a generalization of G's observation. It turns out that for the particular 'theory of orders' I considered, the extension stops quickly by a result of C. Spector (*JSL*, vol. 20, 1955, pp. 151–163), according to which any ordinal definable in a theory of orders indexed by a recursive ordinal is again a recursive ordinal (compare *MP*, pp. 127–128). [In the summer of 1957, Spector, G. Kreisel, and I discussed the matter (at Ithaca), and we had three different views. Kreisel wanted to restrict the orders to provable well-orderings (which stop below the first nonrecursive ordinal number), Spector wanted to stop at that ordinal, and I wanted to go beyond by using devices such as inductive definitions, which appear to me to be unobjectionable, even to those who object to the unrestricted use of impredicative definitions. (In this connection I had previously already been struck by the intuitive appeal of inductive definitions and considered some simple examples in a more restricted context in *JSL*, vol. 18, 1953, pp. 49–59).]

The vicious circle principle is at the center of what G calls 'the most important of Russell's investigations in the field of analysis of the concepts of formal logic, namely those concerning the logical paradoxes and their solution' (p. 215). 'The principle,' Russell says, 'may be stated as follows': 'Whatever involves *all* of a collection must not be one of the collection'; or, conversely: 'If, provided a certain collection had a total, it would have members definable only in terms of that total, then the said collection has no total' (*PM*, I, p. 37). Russell also speaks of 'presupposing or involving' a totality (e.g., p. 39). Clearly Russell views 'definable in terms of,' 'involving,' and 'presupposing' as equivalent in the context, but G sees three different principles, of which the first is less plausible than the other two. In addition, G observes that a fourth principle has to be added, in order to prevent the intensional paradoxes (*BP*, pp. 217–218).

It is a little hard to keep track of G's discussion of the three forms. The first form (call it the strong form) is, in G's words, No totality can contain members *definable only in terms of* this totality. According to G, 'Only this one makes impredicative definitions impossible and thereby destroys the derivation of mathematics from logic, effected by Dedekind and Frege, and a good deal of modern mathematics itself.' G considers this a proof that the principle (rather than classical mathematics) is false. The principle applies *only if* one takes the nominalistic standpoint. For sets and concepts as objectively existing, there is no objection to describing some of them by reference to all. Moreover, G refers to his sentence (in his incompletability proof) about its own formal demonstrability as an approximation to the self-reflectivity of impredicative principles 'within the domain of constructivistic logic,' and gives an example in ordinary language: 'Every sentence (of a given language) contains at least one relation word.' He is, I believe, suggesting that self-reference is sometimes admissible even outside of the realist outlook. (This paragraph summarizes G's discussions on pp. 218–221 of the first form of the vicious circle principle.)

Of the other two (closely related) forms (which may be called the weak form), G considers the extent to which they contradict the realist position.

First, G argues that impredicative definitions do not violate the weak form of the principle: If 'all' means an infinite conjunction, an impredicative description (i.e., unique characterization) of a thing does not contradict the second form because it does not 'involve' the totality; nor the third form, if 'presuppose' means 'presuppose for the existence,' not 'for the knowability' (p. 219). (Incidentally, contrary to the contrast here, a set presupposes its members 'for existence' but not 'for knowability.') Second, for sets, one may assume, G says, that the second form applies (or that it is not contradicted) and get axiomatic set theory; G also suggests the possibility that it may not apply, but I feel that he has since given up the idea (p. 222). In other words, set theory according to the iterative concept does not violate the second form; moreover, if 'presuppose' means 'presuppose for existence,' it does not, I believe, violate the third form either.

(4) Some details

I propose to list a few minor and supplementary points regarding the Russell essay, including a number of changes G has suggested, some of which have been mentioned before.

1. The change of the term 'constructivistic' as explained above.
2. The replacement of 'class' by 'set,' the contrast of concepts with objects (including sets), and the need of a term including both (being, thing, or entity).
3. The replacement of 'physical bodies' by 'physical objects' on p. 220.
4. Replace 'primarily given' (p. 216, line 7) by 'arrived at first starting with the primitive terms of the language.'
5. I would have liked to quote and discuss footnotes 5 (p. 214) and 10 (p. 216).
6. Should the word 'second' (line 7, p. 217) be 'first'?
7. Insert '(in the first sense)' between 'false' and 'than' in line 12, p. 219.
8. Delete footnote 24 and the sentence in the text to which it is attached (p. 220).
9. G points out, in regard to the last complete sentence of p. 221, that, while a concept may contain itself as a constituent, this is unnecessary for the justification of intensional impredicative definitions.
10. Delete the two sentences ending with the first complete sentence of p. 221. (G said that the reference to structures had been connected with some idea of his that he no longer thought relevant.)
11. I wonder whether 'recursive' is the right word in line 18 from the bottom, p. 227.

12. Footnote 23 (p. 223) refers to the construction of predicates and relations such as 'red' or 'colder' by certain similarity relations in appendix C of the second edition of *PM*. There is a related reference (p. 220) to Russell's admitting 'universals' [primarily the similarity relation, as I recall] in *An Inquiry into Meaning and Truth*, 1940.

13. Footnote 47 (p. 230) appears to be relevant to the question about the primitive concepts of logic and the relation between the principle of contradiction and the truths of reason according to Leibniz. (The word 'class' should be replaced by 'set'.)

14. The considerations on p. 225 are relevant to the discussion on p. 99 of *BA*.

15. After I had written this section, I reread the review of G's essay by Bernays in *JSL*, vol. 11, 1946, pp. 75–79. The review contains a helpful summary of the essay, as well as several interesting ideas of the reviewer. I believe that this section and the review complement each other in some ways. At some places I find Bernays to have given a better formulation of ideas that I have also tried to present in this section. I would like to quote three particularly apt formulations from the review. (1) G points out in the essay, Bernays says, 'that it is just Russell's refraining from a more decided realism towards the logical and mathematical objects, to which are due the known difficulties of *PM*.' (2) Russell in *PM* does not separate the general requirements of a solution of the paradoxes from those from a 'constructivistic' point of view. (3) By detaching the system of (the first edition of) *PM* from the original aim of the no class theory, one arrives at the simple theory of types, from which, by removing some artificial restrictions, we get axiomatic set theory, that is, however, based not on the vicious circle principle, but on what Russell calls 'the limitation of size.' I believe these explanations of some aspects of G's essay make it easier to follow G's own presentation of his lines of thought on these aspects.

Index